GW01374712

THE UNFINISHED REVOLUTION

The Unfinished Revolution

SUN YAT-SEN
AND THE STRUGGLE FOR
MODERN CHINA

Tjio Kayloe

Marshall Cavendish
Editions

© 2017 Tjio Kayloe

Reprinted 2018

Published in 2017 by Marshall Cavendish Editions
An imprint of Marshall Cavendish International

A member of the
Times Publishing Group

All rights reserved

No part of this publication may be reproduced, stored in a retrieval system or transmitted, in any form or by any means, electronic, mechanical, photocopying, recording or otherwise, without the prior permission of the copyright owner. Requests for permission should be addressed to the Publisher, Marshall Cavendish International (Asia) Private Limited, 1 New Industrial Road, Singapore 536196. Tel: (65)6213 9300.
E-mail: genref@sg.marshallcavendish.com
Website: www.marshallcavendish.com/genref

The publisher makes no representation or warranties with respect to the contents of this book, and specifically disclaims any implied warranties or merchantability or fitness for any particular purpose, and shall in no event be liable for any loss of profit or any other commercial damage, including but not limited to special, incidental, consequential, or other damages.

All photographs in this book, unless otherwise specified, are believed to be in the public domain. If you have additional information pertaining to the ownership of the photographs, please contact the publisher so that the relevant credit can be given.

Other Marshall Cavendish Offices:
Marshall Cavendish Corporation. 99 White Plains Road, Tarrytown NY 10591–9001, USA • Marshall Cavendish International (Thailand) Co Ltd. 253 Asoke, 12th Flr, Sukhumvit 21 Road, Klongtoey Nua, Wattana, Bangkok 10110, Thailand • Marshall Cavendish (Malaysia) Sdn Bhd, Times Subang, Lot 46, Subang Hi-Tech Industrial Park, Batu Tiga, 40000 Shah Alam, Selangor Darul Ehsan, Malaysia.

Marshall Cavendish is a registered trademark of Times Publishing Limited

National Library Board, Singapore Cataloguing-in-Publication Data

Names: Tjio, Kayloe.
Title: The Unfinished Revolution: Sun Yat-Sen and the Struggle for Modern China / Tjio Kayloe.
Description: Singapore : Marshall Cavendish Editions, 2017. | Includes bibliography and index.
Identifiers: OCN 992165607 | 978-981-4779-07-4 (hardcover)
Subjects: LCSH: Sun, Yat-sen, 1866–1925. | Presidents—China—Biography. | China—History—1912–1928. | China—Politics and government—1912–1928.
Classification: DDC 951.041092—dc23

Printed in Singapore

In memory of my father, Tjio Ie Tjhay,

and my father-in-law, Lourenço Lui Hac-Minh,

two of the finest gentlemen from the Old Country,

who did not live long enough to see the modernization of

their fatherland but never wavered in their conviction

that it would happen during my lifetime.

CONTENTS

List of Illustrations   ix
List of Maps   x

Preface   xi
Acknowledgements   xvi
Notes to Readers   xviii
Cast of Characters   xx
Glossary   xxv

Prologue: Mandate Under Siege   1

CHAPTER 1   Hope of the Nation   20

CHAPTER 2   Baptism by Fire   40

CHAPTER 3   Man of High Purpose   63

CHAPTER 4   Coalition of the Unwilling   82

CHAPTER 5   The Turning Point   102

CHAPTER 6   A Marriage of Convenience   122

CHAPTER 7   The Nanyang Pivot   142

CHAPTER 8   Battle Cries for a Republic   166

CHAPTER 9   The Winter of Discontent   184

CHAPTER 10   The Spark that Started the Fire   206

CHAPTER 11   Betrayal of the Revolution   229

CHAPTER 12   Chaos Under Heaven   245

CHAPTER 13   Dances with Bears   267

CHAPTER 14   The Final Journey   292

CHAPTER 15   The Road to Purgatory   303

CHAPTER 16   The Man and His Legacy   322

Epilogue   341

Notes   347
Bibliography   371
Index   385

ILLUSTRATIONS

1. Sun Yat-sen at 17 years old, 1883   25
2. Sir Ho Kai   32
3. Dr. James Cantlie   32
4. Sun with his "Four Bandits" friends, 1888   34
5. Li Hongzhang   37
6. Yang Quyun   43
7. Sun in San Francisco, 1896   55
8. Kang Youwei   70
9. Liang Qichao   70
10. Empress Dowager Cixi   73
11. Guangxu Emperor   73
12. Sun with his Japanese friends in Tokyo, 1900   89
13. Yuan Shikai   99
14. Zhang Binglin   109
15. Huang Xing   114
16. Song Jiaoren   133
17. Hu Hanmin   133
18. Wang Jingwei   133
19. Sun with Tongmenghui Singapore founding members, 1906   149
20. Homer Lea   193
21. Sun with his son Sun Ke in Hawaii, 1910   199
22. Li Yuanhong   213
23. Official portrait of Sun as provisional president, 1912   223
24. Sun with Tang Shaoyi in Nanjing, 1912   230
25. Sun with Song Qingling in Tokyo, 1915   242
26. Chen Jiongming   252
27. Sun's former residence in the French Concession, Shanghai   254
28. Mikhail Borodin   279
29. Sun with Chiang Kai-shek at Huangpu Military Academy, 1924   286
30. Sun's burial at the Sun Yat-sen Mausoleum, 1929   305
31. Sun depicted with Lincoln on a U.S. postage stamp, 1942   343
32. Sun commemorated on a set of PRC postage stamps, 2016   343

MAPS

1. Xingzhonghui offices   80
2. Tongmenghui offices in Asia and America   138
3. The ten uprisings planned/organized by Sun Yat-sen, 1895–1911   183
4. 1911 Revolution: Independent provinces as of December 1911   217

PREFACE

In October 2013, during his state visit to Indonesia, Chinese President Xi Jinping proposed the creation of the Asian Infrastructure Investment Bank (AIIB) to fund infrastructural projects in Asia. He announced the 21st Century Maritime Silk Road initiative in the same speech, which came a month after unveiling the Silk Road Economic Belt initiative during his visit to Central Asia. These pronouncements were greeted with anxiety by the United States, which saw them as part of a Chinese blueprint to expand her economic and geopolitical footprints in the Eurasian landmass and beyond. The U.S. expressed concern that the AIIB might compete with existing institutions, as well as compromise humanitarian and environmental standards in its pursuit of economic development. Nevertheless, 56 countries have joined the Chinese-led bank as of August 1, 2017, with another 24 in the pipeline. In spite of American pressure on her allies to stay out, Japan is the only major country that has not joined.

The AIIB opened for business on January 16, 2016. During its first year of operations, it made loans totaling US$1.7 billion to nine infrastructure projects in partnership with other international financial institutions, including the World Bank. More significantly, the AIIB adopted the best practices of these organizations and has been assigned the highest possible credit ratings by Fitch, Moody's and S&P. America's fears have not been borne out.

The U.S. has her own reasons for not joining the AIIB, but the implication is quite different when she pressures her allies not to join. Suspicion is a divided highway. Many Chinese see the U.S. reaction as a throwback to the Cold War era, and the attempt to thwart the AIIB as part of a larger conspiracy to contain China and impede her rise. Support for better relations with the United States has been waning among increasing numbers of Chinese and threatens to derail a relationship that for more than 30 years has proved mutually beneficial and contributed to a more secure world.

Relations between China and the U.S. have been marred by mutual suspicion ever since the Communist Party of China assumed power on the Chinese mainland, continuing even after the end of the Cold War and extending up to the present day. A case in point is the incident that took place in Yugoslavia in 1999. On May 8, a U.S. B-2 stealth bomber shelled the Chinese Embassy in Belgrade, killing three Chinese journalists. Most Americans believed it was an accident due to an "old map," as claimed by U.S. officials. Contrastingly, virtually every Chinese believed it was deliberate; they found it inconceivable that technologically advanced America could make such a stupid mistake. Angry students took to the streets across China. In Beijing, crowds gathered and hurled insults, rocks and garbage at the U.S. Embassy. Western media assumed that the protests were orchestrated by the Chinese leadership to incite nationalistic fervor and divert attention away from domestic problems. This view became all the more convincing after it was discovered that the Chinese government had been busing student demonstrators to the U.S. Embassy.

The truth was very different. The Chinese authorities did transport the students to the U.S. Embassy, but the motivation was not to exacerbate the protest but rather to contain it. According to an insider, a member of the Politburo, Chinese leaders did not want masses of students marching across the capital vilifying the Chinese leadership for its weak response to the American outrage, and drawing others to join their cause, as happened in the Tiananmen Square incident ten years earlier almost to the month. The leaders wanted to give a measured response, one that was strong enough to placate the students but not so excessive as to hurt relations with the U.S.[1]

Unlike the Soviet Union, which challenged the U.S. for global hegemony, China shows little interest in challenging the U.S., much less dominating the world. China needs many more decades of peace and stability to bring about a moderately prosperous society. There is no ideological conflict between China and the U.S., and while competition may be inevitable, conflict is not. Why then do so many Americans in the government, military and media harbor negative feelings about China? A big part is undoubtedly the realization that China is the only other country with the potential to be both a continental and maritime power. This, coupled with her rapidly growing economic clout, has Americans convinced that it is only a matter of time before China becomes a superpower, and a threat to the U.S. and the existing world order.

PREFACE

These concerns have been reinforced by China's construction of islets in the South China Sea and the installation of military bases on them. Many Americans see this as evidence of China's intent to challenge America's preeminence in the region and reinforce China's claims to the substantial oil and gas reserves that are believed to lie under the seabed. Territorial disputes in the region began soon after the end of World War II and involved half a dozen claimant countries. But the disputes did not escalate to the present level until the Obama administration announced in 2011 its "rebalance to Asia" (also known as the "pivot to Asia") policy to shift the U.S. global security focus and divert more of her diplomatic and military resources to Asia-Pacific. Obama followed this up with other provocative moves. During his April 2014 visit to Japan, he publicly declared that the Diaoyu/Senkaku Islands are covered by the U.S.-Japan Security Treaty. The U.S. also restarted rotational deployment in five military bases in the Philippines and lifted the ban on arms sales to Vietnam.[2]

The South China Sea is a fulcrum of world trade. By some estimates, half the world's maritime trade and natural gas, and a third of her crude oil, goes through the Strait of Malacca. A blockade in this narrow and strategic body of water would grind the economy of some countries to a screeching halt. China's vulnerability in this respect has been recognized by the Chinese government as one of the country's greatest strategic weaknesses. It is small wonder that Obama's rebalancing policy stoked Chinese suspicion over U.S. intentions. This has instigated the Chinese leadership to substantially increase China's military budget to upgrade her military hardware, reform her armed forces and construct the islets in the South China Sea to enhance her maritime power. China's aggressive response has in turn heightened America's suspicions about China's intentions and sharpened America's resolve to take a harder line against China. The construction of military installations on the islets only began in 2014 but already it is shaping up to be one of the hottest spots in the world, with the potential to spark a major conflict between China and the U.S., one that would have a most devastating impact on the rest of the world.

China today is a land of superlatives – home to the biggest hydroelectric facility, the longest bridge, the fastest supercomputer, the speediest trains, the longest network of expressways and navigable waterways, space-age airports, the biggest population, the largest standing army, and the most number of skyscrapers, millionaires, and Internet and mobile cellular users. She is also the world's largest trading power, with vast holdings of U.S. Treasury bonds, and a global power with significant influence in shaping the world political order.

This image of China is in sharp contrast to her state on the cusp of the 20th century. For a time, it appeared that the once proud and mighty Celestial Empire might go the way of the Sumerians. Beginning with the Opium War in 1839 and for over 100 years thereafter, China was rent asunder by predatory foreign powers in a mad scramble for privileges and concessions while she struggled to preserve her sovereignty and dignity, escape her backwardness and join the modern world. This was China's century of humiliation, a period during which she was bullied, and sullied as the Sick Man of Asia. China's salvation from the precipice of a slippery slope to emerge as one of the world's most dynamic economies was the work of a few outstanding individuals. Sun Yat-sen was the first of these remarkable men. Through the ideas he spawned and the deeds he performed, Sun laid the groundwork that half a century later led to China's resurgence.

Born in maritime China and educated in missionary schools abroad, Sun Yat-sen was a product of East and West, a rarity in his time. During his formative years, China was ruled by a decrepit conquest dynasty, preyed upon by foreign powers and on the brink of collapse. Sun's foreign education and his encounters with the modern world instilled in him a strong desire to see China playing a role in that world. Sun wanted to contribute to the process as an insider, as a member of the bureaucracy. Rejected, he turned to revolution to bring about a regime change. He began by organizing peasant uprisings with the aid of secret societies but eventually got himself accepted by intellectuals and became the leader of a nationalist revolutionary party, the Tongmenghui, or the Revolutionary Alliance. After the 1911 Revolution that overthrew the Manchu Qing dynasty, he was briefly president of a republic, which after his resignation quickly degenerated into a dictatorship and then fragmented into warlordism. Inspired by an unshakeable faith in China's potential for greatness and in his own mission, Sun formed three successive military governments in Guangzhou to mobilize progressive forces and seize power from the militarists in Beijing.

PREFACE

The hostility of foreign powers forced him to forge an alliance with Soviet Russia, with whose help he reorganized his political party, the Zhongguo Guomindang, or Chinese Nationalist Party. He refined his political doctrine, The Three Principles of the People, as a blueprint for China's modernization drive but died before his dream of a strong, united and modern China could be realized.

No one personifies the crisis mood of that period better than Sun himself. A reading of his biography will not transform the reader into an instant expert on modern China, nor will it give more than a partial view of China's difficult transformation to modernity. But it is a good starting point toward understanding how China's leaders, officials and intellectuals think. As Ord Arne Westad reminds us: "The past is inscribed in China's mental terrain in a calligraphy so powerful that it determines most of its approaches to the present. History therefore influences Chinese ways of seeing the world in a more direct sense than in any other culture."[3] The century of humiliation and the history of that period, of which Sun was one of the most important actors, still shape the way the Chinese see themselves and the world. An appreciation of how China's leaders think will hopefully help to mitigate the suspicions and counter the distortions about China's intentions as a superpower in waiting.

Drawing on several landmark works – by Marie-Claire Bergere, Harold Z. Schiffrin, C. Martin Wilbur and Yen Ching-hwang – I have tried to present a balanced and comprehensive account of Dr. Sun's life that reveals his strengths and weaknesses, his triumphs as well as his disappointments, and above all his bold vision and struggle for a modern China. Context is essential to the drama and my narrative tries to elaborate on the turbulent history and intellectual climate of his time, which a reader needs to make sense of Dr. Sun's life. I have also given considerably more real estate to his relations with the Chinese in Southeast Asia than in his other biographies available in English. Virtually all the citations in this book are to readily available secondary sources in English from which more serious readers may obtain additional information.

ACKNOWLEDGEMENTS

This book began as a manuscript on Dr. Sun's relations with the Chinese in Southeast Asia. The catalyst was a pair of essays that University Professor Wang Gungwu, National University of Singapore, wrote in 1953 as theses for his baccalaureate. The first was about Dr. Sun's eight visits to Singapore, and the second on the activities of Chinese reformists and revolutionaries in the Straits Settlements. Before reading these essays, I was quite unaware that Dr. Sun's relations with the Chinese overseas ran so deep and so extensively. Thus began a journey of discovery as I read the works of other historians who expanded on Professor Wang's pioneering essays and extended his inquiry to other parts of Southeast Asia. I have relied on a number of these works in this book.

Professor Wang's imprint is not just in this book's germination. In the past several years, I have had the pleasure of meeting Professor Wang on many occasions and hearing his views on a host of subjects, some of which have helped to shape this book. A number of them have since been recorded for posterity in Ooi Kee Beng's *The Eurasian Core and its Edges*[4], but to listen to Professor Wang expound his views over lunch and to ask him questions, is a unique privilege for which I am most grateful.

The stimulus to rewrite my manuscript as a whole-life biography originated with Dr. Lee Seng Tee, Chairman of the Lee Foundation, Singapore. An amateur military historian, one of Dr. Lee's interests is to promote understanding between East and West. Among his many personal endowments to scholarship and education around the world is a professorship chair in U.S.-Asia Relations at the Kennedy School of Government at Harvard University. In addition, the Lee Foundation has endowed a U.S.-China Relations chair at the Lee Kuan Yew School of Public Policy, Singapore. Over the past two decades, I have had the privilege of lunching regularly with Dr. Lee. It was at one of these lunches a few years ago that he encouraged me to expand the scope of my manuscript. This of course made perfect sense as Dr. Sun's most recent biography available in English was written more than 20 years ago, and much new findings have emerged since. In support of my endeavor, the Lee Foundation is donating copies of

ACKNOWLEDGEMENTS

this book to many educational and other public institutions in Singapore. Dr. Lee and the Lee Foundation's interest and support of my work mean a lot to me, and for that I am very thankful.

I have piled up a number of obligations in the course of writing this book, and would like to express my thanks and gratitude to the following people for their help, support and encouragement: Dr. Tan Teng Phee, immediate past General Manager of the Sun Yat-sen Nanyang Memorial Hall, Singapore, for his valuable input and for making the resources of his organization available to me; Professor Leo Suryadinata, former Director, Chinese Heritage Centre, Singapore, for his advice and guidance; Choo Wai Hong, author of *The Kingdom of Women*, and Aileen Boon, founder and editor of Suntree Publishing, for reading parts of my manuscript and offering valuable comments and suggestions; Ang Taie Ping and Henry C.Y. Wong, for their help with translations; James Tan, for permission to use the library of the East Asian Institute, Singapore; Yap Soo Ei, Curator, National Heritage Board, for her help while this book was in its conceptual stage; Serafina Basciano, graduate student in Linguistics at King's College London for test-reading my manuscript; and others who have helped in one way or another: Chew Loy Cheow, Annemarie Clarke, Harjana, Chester Ho, Clifton Kwek, Joyce Kwek, Tessa Kwek, June Leong, Lu Caixia, Elaine Tan, Mintoro Tedjopranoto, Hans Tjio and Wong Hiu Man.

Most of all, I would like to express my thanks to my editor Justin Lau for the enthusiasm, expertise and dedication that he brought to the task. His sharp critique has helped to make this a much tighter, clearer and more readable book.

Last but not least, I want to thank my daughters Leona Hoyin and Arianne Sunyin for their advice and loving encouragement every step of the way.

NOTES TO READERS

ROMANIZATION OF NAMES

This book uses the *pinyin* system of romanization for Chinese proper names except for those better known in other forms, for example Sun Yat-sen instead of Sun Yixian, Chiang Kai-shek instead of Jiang Jieshi and Hong Kong instead of Xianggang, or where an official transliteration already existed, for example in British Malaya and Hong Kong – thus Tan Chor Nam instead of Chen Chunan and Lim Nee Soon instead of Lin Yishun.

Chinese, Japanese and Korean personal names are written with the family name first followed by the given name, except where a Western given name is used, as in Wellington Koo and Eugene Chen.

THE NAMES OF SUN YAT-SEN

Like many Chinese of his day, Sun Yat-sen used different given names at different periods of his life. His name in the genealogical records of his family is Sun Deming (孙德明). Traditionally, Chinese families would wait a few years before officially naming their children. In the meantime, they used a "small" name, which in the case of Sun was Dixiang (帝象). His "big" name, the one that he used when he started schooling, was Wen (文). Sun Wen was the name he used to sign official documents later on in life. He adopted the baptismal name Rixin (日新) in 1883 but his Chinese tutor Qu Fengzhi later changed it to Yixian (逸仙). When he took refuge in Japan in 1895 after the failure of the Guangzhou Uprising, Sun assumed a Japanese pseudonym, Nakayama Sho (中山樵), as a cover. Nakayama in Japanese means "central mountain," which in Chinese is Zhongshan (中山), the name that he used later in his life. Sun also had a Hawaiian pseudonym, Dr. Alaha, which he used when visiting Japan after his banishment from the country.

Of his various names, two or three have persisted. The West knows him as Sun Yat-sen, the Cantonese pronunciation of Yixian. This was the name that he used in his contacts with Westerners. In China, usage is more varied. Apart from Sun Yixian, the most common variations are Sun Wen and Sun Zhongshan.

NOTES TO READERS

MONETARY UNITS

The currency denoted by the C$ sign is the Chinese yuan. The U.S. dollar is denoted as US$, the Straits Settlements dollar as S$ and the Hong Kong dollar as HK$. The Chinese yuan, the Japanese yen, the Straits dollar and the Hong Kong dollar were all valued at roughly half an American dollar circa 1900.

CAST OF CHARACTERS

Blake, Sir Henry Arthur (1840–1918): Governor of Hong Kong from 1898 to 1903, he favored an alliance between Sun Yat-sen and Li Hongzhang to insulate the British colony from the Boxer upheaval.
Borodin, Mikhail (1884–1951): Comintern agent who helped to reorganize the Guomindang and set up the Huangpu Military Academy.
Cai Yuanpei 蔡元培 (1868–1940): Sun's envoy in negotiations with Yuan Shikai and later president of Peking University.
Cantlie, Dr. James (1851–1926): Scottish doctor who taught Sun at the Medical College in Hong Kong and later became of one of Sun's staunchest supporters.
Chen Duxiu 陈独秀 (1879–1942): Founder of the popular Shanghai journal *New Youth*, and head of the School of Letters at Peking University; co-founded the Communist Party of China in 1921.
Chen, Eugene 陈友仁 (1878–1944): Trinidad-born lawyer who was foreign secretary in Sun's third Guangzhou government.
Chen Jiongming 陈炯明 (1878–1933): Originally a supporter, he broke with Sun during the latter's second Guangzhou government and became a bitter enemy.
Chen Qimei 陈其美 (1878–1916): An ardent supporter of Sun and the protector of Chiang Kai-shek, whose career he helped to shape; assassinated by Yuan Shikai.
Chen Shaobai 陈少白 (1869–1934): One of the "Four Bandits" and one of Sun's lieutenants during the Xingzhonghui period.
Chen Tianhua 陈天华 (1875–1905): Anti-Manchu pamphleteer who committed suicide in 1905 to protest repressive Japanese policies against Chinese students.
Cixi, Empress Dowager 慈禧太后 (1835–1908): Consort of the Xianfeng Emperor, she ruled over the Chinese empire from behind the silk screen after his death in 1861.
Deng Ziyu [Teng Tzu Yu] 邓子瑜 (1878–1925): A veteran of the Huizhou Uprising in 1900, he took refuge in Singapore, where he helped to start a revolutionary movement.

CAST OF CHARACTERS

Duan Qirui 段祺瑞 (1865–1936): Leader of the Anhui clique who served as prime minister of the republic (1916–17) and later as chief executive (1925–26).

Feng Guozhang 冯国璋 (1859–1919): Leader of the Zhili clique who served as president of the republic in 1917–1918.

Feng Yuxiang 冯玉祥 (1882–1948): Known as the Christian General, he led a coup against Wu Peifu and later formed the Guominjun.

Feng Ziyou 冯自由 (1881–1958): The Tongmenghui's representative in Hong Kong and southern China who served as Sun's private secretary during his brief presidency.

George, Henry (1839–1897): American social reformer whose single-tax idea deeply influenced Sun's thinking.

Goh Say Eng [pinyin: Wu Shirong] 吴世荣 (1875–1941): Chairman of the Penang branch of the Tongmenghui.

Guangxu Emperor 光绪帝 (1871–1908): Eleventh emperor of the Qing dynasty; he was placed under house arrest by the Empress Dowager Cixi, his aunt, for initiating the Hundred Day Reform.

Ho Kai [pinyin: He Qi] 何启 (1859–1914): Founder of the College of Medicine for Chinese in Hong Kong and one of Sun's early benefactors and role models.

Hu Hanmin 胡汉民 (1879–1936): One of Sun's principal lieutenants during the Tongmenghui period who became the first republican governor of Guangdong.

Huang Naishang 黄乃裳 (1849–1924): Father-in-law of Lim Boon Keng who became a staunch supporter of Sun.

Huang Xing 黄兴 (1874–1916): Leader of the Huaxinghui who became Tongmenghui's number two and remained loyal to Sun throughout the Tongmenghui period.

Inukai Ki [Tsuyoshi] 犬養毅 (1856–1932): Japanese journalist and politician who was one of Sun's benefactors.

Joffe, Adolf (1883–1927): Soviet operative who signed an agreement with Sun on Soviet aid to the Guomindang.

Kang Youwei 康有为 (1858–1927): Chinese scholar who inspired the Hundred Day Reform and founded the Baohuanghui (Society to Save the Emperor).

Khoo Seok Wan [pinyin: Qiu Shuyuan] 丘菽园 (1874–1941): Kang Youwei's host in Singapore in 1900 who reportedly gave S$250,000 to the Baohuanghui.

Kong Xiangxi [H.H. Kung] 孔祥熙 (1881–1967): Sun's brother-in-law by virtue of his marriage to Song Ailing, the elder sister of Song Qingling, he mediated between Sun and the Northern generals.

Lea, Homer (1876–1912): Hunchbacked American adventurer who served as military adviser to Sun Yat-sen before the 1911 Revolution.

Li Hongzhang 李鸿章 (1823–1901): Doyen of the Self-Strengthening Movement who became the second most powerful person in the empire after the Empress Dowager Cixi.

Chiang Kai-shek [pinyin: Jiang Jieshi] 蒋介石 (1887–1975): Commandant of the Huangpu Military Academy who became head of the Nanjing government (1927–37).

Li Liejun 李烈钧 (1882–1946): 1911 Revolution veteran who joined the Yunnan generals to launch the anti-monarchic campaign against Yuan Shikai and rallied to Chiang Kai-shek after Sun's death.

Li Yuanhong 黎元洪 (1864–1928): Leader of the 1911 Revolution who served as vice president under Sun and Yuan Shikai.

Liang Qichao 梁启超 (1873–1929): Kang Youwei's disciple who supported Kang's constitutional monarchy but later advocated liberal republicanism.

Liao Zhongkai 廖仲恺 (1877–1925): Minister of Finance in Sun's third military government, he became the leader of the Guomindang's left wing after Sun's death; assassinated in August 1925.

Lim Boon Keng [pinyin: Lin Wenqing] 林文庆 (1868–1957): Chinese community leader in Singapore who helped Sun to secure the release of his Japanese friends from incarceration.

Lin Shouzhi [Lim Shou Chih] 林受之 (1873–1924): A veteran of the 1900 Huizhou Uprising, he helped to organize the two Chaozhou uprisings.

Lu Haodong 陆皓东 (1872–1895): Sun's friend and accomplice in desecrating the village idol in Cuiheng; executed in the aftermath of the Guangzhou Uprising in 1895.

Miyazaki Torazo [Toten] 宫崎滔天 (1871–1922): Japanese adventurer who became Sun's lifelong friend and one of his most ardent supporters.

Puyi 溥仪 (1906–1967): Last emperor of the Qing dynasty; abdicated in 1912 but from 1934 to 1945 was puppet emperor of Japanese-controlled Manzhouguo.

Song Jiaoren 宋教仁 (1882–1913): Guomindang leader who was assassinated at the Shanghai Railway Station by Yuan Shikai's henchman.

Song Qingling, Rosamonde 宋庆龄 (1893–1981): Second of the three Song sisters, she married Sun and later supported the Communists.

Sun Ke [Sun Fo] 孙科 (1891–1973): Only son of Sun Yat-sen, he served as Mayor of Guangzhou from 1922 to 1924.

Sun Mei 孙眉 (1854–1915): Sun Yat-sen's elder brother, who financed his education and revolutionary career.

Tan Chor Nam [pinyin: Chen Chunan] 陈楚楠 (1884–1971): Co-founder of the *Thoe Lam Jit Poh*, he was the first chairman of the Singapore branch of the Tongmenghui.

Tang Shaoyi 唐绍仪 (1862–1938): Chief negotiator for the Qing dynasty in 1911 who became the first prime minister of the Republic of China.

Tao Chengzhang 陶成章 (1878–1912): Leader of the Guangfuhui faction in the Tongmenghui who accused Sun of financial mismanagement and campaigned to oust him.

Teng Tse Ju [pinyin: Deng Zeru] 邓泽如 (1869–1939): Chairman of the Kuala Pilah branch of the Tongmenghui and one of Sun's strongest supporters in British Malaya.

Teo Eng Hock [pinyin: Zhang Yongfu] 张永福 (1872–1957): Co-founder of the *Thoe Lam Jit Poh* whose villa Wanqingyuan served as the headquarters of Tongmenghui Singapore.

Too Nam [pinyin: Du Nan] 杜南 (1854–1939): Sun Yat-sen's Chinese tutor in Hawaii who later became one of his main supporters in Malaya.

Uchida Ryohei 内田良平 (1873–1937): Japanese ultranationalist who founded the Kokuryukai, the Black Dragon Society.

Umeya Shokichi 梅屋庄吉 (1868–1934): Japanese impresario who helped to secure arms for Sun's first Guangzhou Uprising in 1895 and remained a lifelong friend and supporter.

Wang Jingwei 汪精卫 (1883–1944): Imprisoned for an assassination attempt on the prince regent in 1910, he later became Sun's heir apparent but was outmaneuvered by Chiang Kai-shek.

William, Maurice (1883–1942): American socialist whose *Social Interpretation of History* was supposedly responsible for Sun's refutation of Marxist philosophy.

Wu Peifu 吴佩孚 (1874–1939): Beiyang Army general who became leader of the Zhili clique and controlled the Beijing government from 1922 to 1924.

Wu Tingfang 伍廷芳 (1842–1922): First ethnic Chinese to be called to the English bar, he was the chief negotiator for the revolutionaries in the North-South negotiations in 1911.

Xu Xueqiu [Koh Soh Chew] 许雪秋 (1875–1912): Tongmenghui member who played the key role in the two Chaozhou uprisings in 1907.

Yang Heling 杨鹤龄 (1868–1934): One of the "Four Bandits" whose shop was used as the group's meeting place.

Yang Quyun 杨衢云 (1861–1901): Sun's partner and rival for leadership of the Xingzhonghui, he was poisoned after the failed Huizhou Uprising.

You Lie 尤列 (1864–1936): One of Sun's "Four Bandits" friends, he took refuge in Singapore in 1901 in the wake of the failed Huizhou Uprising and formed branches of the Gonghedang in British Malaya.

Yuan Shikai 袁世凯 (1859–1906): Kingpin of the Beiyang Army who succeeded Sun as president and later tried to found a new dynasty.

Yung Wing [pinyin: Rong Hong] 容闳 (1828–1912): A graduate of Yale, he was the first Chinese to graduate from an American university.

Zhang Binglin 章炳麟 (1868–1936): The editor-in-chief of *Subao* who was incarcerated together with Zou Rong in the Subao Affair.

Zhang Zuolin 张作霖 (1875–1928): Known as the Old Marshall, he was the warlord of Manchuria as head of the Fengtian clique.

Zhang Renjie 张人杰 (1877–1950): Sun's wealthy patron with many connections in Parisian society.

Zheng Shiliang 郑士良 (d. 1901): Sun's classmate at the Boji Medical School and the Xingzhonghui leader responsible for liaison with the secret societies.

Zhu Zhixin 朱之鑫 (1885–1920): A gifted *Minbao* polemicist, he was the ghostwriter for *The International Development of China*.

Zou Rong 邹容 (1885–1905): Author of *The Revolutionary Army* who was incarcerated together with Zhang Binglin in the Subao case.

GLOSSARY

1912 Constitution: The provisional constitution promulgated by the provisional parliament on March 12, 1912, under which executive power was exercised by the president together with the cabinet whose members had to be approved by parliament. This was the constitution that Sun tried to restore in 1917 when he set up his first military government in Guangzhou.

1914 Constitution: The constitution introduced by Yuan Shikai on May 1, 1914, which did away with all the restrictions on the president's executive power and extended the presidential term to ten years, renewable by re-election without limit. It empowered the president to nominate his own successor, thus assuring Yuan of an indefinite tenure as well as the right to pass it on to his offspring.

Anglo-Japanese Alliance: Signed on January 30, 1902, the alliance was directed specifically against Russian expansionism and bound Britain and Japan to joint action in the event a fourth power joined with Russia. It was the first treaty between an Asian and a Western power against a Western rival and marked Japan's coming of age in international diplomacy. The alliance served Japan in the Russo-Japanese War by discouraging France from aiding her ally Russia. The Alliance was renewed in 1905 and 1911 but was replaced in 1922 by the Four-Power Treaty signed between Britain, France, Japan and the United States at the Washington Naval Conference.

Baohuanghui 保皇会: The Protect the Emperor Society (official English name: Chinese Empire Reform Association), founded by Kang Youwei in British Columbia, Canada, on July 20, 1899. Its goal was to restore the Guangxu Emperor to the throne and to introduce constitutional monarchy in China. It lost its raison d'être after Guangxu's death and renamed itself Xianzhenghui (Constitutional Party).

Black Dragon Society (Kokuryukai): A Japanese paramilitary, ultranationalist right-wing group founded in 1901 by Uchida Ryohei to support efforts to keep Russia north of the Amur River and out of Asia. Its members included cabinet ministers, high-ranking military officers as well as secret agents, and it initially distanced itself from the criminal activities of its predecessor, the Genyosha. Over time, it found the use of criminal tactics a useful means of achieving its aims. The Society supported pan-Asianism and gave financial support to revolutionaries like Sun Yat-sen and Emilio Aguinaldo in the Philippines. It evolved into a mainstream political party in the 1920s and expanded its activities globally in the 1930s. The Society was disbanded by order of the American Occupational authorities in 1946.

Boxer Uprising: An anti-foreign and anti-Christian uprising initiated by a group called the Yihequan ("Righteous and Harmonious Fists"). In May 1900, bands of Boxers were roaming the countryside around Beijing. On June 20, they laid siege to the foreign legations quarter, which was lifted on August 14 by an eight-nation expeditionary force that looted the capital. The Boxer Protocol signed on September 7, 1901, provided for, among other things, payment of indemnities to the foreign powers.

British Malaya: The term loosely describes the states in the Malay Peninsula and Singapore that came under British control in the late 19th and early 20th centuries.

Century of Humiliation: The intervention and imperialism by Western powers and Japan in China from the Opium War in 1839 to the Communist victory in 1949.

China Proper: A term used by many Western writers of the Qing period to distinguish China's 18 "historical" provinces from more recently acquired territories on her northern and western frontiers, notably Manchuria, Mongolia, Xizang (Tibet) and Xinjiang. There is no direct translation of this term in Chinese and its use today is controversial as it implies that the frontier regions are somehow separate territories. The 18 provinces were Anhui, Fujian, Gansu, Guangdong, Guangxi, Guizhou, Henan, Hubei, Hunan, Jiangsu, Jiangxi, Shandong, Shaanxi, Shanxi, Sichuan, Yunnan, Zhejiang and Zhili.

Chinese Exclusion Act: A U.S. Federal law that prohibited immigration of Chinese laborers. Signed by President Chester A. Arthur in May 1882, it was intended to last ten years but was renewed in 1892 and made permanent in 1902. It was repealed in December 1943.

GLOSSARY

Chong Shing Yit Pao 中兴日报 (Renaissance Daily): The first official newspaper of the Tongmenghui in Singapore.

Civil Service Examination: The system used to select candidates for the state bureaucracy, consisting of three levels. The lowest degree, the *shengyuan*, was awarded on the basis of strict quotas established by the central government. Successful candidates, known colloquially as *xiucai*, or "flourishing talents," traveled to the provincial capital in the fall to sit for the *juren* degree. Every third year, *juren* graduates traveled to the capital to sit for the highest-level metropolitan *jinshi* degree, with a final examination presided over by the emperor to rank the candidates. Some would be appointed to the prestigious Hanlin Academy, while others would gain jobs in the bureaucracy. The civil service examination system was abolished in 1905.

Constitution Protection Movement: A movement launched by Sun's first Guangzhou military government in 1917 to reinstate the 1912 Constitution after Duan Qirui tried to call a new provisional parliament in November 1916 instead of reconvening the old parliament that Zhang Xun had forced Li Yuanhong to dissolve on June 12, 1916.

CPC: Abbreviation for Communist Party of China; sometimes also abbreviated as CCP, Chinese Communist Party.

Datong Ribao 大同日报 (Great Harmony Daily): A newspaper published in the San Francisco Bay area that had a correspondence relationship with *Thoe Lam Jit Poh*.

Fengtian 奉天: This may refer to the province now known as Liaoning but it was also used to refer to the whole of northeast China, covering the three provinces of Jilin, Heilongjiang and Fengtian (renamed Liaoning in 1929, revived under the Manzhouguo regime, and in 1945 again renamed Liaoning).

Five-Power Constitution: Proposed by Sun Yat-sen as a means of implementing democracy in China after the overthrow of the imperial regime, it provided for a central government composed of five *yuan*, or branches. Apart from the legislative, executive and judicial *yuan*, there would be an examination *yuan* to administer the selection of candidates for the bureaucracy, and a censorate or control *yuan* to check on the honesty and efficiency of the government.

Furen Wenshe 辅仁文社: The Literary Society for the Development of Benevolence, Yang Quyun's revolutionary organization that was merged into the Xingzhonghui.

Gelaohui 哥老会: The Society of Elder Brothers, a secret society active in the Yangtze region, particularly in Hubei and Hunan provinces.

Gemingdang 革命党: See Zhongguo Gemingdang, or Chinese Revolutionary Party.

Gongjinhui 共进会: The Society for Common Progress was one of the separatist groups of the Tongmenghui which along with the Wenxueshe, another breakaway group, subverted the New Army in central China that sparked the Wuchang Uprising.

Guangfuhui 光复会: The Restoration Society, established by Cai Yuanpei in Shanghai in 1904, was a revolutionary organization which drew its members from Zhejiang and Anhui. It joined the Tongmenghui in 1906 under the leadership of Zhang Binglin and Tao Chengzhang.

Guomindang 国民党: The successor organization of the Tongmenghui after the absorption of several political parties into its fold. On October 10, 1919, Sun announced the creation of the Zhongguo Guomindang, or Nationalist Party of China, which in a sense was a new organization rather than a resurrection of the original Guomindang.

Huaqiao 华侨: See Overseas Chinese.

Huaxinghui 华兴会: The Society for China's Revival was founded in Hunan in December 1903 and drew its members largely from the Yangtze valley, particularly Hunan and Hubei. Under the leadership of Huang Xing and Song Jiaoren, it merged with several other revolutionary organizations in 1905 to form the Tongmenghui.

Hundred Day Reform: The 103 days during which Kang Youwei and his followers influenced the Guangxu Emperor to issue edicts on political and economic reform. It ended when Empress Dowager Cixi staged a coup, imprisoned the emperor and executed six reformers.

Kokuryukai: See Black Dragon Society.

Manchuria: The term used by Westerners and Japanese to refer to northeast China. Within China, it is known as Dongbei, or Northeast, and comprises the three provinces of Heilongjiang, Jilin and Fengtian (now Liaoning).

May Fourth Movement: An intellectual and cultural revolution that began in 1915 with the launch of *New Youth,* a monthly magazine edited by Chen Duxiu to agitate for reform. As part of this New Culture Movement, supporters attacked traditional Chinese thought and exalted Western ideas, particularly science and technology. A high point of this movement was the student demonstration on May 4, 1919, when more than 3,000 students in Beijing held a mass protest against the decision of the Paris Peace Conference to transfer the former German concession in Shandong to Japan. The demonstrations sparked national protests and marked the upsurge of Chinese nationalism, a shift towards political mobilization and away from cultural activities, and a move towards a populist base rather than intellectual elites. Many political and social leaders of the following decades emerged at this time.

May Thirtieth Incident: A major labor and anti-imperialist movement that began when municipal police officers opened fire on Chinese protesters in Shanghai's International Settlement on May 30, 1925. The shootings sparked international censure and nationwide anti-foreign demonstrations and riots.

Meiji Restoration: The political revolution that returned state power from the Tokugawa shogunate to the Meiji Emperor. It began an era of major politico-socio-economic change that led to Japan's modernization and Westernization.

Minbao 民报 (People's Journal): The official organ of the Tongmenghui after *Twentieth-Century China* was banned by the Japanese government in late 1905.

Nanjing Decade: An informal name for the decade from 1928, when Chiang Kai-shek took control of Nanjing, to 1937 when his government retreated to Wuhan as a consequence of the Second Sino-Japanese War.

Nanyang 南洋: Literally Southern Ocean, this is the Chinese term for what is today's Southeast Asia, though the two terms are not exact equivalents. Nanyang used to refer to the countries immediately to the south of China. This included British Malaya, British Burma, Dutch East Indies, French Indochina, Siam and sometimes also

Ceylon and British India. Today when we speak of the Nanyang Chinese, we are referring to those Chinese settled in countries reachable by sea, i.e., Indonesia, Malaysia, Philippines and Singapore. It does not include those Chinese who migrated overland to countries on the Asian landmass from neighboring Chinese provinces.

National Protection Movement: Also translated as Movement for the Protection of the Country, this movement emerged in late 1915 after Yuan Shikai proclaimed himself emperor. Warlords Cai E and Tang Jiyao of Yunnan declared their independence and organized the National Protection Army for an expedition against Yuan. A number of other provinces followed suit with their own declarations of independence. The movement was declared a success after Yuan's death and the provinces rescinded their independence.

New Culture Movement: See May Fourth Movement.

Overseas Chinese: A generic term that encompasses all Chinese who reside outside of China, regardless of nationality. The Chinese equivalents are more specific. Ethnic Han Chinese residing outside of Greater China are known as *huaqiao* if they are Chinese nationals, and as *huayi* if they are not. An ethnic Han Chinese, regardless of nationality or domicile is referred to as *huaren*, and as *haiwai huaren* if he resides outside of China. A *zhongguo ren* is anyone who is a national of the People's Republic of China or the Republic of China, regardless of whether he is a Han Chinese or an ethnic minority.

Pan-Asianism: An ideology advocating and promoting the unity of Asian peoples against Western imperialism. Its roots go back to the mid-19th century when China and Japan, forced to open up, struggled to redefine their place in the international order. The Kokuryukai under Uchida Ryohei emerged as the leading pan-Asian organization advocating the idea of Asian solidarity against the government's policy of cooperation with Western powers. The ideal was later distorted by the Japanese military government into a brutal ideology of imperialism that sought to conquer rather then liberate Asia.

Revolutionary Army, The: A nationalist anti-Manchu tract authored by Zou Rong in 1903 that advocated social and political revolution. See also Subao Case.

GLOSSARY

Russo-Japanese War (1904–1905): A war fought over rival ambitions in Manchuria and Korea. The major theaters of operations on land were in China, specifically the Liaodong peninsula and southern Manchuria. The war ended with Russia's defeat and the Treaty of Portsmouth mediated by U.S. President Theodore Roosevelt.

Scramble for Concessions: The competition among imperialist powers for territorial concessions in China following the Treaty of Shimonoseki which ceded several Chinese territories to Japan. Until this time, the Western powers had been content to establish spheres of influence in China.

Second Revolution: The civil war that ensued after seven southern provinces rebelled against Yuan Shikai following the assassination of Song Jiaoren and Yuan's various violations of the constitution and the lack of due process in his governance.

Self-Strengthening Movement: A movement to initiate institutional reforms after the defeat of the mid-19th-century rebellions. The objective was to consolidate the power of the Qing regime and to strengthen China by introducing Western technology. Most assessments of Self-Strengthening present it as an inadequate policy that sowed the seeds of a modern military and military-industrial complex but failed to make China strong enough to resist foreign imperialism, as shown by China's defeat in the Sino-Japanese War in 1895.

Shimonoseki, Treaty of: See Sino-Japanese War.

Sino-French War (1884–1885): A war fought over the sovereignty of Indochina. China lost the war but was not required to make reparations.

Sino-Japanese War (1894–1895): An armed conflict over the sovereignty of Korea. China lost, and was required under the Treaty of Shimonoseki signed on April 17, 1895, to recognize the independence of Korea, cede Taiwan, the Pescadores and the Liaodong peninsula to Japan, and pay Japan an indemnity of 200 million taels. On April 23, the Triple Intervention of Russia, France and Germany forced Japan to return the Liaodong peninsula to China in exchange for a higher indemnity. The indemnity more than covered Japan's war costs and funded a massive rearmament program. In 1898, Russia took the Liaodong peninsula for herself.

Subao Case: A situation precipitated by the arrest in July 1903 of six Chinese nationals by the Shanghai International Settlement authority on charges of treason against the Chinese state. The arrest provoked an international crisis as the Qing government and the Settlement's authorities tussled with each other on where and how the men should be tried. The affair was finally resolved in May 1904 when a specially constituted court brought the case to a close by entering sentences against two of them, Zou Rong and Zhang Binglin. The trial, known as the Subao Case (after the name of the newspaper with which the defendants were associated), marked the moment when the radicals who called for the end of dynastic rule and the creation of a republic split from the reformers who sought the creation of a constitutional monarchy.

Straits Settlements: The group of territories in Southeast Asia established in 1826 as part of the domain controlled by the British East India Company. The Straits Settlements came under direct British control as a crown colony on April 1, 1867, until 1946, when it was dissolved as part of the British reorganization of its Southeast Asian dependencies following the end of World War II.

Thien Nan Shin Pao 天南新报: The organ of the reform movement in Singapore.

Thoe Lam Jit Poh 图南日报 (Daily for Closer Relations with the South): The Singapore revolutionary newspaper started by Tan Chor Nam and Teo Eng Hock.

Tongmenghui 同盟会: Translated variously as Revolutionary Alliance or United League, its official name in English was The China Federal Association. This was Sun's second revolutionary organization, formed in Tokyo in 1905 through the merger of his first revolutionary organization, the Xingzhonghui, with the Huaxinghui and several smaller revolutionary groups, and joined the following year by the Guangfuhui. Sun was elected its *zongli,* or party president. The Tongmenghui was transformed into a political party in March 1912 and later merged with several smaller political parties to form the Guomindang in preparation for its participation in parliamentary elections. Sun remained as *zongli* but delegated his authority to Song Jiaoren.

GLOSSARY

Treaty Ports: See Unequal Treaties.

Triple Intervention: See Sino-Japanese War.

Twentieth-Century China: Official organ of the Guangfuhui, inherited by the Tongmenghui and renamed *Minbao*.

Twenty-One Demands: A set of demands made by Japan to Yuan Shikai's government in January 1915 while the West was preoccupied with World War I. The demands were for economic rights for Japanese in Manchuria, the right to station police and economic advisers there, and major economic concessions in China Proper. Divided into five groups of demands, the fifth group would have given Japan significant control over the entire Chinese economy and effectively ended the Open Door Policy. Japan was forced by Britain and the United States to drop the fifth group of demands but obtained the first four groups in a treaty with China in May 1915.

Unequal Treaties: China's defeat by Britain in the Opium War, the first in a series of armed conflicts between China and Western powers, led to the signing of the Treaty of Nanjing in August 1842, which forced China to open five "treaty ports" for trade – Guangzhou, Xiamen, Fuzhou, Ningbo and Shanghai – while Hong Kong was ceded in perpetuity to Britain. China was later forced to make additional concessions: the inclusion of a most-favored-nation clause in the treaty; fixed tariffs on trade and extraterritoriality in the Treaty Ports. The Nanjing treaty was followed by similar treaties with other Western powers. By virtue of the most-favored-nation clauses, these powers were granted the same privileges and rights accorded to Britain. The Chinese viewed these treaties as unequal because they were imposed on China through gunboat diplomacy and because they encroached on China's sovereign rights. Most of these unequal treaties were abrogated during the Second Sino-Japanese War. A few survived, most notably the treaties concerning Hong Kong and Macau, which were finally resolved with their respective handovers to China in 1997 and 1999.

United Fronts: The two instances of cooperation between the Communist Party of China and the Guomindang to realize national goals. The first United Front (1923–1927) aimed at reclaiming China from the warlords, while the second United Front (1937–1945) sought to resist Japan in the Second Sino-Japanese War.

Versailles, Treaty of: One of the most important treaties that brought an end to the state of war between Germany and the Allied Powers in World War I. The other Central Powers signed separate treaties. Although the armistice signed on November 11, 1918, ended the actual fighting, it took six months of negotiations at the Paris Peace Conference to conclude the peace treaty, which was finally signed on October 21, 1919. China refused to ratify the treaty due to the provisions which allowed Japan to retain the former German concessions in Shandong. See also May Fourth Movement.

Washington Naval Conference: A disarmament conference called by U.S. President Warren Harding to limit and balance the level of naval power in the various Pacific territories after Japan obtained concessions in the region under the Treaty of Versailles. It was held in Washington, D.C., from November 12, 1921, to February 6, 1922, and attended by nine nations: Belgium, Britain, China, France, Italy, Japan, Netherlands, Portugal and the United States. Neither Russia nor the Central Powers defeated in World War I were invited.

Wenxueshe 文学社: Literary Institute, one of the separatist groups of the Tongmenghui which along with Gongjinhui, another breakaway group, subverted the New Army in central China that sparked the Wuchang Uprising.

Wuchang Uprising: The catalyst for the 1911 Revolution, the Wuchang Uprising began with the accidental explosion of a bomb that was being assembled by revolutionaries in Hankou on the evening of October 9, 1911. The next day, a mutiny broke out among the troops stationed in neighboring Wuchang as a consequence of the explosion.

Xinghanhui 兴汉会: The Revive Han Society was a short-lived revolutionary organization created by Sun in collaboration with the Gelaohui.

Xingzhonghui 兴中会: The Revive China Society was Sun Yat-sen's first revolutionary organization, founded in Honolulu in 1894.

Xinhai Revolution 辛亥革命: An alternate name for the 1911 Revolution, which took place in the Xinhai year of the traditional Chinese calendar.

GLOSSARY

Zhili 直隶: From the 18th century until its dissolution, Zhili province encompassed parts of today's Beijing and Tianjin municipalities, Hebei province, western Liaoning, northern Henan and the Inner Mongolia Autonomous Region. In 1928, the Nationalist government assigned portions of northern Zhili to its neighbors and renamed the remainder Hebei province.

Zhongguo Gemingdang 中国革命党: The Chinese Revolutionary Party, founded by Sun in July 1914 after Yuan Shikai outlawed the Guomindang. Virtually all overseas branches continued to identify themselves as belonging to the Guomindang since Yuan's ban affected only the domestic branches.

Zhongguo Guomindang 中国国民党: See Guomindang.

Zhonghetang 中和堂: The revolutionary society formed by You Lie in Yokohama in 1900 following the failure of the Huizhou Uprising. Branches were later set up in British Malaya after he moved to Singapore.

Zongli Yamen 总理衙门: The Office for the Management of All Foreign Countries, established by the Qing court in 1861 to deal with the crisis provoked by Western powers. Under the leadership of Prince Gong, it was involved not only in treaty negotiations but in Self-Strengthening projects, including the establishment of language schools with Western curricula, and the study of Western forms of government and international law.

THE UNFINISHED REVOLUTION

Prologue

MANDATE UNDER SIEGE

THE MANCHUS who ruled China as the Qing dynasty from 1644 to 1912 were neither Chinese by pedigree nor Chinese in the eyes of the Han Chinese who, then as now, constituted over 90 percent of the population. The Manchus were the descendants of Jurchen tribes who originated in the region beyond the Great Wall known as Manchuria.[1] The Jurchens had a long history of interaction with China. In 1122, they conquered northern China and ruled over the area together with their own territory as the Jin dynasty. The Mongols drove them back to their ancestral homeland in 1234, but by the late Ming dynasty (1368–1644), they were once again pressing on China's northern border. In response Ming China incorporated the Jurchens' territory into her domain, granting Jurchen chiefs honorific titles and trading privileges.

Nurhaci, chief of the Jurchen Aisin Gioro clan, was granted a title by the Ming emperor, but in around 1610 he severed his relations with the Ming court. Six years later, he declared himself Khan of the Later Jin dynasty and began making incursions into territories that the Ming considered as essentially China's. Nurhaci revealed his intention of attacking China Proper[2] as early as 1622 but died four years later before he could realize his dream. His son and successor, Huang Taiji, inherited his ambition and resumed the Jurchen advance on China. Realizing that he could not hope to subjugate the Chinese by military force alone, Huang began adopting features of Chinese government alongside Jurchen institutions beginning in 1631, as well as making increasing use of Han Chinese both in the government and in the armed forces. In 1636, Huang severed his state's link with its tribal past by adopting a new name for his people, Manchu, and declaring a new dynasty, Qing, literally "pure" or "clear." He made a number of spectacular raids across the Great Wall, with one within striking distance of the Ming capital of Beijing. His untimely death in 1643, however, and his succession by an infant son dimmed the Manchus' prospects for further advances.

In the spring of 1644, a rebel force seized Beijing. To spare himself the degradation, the Chongzhen Emperor hanged himself. His commander in charge of the region northeast of Beijing now made the same mistake that had been played out so many times in Chinese history: he enlisted the barbarians to help him recapture the capital and put down the rebellion. The Manchus obliged. On June 5, Manchu forces captured Beijing and put the rebels in flight. Once they occupied the Forbidden City and declared Heaven's Mandate forfeit, it was clear that they meant to stay.

With the Manchus having been "invited" into the capital, the conquest of northern China proceeded relatively smoothly. Central and southern China was a very different story. Here Ming pretenders and loyalists and other disgruntled people continued to resist the new conquest dynasty. It would be another 40 years before the Qing had firm control of China Proper. The conquest of the central and southern provinces was accompanied by massacres, notably the 10-day sack of the commercial city of Yangzhou in May 1645. These brutalities would long be remembered by the Chinese and were invoked in the rallying cries of the revolutionaries who fought the Manchus in the late 19th and early 20th centuries.

Dorgon, the regent for the infant Shunzhi Emperor, was well aware of the problems that could arise between a Manchu aristocracy accustomed to the use of military power and a Chinese bureaucracy split between those who accepted the Manchus and those who opposed them. To reassure the Chinese, Dorgon retained the Ming civil service examination system and invited Ming officials to remain in their posts and perform their duties alongside Manchu appointees. The Confucian philosophy emphasizing the obedience of subject to emperor was enforced as the state creed, and the Confucian court practices and temple rituals over which Chinese emperors had traditionally presided were continued. To retain the confidence of the Manchu nobles, Dorgon adopted policies that asserted Manchu dominance. In spite of the Chinese-Manchu diarchy, Chinese were barred from the highest metropolitan posts, though they predominated over Manchu officeholders outside the capital in non-military positions.

To prevent the absorption of the Manchus into the dominant Han Chinese population, the latter were prohibited from migrating to the Manchu homeland and from taking Manchu brides. Chinese men were required to adopt the Manchu hairstyle by shaving the front of their forehead and braiding the rest of their hair into a *towchang*, or pigtail. Such discriminatory policies amplified their racial distinctiveness and caused considerable resentment among the Chinese. But so long as the economy was steaming along nicely and the vast empire was prosperous and at peace, anti-Manchu sentiments remained latent.

Happily, the Qing dynasty ruled commendably over the vast Chinese empire for the first 150 years. A succession of three remarkable emperors[3] extended China's borders to her greatest extent ever and brought a long period of stability and prosperity that harkened China back to the ancient glories of the Tang dynasty (618–907). By 1775, China was easily the most extensive, populous, powerful and prosperous nation in the world. But the reign of Qianlong, the last of the three great emperors, proved to be a watershed in the Qing dynastic cycle. The success of the Qing in maintaining the traditional order, and the long period of peace and prosperity discouraged change in the attitude of the ruling elite. The cultural superiority of Chinese civilization and the position of the Chinese empire at the center of the known world were accepted as axiomatic. To question this self-evident truth, to propose innovation or to promote foreign ideas were punishable as apostasies. At the same time, China's population grew phenomenally in the 18th century. Lacking the technology to improve production efficiency, per capita production fell. This paved the way for overpopulation and all the ills associated with it. With age, Qianlong's judgment faltered; court intrigues and corruption became rampant. Military campaigns to distant lands exhausted the treasury while graft and profiteering undermined the morale of the army. The serious financial situation was aggravated by court extravagances that became the template for conspicuous consumption among officials and the upper class. Revolts erupted in various parts of the empire in the early 19th century. Secret societies combining anti-Manchu subversion with banditry emerged to capitalize on the growing discontent of the masses.

Qianlong's successors inherited a crumbling empire. They were not the equal of their distinguished forebears and proved even more unequal to the task of arresting the empire's decline. The emphasis of their Confucian upbringing on scholarship and virtuous behavior left them ill equipped to deal with situations that called for radical solutions. The empire's treasury was empty and there were widespread rebellions, which the Qing military, saddled with corruption, found difficult to suppress. The majority of Manchu families, other than those in the military and civil service, had done little except to draw pensions from the state over a period of five generations. Their decadence as a ruling and privileged class coincided ominously with the new threat from the West.

The Portuguese merchants who landed at the southern city of Guangzhou (Canton) in 1514 were the first Europeans to have extensive contacts with China. They established a foothold at Macau, from where they monopolized China's foreign trade. They were soon followed by the British and the French, the former eventually becoming the dominant Western traders in China. Such trade was conducted under the guise of tribute and these Western traders were obliged to follow the same elaborate, centuries-old rituals imposed on envoys from China's many tributary states. There was no conception in the imperial court that the white barbarians deserved to be treated as cultural or political equals. The one exception was Russia, China's powerful neighbor with which she shared a long border. Sensitive to the need for security along this frontier, the Qing court was prepared to be realistic in its relations with Russia. The Treaty of Nerchinsk in 1689 with Russia to end a series of border disputes was China's first treaty that accepted the principle of diplomatic equality with another state. Western attempts to expand trade on the same basis were rebuffed since China had no need for foreign products, which were assumed to be inferior. Despite this attitude, trade flourished. Maritime trade was initially allowed at several southern ports but from 1760 it was confined to Guangzhou and only with the group of Chinese merchants known to Westerners as the Cohong. Foreign merchants were subject to strict regulations and were only permitted to remain in Guangzhou during the trading season.

Trade was not the only basis of contact between China and the West. Catholic missionaries had been attempting to establish their church in China since the 13th century. The Jesuits, especially, contributed greatly to Chinese knowledge in architecture, art, astronomy, canon casting, cartography, geography, mathematics and music. Their willingness to compromise on the Chinese practice of ancestor worship was condemned by a papal decision in 1704 which proscribed the tolerance. This weakened the Christian movement so that by 1800 only a few hundred thousand Chinese souls had been saved from eternal damnation.

In the early 18th century, Britain's trade with China was conducted exclusively through the British East India Company (EIC) and comprised the exchange of Chinese tea, silk and porcelain for British goods. By mid-century, the British public had developed such a voracious appetite for the beverage that the value of Britain's imports from China far exceeded her exports to China. The result was a massive outflow of silver to the Celestial Empire. To help bridge the trade deficit, raw cotton was exported from the EIC's fields in India to China on board ships owned by private British merchants known as "country traders." Alongside this was a small but lucrative trade in opium grown on the EIC's plantations in India.[4]

Relations between British merchants and the Cohong merchants were generally cordial at first. But after the Napoleonic Wars, which confirmed Britain as the leading naval power in the world, the British became more assertive, and tensions with China increased. In 1816 a British trade mission to the Qing court to request an improvement in the arrangements for trade returned empty-handed. Thereafter opium smuggling began to escalate. By 1820, the volume of opium being smuggled into China was so large that silver began flowing in the reverse direction, from China to Britain. This was in spite of the fact that the import of opium was prohibited by imperial decree, but made possible through the connivance of treacherous merchants and a corrupt bureaucracy.

The British government assumed responsibility of the China trade when the EIC's monopoly came to an end in 1834. Lord Napier was appointed commissioner of trade in China and instructed to negotiate improvements in the arrangements for trade with the Qing court. Without first obtaining permission as required by Chinese regulations, Napier proceeded directly to Guangzhou. For his disregard of protocol, he was refused a meeting and was only allowed to leave under humiliating circumstances. In London, the debacle only served to harden the resolve of those in favor of unrestrained commerce. While these free traders were demanding that China be forced to open additional ports, a debate was raging in Beijing among officials on how to stop opium smuggling. Convinced that there was no way to stop it, one group recommended that the government legalize and tax the import of opium, and allow opium poppy to be grown in China. This proposal aroused the ire of another group of officials, who argued that opium was a moral and financial issue on which there could be no compromise. They demanded that the law be strictly enforced to suppress the opium trade.

The Daoguang Emperor was persuaded. In 1839, he dispatched Lin Zexu to Guangzhou as imperial commissioner to suppress the opium trade. Lin acted with ruthless efficiency on his arrival, arresting drug addicts and seizing illegal stocks of opium owned by Chinese dealers. Next he wrote a letter to Queen Victoria appealing to her sense of moral decency and seeking her cooperation to bring an end to the opium trade.[5] He then called on the foreign merchants to hand over their opium stock and to sign pledges that they would cease trading in the narcotic. To convince them that he meant business, Lin suspended all trade and blockaded them in the trading area outside Guangzhou known as the Thirteen Factories. There they were to remain until they complied.

Meanwhile, Lin's arrests of addicts had collapsed the demand for opium, leaving the Western merchants sitting on a mountain of unsold stock. This was a serious problem for the British. Profits from the illegal opium trade had been financing the legal trade in tea and silk, as well as the administration of India. The earnings remitted back to London enabled merchants to finance the purchase of American cotton for the mills of Lancashire, whose products were sold to Indian consumers.[6] A disruption in the flow of funds from the illicit drug trade could conceivably stop the music on this intricately structured trade network. Thus when Charles Elliot, the Chief Superintendent of British Trade in China, assured the British merchants that the Crown would compensate them for their stock of opium that he was about to turn in to Commissioner Lin, they were elated. Over 20,000 chests of opium were delivered to Lin, who lifted the cordon on the Thirteen Factories as promised and allowed the foreigners to go on their way.

Commissioner Lin had won the battle against the foreign merchants but no one could have foreseen that his actions would lead to war with Britain. In London, drug lords and textile barons lobbied Parliament to take retaliatory action. Many in England, including the opium merchants, recognized the immoral nature of the trade but neither they nor the British government could accept the idea that British subjects should be subjected to Qing law when on Chinese territory. More importantly, no other product could match the obscene profits from the narcotic trade. At the end of the day, British national pride and commercial avarice took precedence over moral arguments. An expeditionary force was dispatched forthwith to the China coast to demand satisfaction.

Fighting began in earnest in 1840. Better equipped and better trained, the British used their awesome naval and gunnery power to inflict a quick and decisive victory. Lin Zexu was exiled to faraway Chinese Turkestan to atone for his "sin" while the Daoguang Emperor authorized negotiations to end hostilities. The Treaty of Nanjing, signed on August 29, 1842, a "date that would forever live in infamy," marked the start of a hundred years of humiliation for the Chinese and the inauspicious start to the struggle for modern China.

The Treaty of Nanjing required China to open five treaty ports[7] to British trade, cede Hong Kong in perpetuity to the British Crown, abolish certain trade restrictions and agree to a uniform tariff. To top it all, China was forced to pay a huge indemnity of 21 million silver dollars. This was the first of a series of unequal treaties forced upon a hapless China by foreign powers. A supplementary agreement later granted British citizens immunity from Chinese laws, and conferred upon Britain most-favored-nation status, whereby she would be accorded whatever concessions China might thereafter grant to other powers. The British had drawn first blood and these treaties became the template for other foreign powers as they picked up the blood trail and joined in the "slicing of the Chinese melon." The once mighty empire was now a de facto "colony of many nations but the responsibility of none."

The Opium War occurred on the downward phase of the Qing dynastic cycle. It hastened China's descent from its lofty height as the Celestial Empire to its terrestrial nadir as the Sick Man of Asia. Those who thought that Heaven was about to withdraw its Mandate found plenty of evidence to reinforce their belief. China's principal waterways, the Yangtze and the Yellow River, overflowed and flooded the surrounding areas. Drought scourged the northern provinces and hit the grain crop, which also suffered extensive damage from natural calamities. The Qing court's inability to deal with these natural disasters and provide relief to a population already impoverished by oppressive taxes fueled anti-dynastic sentiments. Resentment eventually erupted in rebellions that came close to rupturing the dynasty's tenuous hold on Heaven's Mandate.

An ineffectual emperor ascended the throne at the very moment when the empire needed a fiery dragon at the fore rather than the lame duck that the Xianfeng Emperor turned out to be. During his entire 11-year reign commencing in 1850, China was tortured by insurrections, the most destructive of which was the Taiping Rebellion.[8] It was unlike any previous popular revolt in China and had its roots in the extraordinary experience of a single individual, Hong Xiuquan. The failed scholar son of a Hakka farmer in Guangdong, Hong experienced delusions after reading a Christian tract, *Good Words to Admonish the Age*. These visions convinced him that he was the younger brother of Jesus, the second son of Jehovah charged with the mission to return the Chinese to the "Heavenly Way" and kill the devil-demons (meaning the Manchus and their Chinese collaborators) who were leading them astray. His victory would usher in a period of *taiping* (Heavenly peace).

In 1843 Hong began roaming the dangerous countryside of Guangdong and Guangxi making converts to his "God-Worshipping" religion. Some converts experienced spirit possession, others had visions of Hong's coming greatness. As their numbers grew, local governments and local elites began to view them as a cult. In 1850, a government attempt to suppress the movement pushed them into open rebellion. Pursued by Qing soldiers, their men, women and children swept through the countryside, sometimes taking and holding towns for weeks and winning new converts and supporters.

In March 1853, the Taiping captured the city of Nanjing. Here Hong Xiuquan and his flock, now a million strong, established the capital of the Kingdom of Heavenly Peace. While on the march, Hong and other top Taiping leaders continued to refine their religious teachings – an eclectic mix of the Christian Bible, the Confucian classics and Chinese folk culture. The Manchu rulers, Daoism and Buddhism were to be destroyed and replaced by the worship of Jehovah. Hong would rule over an egalitarian utopia where every man, woman and child would enjoy complete equality. The sexes were strictly segregated except for conjugal visits for the purpose of reproduction. They worked the fields together and stood side by side on the battlefield. Land was taken from landlords, and such confiscated wealth went into a communal "Heavenly Treasury." But Taiping society was anything but egalitarian. Goods were distributed according to rank, while Hong and his top lieutenants helped themselves to the Heavenly Treasury. They lived in luxurious palaces stocked in abundance with food and drinks, and women serving as playmates. The leaders fought among themselves, which sparked a series of bloody purges in which 20,000, including some Taiping leaders, were killed or driven away, leaving Hong in complete control. Despite the deaths, the Taipings were at the height of their power in 1856.

While the Taiping was establishing itself in Nanjing, the Small Sword Society launched a tax revolt at Shanghai in September 1853, disrupting essential services and driving the Qing customs superintendent out of business. In response, the Americans, British and French created the Shanghai Municipal Council to serve their needs. In 1862, the French dropped out of the arrangement to form their own French Concession; the following year, the Americans and the British jointly created the Shanghai International Settlement. As an emergency measure, the British, French and American consuls also established a system of consular administration of foreign trade. This system of consular control came to an end in May 1855 and customs administration was brought under the Qing government's jurisdiction. From this date until 1949, the Imperial Maritime Customs Service (renamed Chinese Maritime Customs Service after 1911) calculated the duties on foreign trade in the treaty ports. Largely staffed by expatriates at the senior levels, the customs service began to be fashioned into a powerful and efficient bureaucracy with wide-ranging responsibilities. Under its second inspector-general, Robert Hart, who served from 1863 to 1911, its responsibilities grew to include domestic customs administration, postal administration, harbor and waterway management, and anti-smuggling operations. Hart's diplomatic approach and sense of proportion endeared him to the court, which took him into confidence as a trusted servant and an adviser on foreign affairs. On his part, he declined the position of British minister in China in the 1880s in order to remain with the customs service.⁹

While the Qing regime was dealing with the Taiping crisis, tensions with Britain over the opium question were rising to crisis levels. This time the British had grander ideas than just opium; they wanted no less than the extension of their commercial interests across China. Such a concession if granted would have put Britain one step closer to direct imperial control of China. Since the Treaty of Nanjing, other Western powers had also wrested concessions similar to those granted to Britain. Now the French and the Americans were determined to prevent British merchants from developing monopolies in China. Realizing that they now had competition, Britain demanded a revision of the Nanjing treaty to extract more concessions. The Qing government rejected the new demands and the stage was set for another confrontation.

The spark for renewed hostilities was a minor incident off the coast of Guangzhou. On October 8, 1856, Chinese soldiers boarded the *Arrow*, a Chinese-owned schooner with a British registry in Hong Kong. This was a loophole for Chinese ship owners to take advantage of British extraterritoriality to put their vessels beyond the jurisdiction of the Qing government. In this case Chinese coast guards had been tipped off that the *Arrow* was involved in piracy. Probably unaware of the schooner's registry, the coast guards took the crew into custody. Some witnesses alleged that Qing guards had hauled down the *Arrow*'s Union Jack and flung it on deck. Others claimed that the *Arrow* was not flying any flag at all.

The truth mattered little to the British, nor the fact that the *Arrow*'s British registry had lapsed before the incident. The Qing government's refusal to apologize was sufficient cause for war. France promptly joined the fray with her own pretext after a French missionary was killed by a Chinese mob. The Sepoy Mutiny in India prevented the British from attacking China in 1857, but the following year, an Anglo-French expeditionary force reached Tianjin. The Chinese decided to negotiate. Under the Treaty of Tianjin concluded in 1858, China agreed to open more treaty ports, allow foreigners to travel in the interior, legalize the opium trade, accept a resident British minister in Beijing and institute changes to external tariffs and internal transit duties. China signed similar treaties with France, the United States and Russia. When the representatives of the powers returned a year later to ratify the treaties, they were attacked and retreated with heavy casualties. A much larger Anglo-French expeditionary force returned in 1860, marched on Beijing and sacked the Yuanmingyuan, the Old Summer Palace located just 5 miles (8 km) northwest of the Imperial City.[10] Over several days of rampage and plunder, British and French troops with the connivance of their officers destroyed the huge complex of palaces and other exquisite structures that took several emperors over two centuries to build. They looted the vast trove of cultural treasures within, which soon found their way into royal, military and private art collections in Britain. Adding insult to injury, China was forced to pay indemnity of 8 million taels each to Britain and France, and open up Tianjin as a treaty port. In addition, Britain acquired the Kowloon peninsula opposite Hong Kong while France secured the right for its missionaries to own properties in the interior of China. A month later, Russia acquired new territories in China which they promptly named Vladivostok.[11]

The Xianfeng Emperor and his court fled to the Qing summer palace in Jehol (present-day Chengde) beyond the Great Wall when the Anglo-French expeditionary force was advancing towards Beijing in 1860. There he remained until his death in 1861 at the age of 30 from a life of debauchery. His most lasting legacy was to have successfully planted his seed in a concubine – the future Empress Dowager Cixi. Her rise at court began when she gave birth to a son, who became the Tongzhi Emperor.

The Taiping Rebellion lasted as long as it did partly due to the incompetence of the Qing's traditional armed forces. The antecedent of the Qing military was the Eight Banner system created by Nurhaci in 1601. Another military force, the Green Standard, was formed after the Manchu conquest of China and comprised mostly Han Chinese from disadvantaged backgrounds. By the mid-19th century, both had outlived their usefulness. The hereditary nature of the Eight Banners gave rise to complacency while the comforts of a civilian life in the barracks sapped their martial spirit. For the Green Standards, corruption was a major problem. A soldier could obtain a position by purchase and it was not unusual for officers to report non-existent men in their units and pocket the salaries of these phantoms. Both the Banners and the Green Standards lacked modern weapons and competent officers. They were spread throughout the empire, which made them less responsive to rapid mobilization and more difficult to put under centralized supervision.[12]

The main role in the defeat of the mid-century rebellions fell to a new military formation known as the regional armies. When the Taiping swept across Hunan in mid-1852, the court ordered Zeng Guofan, a native of Hunan, out of mourning to organize a militia in defense of his home province. Zeng, then the chief commissioner of the provincial examinations in Jiangxi, realized that a militia would be no match against a crusading force backed by an ideology. To counter them, he would need to raise a well-trained army and indoctrinate it with a sense of mission in defense of Chinese cultural heritage. He began by drawing on his network of family, friends and former disciples to recruit officers, who in turn drew on their own networks to enlist the rank and file. As a result, Zeng's army was closely identified with Hunan province and was known as the Hunan army (or Xiang army, after Hunan's principal river). To pay for his army, Zeng arranged with provincial governors for direct transfers of tax revenues to his coffers. The Qing court gave him leave to sell ranks and titles, and to introduce the *lijin* tax, an internal tax on goods in transit. In 1856, Zeng equipped his army with modern weapons and put them into action against the rebels.

The Hunan army was the first of the regional armies. When a Taiping army threatened Shanghai in 1862, Zeng used his influence to get his protégé Li Hongzhang appointed acting governor of Jiangsu, which made it possible for Li to form his own Anhui army (or Huai army, after the major river of Anhui). Zuo Zongtang, another Zeng protégé, modernized the traditional Qing forces that he commanded as governor-general of Fujian and Zhejiang. All three men used modern weapons and Western training methods against the rebels. By January 1864, Qing forces had isolated the Taiping armies in the field and surrounded Nanjing, the Heavenly Capital. The Hunan army captured Nanjing in July, slaughtering over 100,000 rebels. Hong Xiuquan met his inglorious end during the assault. The remaining Taiping armies, including some leaders, were defeated, captured and executed over the next few years. With the defeat of the Taiping, the Hunan and Huai armies went on to assist in the suppression of the Nian rebellion in northern China and the Muslim revolts in the northwest.

IN JUNE 1853, three months after Taiping rebels seized Nanjing, Karl Marx had written that the Qing dynasty's "dissolution must follow as surely as that of any mummy carefully preserved in a hermetically sealed coffin, whenever it is brought into contact with the open air."[13] Indeed, in 1860 when the Taipings were on the verge of capturing Shanghai and the Anglo-French expeditionary force was sacking Yuanmingyuan, the collapse of the dynasty appeared imminent. What is surprising is that the dynasty did not just survive; it reversed the dynastic decline and hung on to Heaven's Mandate for another half-century.

Qing officials attributed their regime's revitalization to a "restoration." The Tongzhi Emperor, whose name is given to this restoration, was only five when he ascended the dragon throne. Tensions soon arose between his regents and his mother, Empress Dowager Cixi. With the connivance of her fellow empress dowager Ci'an and her brother-in-law Prince Gong, they deposed the regents in a palace coup and took over the regency. Weak and uninterested in matters of state, Tongzhi spent more time in the pleasure courtyards of Beijing than the imperial court in the Forbidden City. He lived his entire life under the shadow of his mother, who ruled the empire from behind the silk screen.

The task of the Tongzhi Restoration encompassed the suppression of the mid-century rebellions, the revival of the economy, the reinstatement of the traditional order, the pursuit of peace with foreign powers, and the initiation of the Self-Strengthening Movement. The last of the major rebellions, the Muslim Revolt in Chinese Turkestan led by Ya'qub Beg, was finally defeated in 1877. The recovery of territory was a more difficult task and it took several years of negotiation to get Russia to withdraw from the Ili valley in Chinese Turkestan under the Treaty of St. Petersburg in 1881. In 1884, the region was incorporated into the empire as Xinjiang province.[14]

To resuscitate the agrarian economy, abandoned areas were repopulated by sponsored migrants, who were supplied with tools and seeds. Agricultural taxes were reduced or remitted in areas that had suffered badly, and irrigation systems were repaired. Steps were taken to attract men of talent for public service, and gentry leaders were encouraged to open or reopen schools and to refurbish libraries. The examination system, which had been disrupted in areas occupied by rebels, was reinstated. Quotas for degrees were increased in the affected provinces to recognize military and financial contribution. In the capital, the government pursued cordial relations with the powers so as to give the country a chance to engage in reconstruction.[15]

However, nothing could reverse some of the changes that had taken place. The Taiping failed to destroy the traditional order, but it forced the dynasty to adopt policies that disturbed the old balance of power, and brought about changes that were to have the most profound impact on the fate of the dynasty. Politically, it caused the transfer of government power from the Manchus to the Chinese. After the defeat of the Taiping, officers of the regional armies were rewarded with important assignments; key governor-generalships and governorships previously held by Manchus now passed to the Chinese. Li Hongzhang, in particular, as governor-general of Zhili and commissioner of trade for the northern ports, was China's de facto prime minister. More and more Chinese were appointed to the Grand Council until they eventually outnumbered the Manchus. The post-Taiping period also saw the growing influence of provincial officials in national affairs. Whereas the Qing government had been highly centralized and decided policies for the provinces, the court was so weakened by the Taiping that it often had to consult high provincial officials on national issues and defer to their opinions, or solicit the views of local authorities in order to win their support. At times, powerful governors-general and governors would act independently of the central government. The most blatant instance of provincial independence would take place in 1911 when provincial authorities declared their support for the Wuchang Uprising and in so doing precipitated the downfall of the Qing dynasty.[16] Militarily, the tradition of the regional armies was inherited by the Beiyang Army. Yuan Shikai as supremo had the total allegiance of the generals under his command, a power which made it possible for him to dictate the fate of the dynasty. Finally, Taiping remnants who went underground joined the Tiandihui, the Heaven and Earth Society, and kept alive the idea of racial and nationalistic revolution against the Manchus. This became a source of inspiration for Sun Yat-sen and other revolutionaries.

The Tongzhi Restoration bought the dynasty some breathing space, "an Indian summer in which the historically inevitable process of decline is arrested for a time."[17] But like similar restorations that had occurred during the Han (206 BCE – 220 CE) and Tang dynasties, the Tongzhi Restoration was no more than a stay of execution, not a commutation of the death sentence on the Manchu regime.

When the Xianfeng Emperor and the imperial family fled to Jehol in 1860, his younger brother Prince Gong had remained in Beijing to negotiate with the foreigners. The peace process transformed him from a xenophobe into an admirer of the awesome power of the West. He began to adopt a new policy of diplomatic accommodation to gain peace and allow China to build up her military strength. The West, too, recognized that the enjoyment of her treaty rights and increased opportunities for trade were dependent on the survival of the Qing regime. Policy reorientation on both sides resulted in a decade of relative peace and harmonious cooperation, a conducive climate for China to embark on her diplomatic and military modernization.[18]

Diplomatic reforms began with the establishment of the Zongli Yamen (Office of General Management) in March 1861 to direct China's foreign relations. This was not the Foreign Office that the powers might have hoped for but it was an improvement over the practice of treating all foreign nations as tributary states.[19] Where it failed as an effective foreign office, it succeeded reasonably well as a promoter of modernization. It was China's first major institutional innovation in response to the Western impact. The Zongli Yamen engaged not only in foreign affairs but also functioned as a promoter of projects carried out under the rubric of what came to be called the Self-Strengthening Movement. These included the establishment of modern schools, the adoption of Western science, industry, and communications, and the investigation of Western laws.[20]

The idea of learning from the West originated more than two decades earlier when opium commissioner Lin Zexu championed it. He had foreign newspapers and Western works on law, history, politics and geography translated. In 1842 Wei Yuan, an adviser to Lin, voicing concern about the military superiority of the West, outlined a plan for maritime defense. Noting the traditional strategy of "using barbarians to control barbarians," he recommended the study of the superior techniques of the West.[21] In 1860, Feng Guifen, another Lin associate, called for the adoption of Western knowledge and the manufacture of Western-style weapons.

Later Zhang Zhidong encapsulated the same sentiment in the phrase "Chinese learning as the base, Western study for use." This became the mantra of the Self-Strengthening Movement.

Beginning in the early 1860s and for the next three and a half decades, Self-Strengtheners invested heavily in education, military modernization and supporting industries. In the initial phase of the movement, from roughly 1861 to 1872, the emphasis was on education and training, the adoption of Western weaponry and the acquisition of scientific knowledge. One of the earliest Self-Strengthening projects was the Tongwen Guan, or Foreign Language College, established at Beijing in 1862 under the auspices of the Zongli Yamen to train specialists in foreign languages for service in China's diplomatic corps. So long as social success required mastery of the Confucian classics, Western-oriented schools had minimum appeal to scholarly and gentry families. It was only among the children of commoners who attended Christian missionary schools that Western learning made any inroads.[22] By the 1870s, the Zongli Yamen had all but abandoned the Tongwen Guan. In 1889, it was absorbed into the Imperial University of Beijing, the forerunner of today's Peking University, or Beida.[23]

An innovative Self-Strengthening enterprise was the Chinese Educational Mission proposed by Yung Wing, the first Chinese to receive an American university degree. In 1872, he led a batch of Chinese boys to Hartford, Connecticut, where they lived with American families and studied at various schools in the area. By 1875 there were 120 in all. Immersed in the social and school environments of this American city, it was hard for the boys to maintain the traditional cultural values insisted upon by Qing officials. The surge in anti-Chinese sentiment in the U.S. soon raised questions and concerns about the wisdom of continuing the program. The final straw was the U.S. government's refusal to allow the Mission's students to attend West Point and Annapolis in spite of the most-favored-nation clause granted to China. The Mission was terminated in 1881 and all the students were recalled home.[24]

Paralleling Prince Gong's diplomatic modernization were efforts to create a modern Chinese military through the adoption of Western technology. In 1865, the Jiangnan Arsenal was established in Shanghai with machinery purchased from the U.S. by Yung Wing. It produced not only guns and cannons but also constructed five ships, the last in 1872. In 1866, a dockyard was constructed near Fuzhou. Although these government undertakings adopted modern production techniques, they retained the old management style and a blind faith in the ability of foreigners.

As the Self-Strengthening Movement progressed, there was greater emphasis on the development of profit-oriented enterprises in the second phase from 1872 to 1885. Foremost among these were the China Merchants' Steam Navigation Company, the Kaiping Coal Mines, the Shanghai Cotton Cloth Mill, and the Imperial Telegraph Administration. Capital for these enterprises came primarily from private sources. The bottom line was the responsibility of the merchants but they were barred from the management, which was mostly in the hands of government-appointed officials. These companies suffered the usual bureaucratic inefficiency, corruption and nepotism. They tended to monopolize business through government favors, monopolies or intervention and thus discouraged private competition. In the third and final phase from 1885 to 1895, while the emphasis on military and naval buildup continued, the idea of enriching the nation through light industry gained favor. Industries such as textile and cotton-weaving gathered momentum.

Li Hongzhang emerged as the leading light of the Self-Strengthening Movement, responsible for over 90 percent of the modernization projects. Though a provincial official as governor-general of Zhili, he performed a number of central government functions due to his proximity to the capital and Cixi's trust in him. Among his fellow Self-Strengtheners, Zeng Guofan died in 1872 and Zuo Zongtang was preoccupied with the suppression of the Muslim rebellions in the northwest. Prince Gong had lost much of his clout in court after two brushes with Cixi and China's defeat in the Sino-French War of 1884–1885.

Most assessments of Self-Strengthening present it as an inadequate policy that sowed the seeds of a modern military and military-industrial complex but failed to make China strong enough to resist foreign imperialism. Various arguments have been advanced to explain the movement's failure. The vitality of China's cultural and intellectual traditions and their incompatibility with the needs of a modern state have often been cited. Many efforts were frustrated by a scholar class whose fortunes were tied to Chinese learning. Distribution of translations of Western works was limited and few Chinese scholars felt the inclination to read them. At the same time, there were no attempts to assimilate institutions and cultures as part of the crusade for modernization. Self-Strengthening thus became the plaything of a few high officials who recognized the need but received no firm or consistent backing from Cixi, who allowed the ideological conservatives at court to stalemate the innovators so she could hold the balance of power.[25]

Another line of argument puts the blame on Western imperialism, which entered a more aggressive phase in the 1870s after a decade of relative peace. Western businessmen, unhappy that they had failed to develop markets in China commensurate with their expectations, became more demanding. As they became increasingly vocal, Chinese public opinion also began to harden against the Western presence. The Treaty of Tianjin had opened the interior to Christian missionaries whose appearance in rural society provoked much resentment. The staunchest opposition was from the gentry, who saw missionaries as a threat to their privileged position in rural society. That missionaries often helped the cause of their converts in litigations did not make matters easier.

Anti-missionary protests became more frequent. One of the most important was the incident at Tianjin in the summer of 1870. Rumors had been circulating that Catholic priests and nuns were kidnapping and sexually abusing children as part of their strange rituals. Civic leaders demanded an investigation and judicial officials were dispatched to inspect the cathedral. The French consul regarded this as a national insult. He rushed to the *yamen* of the city prefect and ended up killing a policeman. The crowd went berserk with rage and within moments had torn the consul to pieces. Rioting then spread across the city. The French consulate and cathedral were razed, resulting in the death of about 20 French subjects. When reports of the incident reached Beijing, court officials expected the worst and made preparations for war with France.[26]

France did not go to war with China because she was already engaged in one with Prussia but this did not stop her from demanding an indemnity and the execution of the officials involved. The incident put an end to the era of cooperation with the West. As imperialism intensified, Li

Hongzhang's readiness to assume responsibility for China's foreign relations made him the most powerful man in the empire after the emperor, or rather the Empress Dowager Cixi.

Cixi continued to rule from behind the silk screen even after Tongzhi reached his majority in 1873. His death two years later provoked a succession crisis. She appointed her infant nephew as heir and thus extended her regency for another 15 years. His enthronement as the Guangxu Emperor scandalized the court for it contravened the Qing succession rule which required that an imperial successor had to be from a later generation so he could properly perform the filial ancestral ceremonies in memory of the deceased emperor. Cixi deflected the opposition by promising that Guangxu's future son would be adopted as the son of the late Tongzhi Emperor. Especially after the death of her co-regent Ci'an and the dismissal of Prince Gong, Cixi reigned supreme over the vast Chinese empire. Insulated from the world beyond the imperial abode by a retinue of obsequious mandarins and sycophantic eunuchs, she never appreciated the dire state of the empire. She raided the imperial treasury at will to satisfy her insatiable appetite for luxuries and penchant for opulent festivities. Her reputation for ruthlessness and violent rages deterred criticisms and unwelcome news. Under her stewardship, the empire's downward spiral continued unabated.

Chapter 1

HOPE OF THE NATION

ONE OF THE most disturbed regions in mid-19th-century China was the southern province of Guangdong. Isolated from the power center by mountain ranges to the north, the Pearl River Delta region around the provincial capital of Guangzhou was a fertile breeding ground for rebels and rebellions. The flourishing opium trade after 1820 helped to finance a corresponding increase in illegal activities and the involvement of secret societies and other criminal elements. Pressured by overpopulation and rural poverty, the area around Guangzhou became a hub of these clandestine groups and their nefarious exploits. A secret society proclamation declared:

> The ancient books tell us that once in five centuries some man of talent beyond his fellows will appear, on whom the hope of the nation will depend. That period has elapsed since the rise of the Ming dynasty, and it is full time that a hero should come forward and save the nation.[1]

Indeed, it was on November 12, 1866, two years short of 500 since the rise of the Ming dynasty in 1368, that Sun Yat-sen was born in the Pearl River Delta. The Taiping Rebellion had met its end just two years earlier. Though it would be several more before the Nian and the Muslim rebellions were brought under control, the little farming village where Sun was born had more or less returned to normal. His birthplace Cuiheng was a small hamlet in the countryside of Xiangshan district (renamed Zhongshan in 1925 to honor her most famous son), one of many that dotted the rich delta. Within a day's journey to the north was Guangzhou; the bustling British colony of Hong Kong lay to the East; and across an expanse of water to the south was the Portuguese colony of Macau.

The delta was the oldest link between China and the maritime nations of Europe. Guangzhou was the major port of trade with the West after the arrival of the Portuguese in 1517. In the century before the Opium War, it was the only legal point of entry on the China coast. Xiangshan was particularly noted for its compradors, agents of European firms whose bicultural competence facilitated trade with local businesses. A number of these men had gone on to become successful entrepreneurs and reformers, such as the great comprador Zheng Guanying. The district also produced large numbers of emigrants who achieved prominence in the cosmopolitan centers of China and in overseas communities. Yung Wing, the first Chinese to graduate from an American university, and Tang Shaoyi, who would become the first prime minister of republican China, were both Xiangshan natives.

Thus, far from being a rural village where time had stood still, Cuiheng sat on the fringe of a wider world that had been exposed to modernity for a while. The hundred or so families in Cuiheng were engaged in agriculture and fishing; life was extremely hard for these people and most lived in abject poverty. The Sun family was no exception, and the prospect of a decent education or social advancement was extremely remote for people of Sun's generation trapped in little hamlets such as Cuiheng. Like millions of others in rural China, they had to work very hard merely to survive. Land scarcity, always a problem in densely populated Guangdong, was particularly acute in Cuiheng, which was sandwiched by high mountains to the north and the sea in its backyard. Farming in this rocky and sandy terrain was limited and many of the hundred or so families in the village had to supplement their meager income from other occupations, often in nearby towns.

Sun's father, Dacheng, owned a plot of land but it was too small to support the family; he had to take on occasional work as a tailor in nearby Macau. Sun's mother, 15 years younger than her husband, was illiterate. Like most Han Chinese women of her day, she had her feet bound, a millennium-old practice that was the standard of feminine beauty and a mark of good breeding. The hardworking couple had three other surviving children: Sun Mei, their elder son, who was 12 years older than Sun Yat-sen, and two daughters. The household also included the widows of Dacheng's two younger brothers, who had left the village and set out for California during one of the gold rushes in the 19th century. One died at sea off the coast of Shanghai, while the other met an early end in California. This was a common tragedy in southern China, but social and economic distress at home forced many from the coastal communities of southern China to seek employment in plantations, mines and railroad construction in the Americas and Nanyang[2]. It was the only alternative to an otherwise impoverished and grim existence at home.

Remarkably little is known about the first 12 years of Sun's life in Cuiheng. Presumably he would have attended the local elementary school and studied the *San Zi Jing*, or Three Character Classic, the classical text that Chinese school children in those days were required to memorize even before they could read. Like the other children in the village, he would also have helped his father in the field. One of Sun's teachers had fought with the Taipings. He escaped capture at a battle in eastern Guangdong and returned to Cuiheng to teach at the village school, regaling his students with tales of the Taiping's campaigns. This was the beginning of Sun's admiration for the Taiping's iconoclastic leader Hong Xiuquan, whose birthplace Fuyuanshui in Hua county was just 75 miles (120 km) from Cuiheng.

Having lost both his brothers, Sun Dacheng would have been aware of the peril for young emigrants, but poverty did not offer him the luxury of choice. So it was that in 1871 Sun Mei left for Hawaii with an uncle who had a business there. He first hired himself out as an agricultural laborer to other Xiangshan emigrants. Working hard and with the help of his uncle, he saved enough money to buy a store and then entered into the business of recruiting Chinese laborers to Hawaii. Having done well, Sun Mei returned triumphantly to his native village in 1878 to visit his parents and marry the girl they had chosen for him. This brought Sun Yat-sen's rustic childhood to an abrupt end. His parents decided that he should join his elder brother in Hawaii. Enthralled by his elder brother's tales of Hawaii and the Islands' riches, it was an opportunity that Sun must have looked forward to with excitement. Accompanied by his mother, Sun set sail for Honolulu the following year.

Hawaii had been touched by Western commercial and religious influences for well over half a century. At the time of Sun's arrival, she was being drawn closer to the American orbit. The Treaty of Reciprocity signed four years earlier with the United States was essentially a free trade agreement that guaranteed a duty-free market for Hawaiian sugar. But it was also a prelude to American political and economic dominance.[3] The modern buildings and ships busily discharging and loading cargoes that Sun would have seen when his ship docked in Honolulu was a world in the process of modernization under the influence of the West. Sun could have settled down and participated in her prosperity without stepping outside the Chinese community, as many before him had done. But Sun Mei was determined that his younger brother should first complete his studies. The problem was that there was no Chinese school in the Islands. The only alternative was one of the foreign schools but even those had few Chinese students. After a short stint in his brother's business, where he learned to use the abacus and other skills, Sun enrolled as a boarding student at the Iolani School. This was an Anglican missionary institution that catered primarily to Hawaiian and half-Hawaiian children.

In spite of the strong American influence in Hawaii, Iolani was a bastion of anti-Americanism. Bishop Alfred Willis, the headmaster of the school, was British, as were all but one of the teachers. The textbooks were published in England, and English history was taught instead of American history as was the norm in most of the other schools. Consequently, Sun's education and introduction to Western history and institutions had a decidedly British flavor, and gave no hint of his later embrace of revolution and republicanism. Indeed, Bishop Willis felt constrained to deny any connection. In 1896, the year after Sun gained global notoriety for leading a failed revolt against the Qing dynasty, the bishop declared in the *Diocesan Magazine* that his former student's "school days gave no indication of his future career. He has left no tradition of hatching plots against magisterial authority. Nor will any one suppose that he was indoctrinated at Iolani with the love of a republican form of government, much less with the desire of revolutionizing the Celestial Kingdom after the model of the Hawaiian Republic, which was then unborn."[4] On the other hand, Bishop Willis' championing of Hawaii's independence against the plots of pro-American annexationists might perhaps explain Sun's anti-imperialism and sensitivity to Western aggression against China in his later revolutionary career.[5]

Nevertheless, Sun's education at Iolani during his impressionable years would have exposed him to English and American ideals of constitutional government, the histories of the English people's struggles against absolute monarchy, and America's struggle for independence from Britain. He would have been impressed with the administration of justice and a judicial system that made possible his brother's rapid economic success and the protection of his property from arbitrary confiscation. These ideas were to have the most profound influence on Sun.

Church attendance in St. Andrew's Cathedral on Sundays was an integral part of student life at Iolani. Eager that the seven Chinese boarders in his school convert to Christianity, the bishop hired a young Chinese evangelist to instruct them in biblical studies every afternoon. This gradually drew Sun to Christianity, which might have exerted a powerful influence in shaping his later political career. Sun had entered Iolani without knowing a word of English but his mastery of the language had improved to such an extent that by the time of his graduation three years later, he was presented the second prize in English grammar by King David Kalakaua. Sun had acquired an elementary education in Cuiheng but this had been interrupted by the family's poverty so it was really at Iolani that Sun began his systematic education.

Not long after Sun's matriculation, Sun Mei had moved his family to the island of Maui, where he established himself as a sugar planter, cattle rancher and dealer of farm equipment. He became quite wealthy and the islanders addressed him affectionately as "the king of Maui" in recognition of his leadership and generosity. After graduating from Iolani, Sun spent the next few months on Maui helping Sun Mei, who was now making even more money. Finding business boring, Sun persuaded his brother in the fall of 1882 to allow him to further his studies. There was no college or university, which limited his choice to the prestigious Oahu School, then the highest center of learning in the Islands. It offered instruction at the college level but never acquired the status of one. Founded in 1841 by American Congregationalists, it was the school most influenced by American Protestant missionaries. Almost a century later, Barack Obama would attend the school, though by then it had been renamed the Punahou School.

Earliest known photograph of Sun Yat-sen, aged 17, in 1883

The Oahu School was a popular choice for many of the children of the missionaries from the Hawaiian Evangelical Association. In this environment, Sun's feeling for the Christian faith grew even stronger. He developed interests in both government and medicine and even toyed with the idea of going to America to further his studies. At the same time, he did not neglect his Chinese studies, and would regularly consult Too Nam, a Chinese from Malaya who was teaching Chinese to American officers based in Honolulu. Too Nam would later re-emerge in Sun's life as one of his most ardent supporters in British Malaya.[6]

Sun Mei was pleased with his younger brother's progress in school and even registered a piece of property in his name. But Sun's growing interest in Christianity brought him into open conflict with his elder brother. Sun Mei was concerned that his young charge might convert to Christianity. This would be a betrayal of their ancestors and their Chinese heritage. Barely a semester later, when Sun's conversion appeared imminent, his infuriated brother shipped him back to Cuiheng on a one-way ticket so their father could "take this Jesus nonsense out of him."[7]

It was too little too late. The young man had already been grafted with the spirit of rebellion. Having been exposed to modernity and Christianity,

Sun felt only indignation for everything in his home village. With the connivance of a village friend, Lu Haodong, who had studied in Shanghai, they shocked their families and the entire village by breaking into the local temple and desecrating the wooden idols of the local deity. This provoked an uproar in the village, for the memory of the Taipings and their attacks on Chinese religious traditions was still very much alive. Alarmed by the scandal that Sun had caused and to protect him from the wrath of the villagers, his parents sent him to Hong Kong to continue his studies.

Hong Kong, Britain's trophy for her victory in the Opium War, was "a barren island with barely a house upon it" at the time of her cession to Britain in 1841, but gradually developed into a modern and prosperous metropolis. In spite of the circumstances in which it was acquired, the Qing regime soon resigned itself to the fact that the island was an integral part of the British presence on Chinese soil. The British colonial administration on its part pursued a deliberate policy of harmonious relations. With the peaceful coexistence, there was almost an open frontier between China and Hong Kong. People from southern China came to Hong Kong to trade and to seek work. Parents who were more liberal and financially able sent their sons to Hong Kong for further studies, as did mercantile families who did not expect their sons to become scholars or bureaucrats.[8] Or, as in the case of Sun, to get their son away from trouble at home.

In Hong Kong, Sun was accepted into another Anglican institution, the Diocesan School. At the same time, he began to study the Chinese classics with Qu Fengzhi, a Chinese Christian pastor. Although Sun had received tutoring in Chinese during his years in Hawaii, it is quite probable that he did not undertake classical studies until this later period.[9] In April 1884, he transferred to the Central Government School[10], the first public secondary school in Hong Kong that offered instruction up to the sixth form, the equivalent of the American twelfth grade. The curriculum and medium of instruction was English, with Chinese taught as a second language. It was around this time that Sun met Dr. Charles Hager, an American Congregationalist missionary who had recently arrived in Hong Kong. A friendship developed between them and Sun decided to formally embrace Christianity. His baptism in early 1884[11] along with that of Lu Haodong's was performed by Dr. Hager. Sun adopted the baptismal name Rixin but Qu

Fengzhi later changed it to Yixian[12], which in Cantonese is pronounced Yat-sen, the name by which the West would come to know him.

Sun made frequent trips back to his home village. It was on one of these visits that he dutifully married on May 7, 1884, the girl whom his parents had chosen for him. Nuptials in traditional China were rarely based on romantic love but upon a sense of duty to propagate the family line. Sun's wife, Lu Muzhen, was the daughter of a merchant. She was to bear him a son and two daughters, but Sun hardly shared their lives over the next three decades. Not long after the wedding, Sun left to continue his studies while his wife stayed in the home of his parents to raise their children.

Barely three months after his wedding, hostilities broke out in August 1884 between China and France.[13] The conflict was over the sovereignty of Vietnam, one of China's major tributaries and a strategic buffer state bordering the southwestern Chinese province of Yunnan. In 1859, Napoleon III in his ambition to build an Indochinese empire had sent troops to Saigon on the pretext of protecting missionaries, a standard ploy during this period of Western imperialism. In 1862, the French imposed a treaty on Vietnam which among other terms ceded to France three provinces in southern Vietnam known as Cochinchina.

France's defeat in the Franco-Prussian War of 1870–1871 rendered her militarily impotent. Unable to afford another war, she turned her attention to trade with southern China. The discovery that the Red River in Tonking (northern Vietnam) was a better route than the Mekong to China's Yunnan province aroused French ambitions to seize Tonking. In 1874, a new treaty was imposed on Vietnam which effectively reduced her to a protectorate. Preoccupied with other crises in the empire, China took no action to stop the French advance beyond refusing to acknowledge the treaty. The French continued to intensify their activities in Vietnam and by 1882 had stationed troops in Hanoi and Haiphong, dangerously close to the Chinese border. To counter the French advance, the Vietnamese government strengthened its ties with China and sought the aid of the irregular Chinese Black Flag army. This Taiping remnant began engaging French troops. In 1883, the Qing court dispatched regular troops into Tonking, where they engaged in skirmishes with the French.

Li Hongzhang, the doyen of China's Self-Strengthening Movement, opposed the action. He advised against taking on a first-rate European power before the completion of China's naval and coastal defense program. His preference for a negotiated settlement was endorsed by Prince Gong, the Zongli Yamen and leading members of the Grand Council. Challenging them was a group of young officials, brilliant scholars who had little practical knowledge or experience of foreign and military matters. They championed a belligerent course of action. The Qing court, vacillating between war and peace, instructed Li to open negotiations. The resultant agreement, which would have turned Vietnam into a joint protectorate, was rejected by Paris. A subsequent agreement in 1884, the Li-Fournier Convention, called for Chinese recognition of all French treaties with Vietnam, withdrawal of all Chinese troops from Tonking, and a French promise of no demand for indemnity, no invasion of China and no undignified reference to China in future treaties with Vietnam. The French parliament refused to ratify the agreement.

Hostilities resumed. The Chinese scored some early successes, but on August 23 a French fleet launched an all-out attack on Fuzhou. Within an hour, they sank 11 Chinese warships and destroyed the Fuzhou Dockyard that had been built with French aid in 1866. In December the Qing court began to vacillate again. There was a threat of renewed Russian activities on the northern frontier and a Japanese advance on Korea. The inclination toward peace was reciprocated by a similar desire in France, where unstable political conditions, the difficulty of supporting a distant military campaign and a major French defeat by the Chinese at Langson began to weigh on the government and dampened the war spirit. In June 1885 Li and the French minister in China concluded the Tianjin Accord based substantially on the Li-Fournier Convention.

The loss of Vietnam after a short and disastrous encounter with France signaled the failure of the Self-Strengthening Movement. China's weakness prompted the British to emulate the French in another Chinese tributary state, Burma. In 1886 Britain secured a treaty which reduced Burma to a British protectorate. With the loss of these tributaries in the south, the fate of the leading tributary in the northeast, Korea, hung in the balance. The Japanese were too astute not to smell an opportunity there.

HOPE OF THE NATION

Although China was not required to pay an indemnity, the Qing court's failure to protect one of China's longtime tributary states was held against it, especially by those living on the coastal provinces who were always sensitive about their own security. It provoked a rise in nationalism and xenophobic sentiments throughout the country. Young radicals like Sun saw the defeat as a national humiliation and further proof of the Manchus' incompetence.

This was Sun's first wartime experience, and it gave him an opportunity to contrast the fighting spirit of lower-class Chinese with the Manchus' paralysis in protecting the interests of the nation. Responding to a call by the governor-general in Guangzhou to attack French ships and men, Chinese dockworkers in Hong Kong had refused to service a French ship damaged in the attack on Fuzhou. They were soon joined by coolies and other menial workers. Hong Kong harbor was incapacitated for more than a week and the French ship was forced to sail to Japan for repairs.[14]

Toward the end of 1884, word had reached Sun Mei about his younger brother's baptism. Less forgiving than his father, Sun Mei's antipathy to the foreign religion had not abated and he summoned Sun to Hawaii to set him straight. Sun dutifully made the trip but if he was looking for reconciliation, it was a futile hope. Sun Mei was so infuriated he threatened to cut off financial support and demanded the return of the property that he had registered in his younger brother's name. At this critical juncture in his life, Sun had no one to turn to except his Christian friends. When the superintendent of the Hawaiian Board of Mission, Reverend Francis Damon, learned of Sun's plight and his desire to return to China to further his studies, the good reverend raised US$300 from the Christian community for Sun's return ticket to China in the spring of 1886.[15]

The year-long stay in Hawaii brought Sun's high school studies to a close. Without a diploma from the Central Government School, he faced an uncertain future. Having been exposed to the world beyond Cuiheng, farming was out of the question. With his peasant background, it was impossible for him to gain admission to any institution of higher learning, or any military or naval academy. Dr. Hager thought that Sun might make an excellent preacher but there was no seminary in Hong Kong. Law was another possibility but this, too, could not be pursued in the colony. The only option was medicine, a field of study that would satisfy Sun's desire to improve his understanding of Western sciences. Armed with a letter of introduction from Dr. Hager, Sun was admitted into the Medical School of Boji Hospital, an American missionary institution headed by Dr. John Kerr. Established in 1835 as Canton Hospital, it was the first Western-style hospital in China. The Medical School was founded in 1866.[16]

Joining him at the Medical School was his village friend Lu Haodong. A new acquaintance was Zheng Shiliang, a fellow student who shared Sun's anti-Manchu sentiments. The scion of a rich Shanghai merchant, Zheng was the product of a German missionary school in Guangdong. He had many contacts in the secret societies of eastern Guangdong, where his family hailed from. Especially numerous in southern China, these clandestine organizations originated in the late 17th century after the Qing conquest of China, with the avowed aim of overthrowing the alien regime and restoring the indigenous Ming dynasty. The objective remained very much alive despite the passage of more than two centuries. Many of them had turned to crime to finance their seditious activities but they filled an essential void: as a source of financial and other assistance in times of distress for members without families and the dispossessed. It was from Zheng that Sun recognized the revolutionary potential of the secret societies. They would feature prominently in his revolutionary strategy and he relied on them almost exclusively as his primary source of muscle in his earlier uprisings. Sun believed that their solidarity and tight organization would render them invulnerable to government suppression.

Sun also became increasingly conscious of China's political dilemma during this time. Like many educated Chinese of his day, he was concerned with the plight of his country and longed to contribute to her modernization. In line with his growing sensitivity to political developments, he continued with his study of the Chinese classics and history. It was while Sun was studying at the Boji Medical School that his brother Sun Mei finally relented. Resigned to his younger brother's independence and resolve to chart his own path, Sun Mei resumed his financial assistance. From this point on, Sun Mei's remittances would be of crucial importance to his impetuous brother's future. They subsidized his professional training and family support, and gave the first boost to his revolutionary career.

A year later, in October 1887, Sun transferred to the newly opened College of Medicine for Chinese in Hong Kong, the antecedent of today's Li Ka Shing Faculty of Medicine at the University of Hong Kong. The College of Medicine was a new institution founded under the patronage of Sir Ho Kai, a prominent member of the anglicized Chinese elite of Hong Kong. Like Sun, he was a product of Sino-European cultural influences. His father had emigrated to Malacca, converted to Christianity and later embarked upon the career of a missionary before launching himself successfully as a businessman. The senior Ho was well-versed in both Chinese and Western learning and made sure that his son had the same opportunities at the Government Central School. This was interrupted in 1872 when Ho Kai was sent off to study in the United Kingdom at the age of 13. After his graduation from the University of Aberdeen with a medical degree, he qualified as a barrister and was called to the English bar. On his return to Hong Kong in late 1882, he became one of Hong Kong's most distinguished civic leaders and one of the Chinese community's principal representatives with the colonial authorities. He served on the Legislative Council for three terms and sat on almost every major public board.

Ho Kai was one of Sun's earliest contacts among those attempting to modernize China through Westernization. He was a mentor and an early role model for Sun, and enabled his young protégé to make numerous contacts with the Chinese and British elites of Hong Kong. Ho showed Sun that "a Chinese with a modern education was competent to comment on public affairs and need not restrict his expertise to a particular professional field."[17] In an 1887 article to an English-language newspaper in Hong Kong, Ho declared that China's troubles were not the result of Western aggression but China's backwardness, which was not simply a matter of military weakness. In his view, the foreign powers demanded extraterritoriality because they distrusted China's legal system and the officials who administered it. The civil service examination system, which emphasized literary competency, produced officials who were incapable, or unwilling out of self-interest, to modernize China's institutions. It excluded those who were best equipped for this role: the Chinese, like himself, who had been trained in the West. But Ho Kai was not interested in becoming a functionary under China's traditional leaders.[18]

Sir Ho Kai   Dr. James Cantlie

Ho Kai endowed the Alice Memorial Hospital[19] shortly after the death in 1884 of his English wife Alice Walden. Entrusting its management to the London Missionary Society upon its completion in 1887, he later added the College of Medicine. Two Scottish physicians, both fellow alumni of Ho Kai at the University of Aberdeen, were instrumental in the College's founding. Dr. Patrick Manson, the College's first dean, gained international recognition for his research on mosquito-borne diseases. In 1886, he co-founded the Dairy Farm Company in Hong Kong to breed imported cattle to ensure a regular supply of disease-free milk in the colony. His successor, Dr. James Cantlie, was a noted authority on leprosy and tropical diseases. The son of a Scottish family of moderate means, Cantlie took his degree at Aberdeen and served his internship at Charing Cross Hospital, London. He took up the deanship at the College of Medicine in 1884. Cantlie, whose favorite student Sun became, would take him along as a translator when visiting Chinese leper villages for his research that would earn him an international reputation in the field. Cantlie later co-authored a biography of his star pupil.[20]

Ho Kai and James Cantlie were among the first in a complex network of social relations that Sun began forming during his days at the College of Medicine and would continue to build throughout his life. Over time, his connections would grow to include not just Chinese, overseas and otherwise, but also a constellation of foreigners from East and West. Sun moved in all these circles, using them for his own purposes and those of his cause but never being drawn into theirs. This was remarkable even in a society founded upon *guanxi*, the systematic exploitation of interpersonal relations. Sun owed his popularity as much to his force of personality as to his ability to tune his discourses to the wavelengths of his interlocutors so as to navigate the labyrinth of contradictions that he would constantly be confronted with. One commonality shared by his social circles was their marginality in the context of the Chinese society of his day. Yet it was these men he met rather than the books he read that most shaped his thinking.[21]

Sun's interest in politics deepened during his years at the College of Medicine but he seems to have been ambivalent about whether to adopt an anti-Manchu stance or take the more respectable course of reform. Among his close contemporaries, he continued to vent his anger and opposition to the Manchu regime. In Guangzhou, he had only Zheng Shiliang; in Hong Kong he had several. One was Chen Shaobai, a fellow student at the College of Medicine. A Cantonese Christian, Chen had a talent for antagonizing his associates with his sharp tongue. He had studied at the Canton Christian College (later Lingnan College), and was to play a crucial role in the early years of Sun's revolutionary career. They became sworn brothers but Chen soon dropped out of the College although he remained Sun's chief lieutenant over the next decade.

Another close friend was Yang Heling, the son of a wealthy family from Sun's village with a business in Hong Kong. While studying draftsmanship in Guangzhou, Yang became friendly with another apprentice, You Lie, who was working as a clerk in Hong Kong. Yang brought You into Sun's orbit. A student of mathematics, You Lie had been initiated into the Triads, which stimulated Sun's interest in the revolutionary potential of the secret societies. Sun and his three new buddies would spend hours in Yang's store discussing politics and venting their anti-Manchu anger, so much so that their neighbors referred to them facetiously as the "Four Bandits." Sun, who is said to have experimented with bombs in the College's laboratory, was nicknamed "Hong Xiuquan" because of his admiration for the Taiping founder. Sun's old friends from Guangdong, Lu Haodong and Zheng Shiliang, now based respectively in Shanghai and Guangdong, would join them whenever they passed through the colony.

Towards the end of his medical studies and in the hope of finding a niche for himself in the government bureaucracy, Sun submitted reformist proposals to two Xiangshan natives. His first approach was to Zheng Zaoru, a *juren* degree holder who had served as Qing minister to Japan and the United States. In a letter in 1890, Sun wrote that he "raises his head in the hope of being of some use in the world," and proposed the now familiar reformist themes: the adoption of Western practices, the diffusion of education to spread literacy, the eradication of opium, the development of institutions to promote talent, and improvements to advance China's agriculture and sericulture. Holding that the spread of literacy was of particular importance, Sun contended that "If human talent is not in abundance and if customs are not good, then the nation cannot be strong."[22]

The other Xiangshan native whom Sun contacted was the great reformist comprador Zheng Guanying, an important political thinker in the late Qing period. One of the first reformers to master a Western language, Zheng had done extensive research on the Western parliamentary system and was among the first to openly call for it. But unlike other reformers

Sun Yat-sen and his "Four Bandits" friends, circa 1888: (*seated, left to right*) Yang Heling, Sun, Chen Shaobai, and You Lie.

such as Kang Youwei, Zheng had no experience in political and diplomatic interactions with the West. Rather he was the product of the cultural and economic environment of Shanghai, where he moved to as a 16-year-old. Sun is said to have submitted two essays to Zheng, which were incorporated into a famous reformist tract that Zheng wrote in 1893, *Words of Warning to an Apparently Prosperous Age*. The book was an inspiration to both Sun and Sun's reformist rival Kang Youwei. In 1898, it was designated a reformist reader for provincial officials by the Guangxu Emperor to promote his Hundred Day Reform movement.[23]

Sun was able to make contact with these luminaries possibly because of their common geographical origin. But the response to his overtures and other attempts at gaining recognition was negligible. As he discovered, it was not easy for a peasant's son with a foreign education to gain the attention of imperial officials. His spirit was not dampened, however. The relative honesty and efficiency of Hong Kong's colonial administration in contrast to the corruption and backwardness of China convinced him now more than ever that China had to change, and that he could somehow contribute to the process.

Sun read extensively during his studies at the College of Medicine. His favorite author at this time was Charles Darwin, whose magnum opus *On the Origin of Species By Means of Natural Selection*, published in 1859, proposed that all species of life were descended from a common ancestry through the process of natural selection: those best able to adapt were more likely to survive and propagate. Sun developed an interest in the French Revolution, scientific agriculture, works by Jean-Jacques Rousseau, John Stuart Mill and others on subjects that he thought would help him to contribute to the modernization of China. The influence of the ideas he absorbed from his readings was to be lasting and he would later incorporate some of them into his own magnum opus, *The Three Principles of the People*.[24] Neither his reading nor his brainstorming sessions with his "bandit" friends distracted him from his medical studies, to which he gave priority during his entire time at the College.

Sun's diligence paid off. He did well at the College and was awarded a scholarship. In 1892, he and another student out of the original 12 successfully completed the course. In spite of graduating at the top of his class, Sun could not practice medicine in Hong Kong. The College's curriculum did not fully comply with British standards, and this rendered its diploma quite worthless in places where British jurisdiction prevailed. His professional status was thus no better than that of a traditional herbalist. Dr. Cantlie encouraged Sun to complete his training in England, but Sun had neither the interest nor the inclination. Instead he reconciled himself to practicing traditional Chinese medicine in the Portuguese colony of Macau, where he set up the Chinese Western Apothecary to dispense herbal remedies as well as modern drugs. The apothecary was set up with the financial assistance of a traditional Chinese hospital. Instead of paying the interest in cash, Sun treated the hospital's patients and provided it with drugs without taking a fee. He used these opportunities to practice modern surgery under the continued guidance of Dr. Cantlie, who would travel from Hong Kong from time to time to assist in more complicated cases.

The barter trade worked well for a while. Lacking a Portuguese medical degree, he was soon compelled to close his practice and move once again. In 1893, he relocated to Guangzhou and set up the East-West Apothecary in the western part of the city to practice as a herbalist. He did well enough and was soon able to open a branch in a neighboring town in partnership with another physician. He quickly earned an excellent professional reputation, but the rapid expansion caused him financial difficulties.

One day in late 1893 or early 1894, Chen Shaobai received an alarming letter from the East-West Apothecary. The store was running low on cash and Sun was nowhere to be found. Chen rushed to Guangzhou but several days passed before Sun showed up. He had been staying home drafting a petition that he hoped would be his ticket into the establishment. Now nearing 28, Sun realized that his small medical practice would not be the key to his larger ambition of modernizing China. He resolved to make another attempt for political patronage. This time he decided to set his sights higher and would settle for no less than Li Hongzhang, still the second most powerful person in the empire after the Empress Dowager.

This aging mandarin, born in 1823 into an illustrious gentry family in Anhui, showed remarkable ability early in life. After obtaining his *jinshi* degree at the relatively young age of 24, he was admitted two years later into the prestigious Hanlin Academy. His rise to prominence began when he was sent back to his native province in 1861 to recruit an army against the Taiping rebels. The following year he was named governor of Jiangsu. He led his Huai army in the defense of the provincial capital of Shanghai, which by this time had become the center of European activities in China. This was Li's first contact with foreigners and the beginning of his lifelong association with foreigners and his interest in reforms and the modernization of China.

After the suppression of the Taiping Rebellion, Li was given wide civil and military responsibilities. In 1870, he was named governor-general of Zhili, a post he held for an unprecedented 25 years. Because of his talent, his Huai army and his proximity to the capital, he played a leading role in China's international and domestic affairs. As superintendent of trade for the northern ports, he was responsible for all trade negotiations with foreigners in his domain. After 1871, he became virtually a one-man foreign affairs office involved in all of China's negotiations with foreigners and a major influence on China's foreign affairs. His preference for diplomatic solutions rather than armed confrontation in China's relations with the powers did not go down well with the war hawks at court who branded him a traitor. Li was among the most ardent supporters of the Self-Strengthening Movement. In modernizing China's military, industries and institutions, he was bucking a conservative, self-seeking system that was opposed to anything Western or that involved change. With the half-hearted support of Cixi, he was able to hold the conservatives at bay until the mid-1890s.

Li Hongzhang

Not one to ruminate on the possibility of failure, Sun shuttered his East-West Apothecary for good. Accompanied by Lu Haodong, he made the trek to Tianjin, where Li was holding court. They took the circuitous route via Shanghai in order to discuss Sun's plans with Zheng Guanying. Zheng put Sun in touch with Wang Tao, a reformist journalist who had friends in high places. Wang read Sun's manuscript, suggested some amendments and gave Sun a letter of introduction to a friend in Li's entourage. Armed with his petition, Sun left for Tianjin.

Echoing arguments that had been promoted by Dr. Ho Kai and Zheng Guanying, both passionate proponents of economic and social reforms, Sun's petition proposed that China exploit her manpower and natural resources for her economic development. Criticizing the official-gentry's singular emphasis on military means to respond to the foreign threat, Sun argued that the wealth and strength of the Western nations were not derived from their hardware superiority alone, but through better use of human capital, more efficient utilization of their agricultural and natural resources, and the free rein given to commercial enterprises to pursue their profit objectives. Japan's transformation since the Meiji Restoration of 1868, Sun pointed out, was more successful because it had taken reform more seriously, despite the fact that it had begun trading with the West and adopting Western methods later than China. The natural ability of the Chinese people, if properly nurtured, he argued, would enable China to surpass the West within 20 years. Perhaps because of his peasant background, Sun showed particular interest for agricultural modernization. Concern for peasant welfare was an established principle of Chinese statecraft but now Sun urged that Western science and technology be applied to improve agricultural productivity. In his petition, Sun made references to *minsheng* or "people's livelihood," an ancient expression that had cropped up in many reformist tracts and which Sun would later use to propound the third limb of his famous *Sanmin Zhuyi*, The Three Principles of the People.[25]

Not that any of his ideas were particularly original, but Sun's purpose was not to sell his program but to buy his entrée into the ranks of China's elite. Conceding his inability to write an "eight-legged" essay or to qualify for a literary degree, he nevertheless claimed that he had a different skill set to offer:

> I have already passed the English medical examinations in Hong Kong. When I was young, I tasted the experience of overseas study. Western languages, literature, politics, customs, mathematics, geography, physics and chemistry – these I have had an opportunity to study in a general sort of way. But I paid

particular attention to their [the West's] methods of achieving a prosperous country and a powerful army and to their laws for reforming the people and perfecting their customs.[26]

Sun concluded his petition with a bold plea that the governor-general take him under his wing and send him abroad for study so he could contribute to China's modernization. An enlightened official, Li appreciated men of talent and might at least have given Sun an interview. But in June 1894 when Sun was in Tianjin, the specter of war was looming between China and Japan. If there was to be war, Li as the nation's leading diplomat would be called upon once again to serve the nation. In these circumstances, Sun's request for an interview was declined. It is doubtful if the governor-general ever laid eyes on Sun's petition. Its publication in *Wanguo Gongbao* (Globe Magazine), a Shanghai missionary publication popular in reformist circles, was little consolation.[27]

Until the rejection, Sun had hoped that even a minor position in Li's entourage would have given him a chance to demonstrate his skills. It was now clear that the doors to the bureaucracy would remain closed to him. Convinced of the futility of seeking further official patronage, he took no more interest in the reformist themes that were supposed to be his ticket out of marginality into the bureaucratic and social elite. Spurned by the establishment, Sun gave up his medical practice to embark on a crusade for a regime change.

Chapter 2

BAPTISM BY FIRE

THE GATHERING CLOUD between China and Japan was over the suzerainty of a third neighbor, Korea, long an important cog in China's tributary system. Like Japan, Korea had adopted a policy of international isolation. When Japan was forced to open up by the United States in 1853, it became increasingly difficult for Korea to maintain her isolation. In 1867, the Zongli Yamen suggested to Korea that resistance was not practical and that she should open up voluntarily. In 1876, Korea signed an unequal treaty with Japan. Three years later, when Li Hongzhang took charge of Chinese relations with Korea, he advised the Korean government to sign a treaty with the United States so as to deny Japan exclusive access. Meanwhile, Japan had become increasingly involved in Korea's internal affairs, backing the reform faction at court against the pro-Chinese conservatives who supported the royal family of the Joseon dynasty. In 1884, while China was engaged in the Sino-French War, a group of pro-Japanese reformers led by Kim Ok-kyun briefly overthrew the pro-Chinese Korean government in a bloody coup d'état. War between China and Japan was forestalled by the Convention of Tianjin in 1885. This provided for mutual troop withdrawals and advance notification of any future troop movements into Korea. China had in effect surrendered her exclusive suzerainty over Korea, which now became a joint protectorate of the two Asian empires. Kim fled to Japan, which turned down Korean demands for his extradition.[1]

A decade later, in March 1894, Kim Ok-kyun was lured to Shanghai, where he was murdered by a Korean assassin. His body was shipped on board a Chinese warship to Korea, where it was quartered and put on public display as a warning to other rebels. The Japanese government was outraged, taking this as a direct affront to its stature and dignity. Tensions worsened when the Korean king requested the Chinese government to send troops to aid in suppressing the popular Tonghak rebellion. The Chinese did not inform Japan of the decision to send troops, as required by the

Convention of Tianjin. This gave the Japanese a pretext to send an expeditionary force to Korea. Li Hongzhang attempted to negotiate a settlement but when the Japanese sank a Chinese troopship ferrying reinforcements to Korea, conflict became inevitable. The Sino-Japanese War was officially declared on August 1, 1894.

Toward the end of the summer, in the midst of the raging war, Sun departed for Hawaii to begin his career as a professional rebel. He chose the Islands as his initial target for revolutionary agitation because money was to be central to his strategy. It was never his intention to build rebel power in remote jungles or inaccessible mountain caves, or to engage in a drawn-out civil war. His was to be a revolution based on strategy and money. In this he considered his brother the most likely source. With Sun Mei's help he hoped to tap the resources of the 20,000-strong *huaqiao* (overseas Chinese) community in Hawaii. These were the people he knew and understood and whose social origin he shared, for many were from his home district of Xiangshan.

His first stop was Maui, where his brother had earned somewhat of a reputation as a "godfather." Sun Mei, who had been so upset over his younger brother's religious conversion, had no qualms about endorsing his political dissension. His own conversion to republicanism might have been encouraged by the revolution in Hawaii the previous year. A group composed largely of American plantation owners overthrew Hawaii's native monarch in a bloodless coup and established Hawaii as a republic. No one could have foreseen that this liberation of the Hawaiian people from the shackles of monarchical rule was but a prelude to American imperialism. Hawaii would be annexed as a territory, in effect a colony, of the United States five years later in 1898, and remained so until 1959 when it became the 50th state of the American Union.

Even with Sun Mei's introduction and a shared dislike of the Manchus, few *huaqiao* were ready to engage in subversion against the regime for fear of reprisals against family members in China. After months of persuasion, Sun was able to enlist only about 20 people to his cause. All of them were either Christian idealists, motivated by personal ambitions or linked in one way or another to Sun or his family. Their enlistment has a special significance in Sun's career. It marked his entrée into the conspiratorial world of revolution and the network of relations that was to be the hallmark of his strategy. It also set the precedent for *huaqiao* involvement in home politics from which they had been excluded and in which they would play an increasingly important role in the early years of the following century.

On November 24, 1894, Sun gathered his newly minted recruits to form an anti-dynastic organization whose seditious objective was camouflaged behind the innocuous name of Xingzhonghui, the Revive China Society. This was not so much a political organization as a fundraising network to bankroll Sun's conspiratorial activities. The society's charter that Sun drew up at this time dealt mainly with procedural matters, preceded by a preamble that denounced the weakness and corruption of the Qing government and warned foreigners against designs on Chinese territory. There was no mention of republicanism or the overthrow of the Qing dynasty. These might have been incorporated into the oath that members were supposedly required to take, but of that little is known.

The society's income, mainly from subscription fees at five dollars per head, was as dismal as its membership, which however did eventually grow to about 100. Even so, the amount raised totaled a mere HK$23,000 (approximately US$11,500) by the following October when Sun launched his first revolt. More than half was said to be from Sun Mei and a sugar planter friend who sold all his properties. In spite of the poor collection, the months of campaigning in the Islands were not a total waste of time: they revealed a source of finance that Sun would turn to throughout his revolutionary career.

Sun's original plan was to sail on to North America to campaign among the *huaqiao* on that continent. When news arrived that Chinese forces were being routed by Japanese troops in southern Manchuria, Sun saw an opportunity for an early revolt. He cut short his campaigning in the Islands and canceled his American tour. Accompanied by several adventurous daredevils, Sun departed for Hong Kong in January 1895. The British colony was to be "a launching pad for what he hoped would be a paralyzing thrust at the soft underbelly of the Manchu regime."[2]

On the long sea voyage across the Pacific, Sun's ship made a stop in Yokohama. His attempted conversion of fellow *huaqiao* passengers came to the attention of Feng Jingru, a bookseller in Yokohama. Feng had taken refuge in Japan after his father was imprisoned by the Qing government for associating with the Taipings. He made no secret of his anti-Manchu sentiments and invited Sun to come ashore for a talk on "national affairs." As the ship was sailing immediately, Sun handed some Xingzhonghui propaganda to Feng through an intermediary and asked that Feng and his friends organize a local branch. His son Feng Ziyou, who would later become an important emissary and historiographer of the revolutionary movement, became a member when he was just 14 years old.

It was with the founding of the branch in Hong Kong, where Sun arrived on January 26, 1895, that the Xingzhonghui took on its importance and historical significance. The founding members were Sun's "Four Bandits" friends of his youth, with whom he had so often fantasized about an anti-Manchu insurrection; the few Hawaiian zealots who had accompanied him on the long journey across the Pacific; and a group of young Westernized Chinese in Hong Kong who shared Sun's anti-Manchu sentiments. The latter were members of the Furen Literary Society, a three-year-old organization whose Confucian name belied its revolutionary aims. The merger of the two organizations was the first demonstration of Sun's readiness to collaborate with competing organizations, provided his own supremacy was not challenged.[3]

Most of the 16 original members of Furen were employees of English shipping companies who had attended local missionary schools. Their leader was Yang Quyun, an assistant manager at David Sassoon, Sons & Co., the Hong Kong-based shipping subsidiary of one of the earliest Jewish firms in China, with a long history in the opium trade.[4] Born in Hong Kong in 1861, Yang's background was even more Westernized than Sun's. His grandfather, a native of Fujian, had migrated to Penang in British Malaya but his father decided to return and settled down in Hong Kong. Yang had studied at an English school, and like Sun had only a scant knowledge of Chinese, which he also tried to improve when he entered politics. He apprenticed at a naval dockyard

Yang Quyun

when he was 14 but was laid off after losing three fingers of his right hand in an accident. He went back to school to study English before returning to the job market, first as a teacher at a local high school and later as a chief clerk in the China Merchants Steam Navigation Company. Yang's deputy in Furen was Xie Xuantai, a 25-year-old Cantonese Christian born in Australia, where his family had emigrated. He returned to Hong Kong when he was 15 and completed his studies at Sun's alma mater, the Government Central School. The social backgrounds and professional experiences of the Furen leaders were thus very similar to those of Sun and his inner circle. And like Sun, their political orientation was born of their own perception of China's backwardness in contrast to the prosperity and efficiency of Hong Kong.

Yang Quyun founded the Furen Literary Society in March 1892 when Sun was in the final months of his medical studies in Hong Kong. They had met the previous year but did not immediately establish close relations. At their reunion in early 1895, both were ready to take advantage of the unstable political situation in China in the wake of the Sino-Japanese War. There were good reasons for Sun and Yang to pool their resources and efforts in their common aim to overthrow the Qing dynasty. For one, there were striking similarities between the two men. Neither was born into the scholar-official-gentry class nor schooled in the traditional system. They had picked up ideas in the foreign schools they attended and through contact with foreigners; both also had links with *huaqiao* communities. But Yang was also every bit as ambitious and strong in character as Sun, and this was a problem with respect to the leadership of the merged organization. To avoid a clash between the two headstrong contenders, the top position was kept vacant at the inaugural meeting on February 18, 1895, to establish the Hong Kong branch of the Xingzhonghui.

The charter of the Hong Kong chapter was a modified version of the Honolulu original with a decidedly stronger anti-Manchu overtone. Charging the Qing government with moral bankruptcy, it conjured up a chilling image of a China partitioned by the foreign powers. It called for a unified nation, the education of the masses and the application of modern science to save China and create national wealth and power. Membership in the Xingzhonghui was open to any person with the proper introduction, even foreigners. Contradictory as this may seem given that one of the society's avowed objectives was to prevent the foreign dismemberment of China, it actually reflected pragmatic and ideological considerations. Foreign support, or at least neutrality, would be crucial to their success, and the party's leaders saw no point in alarming foreigners. A modern China, so they believed, would not only be strong enough to deter foreign aggression but by virtue of her modernity would remove the very motivation for the aggression. Given the capital-intensive revolution envisaged by Sun, money was to play an important part. Here, too, the pragmatism exhibited by the leaders was clearly evident in its fundraising strategy. Appealing as much to Chinese patriotism as to the profit motive, bonds purchased by members at HK$10 apiece were to be redeemed for ten times their nominal value "when the country was established." This was the closest hint of revolution in the society's charter. Some witnesses later claimed that the society's charter was complemented by a secret oath to "overthrow the Manchu dynasty, restore China and establish a republican regime."[5]

Present at the inaugural meeting of the Xingzhonghui was an important new recruit, Huang Yongshang, the scion of a prominent anglicized Hong Kong family originally from Xiangshan. Huang's father was one of the first Chinese to study in the United States; he became a member of the Legislative Council on his return to Hong Kong and was one of the "King's Chinese," whose adoption of Western culture and habits did not blunt their patriotism to their fatherland. Huang was one of the first to join the Xingzhonghui and would soon sell one of his apartment blocks for HK$8,000 to help prepare the Xingzhonghui's first uprising, in Guangzhou.

The Xingzhonghui had a number of sympathizers among Hong Kong's Chinese elite. Of these the most prominent was Ho Kai, the patron of the College of Medicine for Chinese, who now assumed the role of a gray eminence to Sun and his comrades. Ho did not join the Xingzhonghui but attended its initial meetings, and was instrumental in convincing the British editors of two Hong Kong dailies to write favorably about the impending uprising. In March, the *China Mail* disclosed in three separate editorials that the "Reform Party" was planning to overthrow the Qing dynasty and establish constitutional rule. They urged foreigners not to repeat the mistake of supporting the dynasty as they had done with the Taiping Rebellion.

This new breed of revolutionaries was different, the newspaper claimed, and their intention was to rid the country of misrule. They were moderate constitutional reformers, quite different from the ubiquitous secret societies, and were therefore worthy of European support and tutelage. The new regime would make liberal use of foreigners as advisers in their reform programs and would recognize all of China's existing treaty obligations and arrangements such as the collection of customs duties. To convey the image of a restrained revolution, the *China Mail* revealed that the aim of the revolution was to establish a new dynasty, not a republic. Sun and his comrades realized that significant change in China would not be possible without the backing of the foreign powers, especially if attempted by people like themselves who lacked a solid social constituency at home. They recognized that most foreigners were skeptical of the prospects of republicanism in China and feared the disruptive effects of a prolonged civil war. They therefore found it expedient to cloak their intentions in terms that would make them more palatable to foreigners. In spite of the *China Mail*'s editorials, the British government stuck to its support for the Qing regime, while the respectability bestowed by this newspaper and Ho Kai did little to alter the international community's perception of Sun and his comrades as opportunistic adventurers.[6]

There was at least one non-Chinese sympathizer, a Japanese photographer-turned-moviemaker by the name of Umeya Shokichi. In 1893, Umeya had set up a photographic studio in Singapore but his attention soon turned to the enormous profits to be made in the new rubber industry in peninsular Malaya and the potential for large-scale Japanese immigration to the region. He obtained the commitment of an influential political figure in Japan to put together the funds and to draw in other important political and cultural figures in support of his scheme, but nothing came out of the plan. With the outbreak of the Sino-Japanese War, the *huaqiao* community in Singapore turned hostile toward Japanese nationals and Umeya decided to move his business to Hong Kong. It was here at his residence on the second floor of his newly established studio that he received a visit from Sun sometime after the latter's arrival in Hong Kong in January 1895. The meeting lasted all day and resulted in Umeya's conversion to Sun's revolutionary cause. Thereafter Umeya entered into a life of clandestine meetings and covert operations in support of Sun. As his business prospered, he diverted significant sums to support Sun's revolutionary activities.[7]

Barely a month after the establishment of the Xingzhonghui, the revolutionary conspirators were already crystallizing plans to seize Guangzhou. Their objective was to capture Guangdong and Guangxi and set up a government for the two provinces to serve as a springboard or to inspire a chain reaction of responsive risings elsewhere. The ultimate hope was of course the collapse of the Qing dynasty. This almost happened without the revolutionaries' help.

In the initial stage of the Sino-Japanese War, most bets were on a quick Chinese victory. The war was indeed brief, but with China at the wrong end. Having modernized their armed forces through the adoption of a Western-style military, the Japanese outgunned and outmaneuvered the Chinese and scored a series of victories on land and sea. With the loss of the port of Weihaiwei and a Japanese attack on the Pescadores, a strategic chain of islands between the west coast of Taiwan and the mainland, the Qing court sued for peace.

Li Hongzhang traveled to Japan to negotiate an armistice, but the Treaty of Shimonoseki signed on April 17, 1895, was a disaster for China. It would have been worse had a Japanese assassin's bullet not wounded Li and shamed the Japanese government before the world. The treaty imposed on the humiliated Qing government a war indemnity of 200 million taels of silver, the opening up of treaty ports to Japanese trade and the granting of most-favored-nation status to Japan. China was also made to renounce her suzerainty over Korea and to cede the Liaodong peninsula, Taiwan and the Pescadores to Japan "in perpetuity." Within a month of the Shimonoseki treaty, the so-called Triple Intervention of France, Germany and Russia forced Japan to give up the Liaodong peninsula. The Japanese reluctantly agreed, in exchange for an additional indemnity of 30 million taels of silver from China. The anger generated by what seemed to the Japanese a diminution of their hard-earned spoils of war was to linger on well into the 20th century.

China's defeat sent shockwaves throughout the country and around the world. In the span of a few months, Japan had negated 30 years of China's Self-Strengthening and altered the international order that had prevailed in East Asia for over half a century. Defeat by a Western power was humiliating enough but surrendering a large chunk of territory to a former beneficiary of China's great culture and civilization was a cruel and traumatizing blow to the Chinese. It revealed China's weakness to the world, which until then had at least some veneer of credibility, even if signs of her political and economic decay had been evident for some time. It stimulated reassessment of the strategy that China had pursued to respond to the challenges of the West.

Until the Shimonoseki treaty, the Western powers had adopted a policy of opening up China for commercial exploitation rather than territorial acquisition. Japan's territorial grab in the wake of her victory rendered the old formula passé. Instead of sharing commercial privileges, the powers now joined by Japan pushed further into the Chinese interior as they rushed to create spheres of influence in a "scramble for concessions." The new privileges obtained included the construction of railways, which had thus far been denied them, and the leasing of Chinese territories. Unlike the concessions in the treaty ports, where the Chinese at least had de jure sovereignty, these leased territories were foreign enclaves where the foreign lessee held all regalian rights. At this point China owed her survival to the pragmatism of the Western powers to exercise restraint among themselves to prevent a total disintegration of the empire.

The Chinese who had been cynical about the Qing regime's reform efforts now had even less reason to hold back. While the majority remained hesitant about a sharp break with tradition, a number emerged to agitate for radical reform. Japan, the cause of their anguish, became overnight the model for their emulation. Disorder spread in the lower reaches of society throughout the length and breadth of the empire as discharged soldiers, demoralized and unpaid, created havoc in the towns and countryside. Nowhere were they more numerous or menacing than in Guangdong province, where there were already multitudes of secret society gangsters, opium smugglers and pirates. The corruption in Guangdong, which had reached "a degree of notoriety rarely surpassed even in China," fostered even greater resentment of the Qing dynasty in the province than anywhere else.

Thus regardless of the overall naiveté of Sun's strategy, Guangzhou was as good a choice as any for an uprising. Plans were elaborated to the minutest detail and completed by the end of August. D-Day was set for Saturday, October 26, 1895, which was the ninth day of the ninth month in the Chinese lunisolar calendar. This was the day of the "Double Ninth" Festival when Chinese visit the graves of their ancestors to make offerings. The expected crowds would provide convenient cover for the insurgents.

A strike force of 3,000 Triad members and bandits recruited from the coastal districts of Guangdong was to assemble in Hong Kong. They would then travel to Guangzhou by ferry with arms and ammunitions, which Umeya Shokichi had helped to procure, concealed in barrels camouflaged as Portland cement. As a means of identification, the rebels were to wear red belts. Upon disembarkation, this "suicide" squad would divide into four companies and storm the offices of the governor-general and the governor as well as the military command headquarters. Their mission was to cripple the administration of Guangdong and Guangxi to pave the way for the establishment of a revolutionary government for the two provinces. The squad's first objective was to kill the officials and military officers, or hold them prisoner, in order to suffocate the command chain in the event of a counterattack. Concurrently, similarly constituted columns were to converge on Guangzhou by way of the Pearl River tributaries. Some of these forces were to be stationed at strategic points leading to the provincial capital to divert and ambush loyalist troops, while a bomb squad was to provide additional distraction and confuse the enemy.[8]

The plan required split-second timing and a good measure of nerve. The vanguard force was probably in the hundreds, rather than the thousands claimed, and many among the rank and file were mercenaries, rather than committed revolutionaries. Sun was not particularly concerned about the size or political orientation of the strike force; he believed that once the shooting began and they had achieved their first objective, sympathetic risings of secret societies and bandits in the hinterland would join to take the movement beyond the two provinces. Sun also hoped to gain support from the Cantonese gentry and, through a friend in high office, that of key military and naval personnel.

With his better connections in Hong Kong, Yang Quyun, the leader of the Furen group, took chief responsibility for finance. In addition to the HK$8,000 from the sale of Huang Yongshang's block of apartments, another HK$10,000 was donated by a secretive merchant who delivered the money to Yang in a cemetery. These funds, together with those remitted from Hawaii and an unspecified sum from Sun, who contributed all his savings from his medical practice, were all the money in the war chest.

Sun was to take charge of operations in Guangzhou, where within sight of the provincial capital he was to weave a subversive web. He was assisted by Lu Haodong, with Zheng Shiliang serving as the principal liaison with the secret societies in the province. Supporting them were about 30 local members of the Xingzhonghui. These included several naval officers whose role was to subvert part of the Guangdong fleet. Two members from the Hawaiian cohort were to lead a contingent of fighters from their home district of Xiangshan. Another supporter was the proprietor of a religious bookstore, the very same store that Sun had rented for his medical practice two years earlier. The rear of the bookstore was a Presbyterian chapel whose pastor also served as manager of the bookstore. He, too, had joined the Xingzhonghui, and the bookstore served as a rendezvous and one of the arms caches in Guangzhou.

To camouflage his covert operation, Sun adopted a public persona as a reformer and in early October set up a new organization which he christened the Agricultural Study Society, with the bookstore listed as its office. Its manifesto, apparently written by Sun, promoted universal education and scientific agriculture:

> If we want China to change from a state of weakness to one of strength, from impoverishment to prosperity, we must promote education ... I am a son of a peasant family, and know the hardships of life in agriculture. When I was young, I went abroad and learned about Western government and civilization, and read extensively and studied everything concerning modern learning, paying special attention to agriculture and botany.[9]

The reformist and educational purpose of the agricultural society was well received in gentry and bureaucratic circles. Having established quite a reputation in Guangzhou through his previous medical practice, Sun managed to get a number of local influentials to help him. Not all were ignorant of his real intentions, however, and at least one was admitted to the inner circle. Liu Xuexun was an ambitious Xiangshan native who had achieved the highest level *jinshi* degree in the civil service examinations, and amassed a personal fortune by taking bets on the results of such examinations. An old-fashioned monarchist, he saw Sun's venture as an opportunity for founding a new dynasty. While avoiding personal risk, he encouraged Sun's plotting, which Sun reciprocated by feeding him hope, believing that the involvement of a prominent gentry could be useful. Liu's wealth and social standing would add an aura of respectability to an uprising led by foreign-educated Christians of humbler origins. Yet it was precisely their foreign background that the conspirators emphasized in Hong Kong when they were trying to win approval from the British there.

The leadership of the Xingzhonghui was finally settled on October 10, a little over a fortnight before the scheduled uprising. What was at stake was more than just the head honcho of the society; it was the presidency of the provisional government. As the man in charge of the society's finances, Yang knew that he held the fate of the rebellion in his hands. He demanded the position, at least until after the rebellion, when it would revert to Sun. The argument became so heated at one point that Zheng Shiliang proposed eliminating Yang. Chen Shaobai, always the cool-headed one, saved the day and the uprising. He argued that killing Yang would invite the intervention of the authorities and compromise the uprising. Sun grudgingly deferred to his rival after Chen convinced him that once the plot succeeded, Sun would be in control in Guangzhou. If the uprising failed, the title would be meaningless anyway. Sun reluctantly agreed to be the president-in-waiting.

The Xingzhonghui had 153 members just before the scheduled uprising, including 112 who had joined in Hawaii. Of the remaining 41, all but one was from Guangzhou or Hong Kong. Seventy-three or almost half of the society's members were from Sun's home district of Xiangshan. Friendships and geographic ties were apparently important factors in bringing these people together. Wealthy merchants and small business owners, traditionally the low-prestige groups in Chinese society, made up the largest block of the membership. There were also significant numbers in vocations that required Western education and training, such as physicians, English teachers, clerks and technicians in foreign enterprises. Some like Sun, Yang

Quyun and his deputy Xie Xuantai had spent a good part of their lives overseas and were only superficially acquainted with Chinese culture; a few even communicated with each other in English. Within the inner circle, Chen Shaobai was perhaps the only one who was proficient in written Chinese. Propaganda played only a minor role in the Guangzhou uprising. The leadership did not try to create a disciplined movement based upon an indoctrinated following. They saw their task merely as a spark to ignite anti-dynastic sentiment. In this they took the path of least resistance and relied on traditional means, the secret societies and bandits.[10]

On October 26, the coup plan was set in motion. Almost immediately, the entire operation started to go awry. That morning, as his men in Guangzhou appeared at the wharf to greet the expected boat with the rebels and weapons from Hong Kong, Sun received a telegram from Yang Quyun informing him that the "goods" could not arrive on schedule but would be sent the following evening, October 27. On the evening of the 26th, Sun and Chen Shaobai decided that an indefinite postponement would be their best option and accordingly sent a telegram to Yang to cancel the "shipment" until further notice and to send the hired guns home to await orders. It was too late. Sun's telegram did not reach Yang on time and the boat arrived on the morning of October 28. When the rebels on board reached the wharf, Guangzhou's police were lying in wait to greet them. The authorities had been tipped off.

Earlier, the Xingzhonghui conspirators had planned on posting a "declaration of war" in and around Guangzhou once the fighting started. The responsibility for drawing up those proclamations fell on Zhu Qi, the sole degree-holder among the members. His complicity in the conspiracy put his family at risk according to the Chinese principle of collective responsibility. His brother, a local official, came to know of the plot. To protect himself and his family, he decided to betray it to the authorities. A day or so before D-Day, he forged Zhu Qi's signature to a confession and sent it to the assistant prefect, who immediately ordered a surveillance on Sun. A report was sent to the governor-general, who laughed the matter off when told that Sun was the suspected culprit. He knew of Sun and had thought of him as a harmless "wild man who would not dare revolt." Without the governor-general's nod, the authorities feared entanglement

BAPTISM BY FIRE

with the foreign missionaries by detaining one from their flock without concrete proof. Moreover, Sun's penchant for publicity had projected an image of himself as an idealistic amateur, not a cold-blooded conspirator. Nonetheless, the red flag had been raised. Meanwhile, Inspector Stanton of the Hong Kong Police learned on October 27 that about 400 fighters had been recruited in Hong Kong and were scheduled to depart for Guangzhou on the SS *Powan*. Later that evening, Stanton discovered that Yang Quyun had also purchased a large quantity of arms and shipped them on the *Powan*. He immediately telegraphed the information to Guangzhou. Thus alerted, the governor-general called for additional troops to reinforce his garrison and sent a police party to intercept the steamer when it arrived in Guangzhou.[11]

The police force was too small to hold the entire group and many got away. Raids on the rebels' secret hideouts yielded arms, ammunition and other battle paraphernalia. Several prisoners were taken, including Lu Haodong. Refusing to divulge any information about the uprising or his comrades, Lu remained defiant to the end. He was executed along with several other captured rebels. Thus ended Sun's first uprising without a shot fired, save those from the firing squad. The ones who were still at large became wandering refugees among the *huaqiao* communities in various parts of the world. The Xingzhonghui would remain dormant for the next five years.

Sun narrowly escaped capture. He found refuge in the home of a Chinese Christian minister in Guangzhou before hastily departing in a sedan chair to Macau and then to Hong Kong, where he arrived on October 29. An attorney referred by Dr. Cantlie advised Sun to leave the colony as soon as possible to avoid possible extradition. Umeya Shokichi arranged the passage for Sun, accompanied by Chen Shaobai and Zheng Shiliang, to take the first available ship out of Hong Kong, which was bound for Kobe, Japan.[12] Their arrival on November 12 attracted the attention of the Japanese press, which announced the arrival of "the leader of the Chinese revolutionary party." The trio proceeded to Yokohama, where there was a Cantonese community of a few thousand. Thus began Sun's 16 years of exile from his motherland, during which he was barred from entering Hong Kong or returning to China.

THE FAILED insurrection in Guangzhou was the first in a series that by 1911 would total ten. It had all the elements of the strategy that Sun would repeatedly use in the other risings: the use of a base beyond the reach of the Qing government; the appeal to hired hands funded by donations from wealthy patrons; and the quest for foreign aid, for which Sun was sometimes all too eager to make significant concessions. His repeated failures underscore the limits of a strategy that was too casual about organization; neglecting the need for propaganda; focusing too much on immediate results; and entrusting to social outcasts the execution of a program that was beyond the scope of their experience.[13]

The Guangzhou debacle introduced an unwelcome dimension into Sun's life. Before the uprising, he was a successful young physician who dabbled in revolutionary babble. After walking the talk, he was a terrorist with a price on his head. Indeed, six months after the uprising, an article in a Chinese newspaper in Singapore portrayed him as a traditional bandit chief. To evade detection, Sun assumed a new persona by clipping his *towchang*, growing a moustache and trading his Chinese robe for a European suit, a transformation that made him look like a modern Japanese of the Meiji period. In Yokohama, Sun, Chen and Zheng established a branch of the Xingzhonghui. Though anti-Manchu sentiment was not lacking, the *huaqiao* were hesitant to consort with a rebel on the run. Of the several thousand Chinese in Yokohama, only 15 attended the inaugural meeting presided over by Sun. Nevertheless, he was able to borrow enough money to pay for his next destination while setting his sights on the larger and more affluent *huaqiao* communities on the American continent. Zheng Shiliang, whose name was not on the Manchu wanted list, was sent back to Hong Kong to lay the groundwork for a future rising, while Chen left for Tokyo.

Arriving in Hawaii in January 1896 under an alias, Sun spent a good six months in the Islands. Although the Xingzhonghui's Hawaiian membership had increased since its formation, news of the Guangzhou failure dampened morale. Sun tried to invigorate the moribund branches through various means, including forming an association to offer military education and a discussion group affiliated with a Chinese newspaper in Honolulu. Though he failed to stimulate the membership, Sun did quite well

Photograph of Sun Yat-sen taken in San Francisco, 1896.

financially and was able to raise enough money to make the journey to North America.

Before leaving Hawaii, Sun had a coincidental encounter with Dr. Cantlie and his wife, who were vacationing in Hawaii on their way home to England for a well-deserved retirement. Surprised to meet his favorite student, Dr. Cantlie invited Sun to visit him in London. Whether Sun had previously planned to visit Europe after America is uncertain, but his promise to visit the Cantlies in London delighted his former teacher who still harbored hopes that his former protégé could be persuaded to resume his medical studies.

The six-month sojourn gave Sun the opportunity to spend quality time with his family. His wife, their son Sun Ke (born in 1891), daughter Sun Yan (born in 1895), and his widowed mother had joined Sun Mei in Hawaii to escape possible reprisals by the Manchu authorities. Another daughter, Sun Wan, would be born in November 1896. His generous and affluent brother took care of his family and paid for their expenses. Once again, thanks to Sun Mei's Confucian sense of family obligation, Sun was able to pursue his revolutionary career free of financial worries.

In San Francisco, the starting point of his American tour, Sun foolishly posed for a photograph. A copy found its way to the Chinese Legation in

Washington, D.C., which instructed its staff throughout the United States to monitor his every move. Unaware of the surveillance, Sun toured the country proselytizing his revolution. Unfortunately for him, the *huaqiao* in America, like their counterparts elsewhere, sought personal success above all else. They had little appetite for Chinese politics but were loyal to the Qing dynasty which since the 1880s had shown increasing concern for the welfare of its overseas subjects. Sun achieved nothing from his three-month tour. When he boarded the SS *Majestic* in New York on September 23, the Chinese minister in the United States alerted his counterpart in Britain of Sun's impending arrival. In London the Chinese minister immediately applied to the Foreign Office to extradite Sun on his arrival in the British Isles, which was turned down. Arriving in London on October 1, 1896, Sun was instantly placed under surveillance by private eyes hired by the Chinese Legation as he moved into the accommodation that Cantlie had found for him at Gray's Inn Place in Holborn.

Almost a year had passed since the Guangzhou coup. During that time Sun had been living the life of a professional rebel on the run in a vain search for constituents. Now ready for some relaxation, he spent his first few days in London taking in the usual tourist sights and rekindling his friendship with the Cantlies. Slater Detective Agency, the firm of private investigators hired by the Chinese Legation, continued to trail him and file reports of his movements. With the only legal recourse of getting Sun back to China denied by the Foreign Office, the Chinese Legation resorted to detaining him.

How did Sun end up a prisoner in the Chinese Legation? We may never know for sure as there are conflicting claims. According to Sun's own account issued after his release, he was walking to the Cantlie residence on Sunday, October 11 to join them for church. On the way, he was approached by two Chinese men who engaged him in conversation. The door of an adjacent house suddenly opened and Sun was "half-jokingly and half-persistently compelled to enter" by the two men. Suspecting nothing, Sun entered in good faith. Only after the door was "hurriedly closed and barred" did it occur to Sun that he might be in the Chinese Legation. He was then taken to a room on the second floor and an elderly Englishman with a white beard presently appeared who informed Sun that he was in the Chinese Legation, where Chinese and not British law applied. He also told Sun that the Chinese minister in the United States had sent instructions for Sun's arrest, and that he was awaiting further instructions from the Zongli Yamen in Beijing.[14]

The elderly Englishman was Sir Halliday Macartney, the secretary of the Chinese Legation. A relative of Lord Macartney, who led the first British mission to China in 1793, Halliday Macartney was an old China hand, having served with the Chinese army fighting against the Taipings. He worked in the Nanjing arsenal for a time until he was employed by the Chinese Legation in London when it was set up in 1877. Macartney gave a different version of how Sun came to be detained. He claimed that Sun had entered the Legation of his own accord to make enquiries. Recognized by the legation staff, Sun was detained on his second visit. There is also a third version, based on statements later made by Sun's comrades. According to them, Sun told them that he had gone willingly to the Legation out of defiance, and had only invented the story of the kidnapping to discredit and embarrass the legation.

Whatever the truth of the matter, what is indisputable is that Sun was taken prisoner and held captive in the Chinese Legation for 12 days. Macartney knew how badly Sun was wanted in China and acted with ruthless efficiency to please his Chinese masters. Three days after Sun's capture, he was negotiating for a ship charter to transport him to China. Sun's numerous attempts to communicate with the outside world were intercepted by Macartney. Salvation came when the legation's English porter agreed to deliver to Dr. Cantlie a message which Sun had scribbled on two calling cards:

> I was kidnapped into the Chinese Legation on Sunday, and shall be smuggled out from England to China for death. Pray rescue me quick; A ship is already charter by the C.L. [Chinese Legation] for the service to take me to China and I shall be locked up all the way without communication to anybody ... O! Woe to me![15]

On receiving this note, there was no stopping Dr. Cantlie from hounding Scotland Yard, the Foreign Office and the *Times* to secure Sun's release.

Typical of English bureaucracy, the matter meandered its way slowly through the various departments while the venerable newspaper sat on the story. Impatient at the slow progress, Dr. Cantlie hired a private eye to keep watch over the Chinese Legation building. Ironically, this detective was from Slater, the same agency engaged by the Chinese Legation. Following the decision of Lord Salisbury, concurrently prime minister and foreign minister, to authorize official intervention, Scotland Yard launched a round-the-clock surveillance of the legation on October 19 while the police kept watch on all ships bound for China. On October 22, the Foreign Office decided to press for Sun's release. Dr. Cantlie, acting on official advice, applied to the Old Bailey for a writ of habeas corpus against the legation, but the presiding judge shifted responsibility back to the Foreign Office. By this time, the hearing at the Old Bailey had attracted the attention of the London *Globe*, which broke the news in a special edition on the same day. The next day, virtually every newspaper picked up the story of Sun's detention. Hordes of journalists, photographers and inquisitive members of the public mobbed the legation. This so embarrassed the Foreign Office that it threatened the Chinese Legation with severe diplomatic reprisals. That afternoon, the legation caved in and released its prisoner. As Sun left the legation building into the custody of Foreign Office officials, he was swarmed by reporters all clamoring for interviews. The 12-day ordeal had taken its toll and Sun, escorted by Dr. Cantlie, left without giving any statements.

After a day of recuperation, Sun was ready to shift into high gear. Having become a *cause célèbre*, Sun made the most of it to project himself as a respectable Chinese patriot to the British public. In a letter to the *Times* and other metropolitan papers on the day after his release, Sun wrote:

> Sir, – Will you kindly express through your columns my keen appreciation of the action of the British Government in effecting my release from the Chinese Legation? I have also to thank the Press generally for their timely help and sympathy. If anything was needed to convince me of the generous public spirit which pervades Great Britain, and the love of justice which distinguishes

its people, the recent acts of the last few days have conclusively done so. Knowing and feeling more keenly than ever what a constitutional government and an enlightened people mean, I am prepared to pursue the cause of advancement, education, and civilization, in my own beloved but oppressed country.[16]

Sun also gave press conferences and granted numerous interviews. Journalists were impressed by his personality and completely convinced by his version of the kidnap. In commenting on his political views, Sun was careful not to mention revolution or republicanism but positioned himself as the leader of the "Reform Party." He also took great pains to disavow any affiliation to the British socialists and to publicize his Christian faith. Not known to be a regular churchgoer, he made it a point to attend church under the watchful eyes of the media. The London *Globe* even implied that Sun would stay on in England to help Cantlie train Chinese medical practitioners.

Sun attracted attention from unexpected quarters as well. The distinguished Cambridge sinologist Professor Herbert A. Giles, who was working on a Chinese biographical dictionary, asked Sun to prepare a short autobiography. Sun also had the satisfaction of having his name mentioned in parliament when in February 1897 questions were raised about the behavior of the Chinese Legation and the personal responsibility of Halliday Macartney. With the help of a "friend," most probably Dr. Cantlie, Sun later wrote an account of his ordeal at the Chinese legation in *Kidnapped in London*. Published in England early the following year and on sale in Shanghai by May, this book did more than anything else to spread the name of Sun abroad. More importantly, the kidnapping episode bolstered Sun's self-confidence and convinced him that he was destined for some higher purpose. In a private letter to his friend and teacher in Hong Kong, the Christian minister Qu Fengzhi, he wrote: "I am like the prodigal son and the lost sheep: I owe everything to the great favor of God. Through the Way of God I hope to enter into the Political Way. I hope you will not cease to write to me about the Way of God."[17]

The British government's indignation at the kidnapping was over the flouting of British law by the Chinese legation. Mistaking this as sympathy for his cause, Sun made a play for British neutrality in March 1897 by promising Britain trade and investment opportunities in China. Writing in the *Fortnightly Review*:

> Nothing short of the entire overthrow of the present utterly corrupt regime, and the establishment of some good government and a pure administration by native Chinese with, at first, European advice, and, for some years, European administrative assistance, can effect any improvement whatever. The mere introduction of railways, or any such appliances of the material civilization of Europe, would (even were it as feasible as those who put their faith in Li Hung Chang seem to think) rather make matters worse, by opening up new channels for extortion, fraud, and peculation ... Here it may be enough to say that the benevolent neutrality of Great Britain, and the other Powers, is all the aid needed to enable us to make the present system give place to one that is not corrupt.[18]

While political neophytes like Dr. Cantlie might have seen Sun as the hope of a better future for the Chinese people, the British government was not taken in by his appeal to Western values and considered him a nuisance and a political liability. British commercial interests in China had nothing to do with constitutional government in China. As Britain competed with other Western powers for valuable concessions in China, she could hardly afford to offend the Qing government by supporting a conspirator against the regime. In fact, right after Lord Salisbury reprimanded the Chinese Legation for their behavior, he was quick to reassure Beijing that he would not allow Hong Kong to be used as a base for agitation on the mainland and to this end he would maintain the prohibition against Sun setting foot in the British colony.

Sun stayed on in London until early July 1897 and took the opportunity to study and enlarge his contacts. He continued to be a frequent guest at the Cantlie residence and regularly accompanied the couple to Sunday service at St. Martin's-in-the-Fields. The Cantlies introduced him to their circle of educated and well-traveled friends whose religious convictions and overseas travels inclined them to take an interest in world affairs. When not in the company of the Cantlies or their friends, Sun spent most of his time reading on politics, law, diplomacy, military affairs and other subjects at the British Museum, where he made a number of new acquaintances. One was Felix Volkhovsky, the Russian editor of *Free Russia* who had recently obtained his freedom after seven years of imprisonment in St. Petersburg followed by 11 years of exile in Siberia. Together they worked on a Russian translation of Sun's *Kidnapped in London*, which was published in 1897.

Another was Minakata Kumagusu, a Japanese botanist who was then employed in vacation research work at the Museum. He confided to Sun that his wish in life was that "Asians will drive out [of Asia] all Westerners once and for all." Until then Sun had never heard of pan-Asianism, the ideology promoting the unity of Asian peoples against Western imperialism. This idealism was to be a source of inspiration for Sun. He also befriended a number of people outside the Cantlies' circle and the British Museum. Of particular interest was Rowland J. Mulkern, a professional Irish nationalist soldier, who volunteered as an occasional bodyguard when Sun moved around London. He would later become the only Westerner to join the Xingzhonghui.

On July 2, Sun set sail for his return trip to Japan via Canada. Chastened by his London experience, Sun became more prudent. He kept to his cabin most of the time and did not join the conversations during mealtimes, so much so that the ship's doctor had to advise him to spend more time on deck and to exercise more. When he landed in Montreal on July 11, he used an alias to hide his movements and made enquiries about the *Empress of India*, which was scheduled to sail from Vancouver to Yokohama in early August. At first he was afraid that Chinese officials who had attended Queen Victoria's Diamond Jubilee celebration would be sailing on the same ship, but then discovered that only the Japanese delegation would be on board. On his overland journey across Canada, Sun continued to press the *huaqiao* for money. He must have been quite successful for he was able to upgrade his accommodation on the *Empress* when he boarded it using his own name. At this point, the Chinese Legation in London called off the surveillance that had been maintained throughout Sun's journey across Canada.[19]

In March 1896 the Hong Kong colonial government had issued a banishment order against Sun in absentia and was enforcing it vigorously under instructions from London. His appeal to the Hong Kong colonial secretary for a review was turned down. In fact, Sun was barred from entering Hong Kong, except for a brief lapse, until after the 1911 Revolution. Thus, forced by circumstances rather than choice, Japan was to be Sun's home and base of operations for the next decade.

Chapter 3

MAN OF HIGH PURPOSE

ON JULY 8, 1853, Commodore Matthew Perry of the U.S. Navy sailed into Edo (modern-day Tokyo) Bay with a squadron of four ships. His mission was to conclude an agreement with the Japanese government for the protection of shipwrecked or stranded Americans and to open one or more ports for supplies and refueling. He returned the following spring to receive Japan's reply with an even larger squadron to convince the Japanese that he was prepared to use his advanced firepower. Without the means to resist the American's demands, the Japanese grudgingly signed the Treaty of Kanagawa on March 31, 1854. By the terms of this accord, Japan would protect stranded American seamen and open two ports, Hakodate on the northern island of Hokkaido and Shimoda about 60 miles (100 km) southwest of Tokyo, for refueling and provisioning American ships. Japan also gave the U.S. the right to station consuls in these ports, a privilege not previously granted to foreign nations. This treaty was not a trade pact and it did not guarantee the right to trade with Japan, though it contained a most-favored-nation clause. It also ended almost two centuries of isolation. Within five years, Japan had signed similar treaties with other Western powers.

These accords with the Western powers were unequal treaties similar in nature and intent to those that been imposed on China two decades earlier. They were forced on Japan through gunboat diplomacy, which the Japanese found profoundly humiliating and a source of national shame. The Tokugawa shogun's inability to defend Japan against the Western aggression sparked a fierce struggle within Japan. Xenophobic samurai claimed that the shogun's compromise with the West ran counter to the will of the emperor. They began a campaign of assassinations targeted at shogunate officials and foreigners. These samurai, in alliance with court officials, secured control of the imperial court and influenced the young Meiji Emperor. Realizing that his days were numbered, Shogun Tokugawa Yoshinobu relinquished his political power to the emperor. The restoration of imperial rule was the start of a period of nationalism and socio-politico-economic restructuring known as the Meiji Restoration.

The shogunate system was abolished, the military modernized, and numerous Western institutions adopted – including a Western legal system and quasi-parliamentary constitutional government modeled on the constitution of the German Empire. While many aspects of the Meiji Restoration were adopted directly from the West, others such as the dissolution of the feudal system and the shogunate were processes that had begun well before the arrival of Commodore Perry. Nonetheless, his intervention is widely viewed as a pivotal moment in Japanese history.

In the years following the Meiji Restoration, Japan sought to distance herself from the rest of East Asia and to identify with the industrialized West. But she could not escape her geographical proximity to the Asian mainland, or insulate herself from developments therefrom. A major concern was Western imperialism, in particular Russian expansionism in northeast Asia, as such maneuvers might portend an attempt to colonize Japan. Victory in the Sino-Japanese War had not brought the desired security, or recognition as a global power. She had created opportunities for imperialism in China, but others were exploiting them to better advantage. While allowed to join in the slicing of the Chinese melon, the choicest spoils were kept out of her reach. This was made clear by the Triple Intervention by which Japan had to return the Liaodong peninsula, only to see Russia claim it as her prize six months later. There was pervasive skepticism whether the West would ever accord equality to any Asian people. In reaction to the "Yellow Peril" theme in the West grew the belief that racial ties would eventually pit the white man against the yellow race. Japan's active participation in the raging "scramble for concessions" in China was accompanied by fears that the premature collapse of China would leave Japan without natural allies, ending up as the isolated victim of a predatory West. The Japanese saw China's modernization as an essential preventive against such an eventuality. Since Japan had successfully extricated herself from the backwardness that China was still mired in, she was in the best position to help her neighbor.[1]

These politics led to a movement to create a continental identity as an antidote against Western hegemony in Asia. At the root of this pan-Asian movement was the recognition of the cultural links that bound Japan to China. Apart from the cultural loyalty that everyone professed, pan-Asianism was interpreted in many different ways. Its partisans came from the Right, the Left and the various shades between.

The nationalistic societies that supported an aggressive foreign policy to preserve Japan's national prestige and Eastern values were headed by Toyama Mitsuru. Born into a family of samurai from Fukuoka on the island of Kyushu, Toyama made his fortune in the local coal mines. He held no public office but used his considerable personal fortune to finance ultranationalist groups that supported pan-Asianism, in particular the Kokuryu-kai, or Black Dragon Society, whose vision was to extend Japan's territory as far as the Amur River in Siberia. This society was founded by Uchida Ryohei, who later became one of the principal promoters of the Japanese fascist movement.

The pan-Asian ideal also gained currency among the Left of the Meiji era who wished to rid Japan and East Asia of the Western presence. At the head of these liberals was Okuma Shigenobu, the leader of the Progressive Party who served concurrently as prime minister and finance minister from 1896 to 1898. Invoking Japan's cultural debt to China, Okuma believed that Japan having modernized owed a moral duty to protect China against Western aggression and to help "a Chinese hero" save his country. This Okuma doctrine, which he formulated in 1898, was taken up by Inukai Ki (a.k.a. Inukai Tsuyoshi), a journalist and liberal member of the Diet allied with Okuma. The son of a scholar of classical Chinese and also one in his own right, Inukai was sympathetic to modern Asian nationalism. Committed to helping out Asian nationalists, his home in Tokyo was a haven for political refugees from all over Asia.

Men as much in the public eye as Okuma and Inukai had to operate through intermediaries who held no public office and would work for anyone for a price. Those who believed that they were also working for an ideal called themselves *shishi*, "men of high purpose." Placing themselves at the service of pan-Asianism, such men brought to their work all the loyalty and devotion inherited from their feudal code of honor. One such *shishi* was the Japanese adventurer Miyazaki Torazo. Better known by his pen name Miyazaki Toten, he was born in 1870 of samurai stock and had a liberal education marked by a religious and moral crisis and a fleeting conversion to Christianity. A second crisis led to a break with Christianity, after which he set off on a series of adventures to China and Siam. In 1896 Inukai Ki entrusted him with funds from the Ministry of Foreign Affairs to travel to China to seek out a *shishi* who, with Japanese help, could save his country from Western imperialism. Working alongside him in the quest for a hero was Hirayama Shu, another trusted aide of Inukai who was often called upon to cooperate with Uchida and Toyama's men. Chen Shaobai learned of the assignment entrusted to Miyazaki and made contact with him. Eager to make an impression, Chen gave him a copy of *Kidnapped in London* and the names of several sympathizers in Hong Kong, Macau and Guangzhou since Miyazaki was about to join other Japanese agents in China. Miyazaki pursued those leads in China but when he learned that Sun was due in Yokohama, he took the first available ship home.

Sun had arrived in Yokohama on August 10, 1897. At his reunion with Chen, it was decided that he would take over the Japanese connection while Chen proceeded to Taiwan to rally the victims of Japanese aggression. That Sun was ready to collaborate with the Japanese in China while Chen prepared to agitate against the Japanese in Taiwan is no more paradoxical than Sun's attempt at collaboration with Britain, who was at the forefront of the imperialist assault on China.[2] Or in today's context, the U.S. seeking China's help to rein in North Korea while continuing to sell arms to Taiwan over China's objections.

The first meeting between Sun and Miyazaki took place in the autumn of 1897 at the home of Chen Shaobai, who had left for Taiwan. Miyazaki went to the meeting with high expectations but his first impression of Sun was far from positive. As he later described the scene: "He [Sun] had not rinsed his mouth or washed his face, and he sat there just the way he'd gotten out of bed. At first I was startled by such casualness, and thought he must be unstable." Bothered by Sun's casualness, Miyazaki initially had doubts if Sun was their man, the *shishi* who could lead 400 million Chinese to solve China's myriad problems. But they warmed up to each other after a while for they had much in common. Both were Western-educated, had converted to Christianity, and were ready to tread outside the perimeter of the law in pursuit of their objectives. Perhaps because of their cultural closeness, there was not the formality or circumspection that Sun invariably felt pressured to adopt with Westerners.[3]

When asked about his "plans" and the "contents of your so-called revolution," Sun told Miyazaki: "I believe that the highest order of government is one in which people govern themselves. Therefore the political principle I advocate is republicanism." Contradicting those who claimed that China was not ready for republicanism, Sun declared:

> Some people argue that republican institutions will not fit a barbarous country like China. But those who take that view are ignorant of the facts. To begin with, republicanism is at the core of our political tradition, and it is a heritage bequeathed to us by our ancient sages. That is, when you think about our country's ancient times you call to mind the examples of the government in the three dynasties [Xia, Shang and Zhou]. But the government of those days actually contained the essence of republicanism ... This republicanism is the finest natural form of government, and it is essential because it suits the Chinese people...

Tuning in to Miyazaki's wavelength in his usual skillful way, Sun now denounced Western imperialism in contrast to his recent enthusiasm for the British respect for rights and the rule of law. He spoke of "a hero [who] rises up to overthrow the Manchu barbarians," and humbly proposed himself for the role:

> Alas, because our territory is so huge and our people are so numerous, we are like a piece of meat on the butcher block. The ravenous tiger who devours it will grow so strong he will come to dominate the world. But now if someone with moral principles responds to this, he will find himself in harmony with the principles of humanity and renowned throughout the world. I would not have been able to stand aside from such a challenge even if I were an ordinary person anywhere in the world, wanting the way of humanity to be preserved. How much more so when it concerns the country of my birth, the land whose distress I have myself

experienced! I know my deficiencies in ability and knowledge, and know that I am not qualified to undertake this great task. But the times do not permit me to stand by waiting for someone else to lead the way. So I am eager to make myself a forerunner of the revolution in response to the times.

Sun made a lasting impression on Miyazaki, who discerned in his new friend "the spirit of sacrifice worthy of a samurai." This was remarkable given that Sun spoke no Japanese and Miyazaki had but a rudimentary grasp of English and even less Chinese. They had to supplement their dialogue by writing out the common characters used to transcribe their respective mother tongues. This first meeting was the beginning of a close friendship that was to endure for a quarter-century until Miyazaki's death in 1922.

Miyazaki lost no time in introducing Sun to his own mentor, Inukai Ki, who was just as taken with Sun. With the influential Inukai as his patron, doors began to open and Sun met other leading figures in Japanese politics, including right-wing ultranationalists for whom pan-Asianism meant Japanese domination of the Asian continent. Sun was considered a good investment by all these circles and was given a house in Tokyo. He was also given a cover identity as a language teacher to Miyazaki and his sidekick Hirayama Shu. This was to satisfy the Japanese Foreign Office, which did not want to antagonize the Qing court by openly supporting one of their avowed enemies. Hirayama understood some English and was appointed Sun's guide around Tokyo. On his first night in Tokyo, Sun adopted the name Nakayama, which Hirayama had noticed on the nameplate of a house they passed. It means "central mountain," which in Chinese is *zhongshan*. So it is as Sun Zhongshan that Sun is most commonly known in the Mandarin-speaking world.

For the next three years until 1900, Sun stayed put in Japan. During that period, China was being transformed politically and militarily. One stipulation of the Treaty of Shimonoseki required the Chinese government to pay Japan a huge indemnity. China lacked the financial resources to meet these obligations and was forced to borrow from Western banks. These high-interest, gold-linked loans were collateralized by China's tax revenues, which were already controlled in part by the Western powers through the Imperial Maritime Customs Service. With the rising price of gold against the Chinese currency, China's indebtedness to the West was actually considerably higher. Indeed, within 40 months of the war, China's foreign debt was almost three times her annual revenue.[4] The Western nations also demanded as a condition for the loans that the Chinese government give them geographically defined spheres of influence, with extensive railroad, mining and timber rights. Many of these spheres in the scramble for concessions of late 1897 and early 1898 lay along the heavily populated coastal areas of northeast China adjoining Russia and southeast China adjoining French Indochina. The Qing court's inability to resist these demands led the West increasingly to deride China scornfully as the "Sick Man of Asia."

The threat of China's dismemberment struck panic into the hearts of the literati. They feared it would be a prelude to the partition of the country and eventually national extinction. It stimulated their patriotism and their fervor for reforms, led by Kang Youwei, a child prodigy from a well-to-do scholarly family in Guangdong who had attracted national attention for his radical reinterpretation of the Confucian classics. Inspired by the work of a contemporary, he argued that the Confucian texts in current use were forgeries by a Han dynasty scholar, created to legitimize a usurper to the Dragon Throne. Criticisms of Kang's conclusions caused his work to be banned. Undeterred and to bolster his case, Kang published another work in 1897 which argued that institutional reforms had been championed by Confucius and other great philosophers of the past, and were therefore not morally wrong. While remaining true to the basic tenets of Confucianism, Kang called for institutional reforms inspired by the Western and Japanese experiences, and the establishment of a constitutional government.

In 1888, Kang had attempted to present a memorial to the Guangxu Emperor, but without a sponsor in court it never reached the throne. In 1895, when Japan was dictating the peace terms at Shimonoseki, Kang and his protégé Liang Qichao circulated a memorial to protest the treaty. Liang, a child prodigy who passed the *juren* provincial examinations at the age of 16, had met Kang while they were both sitting for their *jinshi* metropolitan examinations in Beijing in 1890. Subsequently, Liang decided to study

Kang Youwei   Liang Qichao

with Kang, whose teachings about foreign affairs fueled Liang's interest in reforming China. Together, Kang and Liang gathered the signatures of over 600 provincial graduates who were in Beijing in 1895 for the metropolitan examinations. The memorial urged the Qing court to reject the Shimonoseki treaty, continue the war and initiate institutional reforms. It did not make it past the Censorate to the emperor, but the reform ideas were widely disseminated by the press and found enthusiastic support among certain segments of the provincial literati and elites.

The German occupation of Qingdao in Shandong in late 1897 precipitated another surge of demands for reform and Kang was finally granted an audience with the emperor in the summer of 1898. His idea to institute reforms from above, similar to the Meiji government's method in Japan 30 years earlier, was well received. Beginning June 11, 1898, Guangxu with the assistance of Kang and two of his disciples, Liang Qichao and Tan Sitong, promulgated 40 edicts proposing wide-ranging reforms in education, the armed forces, agriculture and other areas.

The whirlwind of imperial decrees was no more than the shuffling of papers, however. Few, if any, of the proclamations were ever implemented. Nonetheless, the mandarins and the literati felt threatened and rallied to Cixi, who was hostile to the reforms from the start. She appointed her cousin Rong Lu as governor-general of Zhili and commander of the armed forces. Rong was a leader of the conservative faction in the imperial court and was rumored to have been Cixi's lover before her entry into the imperial harem. Suspecting that his aunt was planning a coup d'état to force his abdication, Guangxu summoned the reformers to take preemptive action. On September 18, Tan Sitong called on Yuan Shikai, the commander of the powerful Beiyang Army under Rong Lu, to persuade him to murder his superior and to remove the empress dowager. Yuan feigned agreement but immediately reported the conspiracy to Rong, who rushed to inform Cixi in the Summer Palace. She returned to the capital on September 21, imprisoned Guangxu and ordered the arrest of the reformers. Tan Sitong was among those executed. Kang Youwei and Liang Qichao managed to escape but Cixi's coup d'état was the death knell of the Hundred Day Reform, which lasted all of 103 days.

In Hong Kong, Miyazaki had become aware of the reform movement, which was attracting many young revolutionaries. He tried to mediate between the reformists and the revolutionaries but he was so obviously partial to the latter that his efforts were doomed. His mediation took on a new urgency when word reached him that Kang and his party were about to fall from grace. Liang took refuge in the Japanese consulate in Tianjin and was taken on a Japanese gunboat to Japan. The British helped Kang to get to Shanghai and from there he was taken on a British boat to Hong Kong, where he was met by Miyazaki. Kang did not have a high opinion of Miyazaki and was not at all sure he wanted to go to Japan. Perhaps he was put off by Miyazaki's attempts to poach his followers to join the revolutionaries. It is also possible that Kang may have had an inflated opinion of his own importance because of the British assistance and the Japanese offer of help. Kang also had doubts about his own safety in Japan. Only after Miyazaki assured him of the excellence of Japanese police protection and agreed to accompany him on the trip did Kang finally consent to go to Japan. In Tokyo, Foreign Minister Okuma sent out a ship from Hong Kong for Kang and his party, who were then secretly transferred to the *Kawauchi Maru* bound for Japan, where they arrived five days later.[5]

By early November 1898, China's preeminent revolutionary and principal reformists were all in Japan under Japanese patronage. Kang arrived in Japan just after the fall of the Kenseito cabinet. Okuma could no longer help except on a personal level. The new cabinet was less welcoming of the reformists, and for good reason. The Western powers were beginning to view with suspicion the presence of so many Chinese provocateurs in Japan. The Qing regime on its part protested Kang's presence in Japan. Its fears were not entirely unfounded. A group of loyalists wanted to spirit the Guangxu Emperor, who had been under house arrest since Cixi's coup, to Japan to form a government-in-exile, which would have strengthened Kang's cause. Kang on his part wanted the Japanese to help him overthrow the empress dowager right away so that the Guangxu Emperor could resume his reform agenda for China.

The Japanese did not want to be seen meddling in China's internal affairs in such a blatant manner. They thought that the best way to bring about change in China would be for the reformists and the revolutionaries to come together to form a united front. To that end Inukai Ki invited Sun and Kang to his house for a tête-à-tête. Still hopeful for recognition from the literati, Sun responded enthusiastically to the overture. Kang, on the other hand, showed no inclination to cooperate with Sun or even to meet with him, and instead sent his disciple Liang Qichao. Clash of personalities and literati disdain for a political aspirant with no background in Confucian orthodoxy only partially explain the futility of the Japanese effort to bring the two groups together. It fell flat primarily because Kang, who claimed to have a mandate to save the emperor, would never yield his allegiance to the dynasty. Neither would Sun give up anti-Manchuism and republicanism, which were fundamental to his strategy.

The Japanese found Kang's proposal to reform China's monarchial system more reassuring than Sun's revolutionary aim to replace it with a republic. This was not at all surprising given that Japan herself was a monarchy and that worldwide monarchies still outnumbered republics at the end of the 19th century. Despite their obvious preference, Kang's arrogance and uncompromising haughtiness hurt his standing with the Japanese. He became embittered when he failed to obtain Japanese patronage. The Japanese government finally decided it would be best for Kang to leave the country. An intermediary was given secret funds from the Foreign Ministry to help Kang with traveling expenses, and living expenses for Liang, who remained in Japan.

Empress Dowager Cixi   Guangxu Emperor

    Kang arrived in Canada in April 1899. Following a series of meetings with local merchants, he founded the Baohuanghui (Protect the Emperor Society) on July 20 at the Chinese Theatre in Victoria, British Columbia, to rally international support for the Guangxu Emperor, who was still under house arrest. Kang's primary objective was to raise funds to nurture political resistance against Cixi and the powerful conservative faction in the Qing government. The following summer, the Baohuanghui launched a telegraph campaign that contributed to Cixi's decision to shelve her plan to replace Guangxu as emperor. Liang Qichao made Yokohama the base of the Baohuanghui and traveled to Nanyang, Australia and Hawaii to set up branches. Kang sent other disciples to form chapters in Canada and the United States.[6]

    Before Kang made his exit from Japan in November 1898, Sun and the Japanese pan-Asianists were already toying with the idea of an alliance with the independence movement in the Philippines, a Spanish colony since 1665. Their plan was to help liberate the islands and turn them into a supplementary base for agitations against the Qing dynasty. In 1895, the year that the Xingzhonghui was formed in Hong Kong, the Katipunan, an anti-Spanish revolutionary society in the Philippines, had negotiated an agreement with Japan for the purchase of arms. When they were unable to come up with the advance payment, however, the deal was called off. One of the Katipunan's leaders, Emilio Aguinaldo, then took over the leadership of the independence movement and in November 1897 proclaimed the Republic of Biak-na-Bato in the mountains of Luzon. This ran into difficulties in the middle of the following month, and Aguinaldo took voluntary exile in Hong Kong in exchange for generous payments from the Spaniards.

In April 1898, war broke out between Spain and America. As a Spanish colony, the Philippines became part of the conflict. Aguinaldo returned to the Philippines to help the U.S. rally Filipino freedom fighters against the Spaniards. But when the Americans appeared bent on substituting themselves for the Spaniards as colonialists, relations with Aguinaldo became strained. His junta in Hong Kong sent Mario Ponce to Japan in June 1898 to seek help from the Japanese pan-Asianists. The Japanese were sympathetic but reluctant to offend the Americans. Finding his attempt to purchase and transport arms to the Philippines blocked, Ponce approached Sun, who saw it as an ideal proving ground for pan-Asian solidarity. His thoughts were apparently to use the Philippines, once liberated, as a revolutionary base for his movement to stage uprisings in China. Inukai was equally enthusiastic; he thought Japan had much to gain from two grateful nations if the project succeeded. As he did not wish to antagonize the Americans, however, he placed Sun at the center of the negotiations to make the project seem a Chinese initiative.[7]

The Japanese army and most politicians were for all-out aid but the only arms available were imported from the U.S., which the Foreign Ministry felt could hardly be used against the Americans. A stratagem was required. Inukai suggested Nakamura Haizan, a friend and party stalwart who was condemned to a short life because of diabetes and who Inukai thought would be happy to perform one last noble act for the emperor. The Foreign Office remained adamant in its opposition but a hardcore expansionist general in the army general staff felt it was essential for Japan to have a friendly and grateful group in the Philippines. His intercession tipped the balance and it was finally agreed that army munitions would be quietly sold to a Japanese company, which in turn would sell them to a German who was a friend of Nakamura. Sun was in control of most of the negotiations. An old Mitsui ship, *Nunobiki Maru*, was purchased to transport the arms to the Philippines.

Hirayama Shu and five other Japanese adventurers departed for the Philippines in early summer 1899. The *Nunobiki Maru*, with Japanese fighters, six million rounds of ammunition and materials for the manufacture of more, 10,000 rifles, a canon and ten field guns, sailed for the Philippines on the night of July 19. The overloaded ship went down in a storm on the high sea, taking with it the precious cargo and the lives of 13 men. Meanwhile, Hirayama's advance party had managed to reach Luzon. Shortly after making contact with Aguinaldo, they received news of the munition ship's fate. An embittered Aguinaldo vowed never again to trust the word of the white man and to fight to the bitter end.

With surplus funds at his disposal, Sun outfitted another munition ship but when American troops captured a member of Hirayama's advance party, the Japanese government put an immediate stop to the intrigue. Despite the failure, the incident engendered the solidarity of the Chinese, Japanese and Filipinos involved. The following August, the Philippine junta in Hong Kong issued a public statement expressing regret for the loss of Japanese lives in the cause of Philippine independence. At the same time, letters from Filipino generals expressed their appreciation for the Japanese bravery and sacrifice.

In gratitude for Sun's demonstration of pan-Asian solidarity, the Aguinaldo junta in Hong Kong presented him with 100,000 yen from their war chest. With the money, Sun started a daily newspaper in Hong Kong to serve as the mouthpiece of the Xingzhonghui to challenge the reformists' dominance in journalism. If there was one thing that Sun learned from his abduction in London, it was the power of public opinion. The establishment of the *Zhongguo Ribao (China Daily)* was left to Chen Shaobai, who had grown impatient in Japan and returned to Hong Kong in the fall of 1898. With the help of veteran supporters Ho Kai and Qu Fengzhi, the first issue rolled off the press in late 1899. In spite of periodic financial woes, the *China Daily* managed to survive until 1913, a remarkably long time for an opposition paper during that period.[8]

Without the hoped-for base in the Philippines, Sun turned his attention to reviving the Xingzhonghui in Hong Kong. Its activities had sagged considerably after his departure and that of Yang Quyun in the aftermath of the failed Guangzhou Uprising in 1895. But they did not cease altogether.

Some of his old partisans, You Lie in particular, had been busy recruiting secret society members. Zheng Shiliang, Sun's old companion and principal liaison with the Triads in the Guangzhou Uprising, now returned to join the new campaign. To extend his reach beyond Guangdong and Guangxi and give his movement a national character, Sun sent agents further north to establish contact with the Gelaohui (Society of Elder Brothers), the main secret society in the Yangtze valley that was particularly active in Hunan and Hubei.

Hirayama Shu made the initial contact with the Gelaohui but the close relations that later developed with its leaders were largely the work of Pi Yongnian. A former reformist from Hunan, Pi joined the Xingzhonghui after meeting Sun in Tokyo. In 1899, Sun sent Pi back to China to negotiate with Gelaohui leaders. He was accompanied on this mission by a new recruit, Shi Jianru, a young man with an impeccable literati background who became radicalized after China's defeat in the Sino-Japanese War and the suppression of the Hundred Day Reform movement. His induction into the Xingzhonghui was a sign of the times, when even young gentry were beginning to be infected with revolutionary fever.

The efforts of Sun's agents brought together for the first time the leaders of the Triads and the Gelaohui in Hong Kong. At Pi's suggestion, the leaders of the two secret societies agreed to form an alliance with the Xingzhonghui under Sun's overall leadership. The alliance, baptized the Xinghanhui (Revive Han Society), was sanctified with an offering of pigeon blood and wine, and a special seal cut to symbolize the anti-dynastic nature of the new organization. But this was nothing more than a loose military alliance as none of the constituent organizations surrendered its autonomy. And as Sun would soon find out, an agreement with men whose sole interest was to obtain funds and arms to overthrow the Manchu dynasty but who did not share his revolutionary and republican ideals was bound to be opportunistic and short-lived.

Besides extending his reach to the Yangtze provinces, Sun probably realized at this time that the creation of the Xinghanhui could also give him a pretext to seize the leadership of the Xingzhonghui from Yang Quyun. Yang had left Hong Kong in late 1895 after the failed Guangzhou Uprising, making stops in Saigon, Singapore, Madras and Colombo before arriving in Johannesburg in late 1896. There he set up a branch of the Xingzhonghui with the support of the local *huaqiao* community. The following fall, Yang read in the foreign press about the war chest of several million dollars that Sun was alleged to have amassed in Japan. He decided to return to Asia, and as his own humble contribution, raised several hundred pounds from the *huaqiao* community in South Africa. After a brief reunion with his family in Hong Kong harbor in March 1898, he proceeded to Japan.[9]

Yang's arrival in Yokohama did not please Sun at all. The old competition between the two men for the top spot in the Xingzhonghui was still very much alive. According to Yang, Sun told him one day that the Gelaohui had appointed him "president." Since it would be impossible to have two presidents, he suggested that Yang should leave the Xingzhonghui if he could not accept Sun's leadership. Not wishing to split the party, Yang resigned the presidency in favor of Sun and returned to Hong Kong in January 1900. Sun was now the undisputed leader of the Xingzhonghui but he still had to face competition from the Baohuanghui for money and fighting men for the uprising that each was planning.

Although often touted as Kang Youwei's protégé and deputy, Liang Qichao was not always on the same wavelength as his mentor. Sun's republicanism and Kang's constitutional monarchy were to Liang matters of expediency rather than principles. His writings during this period betrayed little of his preference for either. In Japan he began to drift further from his mentor in both his activities and the ideas he espoused. After Kang's departure for Canada, Liang wavered even more in his reformist convictions and began leaning toward the revolutionary argument. Articles he published became increasingly anti-Manchu, and he even co-authored a number of articles with Sun.[10]

In late 1899, having negotiated an alliance with Sun in which Liang apparently agreed to be second in command, Liang wrote to Kang, co-signed by 12 other members of the reformist camp, suggesting that the master retire from politics and that both reformers and revolutionaries be united under a new organization established on republican principles. Kang had already learned of Liang's planned alliance with Sun from members of the reform movement still loyal to him. In anger, he wrote back to his mutinous disciples, denouncing their intentions and ordering Liang to travel to Hawaii to campaign on behalf of the reformist cause.[11]

Liang obediently submitted to his mentor's wish but remained on friendly terms with Sun, who even gave him a letter of introduction to his brother Sun Mei. Sun was later to regret the kind gesture. In Hawaii, it did not take long for Liang's enthusiasm for cooperation with Sun to cool once he discovered the potency of the Baohuanghui brand. Soon came word that instead of severing his ties with Kang, Liang was making deep inroads into Sun's power base in Hawaii. He depleted the ranks of the Xingzhonghui in Hawaii to establish Baohuanghui as the leading political movement during this period. He wrote to Sun to assure him that he still advocated anti-Manchuism but justified his work for the Baohuanghui as a matter of expediency. He wanted to capitalize on the public furor over what was widely perceived as a plot by the empress dowager to replace the Guangxu Emperor. In his last conciliatory letter to Sun in April 1900, Liang urged Sun to realize that the Baohuanghui brand was too valuable to be given up, arguing that restoring the emperor to power and then making Sun president of the republic would best serve republicanism.[12]

One reason for Liang's success in Hawaii was his skill in exploiting his prestige and eloquence. He had also taken the bold step of joining the Triads, which Sun had not, in order to rally its many members to his increasingly militant cause. Also working in Liang's favor was the timing of his visit, which coincided with the imperial decree naming an heir-apparent to the throne, interpreted by many as a death sentence for the imprisoned emperor. Liang conveyed his concerns to the *huaqiao* in Hawaii, who were excited by the idea of aiding in the rescue of the emperor and responded enthusiastically to his appeals for financial contributions.

The funds solicited by Liang were for an uprising in Hankou that he had first planned in Tokyo with Tang Caichang in 1899. A native of Hunan, Tang was deeply embittered by the execution of his close friend Tan Sitong in the coup that killed the Hundred Day Reform. He followed the surviving reformists to Japan where he and Liang began planning an uprising in the Yangtze area. Through a letter of introduction from Pi Yongnian, Tang met with Sun, whose ideas left a deep impression on him. He was overjoyed to find out that the Gelaohui had responded positively to Sun's call to take up arms against the Manchu regime. Like the Japanese, Tang saw the great potential of an alliance between Sun and Kang, and he volunteered to make another attempt to change Kang's mind. Tang had no more success than the Japanese or any of those who had tried before him.[13]

Tang later met with Sun again in Japan, by which time they were both resigned to the fact that Kang would never agree to open cooperation. They agreed that Tang should maintain his close links with Kang while they took independent actions to achieve the same goal. The plan which they discussed in detail was for Sun and his followers to start an uprising in Huizhou in south China and for Tang to launch a simultaneous uprising at Hankou in central China. While Sun and Tang conceived of their respective plans as ultimately unified in purpose, the bitter rivalry between the reformist and revolutionary camps for donations from the same finite *huaqiao* communities posed serious difficulties for their cooperation. Kang's association with the Guangxu Emperor coupled with his and Liang Qichao's scholar-gentry credentials made them international social and political celebrities who far outshone Sun in newsworthiness.

In the spring of 1900, the Gelaohui heard of the vast sums allegedly being made available by Kang Youwei to Tang Caichang. Tired of waiting for the subsidies that Sun had promised, the Gelaohui transferred its allegiance to the Baohuanghui. Pi Yongnian tried to win over Tang to Sun's cause but Tang was not really interested in the ideological or programmatic difference between the reformists and revolutionaries. The Gelaohui defection and the departure of Pi, who retreated dispirited to a Buddhist monastery, deprived Sun of access to the Yangtze. It would be another five years before he could resume contact with this region. Meanwhile, he had to fall back once more on his own province of Guangdong.[14]

In spite of the setbacks, Sun still had the support of the Japanese pan-Asianists, who found his adventurous spirit well suited to their agenda. With the Qing government embroiled once more with a popular uprising, the time was opportune for another assault on the Manchu regime. Eager to see action, Miyazaki and his cohort of Japanese adventurers were egging Sun on. Tempering this recklessness was the more cautious attitude of Sun, who still wanted to pursue a few other options.

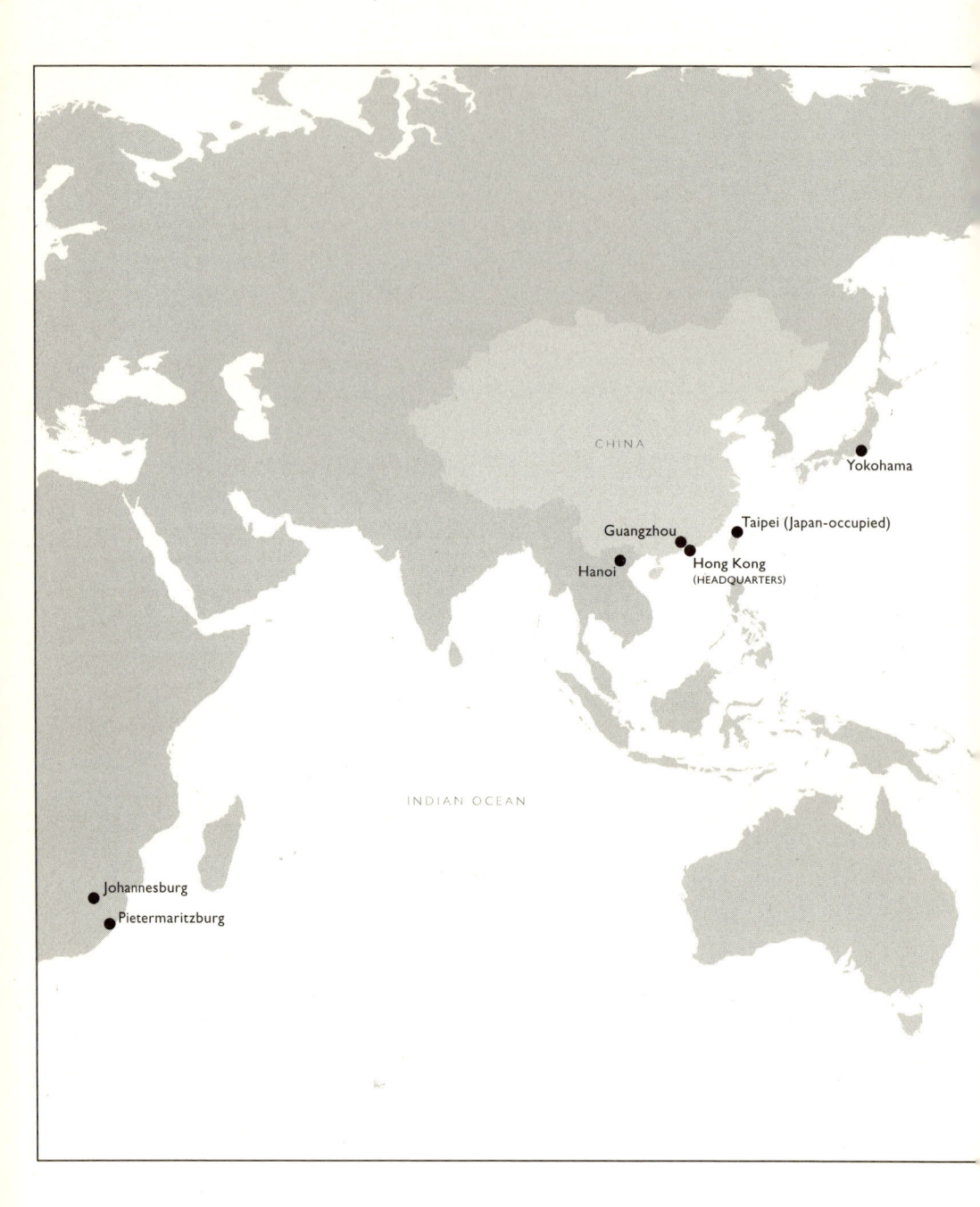

MAP 1

XINGZHONGHUI OFFICES

Chapter 4

COALITION OF THE UNWILLING

THE FINAL YEARS of the century witnessed the continued erosion of the economic and military powers that had propelled the old empires of Asia to dominance. Long the world's pacesetters, these empires had either disappeared or were rapidly disintegrating. Persia, though still territorially significant, exercised little real power. The Ottoman Empire, having lost much of her territory, was an empire only in name. Qing China, under increasing pressure from Western and Japanese imperialism, was sliding into anarchy. In contrast, the new Western empires were continuing to expand their realm as well as their share of world trade. This was especially apparent in Africa, which in the final two decades of the 19th century came under almost complete European domination. Even Italy, Germany and Belgium, with no imperial heritage to speak of, had carved out huge territories in the Dark Continent. The United States, having acquired Alaska in 1867, annexed Hawaii and the Philippines in 1898. More significantly, there had been no major armed conflict in Europe since Napoleon's defeat at Waterloo in 1815. To people in the West, the world had never been more prosperous and peaceful, and there was every reason to look forward to the continued march of progress in the 20th century.

The new century did not start out well for China. In the closing years of the 19th century, foreign powers had increased their outrages against her as they intensified their competition in the scramble for concessions. Germany, using the pretext of an attack on her missionaries in November 1897, seized Jiaozhou in Shandong and pressured the Qing government into leasing it for 99 years. Russia, with her own pretense of protecting China from the Germans, exacted a 25-year lease on Port Arthur and Dalian in March 1898. Not to be outdone, the French leased Guangzhou Bay (now Zhanjiang) on the southern coast of China opposite Hainan Island in April

1898. Alarmed by these developments and fearing for the security of Hong Kong, Britain invoked the most-favored-nation clause and in June 1898 leased the New Territories for 99 years and in the following month leased Weihaiwei for 25 years.[1] Britain also secured a commitment that China would not alienate the Yangtze region to any other power, thus turning the area into a British sphere of influence. Japan, already the colonial master of Taiwan, secured a similar non-alienation commitment on Fujian province. In 1899, the United States, a relative newcomer to the great game in China, adopted an "Open Door" policy, whereby all countries would agree not to deny others access to their spheres of influence in China. This was never formally adopted by treaty or international law, and the policy, which the United States had neither the will nor the power to enforce militarily, was frequently broken with impunity.[2]

In the face of these foreign encroachments, there was pervasive fear among the Chinese that their country was about to go the way of Africa – "carved up like a melon" – and disappear from world maps. The fear of national disintegration permeated every strata of society and gave rise to intense hatred of foreigners, whose very presence was a constant reminder of their country's woes. The sense of injustice intensified by larger factors eventually resulted in an outburst of anti-foreignism.

The influx of imports after the Opium War depressed the native economy. While many who suffered blamed their misfortune initially on the Taipings, they later transferred their anger to foreigners for having inspired the rebels with their alien Christian religion. Adding to the economic hardship was a series of natural calamities. The Yellow River, which shifted its course from Henan to Shandong in 1852, caused serious flooding and inundated hundreds of villages in Shandong in 1898. A severe drought followed in 1900 in most of North China, including Beijing. Victims as well as the superstitious blamed the misfortune on the foreigners who had offended the spirits by propagating a heterodox religion. They and their religion were held responsible for destroying the natural functioning of "wind and water" (*fengshui*, geomancy), and adversely affecting the harmony between men and nature. The invasion of Christianity under the protection of gunboats was deeply resented by the Chinese. The unequal treaties allowed its free propagation and granted missionaries the right to rent and buy land for the construction of churches. Missionaries offered monetary subsidies and protection against lawsuits to win converts who sometimes abused the refuge to bully and take advantage of their fellow countrymen. The churches' blatant display of their power, influence and wealth was an affront to the Chinese who regarded Christianity as a socially disruptive and heterodox sect whose converts' failure to perform traditional rites and participate in local festivities was a constant source of provocation.[3]

It was in this atmosphere of economic hardship and superstition, coupled with the fear and hatred of foreigners and their imperialism and religion, that the Boxer movement emerged in northeast China in the closing years of the 19th century. The movement, descended from the Eight Trigrams rebellion of 1813, was a page out of China's past. Taking the name Yihequan, it was a branch of the ancient calisthenic fighting or boxing art devoted to righteousness and harmony. Practitioners of the ritual were supposed to be possessed by spirits that made them invulnerable to bullets.[4] The Boxer Uprising is sometimes referred to as the Boxer Rebellion – this is a misnomer. The movement started out as anti-dynastic, but the real anger was eventually directed against foreigners, their Christian religion and the Chinese converts. Indeed, their eventual battle cry was "Support the Qing, exterminate the foreigners."

The Boxers emerged in southern Shandong in response to the provocation of Western missionaries and their Chinese converts. Shandong being the birthplace of Confucius and Mencius, its people were particularly sensitive to foreign insults, which the Germans supplied in abundance. Catholic bishops provoked resentment among the Chinese by acquiring rights and privileges equal to those of provincial governors. They encouraged their Chinese converts not to participate or share in the expenses of local festivities, thereby offending their fellow villagers and inciting numerous incidents. A German-built railroad eliminated tens of thousands of jobs and deprived large numbers of Chinese of their means of subsistence. Missionary attacks on Chinese civil and religious traditions and the misdeeds of their Chinese converts reinforced the feeling that foreigners were the cause of their sufferings. Beginning in 1898 the Boxer movement began to threaten Christian converts, calling for the end of the privileges they enjoyed. Attacks on missionaries and converts became increasingly common and violent. By early 1899, the Boxers had destroyed or taken a good deal of property from Chinese converts and killed several in Shandong. Alarmed, the foreign powers demanded that the Qing suppress the Boxers and their supporters.

Aware of the danger of being seen as hostile to a popular movement that for once was not directed against the dynasty, Empress Dowager Cixi issued an edict in January 1900 urging officials to "distinguish between outlaws and those law-abiding citizens who practice ritual arts to protect themselves and their families, or who unite the people of their villages to protect themselves."[5] On January 24, she issued another edict, this one proclaiming the Guangxu Emperor's nephew Puyi to be the true heir to the Tongzhi Emperor.[6] Many saw this as the first step towards deposing the Guangxu Emperor. Cables of protests poured into the capital from *huaqiao* communities all over the world. The edict also triggered the reformists' plan for a rising at Hankou in the Yangtze valley.

On January 27, Kang Youwei departed Hong Kong for Singapore where Khoo Seok Wan, heir to one of the great fortunes in the British colony, had promised to contribute S$250,000 toward the Hankou uprising.[7] Liang Qichao, in Hawaii since the previous December, was setting up Baohuanghui branches in the Islands and raising money for the same uprising from Sun's former supporters. Sun was in Japan following news of the unrest and contemplating how he could best exploit the Qing's entanglement with the foreign powers to topple the dynasty. With his reformist rivals now threatening to surpass him in both money and men, Sun could either seek collaboration with the provincial leaders whose anti-Boxerism threatened to sever their ties to the capital, or side with the invading foreigners.[8]

By May, groups of Boxers began drifting into Beijing and Tianjin terrorizing and killing foreigners and Chinese converts. At the end of the month, when the Boxers began attacking railways, the foreign powers decided on a show of force. An eight-nation expeditionary force was sent to guard the foreign legations in Beijing, where the expatriate communities and many Chinese converts had taken refuge. In early June, another multinational relief force set out for Beijing from Tianjin. Tricked by the pro-Boxer faction at court into believing that these foreign forces were on their way to the capital to remove her and restore the imprisoned Guangxu to power, Cixi saw little reason for restraint. Thus when the Boxers besieged the foreign legations in Beijing on June 19, Cixi put her weight behind them and declared "war" on the foreign powers on June 21. The governors of the central and southern provinces recognized this was one war China could not possibly win. Realizing the suicidal nature of the policy, they distanced themselves from the court's declaration of war on the foreign powers. These powerful officials claimed to the powers that it was not the throne but the Boxers and their patrons in court that had declared war. They pledged to keep the Boxers out of their provinces if the foreign powers would keep their troops and gunboats out of the provinces under their charge.

In late May or early June 1900, before the Boxers' siege of the foreign legations, Sun received an astonishing letter from a former comrade-in-arms, Liu Xuexun, the bookmaking scholar. He had flirted with Sun in the failed Guangzhou Uprising in 1895 but had since joined the entourage of Li Hongzhang. In the letter, he informed Sun that his chief would like to confer with him on a plan to declare the independence of Guangdong and Guangxi, the two provinces under his charge. Liu invited Sun to Guangzhou for a talk.

Except for a brief visit to Japan the previous August when Liu sought Sun's introduction to two Japanese politicians, there had been no contact between them since the Guangzhou Uprising. This may well explain Sun's suspicion and skepticism. He thought it highly improbable that someone of Li Hongzhang's stature in the Qing government would be thinking of secession. He may have lost some favor with the empress dowager, but he had all along been a faithful servant of the court and could be expected to remain so. Sun was apprehensive, too, about the motives of the wily old fox, suspecting that it might be another of the Qing government's tricks to capture him. With officials preoccupied with the Boxer crisis, this, too, seemed unlikely but it was a possibility that Sun could not afford to ignore. On the other hand, the idea might not even have originated from Li Hongzhang but from the Cantonese gentry, who were prepared for desperate measures to keep their province free of the Boxers and foreign invasion. It might even be another of Liu Xuexun's schemes to further his own interests. For whatever it was worth, Sun found the offer too enticing to pass up and decided to give Liu the benefit of the doubt.

Li Hongzhang received marching orders from the court on June 8 to present himself in the capital, but he was in no hurry to do so until he could discern the purpose for the instruction, or to commit himself to the drastic course of secession. On the very same day, Sun sailed on board a French steamer, the SS *Indus*, arriving in Hong Kong on June 17.[9] He was accompanied by Chen Shaobai, Zheng Shiliang, Miyazaki Torazo and two other Japanese, Kiyofuji Koshichiro and Uchida Ryohei. A persona non grata in the British colony for his role in the 1895 Guangzhou Uprising, Sun could not risk landing even though he was traveling under his Japanese pseudonym, Dr. Nakayama. Instead he held a briefing session on board a sampan with his party, joined by several more of his followers, including Yang Quyun and Hirayama Shu, who had preceded him to Hong Kong. To preempt anything untoward that Li Hongzhang or Liu Xuexun might have up their sleeves, it was decided that Miyazaki, Kiyofuji and Uchida would meet with Liu as Sun's emissaries. As Japanese nationals, they enjoyed immunity from Chinese laws under the extraterritoriality terms that Japan and the Western powers had forced on China. It was extremely unlikely that the beleaguered Qing government would risk an international incident by accosting them. With the reformist now threatening to preempt him, Sun agreed to have Miyazaki travel to Singapore after his meeting with Liu to resuscitate negotiations with Kang for a coalition. Sun with a small party would first go to Saigon, where he had some business to attend to, and later join up with Miyazaki's party in Singapore. The stage was now set for the final attempt at uniting the revolutionaries and reformists for another strike at the Manchu regime.

A Chinese gunboat met the *Indus* under cover of darkness to transport the three Japanese up the West River to Liu's spacious mansion in Guangzhou. The talk progressed very slowly. Both Liu and Miyazaki spoke some English but had to augment their conversation by scribbling notes in Chinese. What actually transpired during the all-night exchange is unclear. Miyazaki professed that he could not discern the esoteric details while Kiyofuji and Uchida understood even less. There was apparently an agreement to try once more to line up Kang Youwei in a coalition with Li

Hongzhang and Sun to insulate at least a part of China from the Boxer unrest and possible foreign retaliation. Liu told the Japanese that his chief could not commit himself to any specific course of action while the political situation in the capital was still in flux. Before parting, he handed Miyazaki a large sum of money as a token of aid to Kang from the Cantonese gentry, who he claimed were particularly keen to see a Li-Kang-Sun alliance.

Sun sailed with the *Indus* for Saigon on June 18 just as the gunboat carrying his three Japanese emissaries was returning to Hong Kong, too late for them to brief Sun on their parley with Liu. Sun only learned of the inconclusive meeting via a telegram from Miyazaki when he arrived in Saigon three days later. Beijing's declaration of war on the foreign powers on the same day may have led him to believe that Li Hongzhang would finally proclaim the independence of the two provinces under his charge. To keep the door open, Sun sent a short telegraph to Liu affirming his interest in cooperating with Li.

Miyazaki and his party arrived in Singapore on June 29 and checked into the Matsuo Inn, a *ryokan* popular with visitors from the Land of the Rising Sun. Having helped Kang to escape to Japan in the aftermath of the failed Hundred Day Reform, Miyazaki was certain that Kang would be delighted to meet with him and accordingly sent word through an intermediary to request a meeting. Kang politely but firmly declined the request on the grounds that he was so heavily guarded by the British colonial government that it was impossible for him to receive visitors.

In truth, Kang had received news from his partisans in Hong Kong that a party of Japanese, fresh from a meeting with Liu Xuexun, were on their way to assassinate him. Kang had every reason to take the warning seriously. After Cixi's coup d'état in 1898 and the imprisonment of the Guangxu Emperor, the Qing government had offered a reward for Kang's head. He was particularly suspicious of anyone associated with Liu Xuexun, a protégé of Li Hongzhang who had apparently added 40,000 taels to the 100,000 taels that the Qing court had placed on his life. There were rumors, too, that Liu had been given a contract by the Qing government to eliminate him. Kang therefore wanted nothing to do with the Japanese. So when Miyazaki persisted, Kang reported the matter to the British colonial government. Aware of the price on Kang's head, they promptly stepped in.

Sun Yat-sen with Japanese sympathizers in Tokyo, 1900: *(left to right)* Suenage Takashi, Uchida Ryohei, Miyazaki Torazo, Koyama Yutaro, Kiyofuji Koshichiro, and Sun.

To be sure, the British had no great affection for Kang, the anti-foreign tenor of his writings, his magisterial attitude or his pompous pronouncements against the British Foreign Office. But his support for the Guangxu Emperor, still the legitimate occupant of the Dragon Throne, made it difficult for the British to treat him like a common rebel. Thus when Kang arrived in Singapore on January 31, 1900, Acting Governor Sir James Alexander Swettenham of the Straits Settlements had sent a detachment of Sikh guards to protect him.

While the Singapore police was preparing affidavits for a banishment order against Miyazaki and his party, a Japanese acquaintance warned him that Kang's group suspected that Miyazaki's mission in Singapore was to assassinate Kang. Infuriated, Miyazaki drafted a hasty letter castigating Kang for believing such rumors when it was his intention all along to assist the reformist's cause. Kiyofuji, too, was angered. Uchida was so disgusted that he took the first available ship back to Japan despite Miyazaki's plea to await Sun's arrival. By this time, the warrants of arrest were ready to be served. On the evening of July 6, while Kiyofuji was playing *go* with the houseboy to the accompaniment of Miyazaki's *biwa* in their room at the

Matsuo Inn, the colonial constabulary entered and remanded them both into custody.[10]

Reluctant to disclose the true nature of their business with Kang, Miyazaki told the British officers that he and his party were in Singapore on a pleasure trip and once there had felt obligated to call on Kang Youwei, whom he had previously met in Hong Kong. As for the large stash of cash and two sharp *katana* found during a search of their belongings, Miyazaki explained that a *katana* was as essential to a *shishi* as a cross was to a Christian. It was also not unusual for a *shishi*, Miyazaki insisted, to travel with large amounts of money to meet expenses while on the road. The British were not convinced by their stories nor by the Japanese consul's affirmation of their statements. They were jailed for six days while colonial officials deliberated what to do with them.

Meanwhile Sun, whose principal purpose for visiting Saigon was to see Paul Doumer, failed to meet the governor-general. Earlier in Tokyo, Sun had met with the French minister Jules Harmond to outline his plans to overthrow the Qing dynasty and establish a new social order. According to Harmond's account of the meeting, Sun asked for French arms and military advisers, proposing in exchange to grant France "generous" concessions in southern China once his revolution succeeded. Although Harmond was favorably impressed, he warned Sun that it was not usual for a government to encourage revolution against another with which it had cordial relations. Stressing that French policy in China was to preserve the status quo, Harmond told Sun that France would of course be anxious to establish good relations with Sun's government should the revolution succeed. At the end of the meeting, he agreed to write to Paul Doumer to suggest that he meet with Sun during the latter's visit to Saigon.[11]

Since taking up his post in 1897, Doumer was determined to extend French presence in the Far East. He supported the 1898 French policy of breaking up China and creating a sphere of influence in her southern provinces by building on the French-leased territory of Guangzhou Bay in western Guangzhou and the Tonking-Yunnan railway. In 1900 the policy of the French government was to maintain good relations with the Qing government and to limit itself to economic expansion. Thus when in May–June 1900 Doumer amassed troops on the Tonking-Yunnan border ostensibly to assist the French consul in Kunming who was besieged by xenophobic bands, he was warned by his superiors in Paris to back off.[12]

Sun's timing to meet Doumer could not have been worse. Alerted by a telegram from Harmond, the French foreign and colonial ministers warned Doumer not to entertain Sun, whose request for an interview was thus denied. Sun met instead with a high-ranking official from Doumer's office, to whom he proposed that if France would supply him with arms, ammunitions, money and military advisers, and allow his men to use Indochina as a base to link up with the secret societies across the border in Guangxi, he would reward France with rich concessions once he succeeded in establishing an independent regime in southern China. As to be expected, no French assistance was forthcoming. These initial contacts with the French produced little prospect that the French government would assist Sun's movement. To drive his point home, the foreign minister repeated his warning that France had no interest in establishing ties with Sun, or in any way foment further troubles in southern China.

Having failed to accomplish his mission in Saigon, Sun sailed for Singapore on July 6 to make the rendezvous with Miyazaki and his party, totally unaware that they had been taken into custody on that very day. He was accompanied by Rowland Mulkern and two Japanese who had rendezvoused with him in Saigon. The Irish soldier had kept the promise he made to Sun in London and became the only Westerner to join the Xingzhonghui.

A representative from the Japanese consulate came on board when the ship dropped anchor in Singapore harbor on July 9. He notified the Japanese of Miyazaki and Kiyofuji's incarceration and warned them not to leave the ship as they, too, were under suspicion of plotting to assassinate Kang. Ignoring the warning to take the first ship out of Singapore, Sun led his group ashore to try and secure the release of their imprisoned comrades.[13] It was to a friendship that he had fostered at the College of Medicine in Hong Kong that he now turned. Dr. Goh Kit Moh had since returned to Singapore and Sun managed to track him down at his clinic on South Bridge Road. Considering the severity of the charges against Miyazaki and company, there was little the doctor could have done. Goh suggested enlisting the help of a fellow physician, Dr. Lim Boon Keng.[14]

A Straits-born Chinese, Lim was one of the most influential persons within the local Chinese community as well as the British colonial administration. At 31, he was three years younger than Sun but was already into the second of his three-year term as a Legislative Councilor, having been made a Justice of the Peace at the unprecedented age of 28.[15] Even with Lim's influence and intercession with the British colonial government, Sun needed all his eloquence to obtain the release of his Japanese friends. On July 10, he appeared before Governor Swettenham and two other members of the Executive Council. Since the Qing government was at war with Britain and the other foreign powers, Sun thought it prudent to disclose at least a partial truth. He admitted to the tribunal that he, too, was wanted by the Qing government, though the price on his head was only a third of Kang's. Describing Miyazaki as a "great companion" whom he had met through a Japanese parliamentarian, Sun explained that his two Japanese friends were in Singapore at his behest to see Kang, with whom he hoped to explore the possibility of cooperation.

Sun took the opportunity to impress his British interrogators that he was trying to pacify and provide leadership to the Chinese masses. Though his ultimate objective was to overthrow the Manchus, his immediate aim was to form an independent southern regime. His movement was necessary as China could not otherwise be reformed, but he promised to keep disturbance to the minimum. Claiming a wide following in several southern provinces, Sun told the British that his followers shared the fear that China would be partitioned. Some of his followers were already itching for action, and if nothing was done, they might go over to the Boxers.[16]

Swettenham was not completely sold on Sun's story. He was even less convinced that the Japanese would not resort to violence to stop Kang from interfering with their plans if the reformist could not be persuaded to join Sun. He also suspected the Japanese of planning to purchase arms in Singapore and use the colony as a base for Sun's uprising, a prospect he found disquieting, especially since there was Japanese involvement. On July 11, Miyazaki and Kiyofuji were served with five-year banishment orders and a similar writ issued was against Uchida in absentia. No action was taken against Sun though Swettenham warned him that he would not permit revolutionary activities in his territory.[17] He also tried to convince

Sun that it was "inexpedient for a patriotic Chinese to raise fresh disturbances in China just at the moment it was about to be invaded by foreigners."[18]

As a leader of the Xingzhonghui, which had ties with secret societies in Guangdong, Sun would have been given the contact details of secret society leaders in Singapore. There is no indication that he met with any, and given the fleetingness of his visit, he most probably did not. He did, however, meet Dr. Lim Boon Keng's father-in-law, Huang Naishang. A native of Fujian province, Huang had supported Kang Youwei's reforms. When the movement met with a conservative backlash, he fled to Singapore, where he became one of the leading figures in the local Chinese intellectual circle. His meeting with Sun helped to shed his bias against the revolutionaries, and he became more radical as conditions in China continued to deteriorate. After 1903, Huang became one of the most important revolutionaries in Singapore.[19]

On July 12, members of the colonial constabulary escorted Miyazaki and Kiyofuji on board the *Sado Maru* bound for Hong Kong. Having failed to secure an alliance with Kang, and with the British looking none too kindly on his activities, Sun gathered his other followers and joined the banished Japanese on board, thus ending any hope of cooperation with Kang. Leaving Singapore under these unhappy circumstances, little could Sun have foreseen that he would return to Singapore eight more times and that the Lion City would come to play a substantial role in his struggle for a modern China.

As the *Sado Maru* with Sun and his party on board steamed toward Hong Kong, Governor Sir Henry Blake was prepared to let him land and negotiate with Li Hongzhang's representatives. Earlier in the month, Blake had received word, probably from Ho Kai, that Li was flirting with the idea of an alliance with an "anti-Manchu but not anti-foreigner" movement, which Blake presumed to be a reference to Sun. If true, it would ensure peace in Guangdong, a region close to Hong Kong. This would be advantageous to the colony and to British interests. London concurred with Blake's proposal to let Sun land in Hong Kong provided it had the blessing of Li, who was in the meantime continuing to weigh his options. Not until July 8, when he was reappointed to the key post of governor-general of

Zhili and superintendent of trade for the northern ports, did Li announce that he would shortly leave Guangdong for the north. The news alarmed Blake, who feared that without Li, the Boxers might sweep through the South. Blake proposed to detain Li when he passed through the colony on his way north. On July 17, the day that Li was due in Hong Kong, Colonial Secretary Joseph Chamberlain vetoed Blake's proposal. During his one-day sojourn in Hong Kong, Li pleaded for generous treatment of China by the powers, whose armies had taken Tianjin and were marching toward Beijing. He assured Blake that Guangzhou would remain quiet if the governor repressed agitators in the colony, and hinted that if the powers were looking for a Chinese to replace the Manchu Guangxu as emperor, he would not mind being the one. He showed no sign of wanting to collaborate with rebels. Sun learned of this when the *Sado Maru* arrived in Hong Kong waters on the same day that Li was passing through the colony. It was now clear that whatever Li was planning, there was no role in it for Sun.

Meanwhile, the foreign legations in the capital remained under siege by the Boxers. There was no word from those trapped inside and the powers were ready to believe the worst. On July 16, the London *Daily Mail* reported that "hordes of fanatical barbarians thirsting for [foreign] blood" had massacred every European man, woman and child in the legations. The *Times* lent its prestige to the story the following day. Warning against a "universal uprising of the yellow races," it called for the use of force sufficient to deal with the "hordes of northern China" to "avenge an outrage without parallel in Western experience." On the same day, the Russians slaughtered over 3,000 Chinese, men, women and children, in a town on the Russo-Manchurian border.[20]

The world would soon learn that of the hundreds of besieged foreigners, only 76 had died. The rest, and several thousand Chinese Christian who had taken refuge in the legations, owed their lives to the Boxers' restraint. The world would also soon learn of the destruction of one of China's most significant national treasures. On June 24, shortly after the siege of the foreign legations commenced, the British systematically destroyed the buildings of the Hanlin Academy, the repository of Chinese bibliographical treasures representing centuries of cultural accumulation. Some of the books were taken as booty, others were simply thrown on the ground or tossed into ponds. Most of these books were the only copies available anywhere and are lost to the world forever.[21]

The siege of the foreign legations lasted a good eight weeks. On July 14, an eight-nation expeditionary force captured Tianjin and then marched into Beijing, lifting the siege on August 14. The allied force immediately unleashed its own reign of terror, plundering and looting in areas which had been the scene of Boxer activity. The next day, Cixi fled to Xi'an and was spared the shame and humiliation of having to witness the carnage. Guangxu wanted to remain in the capital to negotiate with the powers but Cixi, shrewd as ever and fearing that she might be upstaged – or worse, replaced – insisted that he accompany her to Xi'an, the ancient capital, where the court re-established itself on October 23.[22]

After leaving Hong Kong on July 18, Li Hongzhang sailed to Shanghai. There he accepted British advice to stay put until the foreign diplomats had been safely conducted to Tianjin. On August 7, the court appointed him plenipotentiary to search for a settlement with the powers; still Li refused to travel north. His hesitation stemmed from a belief that there could be no peace until the Boxers had been suppressed, the siege lifted and the foreign diplomats given safe conduct to Tianjin. A little over a month after the siege was lifted, Li traveled to Tianjin, where he arrived on September 18.

With prospects of a united front with Kang Youwei and Li Hongzhang now all but extinguished, Sun submitted a proposal prepared by Ho Kai asking Britain and the other powers for help. He promised to establish a constitutional government in which the foreign powers would be given tutelary status. Blake raised the idea with Chamberlain. Two days later the colonial secretary telegraphed that Britain could promise nothing. The rejection left Sun with only the independent military option that he had been considering since the summer. A new possibility opened up when he returned to Japan. For some time, the Japanese had been planning to gain control of Xiamen, a treaty port in Fujian province opposite Taiwan. They had been looking for a way that would avoid alarming the other powers. When Kodama Gentaro, the Japanese governor-general of Taiwan, learned of Sun's Huizhou plot, he ordered his governor Goto Shimpei to help Sun seize Xiamen. Sun traveled to Taiwan to meet Goto.

Meanwhile, the reformers' proposed uprising in Hankou was put under the charge of Tang Caichang, whom Kang had encouraged in every way with promises of funds which the *huaqiao* had so generously contributed. Tang worked hard at recruiting his rank and file, mainly from members of the Gelaohui in the Yangtze valley, and grouped them at five different locations to rise simultaneously on August 9, 1900. As the date approached, there was no sign of the funds promised by Kang. Tang was forced to postpone the date of action, first to August 19 and then to August 23. These postponements were made in panic, leaving little time to inform all the group leaders. Qin Lishan, leading the Anhui group, was inadvertently left out of the loop. Unaware of the postponement, he gave the order to attack on the originally scheduled date of August 9. After six days of fighting and suffering heavy casualties, the Anhui group was suppressed by government forces. Qin escaped but many of his men were captured. Based on information obtained from the prisoners under interrogation, Tang Caichang and other important leaders were arrested on the evening of August 21. Their execution the following day put paid to the reformers' rising.

The difficulty in accessing the highly publicized Baohuanghui war chest was undoubtedly the principal reason for the failure of the uprising. Had the promised funds been promptly remitted, there would have been no postponement and no question of Qin Lishan acting prematurely. The financial difficulties of the *huaqiao* in Honolulu as a result of a fire in Chinatown in early 1900, coupled with the interference of the Qing consul there, had prevented Liang Qichao from remitting the funds promptly. On the other hand, Kang Youwei, who had in his hands the single largest donation from Khoo Seok Wan, seemed reluctant to part with the money.[23]

Qin Lishan escaped to Japan and subsequently traveled to Singapore and confronted Kang Youwei about his failure to send the promised money. His accusations that Kang had misappropriated the funds caused a rift between Kang and his benefactor Khoo Seok Wan, who finally severed all ties with the reformist after a quarrel in 1901 over Kang's mishandling of a contribution of S$50,000 from the *huaqiao* in Australia. The Gelaohui chiefs, who ended up empty-handed, were even more upset and planned to take care of Kang in traditional underworld style. Two Gelaohui leaders showed up in Hong Kong several years later and demanded compensation from Kang, who promptly reported them to the police. Infuriated, one of their friends tried to borrow a gun from Chen Shaobai, whose intervention saved Kang from a horrible death.

After the spectacular failure of their uprising in Hankou, the reformers were forced to shelve their plans for Guangdong, leaving Sun with a free hand to pursue his strategy, which was very similar to the Guangzhou Uprising of 1895. The plan was to launch several uprisings in the lower East River area of Guangdong to draw government troops from Guangzhou, followed by an assault on the provincial capital. As before, bandit and secret society gangs would form the shock troops under the direction of Xingzhonghui members. The key figure in the plot was Zheng Shiliang, Sun's old friend who had also participated in the 1895 uprising. One of Sun's original followers from Hawaii, Deng Yinnan, was put in charge of operations in Guangzhou. As in 1895, the conspirators were supported by the network of Christian clergy and converts.[24]

Shortly after the strategy session, Zheng began recruiting fighters from his native district, in eastern Guangdong. This area, in which Huizhou was a prefectural capital, was notorious for pirates, salt smugglers and other outlaws, and easily accessible to outside help. Zheng's base was Sanzhoutian, 5 miles (8 km) from the coast and less than 10 miles (16 km) from the British-held New Territories. By the end of the summer, Zheng had assembled a force of 600 men, mostly Triad members, and was ready for action. They were held back to await the arrival of arms and ammunition that Sun was arranging in Japan, and to give Deng time to make preparations in Guangzhou.

By early October, with rations and prospects of a fight running low, Zheng's men grew impatient; their restlessness aroused the suspicions of the Guangzhou authorities. On October 3, the provincial naval commander took several thousand men and occupied Shenzhen, which was only 12 miles (20 km) southwest of Sanzhoutian. Several battalions simultaneously closed in on the rebels' camp. On October 6, without instructions from Zheng, who was in Hong Kong to await word from Sun, the rebels were forced into a premature uprising. They struck at the government troops and routed them.

The insurrection rapidly spread to neighboring centers. The rebels were warmly welcomed in the villages they passed through or captured. Disciplined and taking care not to attack any Christian missions, they rallied hundreds of villagers to their ranks. In ten days, the number had risen to 10,000. Now all they had to do was join up with the Triad bands who were waiting for them in the suburbs of Huizhou and farther west, and converge on Guangzhou. At about the same moment that the Sanzhoutian rebels began the uprising, Sun received word from his friends that the Japanese colonial government in Taiwan was looking for an excuse to establish a toehold in Xiamen and would be willing to arm the rebels if they could make their way to the Fujian city. Sun immediately informed Zheng in Hong Kong to substitute Xiamen for Huizhou as the campaign objective. By the time Zheng reached his men, they had already fought their way to the outskirts of Huizhou.

On October 17, the rebels headed up a tributary of the East River toward Xiamen. On their long march through unfamiliar terrain, the rebels were harassed by loyalist troops. On October 20, they were finally checked 150 miles (240 km) from Xiamen. Three days later, Sun sent an urgent message to Zheng to abort the campaign. The Japanese had changed their mind on establishing a foothold in Xiamen and reneged on their promised aid. Even if Zheng were to take Xiamen, they could not send help. Realizing the futility of further fighting, Zheng disbanded his men, ending the two-and-a-half-week revolt.

The premature uprising caught Deng Yinnan off-guard. With the rebellion already underway, there was no time to finalize the preparations. The best he could do was to create a diversion and relieve the military pressure on the Huizhou rebels. Shi Jianru, the new young gentry recruit, volunteered to assassinate the provincial governor. By the time he and Deng managed to smuggle the dynamite from Hong Kong, the Huizhou revolt was already near its end. Nevertheless, he went ahead with his plan and on October 28 succeeded in exploding a crude bomb along one wall of the governor's official compound. The explosion killed six people but missed its primary target. Captured, Shi was beheaded a fortnight later. Among those killed by imperial troops was Sun's Japanese courier, Yamada Yoshimasa, "the first foreigner to lay down his life for the Chinese Republic."

Yang Quyun and Zheng Shiliang remained in Hong Kong, but most of the Huizhou leaders fled to Singapore, where they would later help to raise the political consciousness and Chinese nationalism of the *huaqiao* in the British colony.

Li Hongzhang had been in Tianjin since September 18, but the Allied representatives in Beijing refused to negotiate until the Guangxu Emperor was returned to the throne. On the other hand, the empress dowager refused to return to the capital until after the peace settlement. To break the impasse, the southern provincial leaders diverted the Allied attention to the punishment of high officials who had been complicit in the attack on the legations. Yuan Shikai was particularly anxious to adopt this approach. Having betrayed Guangxu during the Hundred Day Reform, he knew that the emperor's return to power would be detrimental to his interests. The court reluctantly agreed to the punishment of the guilty officials, but now the Allies had a hard time agreeing among themselves on the terms. The Germans supported by the British pushed for punitive terms. The Russians, in the hope of gaining a concession on Manchuria, ingratiated themselves with the court. The Japanese, disturbed by Russia's territorial ambition, offered to withdraw their troops to Tianjin. It took the Allies all of three weeks to reach agreement among themselves.

Yuan Shikai

The Boxer Protocol, signed on September 7, 1901, provided for the punishment of 12 high officials in the capital and another 119 officials in the provinces, ranging from reprimands to capital punishment. An indemnity of 450 million taels (about 67.5 million pounds), payable over 39 years at 4 percent annual interest, was imposed on China. In addition, the protocol called for apology missions to Germany and Japan; destruction of the Dagu and other forts in the vicinity of the capital; prohibition of arms imports for two years; stationing of foreign troops at key points from Beijing to the sea; and suspension of the civil service examinations for five years in some

45 cities where the Boxers had been active. The Allied troops evacuated the capital ten days later.[25]

Peace had been restored but Russia's occupation of Manchuria remained unresolved. Under the pretext of restoring order, the Russians had sent in troops in July 1900 and within three months gained control over all of Manchuria. They now proposed a separate pact, independent of the agreement then being negotiated with the other powers. If accepted by the Chinese, it would have turned Manchuria into a Russian colony. The Russians' aggression aroused grave apprehensions among the powers. Japan, whose interests conflicted with Russia's, was especially perturbed, and warned that any concession to Russia in Manchuria was certain to lead to the partition of China. The other powers joined in the chorus to deny Russia special concessions. The Russians on the other hand threatened the incorporation of Manchuria if her demands were not met. Fearful of offending either Russia or the powers, the hapless Qing court passed the buck to Li Hongzhang. He advised the court to accede to the Russian demands and worked behind the scenes to ensure passage. Under pressure from the powers, the Qing court decided in March 1901 to reject the Russian treaty. The Russians did nothing more than issue a weak statement. Pursued by the Russians and ridiculed by his countrymen, Li Hongzhang died on November 7, 1901, at the age of 78. Li's unfinished work was carried on by Prince Qing, the head of the Waiwubu, the Ministry of Foreign Affairs, who had headed the delegation to the Shimonoseki negotiation.[26] Especially after the signing of the Anglo-Japanese alliance on January 30, 1902, the international situation worked against Russia. She signed an agreement with China on April 4 promising to evacuate Manchuria in three stages, in return for Chinese promise to protect Russian assets and personnel. The first evacuation occurred on schedule but at the second stage in April 1903, the Russians did not leave but resorted to the subterfuge of changing her troops' uniform to those of "railway guards." Additionally, she demanded new monopolistic rights and reoccupied some of the evacuated cities. Russia's territorial ambition was to lead to war with Japan in 1904.[27]

The Boxer Uprising and the peace protocol exposed the incompetence and paralysis of the Qing court. Respectable Chinese who had accused Sun of treason for inciting rebellion now saw his advocacy of revolution as the panacea for China's woes. It negated Sun's image as a common rebel and consolidated his reputation as a patriot. The transformation came at a very high cost, however. On January 19, 1901, an assassin hired by the Guangzhou authorities gunned down Yang Quyun while he was teaching an English class at his home in Hong Kong. Seven months later, Zheng Shiliang died mysteriously after a meal. The coroner's report indicated heart attack as the cause of death, but his friends were certain it was the handiwork of Manchu agents.

Sun had lost his best lieutenants and was once again alone and powerless. The disaster at Huizhou forced him to reflect on the inadequacy of a strategy that was almost totally dependent on foreign aid which was uncertain and slow in coming. It made him realize that his revolution needed the legitimacy that even a few intellectuals could provide. In the early years of the new century, the radicalization of the student generation and their nationalist fervor would finally provide the support from the intelligentsia that had so far eluded Sun.[28]

Chapter 5

THE TURNING POINT

WHEN THE EIGHT-NATION expeditionary force entered Beijing in August 1900 to lift the siege on the foreign legations, Empress Dowager Cixi and the Guangxu Emperor fled the capital to the interior city of Xi'an, where a temporary capital was established. Traumatized by the experience, Cixi issued a decree in Guangxu's name on January 29, 1901, declaring the court's intention to institute reforms, and asking all government officials to submit proposals for change. The most significant of these reform proposals were the memorials jointly submitted by Zhang Zhidong, the governor-general of Hubei-Hunan, and his Guangdong-Guangxi counterpart, Liu Kunyi. They proposed in three separate memorials the introduction of Western knowledge and methods that would vastly improve China's educational, administrative and military systems. With imperial sanction, resistance to change withered rapidly, even among conservative bureaucrats who had eschewed radical changes during the Hundred Day Reform in 1898. A consensus eventually emerged within the Qing government to modernize China's traditional institutions. Borrowing ideas from reformers whom it had persecuted, a New Policy was launched to transform China's social, economic and political frameworks. In the years following, steps were taken to implement them.

Army recruitment through the examination system was abolished, provincial academies were established, and young officers sent for training in Japan. The New Army, announced in 1903, was to be organized, equipped and trained along Western lines and placed under the central control of a defense ministry. These measures along with the rise of nationalism helped to improve the poor image of the military. Officers could now be recruited from the sons of gentry, and this helped to blur the traditional divide between the literati and the military. In 1903 a commerce ministry was created with wide powers to take over the direction of economic modernization. To execute its policies, the Qing government centralized its fiscal administration and launched administrative reforms to define the role of the central ministries, as well as judicial reforms based on the introduction of new legal codes. It also had plans to standardize the currency, weights and measures.

It was natural that court officials steeped in Confucian learning gave the highest priority to education. Modern schools began replacing traditional academies, and curricula were enhanced to include Western sciences. The discontinuance in 1905 of the traditional examination system radically changed the status of the literati and encouraged the rise of a modern intelligentsia. Students were encouraged to pursue their studies abroad, which many did in Japan owing to her geographical proximity, the similarity of her written language and her success in recovering national integrity by combining modern learning with traditional East Asian values.

From just 13 Chinese students in Japan in 1896, the number rose to 500 in 1902 and 8,000 in 1905, the year the civil service examination system was abolished. About half the students were on scholarships, awarded mostly by the more solvent provincial governments rather than the debt-ridden imperial government. Some of the students were females, a sign of the changing times. Most of the Chinese students in Japan tended to study the humanities or military studies as the less politically conscious science and engineering students typically chose to go to the West. Many studied at reputable Japanese institutions but many more enrolled at dubious diploma mills. Some did not even matriculate but coalesced with like-minded compatriots in the university quarter in Tokyo's Kanda district, where they kicked up nationalist storms and agitated against the Qing dynasty.[1]

In contrast to their compatriots at home, these students in Tokyo were more aware of China's miserable state, less willing to tolerate it, and became as nationalistic as their Japanese hosts. They envied the Japanese people's nationalism and their country's status in the world. Compared to Japan's *shishi*, their own leaders, in spite of a hardening attitude towards imperialism, appeared undetermined and indeterminate. The convergence of so many angry and frustrated students in one city provided just the setting for Sun to evangelize his cause. But he was not the man the students looked up to for inspiration and intellectual guidance; it was his old nemesis Liang Qichao, who had also taken refuge in Japan since the abortive Hundred Day Reform in 1898.[2]

Liang was the most influential writer of the time through the essays he wrote on virtually every aspect of China's woes. Swayed by Social Darwinism in his vision of modern imperialism, he called on his countrymen to change their mindset, which he found too preoccupied with personal gains. He called on them to identify themselves with China's interests so their motherland could compete with other nations. For a time, he veered close to the anti-Manchu argument, but in 1903, just when support for revolution was gaining traction among the students, he pushed for constitutional monarchy. He feared that revolution would invite greater foreign aggression and derail the modernization efforts in progress. His youthful disciples grew progressively impatient with his gradualism and began adopting views similar to those advocated by Sun.

In spite of this increasing convergence of minds between Sun and the students, it was not a situation that Sun could easily exploit. It was not just the contrast between his peasant background and that of the students, many of whom were from some of the most distinguished families in China. The students regarded themselves as an elite with a traditional link to political power. Sun's ties to the secret societies and overseas Chinese merchants, traditionally regarded as marginal people, troubled them. Sun in turn had his own reservations about the students; he could not see what role they could possibly play in his fundraising campaigns or his recruitment of fighting men for future uprisings.

Though he lived in nearby Yokohama's Chinatown, Sun had little to do with the students who were firing the patriotic circles in Tokyo. In fact, little is known about how Sun spent the years from 1900 to 1902 except that he was enjoying the companionship of his landlord's daughter.[3] The five-year banishment on him having expired in March 1901, Sun took the opportunity to make a visit to Hong Kong, his first since the 1895 Guangzhou Uprising. Arriving on January 28, 1902, on board the Japanese steamer *Yawata Maru*, he met with his partisans to discuss the consequences of Yang Quyun's assassination. He stayed in the apartment above the office of *China Daily* at 24 Stanley Street and rarely left it. Nevertheless, his presence in the colony was discovered and reported by the press. Consequently, a British sergeant visited and persuaded Sun to leave, which he did on February 4 aboard the British ship *Coptic*. This was his last visit to Hong Kong until 1911; the Hong Kong colonial government subsequently extended the banishment order against him for an additional five years.[4]

By the end of 1902, Sun had become restless and was again on the move, this time to Hanoi in Indochina. Ignoring the instruction of his superiors at the foreign ministry in Paris to avoid all contact with Sun, Paul Doumer extended an invitation to Sun to visit the Exposition de Hanoi, which had opened in November 1902. Sun had failed to meet Doumer in June 1900, and the invitation held out the hope that he would finally get to meet the Frenchman. Boarding the *Indus* on December 4, he made a two-day stopover in Hong Kong to collect HK$1,000 from a wealthy supporter. By the time Sun reached Hanoi on December 18, Doumer had been recalled to France. Sun stayed on for a good six months while he acquainted himself with Doumer's successor, Paul Beau.[5]

Unlike his adventurous predecessor, Beau was a straight-shooter who carried out to the letter the policies of his superiors in Paris. As such he decided against meeting Sun himself and had his principal private secretary find out what the revolutionary's plans were. Beau later reported to Paris that what Sun wanted from France was not financial aid but permission to use Tonking as a conduit to transport arms to southern China. Claiming that he had the sympathy of certain officers commanding provincial troops, Sun declared that they would rally openly to his cause if he could supply them with arms and volunteers from Indochina. His ultimate objective was to overthrow the Qing regime, or at least establish a federal republic of the southern provinces. Again, Sun promised substantial concessions in return for French collaboration.

Beau was not seduced, and indeed wrote to Paris that French commercial interests would be seriously compromised if Beijing were to suspect French involvement in Sun's intrigues. He believed that China's dismemberment might lead to outside intervention and encourage rival powers into southern China to the detriment of existing French interests there. Beau therefore decided to forbid the shipment of arms across French territory and issued orders to have Sun watched during his stay in Indochina. Beau's report was fully endorsed by the French foreign minister, who repeated his instructions to French officials to avoid any direct contact with Sun. This did not mean that the French had lost interest in Sun's activities, for the minister also issued instructions to French diplomats in Asia to keep track of and report on Sun's movements. But the official position remained one of hostility toward the revolutionaries.

Sun was thus once again denied a meeting with Doumer, but he used the opportunity to meet with many *huaqiao* in Saigon. One was Huang Ching Nan, who was to become the leader of the radical group in Vietnam. Sun also established ties with a group in Saigon calling itself the "Iron and Blood Society," a group of assassins who would target Qing officials in south China. Apparently Sun advised them to renounce such tactics.[6] While in Saigon, Sun had a chance encounter with Wong Lung Sang (Huang Lung Sheng), a local anti-Manchu Cantonese. He discussed with Wong and his friends about saving China through revolution. When this group of local Chinese found out Sun's true identity (Sun was traveling under the pseudonym Kao Ta-sheng), they enthusiastically formed a branch of the Xingzhonghui in the city, and held their inaugural meeting in a tailor's shop at 20 Rue Paul Bert.[7]

When Sun returned to Japan in June 1903, no more than a dozen of his partisans were still loyal to him; the rest had defected to the reformist camp. Even one of his most ardent supporters, Feng Jingru, the head of the Yokohama chapter of the Xingzhonghui, was now financing Liang Qichao's publications. It was at this time that Sun started giving more serious consideration to the Chinese students in Tokyo. They began visiting him in Yokohama, and some even encouraged him to form a new revolutionary organization. But Sun was not ready. Since the Qing government had stopped private students from enrolling at Japanese military academies, he set up a secret military academy at Aoyama with the help of some Japanese officers to offer an eight-month course on military science. Opening in the summer of 1903, it attracted no more than 15 students and closed after just four months. His Aoyama cadets swore the same oath of loyalty as members of the Xingzhonghui but Sun now added another dimension – the equalization of land rights, an idea he had been working on since his kidnap by the Chinese Legation in London in 1896–7 but not fully clarified until a few years later.[8]

THE TURNING POINT

Until this time, Sun had not stressed socio-economic reforms. The Xingzhonghui platform was restricted to driving out the Manchus, restoring China to indigenous rule, and establishing a republic. Sun had read extensively at the British Museum Library after his release from the Chinese Legation. He returned to the East with a farsighted revolutionary blueprint that incorporated socio-economic solutions. It was from *Progress and Poverty*, the seminal work of Henry George, that Sun derived his land policy.[9] An American political economist, George sought a middle ground between liberal laissez-faire capitalism and revolutionary socialism. He lived in California at a time when new settlers were driving land prices to astronomical heights. These wild price increases struck him as a source of grave social injustice: landlords could make enormous sums of money simply by renting out pieces of unimproved land. This removed the land, which George considered the ultimate social wealth, from productive use, thereby enriching a few at the expense of the rest of society. His solution was to have the government tax the entire "unearned increment" or the price increase on unimproved land. This, he thought, would put an end to harmful land speculation while providing the government with enough revenue to abolish all other taxes.[10]

To this "single tax" solution, Sun added a major caveat. Instead of taxing away all the unearned increment, he proposed to have landowners assess the value of their own land, on which the government would collect one percent of the value as tax. To ensure that landowners did not undervalue their landholdings, the government should retain the right to purchase the land at the owner's appraised value. Sun's version was a lot more moderate than that proposed by Henry George but it would serve the same purpose. Sun was familiar with land speculation because sharp increases in land value had jolted coastal China in much the same way they had jolted coastal California.

As Sun and the students became better acquainted, they began to shed some of their mutual apprehensions and warmed up to each other. The students were impressed with Sun's gentlemanly demeanor, his long history of revolutionary activity and his extensive Western education, all of which they lacked. With a seasoned leader like Sun, they assumed that the revolution would take place quickly and the Western nations would in turn act with restraint. On his part, Sun recognized that some of the students could at least provide him with access to more regions of China. He even contributed a short essay, *On the Preservation or Dismemberment of China*, to the students' journal *Jiangsu*. Writing to a Chinese audience for the first time, Sun revealed his strong anti-imperialist sentiment, which until now he had only shared with his Xingzhonghui compatriots and close friends like Miyazaki. Adjusting his message to the students' wavelength, the Manchus were no longer just depriving China of the full benefit of foreign trade and investment, the picture that he portrayed in his appeals for help from Westerners, but selling out to foreigners. While praising the Boxers' spirit, he condemned Li Hongzhang for failing to drive out the foreign invaders. And if the Manchus and their Chinese henchmen were incapable of protecting China's interests, Sun was certain that the Chinese themselves could foil any attempt to partition the country. He warned those who wanted China partitioned, both Western and Japanese, that the Chinese were too numerous to be subdued. On the other hand, he averred that not all foreigners were necessarily imperialists. Many Europeans, he believed, admired the Chinese people, and Japanese Sinophiles realized that the preservation of China meant their self-preservation. Much depended, he declared, on the policies that China pursued.

This period coincided with a sharp rise in Chinese nationalism. In April 1903, the Russians reneged on their promise to withdraw troops that had been stationed in southern Manchuria since the Boxer Uprising. Now they demanded exorbitant concessions as the price for withdrawal. If China felt menaced, Japan felt threatened by the continued Russian presence in Manchuria, which she saw as a prelude to a takeover of Korea, now under Japan's sphere of influence. It was precisely to preempt such a threat that the Anglo-Japanese Alliance was concluded in 1902. As war fever mounted in Japan, many Chinese students volunteered for active duty in a student army. A group of students returned to China with an offer to help drive the Russians out of Manchuria but their mission did not even earn a hearing. The Qing government was trying to resolve the conflict through diplomatic and political means, fearing that anything stronger would risk disaster. Student militancy on the other hand was a more immediate but still manageable threat. Measures like pressuring the Japanese to outlaw the students' army reinforced impressions that the dynasty feared popular initiative more than foreign invasion.

The Chinese students in Japan were in close contact with intellectuals in Shanghai, where modern schools and the relative immunity of the International Settlement and the French Concession produced a second pivot for militant nationalism. These Shanghai radicals, who followed their Tokyo counterparts and formed the Volunteer Corps to Resist Russia, made their greatest impact as journalists. Since 1895, scores of periodicals, newspapers and translations of Japanese works had appeared and Shanghai was the hub of the new publishing industry. Following Russia's blackmail on Manchuria in April and the Qing government's failure to come up with an effective strategy, the Shanghai radicals started a propaganda war against the Qing government and turned out several revolutionary publications.

In May 1903, the most famous of these publications, *Subao*, hurled insults at the Qing court and the imperial family in a series of seditious articles. The government coaxed the authorities of the International Settlement to suppress the newspaper and detain its colorful editor-in-chief, Zhang Binglin, who had been a leading anti-Manchu rabble-rouser in Tokyo. In his early thirties, Zhang was a brilliant classical scholar, one of a number who had switched his ideology from reform to revolution. The Qing government also tried to settle scores with the precocious Zou Rong, who that year had written the most famous revolutionary tract, *The Revolutionary Army*, at the age of just 18. It went through several reprints and hundreds of thousands of copies eventually reached Chinese throughout the

Zhang Binglin

world. As with Zhang, study in Japan and exposure to Western ideas had helped to convert Zou to revolution. The Qing court demanded the extradition of Zhang and Zou, which the Shanghai Municipal Council rejected, citing the extraterritorial status of the concession. The International Settlement's Mixed Court found both men guilty but the sentences they meted out were much lighter than those that the Qing had wanted. Both men faced the ordeal of imprisonment together. Zou contracted an illness while in prison and died in 1905 at the age of 21, just months before his scheduled release. Zhang was freed in 1906.

After the widely publicized Subao affair, which annoyed the Qing court, the student radicals worked overtime on their virulent attacks from the relative safety of their sanctuaries in Shanghai and Japan. Like earlier publications, they catered to student provincial groups and contained many translations from Japanese, which were in turn often based upon English, French and German originals. Most did not last more than several issues but reprints were frequently made. Thousands of copies reached the mainland, where modern schools were creating an ever-widening readership. Not all student publications were overtly revolutionary, but the focus on modern ideas and current events stimulated radicalism.

All these publications being churned out in Tokyo and Shanghai demonstrated the students' determination to join the mainstream of world history. Democracy, constitutionalism and even socialism were popular subjects if for no other reason than that they were the modern trend in politics, with which the students wanted to identify themselves. But what made the most potent argument for revolutionary convictions was the specter of imperialism, which the students gave full expression to in words charged with emotion. They discussed its origins as well as its brutal consequences, particularly the direct subjugation or economic enslavement of entire races and nations. The Europeans' record in China seemed to fit in with a scheme for domination that was fast approaching its final stage. Their complete subjugation of China, the students concluded, could only be checked by the awakening of Chinese nationalism, of which the overthrow of the Manchus was the first step.

The Social Darwinist view, popular in Japan, gave a strong racial twist to the students' perception of nationalism. From their vista, it was as a racial unit, charged with a spirit of shared destiny, that a modern nation achieved the cohesion, the adaptability, and the toughness required for survival. Such a view made it easier to blame the Manchu rulers for China's weakness. That their overthrow was the key to recovery was an enticing argument, yet it was the foremost proponent of the imperialist danger who tried to refute it. While the Qing court found his proposed constitutional reforms too radical, Liang's disciples found them too mild and demanded the emotional satisfaction that comes with a more radical solution, which Liang feared would be the sole reward of an anti-Manchu upheaval. In the end, Liang's main contribution was in his diagnosis of China's crisis; he had less success with his prescriptive program. This gave Sun his biggest opportunity thus far.

While Chinese students in Tokyo and Shanghai were fine-tuning their nationalistic ideas, war broke out over competing Russian and Japanese imperialistic ambitions over Manchuria and Korea. Negotiations between the two belligerents had been going on since the end of the Sino-Japanese War. Japan lost her patience and on February 8, 1904, launched a sneak attack on the Russian naval base at Port Arthur. Russia suffered multiple losses early in the war but remained engaged to preserve her dignity. But when Japanese naval forces almost completely destroyed the Russian fleet in the Battle of Tsushima in May 1905 and occupied Shakhalin Island, Russia was left with little choice but to sue for peace.

Sun was in Hawaii when the Russo-Japanese War broke out. His arrival the previous September was greeted with the shocking discovery that Liang Qichao had made underhand use of the letters of recommendation that Sun had given him. Liang hijacked Sun's followers in the Islands by blurring the distinction between the reform and revolution. Nor had Liang hesitated in appropriating Sun's strategy: for instance, he advocated an armed rebellion in Guangdong to save the Guangxu Emperor and the reform movement. He had even gone a step further than Sun and actually joined the local Triads to gain acceptance into the Cantonese community, which Sun had never done even though he had used the Triads to promote his cause. Indeed, Liang was so skillful in exploiting his prestige and eloquence that Sun's own brother Sun Mei was now the head of the local cell of the Baohuanghui.

To win back his partisans, Sun turned to the only network that Liang had apparently not challenged him for, that of the Chinese converts. Relying on Chinese pastors to organize political meetings, Sun addressed large *huaqiao* audiences and the press to argue the case for a republic as against Liang's constitutional monarchy. Using a locomotive analogy that he would use on numerous occasions in the future, he argued that when borrowing technology from abroad, it was not necessary to repeat all the stages of development of that technology. It was not necessary for China to construct early locomotive models before acquiring the latest. Rather, it could employ the most up-to-date model without any delay. Likewise, China need not experience constitutional monarchy for a set period of years before moving on to a republican form of government. Rather it should adopt the latest political system of government – republicanism – right away. A people capable of destroying absolute monarchy could easily go a step further. As for the fear of foreign intervention, Sun claimed that the very act of revolting would earn international respect. Echoing student pamphleteers, he accused the Manchus of pacifying the country on behalf of foreigners and presenting the foreigners with large chunks of Chinese territory. Six month of campaigning brought less than 100 recruits. Since the Xingzhonghui was now defunct, Sun inducted them into the "Chinese Revolutionary Army" and had them sign the same oath that he had used for his military academy cadets in Japan.

For the first time in seven years Sun had the chance to be with his family. Though his brother Sun Mei was still taking care of their mother as well as Sun's family, he had suffered financially and could no longer bankroll Sun's political activities. Sun had to depend on the sale of "patriotic bonds," redeemable after the revolution at ten times their purchase price, and other fundraising devices. While in the Islands, Sun joined the local branch of the Triads in the hope that this would give him leverage with the Chinese community in the United States, which he planned to visit next. In order to ease his way through U.S. Immigration, whose ruthless enforcement of the Chinese Exclusion laws was notorious, he obtained false documents attesting to Hawaii as his place of birth. Armed with letters of introduction from the local Triad lodges to their counterparts in San Francisco, Sun set sail on the *Korea* bound for the United States on March 31, 1904.

Baohuanghui members in Hawaii had reported Sun's departure to their fellow members in San Francisco. Thus when the *Korea* arrived on April 6, U.S. Customs Service interpreters who were Baohuanghui members reported him to the immigration authorities, which had meanwhile been informed by the Chinese consul that Sun's deposition attesting to his Hawaiian birth was false. By chance, Sun was carrying a letter of recommendation to two Chinese clergymen. Their intercession, and that of a local secret society head, helped to extricate Sun from the awkward situation.

Next came seven frustrating months of campaigning from coast to coast, visiting at least 26 cities in the company of a secret society head who paid for all the expenses. Denied basic civil liberties, including the right to naturalized U.S. citizenship, the American *huaqiao* may have been intoxicated by Sun's promise of a powerful home government to protect their interests. But fear of reprisals against family members in China put a lid on their commitment to revolution, which fell far short of Sun's expectations. In New York, Sun met with some Chinese students, among them Wang Zhonghui, the son of an old friend. Wang was a student at Yale Law School, where he would graduate later in the year with a Doctor of Civil Law.

With Wang's help, Sun published a pamphlet, *The True Solution of the Chinese Question*, his first appeal to Americans. As in previous pleas to both Chinese and Europeans, Sun maintained that an anti-Manchu revolution would benefit the West as well as China. His talent for fine-tuning his rhetoric to what his audience wanted to hear had by now been honed to an art. Dropping the militantly nationalist line he had taken with Chinese audiences, the Manchus were no longer weak appeasers of foreigners but the cause of the xenophobia that sparked the Boxer Uprising. And the United States was not the imperialist conqueror of the Philippines but one of China's closest neighbors with legitimate interests in the East, interests that would be served by a Chinese revolution. Appealing for American sympathy and support, he expressed the hope that there would be many "Lafayettes" among them.[11]

Ten thousand printed copies of the pamphlet had no greater impact than previous appeals to foreigners. Probably the only bright spot on his U.S. tour was coming across a copy of the *Thoe Lam Jit Poh* newspaper in the San Francisco office of the *Datong Ribao* (Great Harmony Daily), with which the *Thoe Lam Jit Poh* had a correspondent relationship. He was impressed by the revolutionary tone of the editorial and was apparently surprised that he had neither heard of the newspaper nor known that there was a revolutionary movement in Singapore. He promptly wrote to You Lie seeking more information on the paper and the people behind it.[12]

At this time when Sun's one-man campaign hit a brick wall, so had the student revolutionary movement in Tokyo. In late 1903, Huang Xing, a Hunan native who had been studying in Japan and taken part in anti-Manchu demonstrations there, returned to his home province and formed a revolutionary organization, the Huaxinghui (Society for China's Revival). He enlisted the Gelaohui as allies in a planned attack in Changsha, the Hunan provincial capital, on November 16, 1904, when officials would be preoccupied celebrating the Empress Dowager's 70th birthday. His Gelaohui allies were to launch a series of simultaneous risings in five other spots in the province. Forewarned by spies, the Qing government issued a warrant for Huang Xing's arrest on October 24, but he fled to Japan before they could apprehend him. The leaders of another revolutionary organization, the Guangfuhui (Restoration Society), had planned to support Huang Xing's coup with a rising of their own but were forced to shelve their plans when the Changsha plot failed.

Huang Xing

What these abortive uprisings demonstrated was the need for a coordinated attempt under an experienced leader. Not only was Sun ready to assume that role, the students, too, were by now ready to consider him for it. At the end of the year, Sun gladly accepted an invitation from some militant students in Europe to visit them. On December 14, he embarked for Europe on a journey that was to be the turning point in his revolutionary career.

In London, the first stop on his European tour, Sun had a parley with Yan Fu, one of the most important translators of Western works in the late 19th and early 20th centuries. Sent to study naval technology in the naval schools at Portsmouth and Greenwich in England, Yan spent considerable time researching Western political theories and legal practices. On his return to China in 1879, he was assigned to work as a superintendent in Li Hongzhang's Beiyang naval academy. In spite of his many duties, he translated the works of important thinkers like Adam Smith, John Stuart Mill and Montesquieu. Yan advocated parliamentary government initially but later decided that China was not ready. Now a mature man in his fifties, Yan was even more opposed to revolution. When he told Sun that China was not ready for a republican revolution, Sun countered, "How long can a man wait for the [Yellow] River to clear? You, sir, are a thinker. I am a man of action."[13]

Action was what the group of students in Europe were demanding. There was no need to sell the merits of a revolution to this group of hotheads; they were in Europe because the authorities wanted to keep their radicalism out of China. What the students wanted was for Sun to prove his credentials for leading the revolution movement. At his first meeting in Brussels with five leading student activists, Sun spoke about his ideas on nationalism, democracy and socialism, and unveiled his plan for a "five-power constitution." As in the United States, there would be the legislative, executive and judicial branches, or *yuan*, plus adaptations of two traditional Chinese institutions: the examination *yuan* to administer the selection of candidates for public office, and the censorate *yuan* to check on the honesty and efficiency of government.

The students had no quarrel with Sun's program but they had serious misgivings about his strategy of relying on secret societies, which had proved unreliable. They stressed that intellectuals – obviously referring to themselves – were indispensable to the revolution, and insisted that priority be given to their people, some of whom had successfully infiltrated the New Army. Sun needed the support of the students as much as the students needed a leader. But he wanted to enlist them from a position of strength, not weakness. This he could only do if he could justify the strategy in his two uprisings. By establishing the importance of secret societies, Sun would be the natural leader of the revolutionary movement by virtue of his long association with these clandestine associations. Otherwise his position would at best be on par with the students, especially the group in Tokyo. Seen from this perspective, Sun's seeming reluctance to accord leadership status to the students is understandable. After arguing for three straight days, Sun professed to be convinced and concurred with the students that intellectuals were fit to lead the revolutionary movement if they devoted themselves to it.

Sun took in about 30 students at this Brussels meeting. Twelve days in Berlin produced another 20. In Paris, his next stop, another ten students joined. Having signed up 60 of the approximately 100 Chinese students in Europe, Sun became the leader of a "revolutionary party," which after the founding of the Tongmenghui, or Revolutionary Alliance, became its European Headquarters. The new party brought together for the first time secret societies, treaty port modernizers and intellectual circles in the cause of anti-Manchuism. But no sooner had the students sworn loyalty to Sun's program with esoteric oaths and rituals than a few got cold feet and denounced Sun to the Chinese minister in Paris, who fortuitously decided to ignore the matter. It was a betrayal that presented no real threat to Sun's safety or the new organization. All the same, the betrayal fueled Sun's bitterness and his doubts as to whether intellectuals could be trusted to lead a revolution. In the end, all but 14 of the new recruits had second thoughts and dropped out from the revolutionary party. The handful of Hubei extremists remained committed and that was all that mattered. They recommended Sun to their counterparts in Tokyo, where Sun would face the crucial test of his ability to impress non-Cantonese intellectuals.

While in Paris, Sun used the Russo-Japanese War to diversify his search for foreign help. He called at the Quai d'Orsay in Paris, where he met, among others, Raphael Réau, who had shown interest in Sun's plan in 1903. Réau had worked at the French consulate in Hong Kong and understood the troubled situation in southern China. At the meeting, Sun revived the proposal made two years ago to French officials in Hanoi. This time he threw in a sweetener and offered to help counteract the growing influence of Japan, which was then trouncing France's ally, Russia. Japan, he declared, had lost interest in his cause, and proposed that France ought to replace Japan as the principal patron of his revolutionary movement. In return for military and financial aid, Sun promised to mobilize his partisans and the secret society leaders to change the hostility of people of Guangxi and Yunnan towards France into real sympathy. Réau later wrote in his report that Sun held "enormous power" in these provinces and his movement represented "important factors in the Chinese question." This report was favorably received by two high-ranking officials: Philippe Berthelot, the secretary of the Foreign Affairs Ministry, and Paul Doumer, whom Sun had twice failed to meet when he was governor-general of French Indochina. France being Russia's ally, the Russo-Japanese War was causing considerable tension between France and Japan. Any plan to substitute French for Japanese influence in southern China would naturally be looked at with considerable interest by the French Foreign Affairs Ministry as well as the Ministry of War.[14]

The result of these exchanges within the French bureaucracy was the creation of the Intelligence Service on China in May 1905. One of the principal tasks of the new agency was to collect information on southern China, intelligence on Japanese activity in that region and the military response to be taken in Tonking. Headed by Major Boucabeille and headquartered in the Beijing legation, the agency was an autonomous unit that reported directly to the Ministry of War. This intelligence operation, which continued to be operational until October 1906, paved the way for close cooperation between a small group of French officials and Sun and his people. It enabled Sun to mount an incredible propaganda campaign to promote himself as the inspiration behind the disruptions in the central and southern provinces, and the supreme authority recognized by rebels of all persuasion. In short, he was a heavyweight partner worthy of French diplomatic and logistical support.

Sun sailed with the *Tonking* on June 11, 1905, for his return journey to the East. Traveling on the same ship was another Chinese passenger, Zhang Renjie (a.k.a. Zhang Jingjiang), the scion of a wealthy family of silk wholesalers in Zhejiang. Zhang had served as a commercial attaché to the Chinese Legation in Paris. Making the most of his position, he launched himself into the antique trade. Won over by Sun's personality and political program, he offered to subsidize the revolution. They worked out a code in which the letter "A" would signify a request for $10,000 in funds, "B" for $20,000, and so forth up to a maximum of "E" for $50,000. True to his word, Zhang would always remit money whenever Sun needed funds. He remained one of Sun's strongest financial supporters until 1911.[15]

Sun's departure from Marseille coincided with the cessation of hostilities between Russia and Japan. On May 27, the Japanese destroyed two-thirds of the Russian fleet in the Battle of Tsushima. Realizing the futility of the situation and to save the lives of his men rather than his own honor, the Russian admiral ordered the remaining ships under his command to submit. The signal of surrender was hoisted the following day, May 28. Japan's victory over Russia was the first by an Asian nation against a Western power in modern times, and altered the balance of power in East Asia forever. The Treaty of Portsmouth, mediated by U.S. President Theodore Roosevelt and signed on September 5, gave Japan control over Korea. This was the precursor to Japanese colonization of Korea in 1910. The treaty debunked the notion of white supremacy, sending shockwaves throughout Europe and rekindling fear among Europeans of the yellow peril, even among the British, notwithstanding the Anglo-Japanese Alliance.

The reaction throughout much of Asia and the Middle East was a sharp contrast. When the *Tonking* passed through the Suez Canal, an encounter with Arab laborers who fussed over Sun thinking that he was a Japanese revealed the exhilaration that the victory had on Eastern nationalism. Japan's coup, they said, was a triumph for all colored peoples. Further east, the war's reverberations were even more pronounced. Nehru described the victory of "little Japan over giant Russia" as a great "pick-me-up" for Asia that lessened the feeling of inferiority suffered by many Asians, and boosted their self-confidence. And while Japan's own policy towards her continental neighbors was not above suspicion, her prestige was never greater in China and prompted the Qing government to accelerate the implementation of its New Policies.[16]

The Japanese victory was for Sun a validation of the pan-Asian proposition. Since his meeting with the student activists in Europe, he had been looking forward to the dialogue with their counterparts in Japan, which he knew would be the crucial make-or-break for the future of the revolutionary party. He was certain that they would look favorably upon his close relationship with the Japanese. He was excited, too, by the prospect of meeting the Singapore revolutionaries behind the *Thoe Lam Jit Poh*. With these possibilities in the pipeline, Sun now saw many new and different permutations in his revolutionary future. When the *Tonking* made a brief stopover at Colombo, Sun promptly went ashore and cabled You Lie to arrange a meeting with the Singapore revolutionaries. Recalling his ill-fated visit in 1900, Sun thought that there was a five-year banishment order against him, and was not sure if he would be allowed to land. Actually, there was no banishment order against him but You Lie went ahead anyway to obtain police permission for Sun to disembark while the ship remained in port for a day.[17]

Waiting to welcome Sun at Johnston's Pier when the *Tonking* berthed in Singapore on July 11 were You Lie and his Singapore friends Tan Chor Nam, Teo Eng Hock and Teo's nephew Lim Nee Soon. Until this time, the impression that the three Singapore Chinese had of Sun was gleaned from conversations with You Lie and Dr. Lim Boon Keng. In their minds, the Chinese patriot was an expert on matters of the West and worldly affairs. Coming face to face with Sun himself, they were even more impressed, both by his gentlemanly demeanor as well as the sincerity of his conviction. The respect was mutual. Sun was impressed by their enthusiasm and commitment to work for the betterment of China. Complimenting Tan and Teo on their newspaper, he encouraged them to continue with their revolutionary activities. He briefed them on the student anti-Manchu movements in Japan and Europe, and assured them that conditions in China and abroad were highly favorable to the anti-dynastic cause and that the time was ripe for the revolution to progress to the next level. This, he told them, would come about with the formation of an alliance of revolutionary parties that would soon be formed in Japan. He urged them to be prepared and to join it in due course. The pair responded positively to Sun's overture and assured him of their unreserved support. Sun declined their invitation to extend his visit but accepted their hospitality to stay at Little Paradise, a businessmen's club on Balestier Road where the duo, Lim Nee Soon and their radical friends regularly met to discuss the political situation in China and their revolutionary ideas.

It had been five years almost to the week since Sun first set foot in Singapore. In 1900, he failed to form a coalition with the reformist leader Kang Youwei and was unceremoniously escorted together with Miyazaki, Kiyofuji and others to their ship. The experience left a bitter taste and was one of the reasons that Hanoi was chosen over Singapore to base the

Xingzhonghui's operations in the region. Until Sun picked up a copy of *Thoe Lam Jit Poh* in San Francisco and learned of the local revolutionary movement that had burgeoned since his maiden visit, Singapore was completely off his radar. The meeting with You Lie and the three local revolutionaries convinced him that Singapore was better situated than Hanoi as a base for his revolutionary activities in Nanyang. He was no doubt swayed in his assessment by the Chinese patriotism that was on open display during his one-day sojourn: a boycott of American goods in sympathy with similar actions in China.

Less than two months before, on May 20, the Shanghai Chamber of Commerce had passed a resolution to boycott American goods in retaliation against the vigorous enforcement of its Chinese Exclusion Law[18]. The U.S. government did not take the threat seriously, but within two weeks boycotts were started in major cities throughout China. The news spread to Chinese communities around the world, where the movement received overwhelming support. On June 20, about three weeks before Sun's arrival, several hundred Chinese merchants in Singapore had convened a meeting at the Thong Chai Medical Institution in Wayang Street. Tan Chor Nam's motion calling on Chinese merchants in Singapore to stop trading in American goods was unanimously adopted. You Lie, who also attended the meeting, declared that the Chinese Christians would support their compatriots and called on American missionaries to return home. Many merchants complied with Tan's resolution and stopped dealing in American goods, replacing them with imported substitutes from China. The few who ignored the boycott were denounced as "cold-blooded animals," an epithet borrowed from the Shanghai boycott. Although the movement in Singapore was initiated and dominated by the merchants, it soon permeated throughout the Chinese community. Many Chinese refused to use the British-owned tramcars on the erroneous belief that this was an American enterprise. Dock-workers refused to repair a badly damaged American ship that had run aground on the rocks. Even prostitutes, deemed the lowest class in society, supported the boycott. In one incident, a streetwalker snatched the American cigarette that her customer was puffing on and gave him an earful. Amazingly, instead of losing his cool, the customer apologized to his service provider.[19]

THE TURNING POINT

Sun boarded the *Tonking* the following day for the final leg of his journey to Japan. The sun had not shone so brightly in a long time. Whatever doubts he had regarding his revolutionary future dissipated into the blue sky. Unable to contain his excitement, he penned a letter to Tan Chor Nam when his ship arrived in Saigon, confirming his intent to enlist the support of the Singapore Chinese in his plan for another rising. Sun had previously informed Miyazaki that he might linger on a little longer in Nanyang. But with all the new possibilities spinning in his head, he was anxious to return to Japan and decided to keep to his original schedule.

Meanwhile, in preparation for Sun's return visit, Teo Eng Hock renovated the villa that he had purchased for his mother to spend her twilight years. The villa, which Teo had named Wanqingyuan ("Serene Twilight Garden"), would later serve as Sun's headquarters for his revolutionary activities in Singapore and the region.[20]

Chapter 6

A MARRIAGE OF CONVENIENCE

CHINA WAS AT a crossroad when the Russo-Japanese War broke out in February 1904 on her turf. Her own defeat in the Sino-Japanese War nine years earlier and the "scramble for concessions" that followed in its wake had underscored the danger of possible dismemberment, and given rise to a nationalism that found expression primarily in anti-foreignism, as in the Boxer Uprising. Japan's triumph over Russia debunked the myth of white supremacy and gave the Chinese hope of one day shaking off the debasement and exploitation they had suffered under white hegemony, as Japan had done. Consequently, Chinese nationalism became hardened and more assertive after Japan's surprise victory. Nationalism is often thought of as a Western intellectual construct but in China and the rest of the non-white world it was the rising military power of Japan that stimulated the movement. While resenting Japan's growing aggression against China, many Chinese intellectuals now saw the Japanese model and experience as relevant to their own country.

Japan's victory was also seen as the triumph of constitutionalism over autocracy. The Empress Dowager Cixi, whose abhorrence for constitutionalism was exceeded only by her fear of revolution, agreed to send Manchu princes and nobles abroad to study foreign political systems as a prelude to the introduction of a constitution at home. She knew this would be a time-consuming process, which was fine as she was in no particular hurry to implement constitutional governance. Next came the decision to scrap the traditional civil service examinations altogether. By decoupling Confucianism from the foundation of the education system, it weakened the incentive to study the classics. Modern education expanded rapidly and more students opted to go abroad for their studies. As at home, the new learning flamed subversive ideas, which was inspired as well by the Russian Revolution of 1905.

To be sure, nationalism drew broad support across social classes, but the reforms it stimulated favored the gentry and the wealthy while hardly sending ripples of joy to the masses. Education reforms catered primarily to children of established families. The modern schools were located mostly in urban centers which in any event were generally too expensive for all but the wealthy. Economic development was implemented without regard for peasant welfare and aggravated rural poverty. Commercial opportunities lured the gentry to urban centers. Absentee-landlordism became more prevalent and hardened the terms of rural tenancy for peasants. Industry, though growing, could not absorb the influx of rural refugees who converged on the cities in search of jobs, resulting in urban unemployment. The poverty and misery in the countryside and the discontent in the cities often led to disorder, rioting and sometimes rebellions. Such outbursts did not directly threaten the dynasty but they strained its dwindling resources and what little was left of its prestige.

But popular unrest was not the only source of frustration for the dynasty. Nationalism and modernization created pressures that nibbled away at the regime's authority. Chambers of commerce, established under the Qing's auspices, became instruments of gentry and merchant power in the provinces. Like other new local institutions, they reinforced the trend toward regionalism, which in turn became a vehicle for nationalism. The regime, too laden with foreign debt, was also too weak militarily to push the "rights-recovery movement" fast enough to satisfy nationalist demands, provoking local leaders to rush in to fill the void. The anti-American boycott in the summer of 1905 illustrates the regime's dilemma. The foreign powers blamed the Qing court for the mounting anti-foreignism and used gunboats to assert their demands. The Manchu regime blamed the students and intellectuals and resorted to suppression. The intellectuals blamed both the dynasty and the powers, and intensified their pressure on both. This vicious cycle of recriminations sank the empire deeper into chaos.

Sun's plan for a revolutionary party thus made its appearance at a time of heightened nationalism, widespread discontent and a rising potential for revolution. But after almost two years on the road, he had little to show when he returned to Japan in July 1905. He managed to salvage some bits of his Hawaiian following that had been hijacked by Liang Qichao. And he made a number of new acquaintances among foreign officials and diplomats as well as leaders of diverse Chinese communities in America and Europe. With the possible exception of Liang, no other opposition Chinese leader could claim a more varied experience or a larger fan base. But in 1903, Liang had switched his advocacy to constitutional monarchy and thus abdicated his role as the foremost proponent of intellectual radicalism, leaving Sun as the leading advocate of anti-Manchuism. Sun had crossed his first hurdle with the students in Europe but he still had to overcome the Tokyo intellectuals' disdain for his social and educational background. As for him, he had to come to terms with his own distrust of the students.

A whole series of circumstances helped to resolve the mutual misgivings. On the part of the Tokyo intellectuals, the failure of their attempted uprising at Changsha in 1904 revealed the need for unified action while Liang Qichao's volte-face had deprived them of intellectual leadership and the source of their inspiration. That Sun was considered to fill the leadership role may have been partly due to his age. Most of the students were in their twenties while Sun at 39 years old was almost a decade older than Huang Xing, the oldest leader among the radical students in Tokyo. Miyazaki's memoir *My Thirty-Three Year's Dream*, published in 1902, had cast a flattering spotlight on Sun's achievements, and this may have played a part in changing the Tokyo students' perception of him. They were impressed with Sun's Western education and experience, his reputation and expertise as a revolutionary strategist and tactician, and the breadth of his contacts, which the students recognized were well beyond their reach. Above all else he possessed the one attribute crucial to the students' desire for a swift revolution: the cloak of respectability that would forestall foreign intervention. Sun was the only revolutionary leader who had traveled the world and could speak with authority on foreign attitudes. If the powers had to be placated, who but Sun could keep their gunboats at bay and neutralize their threat? With Liang Qichao out of the equation, there was no one more qualified than Sun to lead the anti-dynastic movement. In spite of his less than sterling track record, his reputation among the intellectuals was formidable.[1]

Sun's attitude had also changed in a way that made it easier for the intellectuals to accept him. His earlier attempts to identify himself with intellectuals were all directed at prominent public figures like Li Hongzhang and Kang Youwei, all of which ended in disappointment. Convinced that China was on the edge of a great popular insurrection, Sun's primary focus was on finding fighting men and the funds to recruit them, neither of which the students could provide. His attitude towards the students began to change in 1902 after his emergence from self-imposed isolation in Yokohama. He began making sporadic contacts with the students and participated in some of their activities. In 1902, he accepted an invitation from Zhang Binglin to take part in a ceremony commemorating the fall of the Ming dynasty. In the summer of 1903, he set up a military academy in Aoyama for Chinese students who were excluded from Japanese academies. More significant was his essay, *On the Preservation or Dismemberment of China*. Presenting himself as an expert on international relations, Sun informed his youthful audience that certain sectors of foreign public opinion were favorable to China. Properly handled, they could stave off foreign military intervention against the Chinese revolution.

Sun's lack of success among the Chinese communities in the United States had undoubtedly also made him more amenable to collaboration with intellectuals. This began in Europe in the spring of 1905 when Sun met with the group of young radical students from Hubei. The chasm between them was hard to reconcile initially, for Sun would only trust the secret societies as the revolution's fighting force whereas the students insisted on the importance of the intellectuals and the army. Happily, there was a meeting of minds after three days of intense discussion. The 14 members that Sun recruited briefed their counterparts in Tokyo of their meeting and asked them to make contact with Sun upon his return to Tokyo.

When Sun arrived in Yokohama on July 19, 1905, Miyazaki was in Tokyo singing praises of his friend to Huang Xing as an outstanding leader whose global reputation would be an asset to the Chinese revolution. On July 28 in Tokyo, it was again Miyazaki who accompanied Sun to meet with Huang Xing, Song Jiaoren and Chen Tianhua at the office of *Twentieth-Century China*, the official organ of the Hunanese's own revolutionary organization, Huaxinghui, the Society for China's Revival. At these crucial first meetings, Sun did most of the talking. Stressing the unity theme, he warned that separate and independent risings by provincial groups would not only lead to chaos but also provide the foreign powers with a pretext for intervention and partitioning China. A united approach on the other hand would ensure a smooth transition and keep the foreigners at bay. While lauding the destructive power of the secret societies, Sun conceded that they needed the leadership of intellectuals to exert a civilizing influence upon their "destructive tendencies." In short, what Sun proposed was to continue the Xingzhonghui's strategy of using secret societies as the main fighting force and to extend it with the inclusion of intellectuals.

The Hunanese leaders took time out the following day to discuss among themselves. They needed no convincing for a united front of anti-dynastic forces, their own plot at Changsha having failed the previous year. They also understood that unity meant acceptance of Sun's leadership, which ceased to be a problem. The question uppermost in their minds, as in the minds of their compatriots, was the form the alliance should take. Chen Tianhua was in favor of complete amalgamation, while Huang Xing preferred a formal alliance with the Xingzhonghui while retaining the "spiritual characteristics" of their own organization. Unable to reach a consensus, it was decided that they would open the question to the entire membership of the party and allow each member to have a say.

On July 30, 70 students representing all but one of China's 18 provinces – Gansu did not have any students in Japan – attended the meeting at the home of one of Sun's most active Japanese collaborators, Uchida Ryohei. This was also the headquarters of the most important Japanese ultranationalist organization, Kokuryukai, the Black Dragon Society, founded in 1901 by Uchida. This society had other reasons for supporting revolution in China, but its most cherished hope was the overthrow of the Qing regime. This would leave a vacuum in Manchuria and enable Japan to create a boundary on the Asian continent at the Amur River. The presence of Uchida, Miyazaki and other Japanese at the meeting and its venue was a testament to Sun's strong Japanese connection.[2]

With the Hunanese leaders' unequivocal support, Sun's motion to form a new revolutionary organization easily carried the day. The name chosen, Zhongguo Tongmenghui, or the Chinese Revolutionary Alliance,[3] was a common secret society name and reflected Sun's preference for a secret society model. All present were asked to take the membership oath, which was essentially the same as the one Sun had recently introduced in Europe except for some minor changes. The first three goals – "expulsion of the Manchus, restoration of Chinese rule and the establishment of a republic" – were already winning slogans and needed no elaboration. But the fourth, "equalization of land rights," was a new concept to the students and required Sun's elucidation. Then following Huang Xing's lead and his call for all to sign the oath, the rest followed suit. As in Europe, Sun taught each member the conspiratorial handshakes and passwords adapted from the secret societies. The election of office bearers was deferred to the next meeting when the Tongmenghui was to be formally inaugurated. Meanwhile, excitement rippled through the Chinese intellectual community in Japan when news spread that prominent student leaders had endorsed Sun.

On August 13, more than 700 students crowded into the Fujimiken Restaurant in Kojimachi to hear Sun's first major speech to the Tokyo students. Queues formed outside on the street, as the restaurant was not large enough to accommodate all who wanted to attend. Sun did not disappoint. Exhorting his audience not to sell China short, he spoke of the country's unmatched potential for greatness – the world's largest population and a civilization that for centuries had been the talk and envy of the world. Playing down the foreign threat, he assured his youthful audience that while the powers craved to "carve China up like a melon," they were fearful of popular resistance. Not that Sun anticipated a clash with the West. He believed that if China were to demonstrate resolve by overthrowing the Manchus, the foreign powers would quietly shelve their imperialist designs. What was needed, Sun told his audience, was the leadership of "men of high purpose." In the past, he was alone. Now the students were joining him. Together they could plan for China's future. Using his now familiar locomotive analogy, Sun urged them to choose a republic so China could make a quantum leap and achieve in 20 or even 15 years what it took Japan 30 years to accomplish. Sun's assertion that a perceptive leader with a blueprint of the future could fast-track China's path to modernity appealed to the students. He struck the students' chord better than the reformists, who by charting China's progress according to conventional wisdom offered the grim prospect of China continuing to lag behind other nations. This was the first time that Sun had spoken publicly in Tokyo and his speech was enthusiastically received by his audience. The students who had earlier despised him as an "uneducated adventurer" now acknowledged him as their undisputed leader.

The overt display of anti-Manchuism alarmed the Chinese Embassy in Tokyo, which demanded that the Japanese government regulate the activities of Chinese students more closely. Consequently, the meeting on August 20, 1905, to officially inaugurate the Tongmenghui was held at the spacious residence of Sakamoto Kinya, a member of the Diet who had investments in coal mines in China. More than 300 people attended the historic gathering. The students took an oath before Sun to "expel the Manchus, restore Chinese rule, establish a republic and equalize the land." A board of 30 members was elected and assigned to the management of three departments whose names were evocative of the American government: executive, legislative and judicial. As expected, Sun was elected *zongli*, or party president. Huang Xing was his second-in-command while Song Jiaoren was made a member of the judicial department.

The creation of the Tongmenghui was a clear sign of the popular support for the revolutionary movement among the young intelligentsia in China. Unlike the Xingzhonghui, which was only active prior to insurrections and had only a few branches that appealed primarily to Christians and Westernized Chinese, the Tongmenghui was to be very different. Having enlisted several hundred students from all walks of life and representing virtually every province, the membership grew rapidly to 963 by 1906 – 863 had joined in Japan, with the rest coming from Europe, Hawaii and Nanyang. The Tongmenghui planned to open five regional offices in China, supplemented by four other regional offices for Europe, Hawaii, Nanyang and North America. While students from scholar-gentry families initially dominated, they were soon joined by numerous *huaqiao* merchants whose goodwill and financial support were to prove indispensable.

Several documents were later prepared in 1905 to guide the new organization. The manifesto of the Tongmenghui is of particular significance as it delineates Sun's Three Principles of the People as the new party's revolutionary ideology. Until this time, only the first two principles, nationalism and democracy, had been given prominence by the revolutionaries. The third principle, the livelihood of the people, formally entered into Sun's thought after the establishment of the Tongmenghui. It was at this point, too, that Sun introduced the equalization of land rights. Like Henry George and John Stuart Mill, Sun wanted future appreciation in land values to be appropriated by the state while allowing current values to be retained by the owner. The inclusion of the equalization of land rights in the manifesto raised a few eyebrows but evoked little debate or serious discussion by the students, who in any event were not even quite sure what it meant. More importantly, the students who gathered in the summer of 1905 to form the Alliance were mobilizing purely for the overthrow of the Manchus, who would have no role in a new government, as the manifesto made abundantly clear. The revolutionaries wanted to return China to Chinese rule and considered a republican regime essential in that equal political rights and election of the president by the people would also assure the retention of Chinese control.

Also in the new party's manifesto was Sun's vision of a three-stage revolution to constitutional government. Under this schema, democracy would be deferred in order to avoid chaos and foreign intervention, with the republican regime introduced in three stages. There would first be military rule of three years in areas liberated by revolutionary forces. During this phase, the military government would control all military as well as civil affairs at the district level. Meanwhile, it would cooperate with the local people toward eliminating the old political and social evils, such as slavery, footbinding, opium smoking and bureaucratic corruption. The second stage would be a period of political tutelage, lasting not more than six years, during which time local self-government would be instituted and popular elections held for local assemblies and administrators. However, the military government would still retain control of the central government under a provisional constitution that specified the rights and duties of the military government and the people. At the end of the period of tutelage, the military government would be dissolved and the country would be governed by a civilian government under a new Five-Power Constitution.

The Huaxinghui turned over its party paper, *Twentieth-Century China*, as a dowry to the Alliance to serve as its official organ and continue the polemics against Liang Qichao, who deprecated revolution and republicanism in favor of constitutional monarchy. Relaunched as *Minbao*, People's Journal, after it was banned by the Japanese government for publishing an "offensive" article, *Japanese Politicians' Exploitation of China*, it was again suspended by the Japanese in October 1908. In those three years, it was run by two successive editorial teams. The pioneering group comprised a group of talented Cantonese scholars that included Hu Hanmin, Wang Jingwei and Feng Ziyou, and a few men from the Yangtze valley, notably Song Jiaoren and Chen Tianhua. During this initial phase, Sun was in daily contact with the team. He dictated certain texts and inspired most of the rest but generally left the composition to the team of talented scholars.[4]

Zhang Binglin took over the editorial direction of *Minbao* in November 1906 after his release from prison. Totally committed to the Alliance's cause, he strove to strengthen the theoretical bases of the Three Principles of the People in the numerous commentaries he wrote for the *Minbao*. Under him, the paper enjoyed tremendous success; 7,000 copies were being sold both in China and in *huaqiao* communities. From the spring of 1907 on, however, many difficulties arose. The ban on the paper in China undercut its profits, and Zhang could no longer count on subsidies from Sun, who had lost interest in the paper once he left Tokyo. Thereafter, Zhang went off on a frolic of his own and focused the paper more and more on his moral and philosophical arguments. His antipathy towards the West became more and more obvious as did his skepticism toward material progress. This new orientation coupled with Sun's absence and the organizational decline of the Alliance all combined to make *Minbao* in its later period appear increasingly to be the personal organ of Zhang himself.

The Tongmenghui thus had all the attributes of a modern political party: a hierarchical organizational structure, an ideology, a program for propaganda and a plan for action. As an organization, it was much more structured and formidable than Sun's motley band of Cantonese rebels in the Xingzhonghui. The students who formed the majority of the membership were not the product of treaty ports and missionary institutions but the offspring of established families from the interior of China. But the new party was also riddled from the outset with features that soon impaired its effectiveness and worked to its detriment.

A MARRIAGE OF CONVENIENCE

The Tongmenghui was formed through the merger of existing provincial organizations: Xingzhonghui, Huaxinghui, several smaller ones, and joined in 1906 by Guangfuhui.[5] All but one of China Proper's 18 provinces were represented in the new party, which did not recruit its members directly on an individual basis but inherited them en bloc from the provincial organizations. The unity of the new party and the authority of the *zongli* were therefore dependent upon the cooperation of the provincial leaders and the obeisance of their respective constituencies. Although Sun emerged as the undisputed leader, his leadership in the Alliance was definitely conditional. His Cantonese entourage was outnumbered at every level of the organization. Of the 70 founding members who attended the July 30 meeting, only ten were from Sun's entourage, and three of them were Japanese. At the board level, only two out of the 30 members were from the Xingzhonghui. And while the Cantonese made up almost the entire membership of the Xingzhonghui, they now constituted only a minority of 112 out of the 963 members enrolled in the Tongmenghui as of 1906.[6]

The members of the Huaxinghui, with its cohort of 263 students from Hunan and Hubei provinces, were the most numerous within the Alliance. Cut off from foreign influences until the end of the 19th century, the militants from these inland provinces had a strong attachment to tradition and a distrust of foreigners. Their leader Huang Xing, 29 years old, was from a modest but educated Hunan family. He had qualified for the basic *jinshi* degree when he was only 22 years old and was selected by the government of neighboring Hubei province to further his studies in Japan, where he helped to organize the Resist Russia Volunteer Army to protest Russia's continued occupation of southern Manchuria after the Boxing Uprising. Returning to China in 1903, he founded the Huaxinghui with Song Jiaoren and others. In 1904, the Huaxinghui in cooperation with several other revolutionary organizations planned an uprising in Changsha during Cixi's 70th birthday celebration. The plot was discovered and Huang Xing with several other leaders were force to seek refuge in Japan. Song Jiaoren, his deputy and fellow provincial, was the son of a small landowning family. He studied the classics but being more interested in world affairs did not pursue the civil service examinations. He met Huang Xing in 1902 and the following year began teaching at a prestigious school in Wuchang. His revolutionary activities were discovered and he was forced to flee to Japan at the end of 1904. In Tokyo, he studied Western political thought and made contacts among the expatriate Chinese student community and Japanese pan-Asianists.[7]

The members of the Guangfuhui, or Restoration Society, did not join the Alliance until late 1906. They were mostly students from Zhejiang and Anhui provinces whose nationalism and xenophobia reflected the mindset of their leaders, Zhang Binglin and Tao Chengzhang, both natives of Zhejiang. Two years younger than Sun, the precocious and erudite Zhang was born into a wealthy and scholarly family. He made contact with Kang Youwei and Liang Qichao following the Sino-Japanese War but after the failed Hundred Day Reform was forced to seek refuge in Japan where he met Sun, whose anti-Manchu sentiments he shared. Back in Shanghai in 1902, he found himself entangled with the Subao Affair, for which he paid the price of imprisonment. Tao Chengzhang, a decade younger than Zhang, came from a family of lower gentry but shared his partner's social and cultural conservatism. Like most Chinese students in Japan, where he was trained at a military academy between 1902 and 1904, Tao had received a classical education before embarking on modern studies. On his return to China, he organized the Guangfuhui with the aim of launching revolutionary action in the provinces of the lower Yangtze, particularly in his home province.

The Cantonese group constituted Sun's power base in the Tongmenghui. Its members were mostly students, many with scholarships from the Guangdong provincial government. Coming from a region long open to the outside world, they were distinguished by their cosmopolitanism, interest in the West and a desire to cooperate with it. Unlike Sun's first-generation followers in the Xingzhonghui who were from the despised circles of the treaty ports, these latter-day Cantonese revolutionaries were from families of scholars and merchants. Hu Hanmin, born in Guangzhou into a family originally from Jiangxi province, had studied the classics and obtained a degree before going abroad. In 1902, he was sent on a provincial scholarship to pursue his law studies in Tokyo. His fellow student Wang Jingwei was also born in Guangzhou and began his classical studies at home. In 1903, he won a provincial government scholarship to study in

Song Jiaoren Hu Hanmin Wang Jingwei

Japan, where in 1906 he obtained a diploma in constitutional law and political science. Zhu Zhixin studied the classics and mathematics. He won a provincial scholarship to continue his studies in Tokyo, where he mingled with the group of patriotic students from Guangzhou. He wrote numerous articles for *Minbao* on Marxism. From 1905 to 1907, Hu, Wang and Zhu were rated among the most brilliant and most prolific polemicists on *Minbao* and played essential roles in the creation of the ideology of the People's Three Principles. Another notable Cantonese was Feng Ziyou. His father was head of the Yokohama branch of the Xingzhonghui, which Feng joined when he was just 14 years old. The younger Feng attended Waseda University and took part in the patriotic activities of the Chinese students in Tokyo. He was appointed by Sun as the Tongmenghui's representative in Hong Kong and southern China.

The various provincial groups held divergent views that influenced their ideological beliefs and strategic choices. The Yangtze revolutionaries were more tradition-bound than their Guangdong counterparts. While the Cantonese were ready to turn to foreigners for financial and even military aid, the Yangtze intellectuals were less inclined to do so. Their antipathy towards foreigners was particularly acute where it concerned the Japanese. Sun still trusted his Japanese friends, especially Miyazaki, whose sincerity and loyalty he never doubted. The Yangtze students, incensed by the discrimination they suffered in Tokyo and alarmed at the rise of Japanese chauvinism, were ready to turn their backs on the cooperation that was now being offered even more reluctantly. Sun's sympathy for the Japanese and the Yangtze revolutionaries' nationalism that favored a struggle against Japan's imperialism in China would later lead to conflict.

Regional factionalism also played a big part in the clashes over theaters of operation. No one doubted the need for armed insurrections but Sun insisted on theaters in the south around Guangdong and its neighboring provinces. This was his backyard where he had many contacts with the secret societies, who in his vision would continue to play a big part in his revolution. Due to its vast distance from the capital, this region was much less well controlled and thus presented a better chance of successful risings. But success at such a great distant from the center was unlikely to bring about the overthrow of the Qing regime. For this reason, Song Jiaoren rejected Sun's southern strategy and considered the Yangtze region as offering the best chance of bringing down the Manchus. There was relative freedom of movement there and because of its relative proximity to the capital, a successful insurrection in the Yangtze had a much better chance of spreading northward to the capital.

Within days of Sun's arrival in Japan, prominent student leaders who had just met him for the first time had endorsed his leadership. It took them only three days to make the basic decision to form the Alliance and a little over three weeks to translate that decision into reality. The swiftness attested to the force of Sun's personality as well as the sense of urgency and hunger for action among the students. Although Sun had not entirely dispelled the doubts about his learning and he still did not command intellectual respect, he had proven himself to be more than an "artful conspirator." His impressive performance in Tokyo confirmed what the intellectuals had known about only through hearsay. And when they discovered that he was not the illiterate country bumpkin that some people had made him out to be, there was no need for further due diligence. They wanted a job done, and Sun was the man with the contacts, the experience, the confidence and the gumption to get it done, even though his pragmatic nationalism did not always go down well with the young idealists from the Yangtze valley.[8]

The formation of the Tongmenghui occurred at a time of rising potential for revolution. The Qing regime had been considerably weakened.

There was widespread discontent among the intelligentsia, and the masses were ready for desperate action. There were ample opportunities to incite and exploit outbreaks of violence. But the Alliance never achieved the cohesiveness to threaten the regime. At least in form if not in substance, the Tongmenghui was closer to a political party. In reality, it was far from one, and Sun's authority was about to be constrained by the organization over which he presided but had little control, an organization whose path for several years thereafter would deviate from that of its *zongli*.

Nevertheless, the creation of the Tongmenghui was an important marker in Sun's revolutionary career. It transformed him from a common rebel to a national figure, the respected leader of a political party dominated by intellectual elites. It conferred upon him the status that until then he had only claimed. Moreover, he could now draw on the talent pool within the Alliance wherein were to be found some of the finest theorists, polemicists and strategists. But the shift from the Xingzhonghui to the Tongmenghui did not substantially change Sun's own strategy. He remained focused on foreign aid and *huaqiao* contributions, and he continued to place his hopes on secret society insurrections to "spark an anti-dynastic chain reaction." Indeed, barely two months after the formation of the Tongmenghui, Sun resumed his travels and his search for money and foreign allies, leaving his new lieutenants to launch the ideological battle against Liang Qichao and the reformists, and to exercise authority over the Alliance's members. Scattered far and wide throughout Tokyo, the members interacted mostly with fellow provincials and had little to do with the head office, which was often inactive for long stretches when Sun and other leaders were absent.

On October 7, 1905, Sun took the French steamer *Caledonia* to Saigon by way of Hong Kong. During a brief stopover in Shanghai harbor on October 11, he had a visit from Major Boucabeille, the French intelligence officer who was on a mission to create an intelligence network in southern China. What actually transpired during the eight-hour meeting is unclear. According to Boucabeille's report, he expressed interest in Sun's movement and hinted that his government might "take a certain interest in your endeavors if it can first be demonstrated that your party is a powerful one." To make that determination, Boucabeille offered to place three

French officers at Sun's disposal for a tour of the southern provinces and to meet with anti-dynastic groups in that region. In return, Sun promised that his movement would act as an information service for Boucabeille in southern China. Sun's own account credited Boucabeille with firmer commitment. Boucabeille is said to have presented himself as the representative of the French war ministry with instructions to offer active support to Sun's movement.[9]

Whatever the truth of the matter, Sun organized several intelligence missions between the winter of 1905 and the summer of 1906, and assigned several of his trusted aides to act as guides to Boucabeille's lieutenants. The Frenchmen were soon won over to the revolutionaries' cause and gave a very favorable account of Sun and his movement in their reports. The prospect of French assistance so soon after the formation of the Tongmenghui undoubtedly raised Sun's hopes for a successful revolution in southern China with French support, or at least their benevolent neutrality.

Boucabeille, however, ran up against the hostility of the French minister in Beijing who rejected his lieutenants' reports and refused to have anything to do with Sun. Thus, when in the fall of 1906 the Qing government officially complained about the subversive activities of French officers in southern China, the French authorities quickly disowned Boucabeille, recalled him back to Paris and terminated the intelligence service in China. Sun abandoned a planned uprising scheduled for the fall of 1906 when the Qing government began cracking down on revolutionary groups in the wake of the Boucabeille mission. The government of French Indochina also tightened controls and blocked attempts by a revolutionary group in Yunnan to purchase arms in the French colony. But such repressions and tightening did not dissuade Sun from planning insurrections in southern China. He would try again at the beginning of 1907 when conditions in Guangdong, Guangxi and Yunnan became more favorable to revolutionary agitation.

The *Caledonia* made an overnight stop in Hong Kong on October 16. Sun could not go ashore as the banishment order against him had been extended for another five years following his brief visit in early 1902. Chen Shaobai and several others went on board to meet him. That same afternoon, Sun presided over their oath-taking as the founding members of the

Hong Kong branch of the Tongmenghui. The *Caledonia* with Sun on board departed the following day for Saigon.[10]

Arriving on or about October 22, Sun met with leaders of the radical Chinese community to form a branch of the Tongmenghui in Cholon, the Chinese quarter about 10 miles (16 km) west of Saigon.[11] This organization was no more than a conglomeration of splintered groups that had neither "the unity of purpose or organizational cohesion" to support Sun in his cause.[12] Nevertheless, the formation of the Cholon branch was an important event in the annals of the 1911 Revolution: it was the first branch of Sun's new coalition in Nanyang, a region that would shortly serve as the new pivot for his revolution.

MAP 2

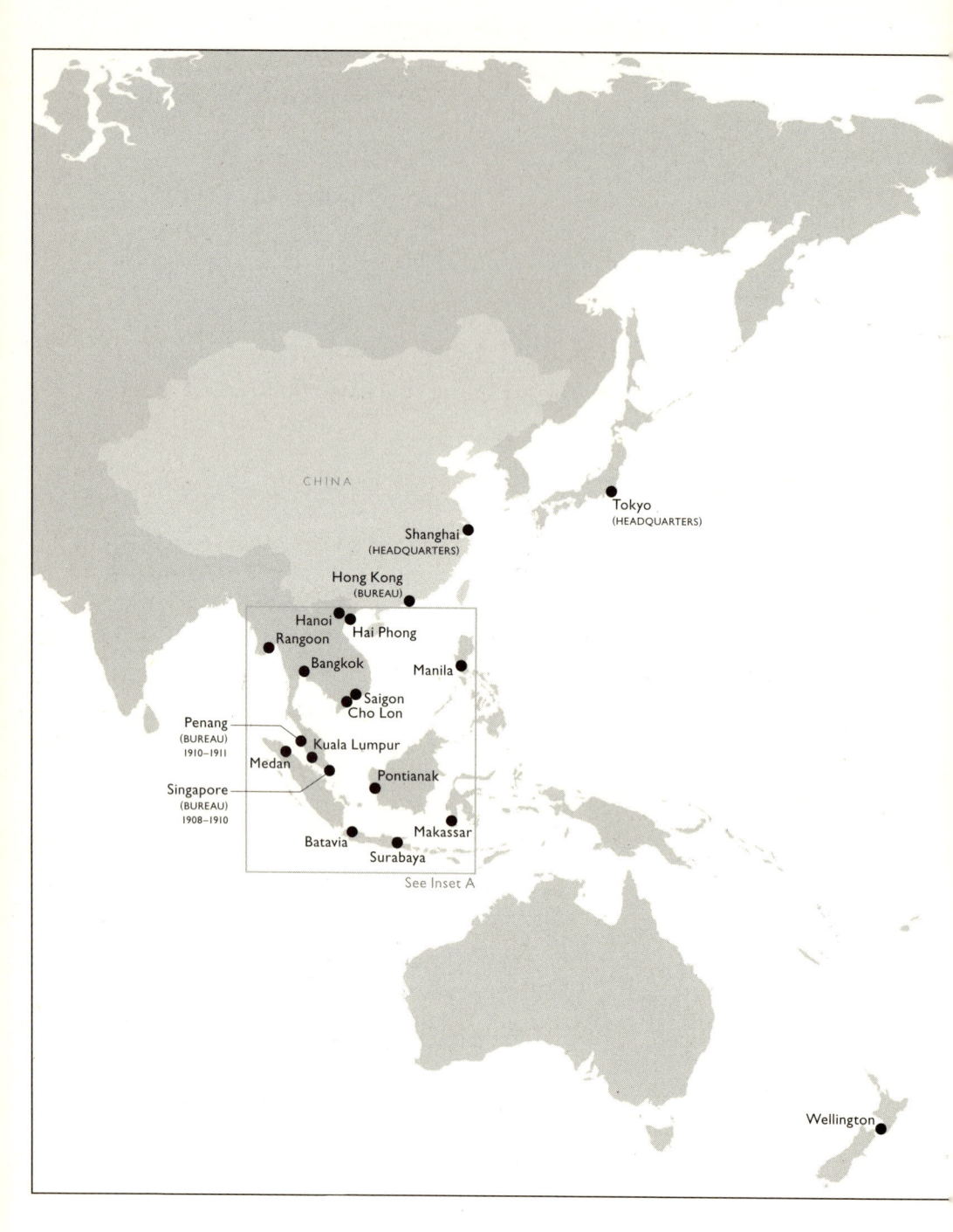

TONGMENGHUI OFFICES

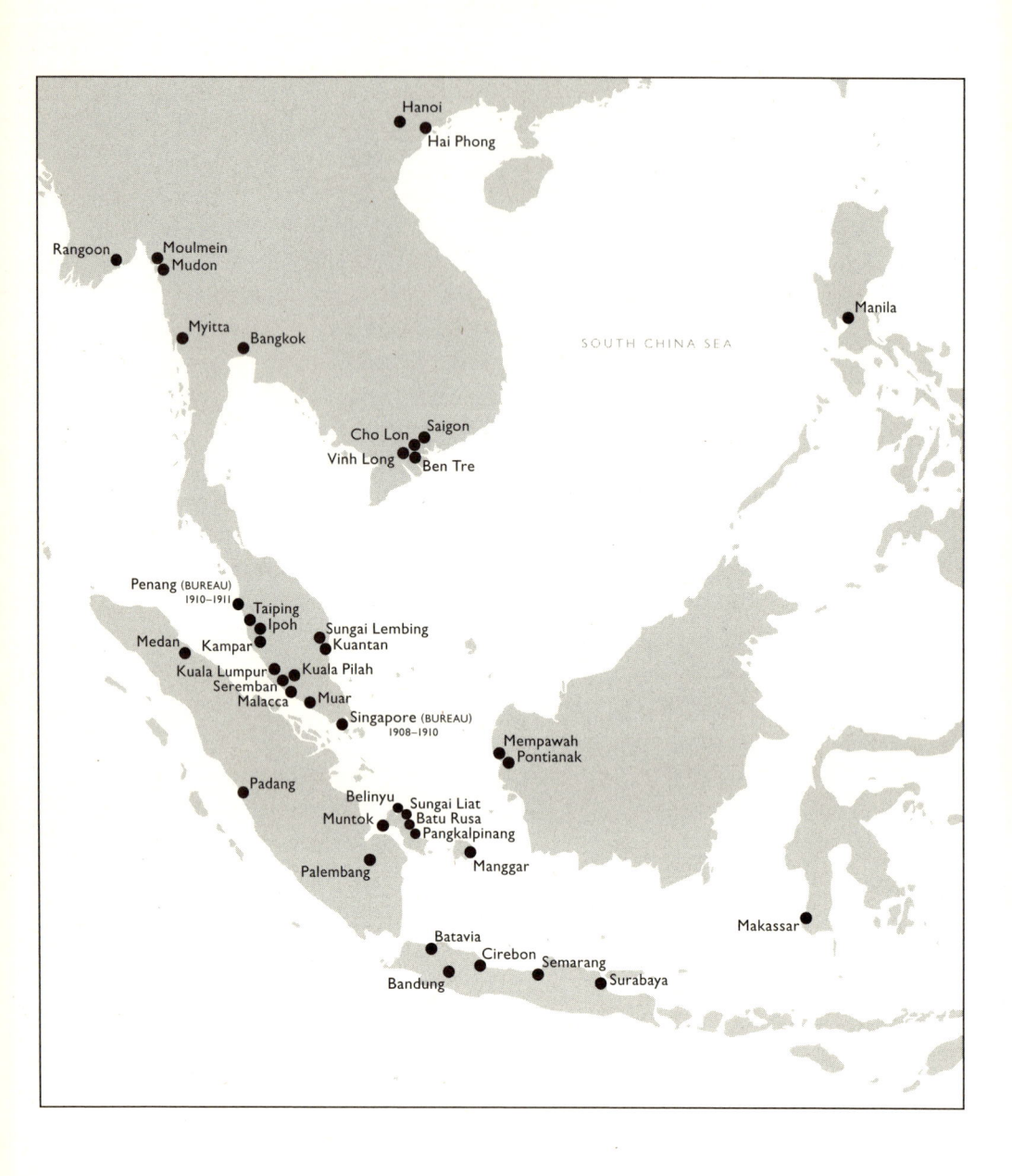

INSET A · TONGMENGHUI OFFICES IN SOUTHEAST ASIA

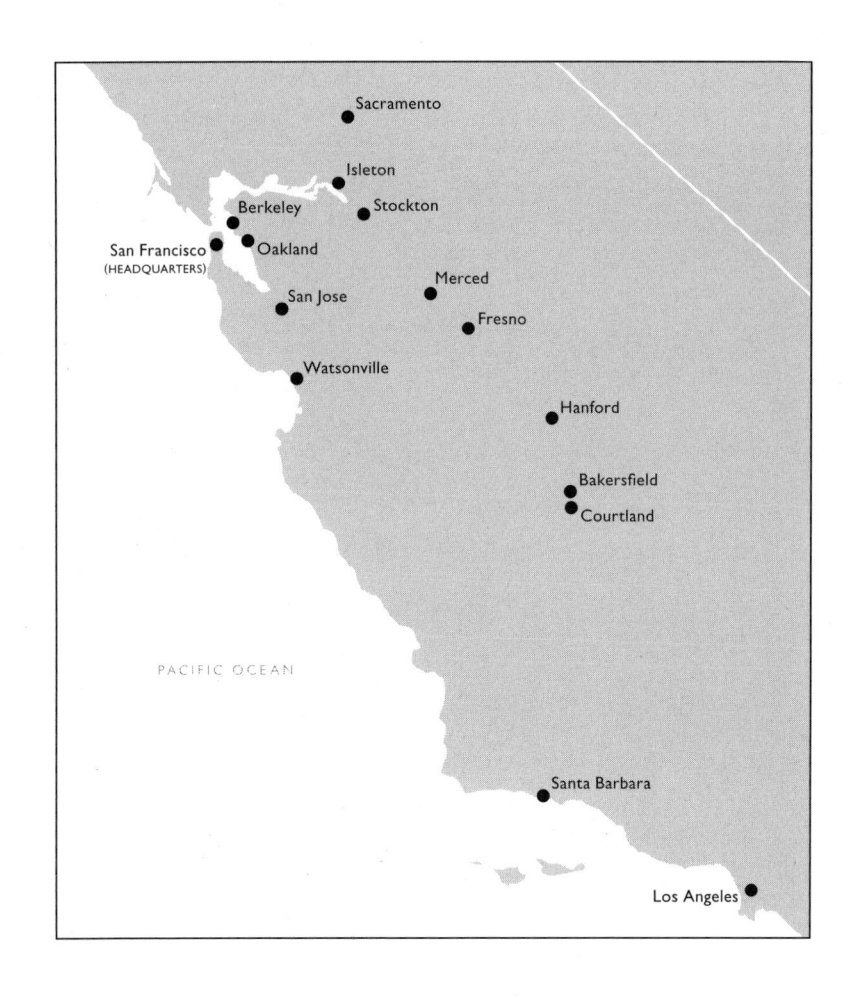

INSET B · TONGMENGHUI OFFICES IN CALIFORNIA

Chapter 7

THE NANYANG PIVOT

THERE HAVE BEEN Chinese communities in Nanyang since at least the beginning of the Yuan dynasty in the 13th century. Going further back, Chinese traders were conducting trade in the region as early as the third century BCE.[1] But it was only with the Manchu conquest of China in 1644 that the first wave of mass migration to Nanyang took place. While the Manchus were able to conquer most of northern China without much of a fight, in central and southern China they faced much greater resistance, and responded to it with cruelty and sometimes massacres. One consequence of these brutalities was to drive many Ming loyalists in the south to take refuge abroad. According to one source, more than 3,000 political refugees fled to Nanyang with their families in nine ships after the fall of the Zheng Chenggong (Koxinga) regime on Taiwan in 1683. Three landed in the Philippines, another three headed for the Dutch East Indies, two sailed for Malacca in Malaya, and one landed in Siam.[2]

Owing to the dearth of women among their numbers, these and earlier immigrants intermarried with local women. Their descendants formed a unique community whose members adopted the language, customs, attire and food of their mothers. Most would have lost their proficiency in Chinese and communicated in the local tongues. In British Malaya and the Dutch East Indies they were known as Chinese *peranakan* ("local born" in Malay), and as Chinese *mestizo* ("half blood" in Spanish) in the Philippines. Prior to the mid-19th century, the small numbers of new immigrants were quickly absorbed into the acculturated community. But as their numbers grew and more women arrived, the new immigrants formed a separate community whose members continued to speak Chinese and retained their Chinese traditions and cultures. These newcomers were called *sin-khek* ("new guest" in Hokkien) in British Malaya, and *totok* ("pure blood" in Malay) in the Dutch East Indies.

The economic and social dislocations caused by the mid-19th-century rebellions sparked a diaspora from southern China. Many set out for Latin America, where several countries were experiencing rapid economic growth. The first great wave of Chinese migration to the United States occurred during the California Gold Rush of the 1850s. Few made lucrative strikes, and most drifted into other lines of work, many in the construction of the transcontinental railroads. After the Civil War, plantation owners lured many Chinese to the South to work fields abandoned by freed black slaves. By 1890, there were Chinese in every state of the American Union.

Migration to Nanyang was easiest and cheapest due to its geographic proximity. Moreover, Western colonization of almost the entire region had opened up economic opportunities for the industrious Chinese. These developments set off an exodus of Chinese migrants to Nanyang so that by 1907 there were close to 7 million Chinese in the region, representing roughly 95 percent of the total overseas Chinese population worldwide: 2.8 million in the Dutch East Indies, 2.7 million in Siam, 1 million in British Malaya, 200,000 in French Indochina, 134,000 in British Burma and 83,000 in American Philippines.[3]

Until the last quarter of the 19th century, the Qing regime had strict laws prohibiting any form of external migration. This changed in 1876 when the court decided to set up consulates abroad to harness the loyalty of its overseas subjects by promoting interest in Chinese culture and education. The first Chinese consulate was established in Singapore in 1877, the same year that the first Chinese legation abroad was set up in London. The consulate's activities were neither political nor anti-British but they changed the attitude of the Singapore *huaqiao* towards China. They began to express their loyalty to the Qing regime, towards which they had hitherto been apathetic at best.

In the closing decade of the century, the Qing court stepped up its efforts to tap the wealth and talent of its overseas subjects in the service of the fatherland. In 1891, the Singapore consulate was elevated to consulate-general. Two years later, the Qing government repealed its anti-migration law, and consulates were established in major *huaqiao* communities around the world. The prestige of the Qing regime rose to its peak but this was badly shaken by China's defeat in the Sino-Japanese War. By then a number of Western countries had also begun adopting exclusion laws against Chinese.[4] There were treaties according Chinese the right to work in those countries, but these treaties proved increasingly difficult to enforce. The inability of the Qing court to protect the rights of its overseas subjects against foreign discrimination gave rise to considerable resentment and ill will towards the dynasty. It was particularly strident in Singapore, where the large reservoir of Chinese migrant workers feared that the British might adopt a similar exclusion policy.[5] During the last years of the century, the Singapore consulate-general put aside its cultural activities and gave priority to raising money for investment in railways and other enterprises in China to reduce her dependency on loans from the West.

Meanwhile, the consulate-general's cultural activities were taken over by a group of Singapore Chinese who had studied in China or the West. The Hundred Day Reform in 1898 met with enthusiastic response from this group of young educated Chinese such as Khoo Seok Wan who started a progressive newspaper, the *Thien Nan Shin Pao*, to support the local Chinese reform movement. After the coup d'état that ended the Hundred Day Reform, Singapore became a fertile field for exiled royalist reformers. Kang Youwei's visit in 1900 aroused considerable interest among the China-born, as well as the China-educated and English-educated *peranakan*.

In the wake of Kang's successful visit to Singapore, the Qing court finally awoke to the importance of their overseas subjects, whose financial support was a safer engine for China's modernization projects than predatory loans from imperialist powers. Their support would also reduce the base of support for dissident groups like the Baohuanghui. The Manchus thus broke with their long tradition of disdain towards *huaqiao* and sent their emissaries abroad to garner as much financial support as possible. This they invariably did by selling official positions and titles to the wealthy *huaqiao*, whose recognition by their home government was the one thing they desired above all else.

Sun first visited Singapore in July 1900, but until 1904, when he came across a copy of *Thoe Lam Jit Poh* in San Francisco, he showed little interest in the island. His presumed banishment was no doubt a factor but he might have felt differently had he known of the group of radical young men across the Johor Straits. In 1897, 18 Chinese youths gathered in the small town of Tangkak in Johor state near the Malacca border to start a movement with the lofty aim of overthrowing the Qing regime and saving China. Calling themselves the "Eighteen Saviors," the group remained an independent movement until 1908 when they were merged into the Malacca branch of the Tongmenghui.[6]

Several leaders of the Huizhou Uprising in October 1900 took refuge in Singapore after it was suppressed. A couple of them had ties with the Triads in southern Guangdong, which maintained close links with the secret societies in Nanyang. Singapore was an important cog in this underground world and her secret societies exerted strong influence over the predominantly Chinese population. The sizable Cantonese community in the colony meant that any Chinese speaking the dialect could easily fit in with little risk of discovery. As a free port under British administration, Singapore's immigration laws were rather lax, which made it relatively easy for anyone to enter and make a living, especially since the colonial government was actively encouraging Chinese immigration by way of Hong Kong and the treaty ports. Singapore was thus an ideal sanctuary for these political refugees. To avoid attention and to enhance their opportunity of contact with the masses, they ran establishments that catered primarily to the poor Chinese. The most prominent of these exiles was Deng Ziyu (Teng Tzu Yu), who was a liaison between the Xingzhonghui and the secret societies in the Huizhou Uprising. In Singapore he owned two hotels which became popular rendezvous for political refugees.[7]

The Huizhou refugees were joined the following year by You Lie, one of Sun's "Four Bandits" comrades. He fled to Yokohama after the abortive Huizhou Uprising, and there founded the Zhonghetang as a workers' recreational club to proselytize revolution among Chinese workers and secret society members. Finding prospects rather limited because of the small Chinese population, he decided to relocate to Singapore. Like his Huizhou comrades, You Lie settled down in Singapore's Chinatown and there set up a clinic specializing in the treatment of venereal diseases. In women-deficit Singapore of the time, his services produced an endless stream of grateful patients. With the help of his secret society friends and people from the lower reaches of society, You Lie established a branch of the Zhonghetang, which soon grew into an impressive network with branches in various parts of peninsular Malaya.

The year 1901 also witnessed the emergence of an indigenous group in Singapore advocating a more radical solution to China's woes. Like the Eighteen Saviors, this group comprised young rich Chinese merchants who were alarmed by China's decline. As an international entrepôt, Singapore was more cosmopolitan than Tangkak, and revolutionary literature published elsewhere was freely available. This Singapore group was thus more in tune with revolutionary ideology and better informed of developments in China. Among the most prominent in this group were the duo behind the *Thoe Lam Jit Poh*, Tan Chor Nam and Teo Eng Hock.[8]

Though their ancestors hailed from different provinces in China and they spoke different dialects, Tan and Teo had much in common. Both were born in Singapore, young and wealthy. Tan's father was a native of Fujian and owned a lumberyard on Beach Road. As a young man, Tan had often heard stories about Zheng Chenggong's heroic resistance against the Manchus in southern Fujian, tales that had nurtured anti-Manchu feelings among the young overseas Chinese. Tan is said to have written several articles under a nom de plume for the reformist *Thien Nan Shin Pao* newspaper that were highly critical of the Qing regime. Teo's father was a Teochew from Guangdong province and owned a textile shop, also on Beach Road. Thirteen years younger than Tan, he was a member of the Chinese Philomathic Society, founded to provide cover and support for reformist activities. In 1899, along with 76 other Chinese in Singapore, he put his signature on a petition against the suspected plot of the empress dowager to force the abdication of the Guangxu Emperor.

Brought up in the Confucian tradition, Tan and Teo were naturally drawn to the reform movement, influenced in no small measure by their close association with Khoo Seok Wan. Neither played a leadership role in the reform movement but were active in promoting the cause. Khoo's defection to the dynasty profoundly affected them but instead of following Khoo's lead, they inclined in the opposite direction, towards the revolutionaries. They were persuaded by the steady growth of revolutionary literature in China at the turn of the century. Prior to 1900, few were published but between 1901 and 1903, the number increased dramatically. A few became bestsellers. Tan and Teo were particularly moved by *Ten Days of Yangzhou*, an eyewitness account of Manchu atrocities during their conquest of China, and Zou Rong's *Revolutionary Army*. Long banned by the Qing government, this was reprinted by the Xingzhonghui office in Yokohama to stir up hatred against the Manchus after the failure of the Guangzhou Uprising in 1895.

The vengeful tone of Zou Rong's tract struck a chord with the duo, whose ancestors' home counties experienced some of the worst atrocities during the Manchu conquest of southern China. They met regularly with their circle of like-minded friends at Xiao Tao Yuan, the Small Peach Garden Club, to vent their anger and frustration against the Manchus. Their political orientation became even more radical after their intercession in the Subao affair in 1903. The Qing authorities had demanded the extradition of Zhang Binglin and Zou Rong to stand trial under Chinese law. Risking deportation by the Straits Settlements government, Tan and Teo cabled the British consul in Shanghai to reject the Qing's extradition demand. This was the first time that any overseas Chinese had taken such a bold action against the Qing government. A few had petitioned for the restoration of the Guangxu Emperor in 1899 but that was done out of loyalty to the emperor. By directly going against the will of the imperial government, they went far beyond that, as Zou Rong and Zhang Binglin were both considered enemies of the state.

Tan Chor Nam and Teo Eng Hock's political metamorphosis reflected the disappointment of the Chinese at home and aboard with both the Qing dynasty and the reform movement. Doubts were already expressed following the house arrest of the Guangxu Emperor after the Hundred Day Reform as to whether the dynasty could reform itself, resist the foreign intrusions and arrest its own decline. Up to that point, the Chinese abhorred the foreign presence but tended to sympathize with the dynasty. After the Boxer Uprising, the exasperation with the empress dowager's rule gave way to disillusionment with the reformists as well.

The revolutionary movement in Singapore took a quantum leap forward in 1903 after the duo met You Lie through the assistant editor of *Thien Nan Shin Pao*. The result was the establishment of *Thoe Lam Jit Poh*. The first issue, which rolled off the press in early 1904, marked the emergence of the revolutionary movement in Singapore from the underground into the open. No local Chinese paper had been so daring before in openly advocating the overthrow of the Qing government. Unlike You Lie's covert activities, which were aimed at members of the secret societies and people from the lower classes, the *Thoe Lam Jit Poh* was meant to appeal to Chinese of all classes. After the launch, it began attacking both the Qing regime and the reformists. Articles advocating revolution were published in the editorial column or reprinted from other revolutionary organs.

The emergence of the *Thoe Lam Jit Poh* brought angry reactions – from the Qing consul-general in Singapore, the conservative merchants who saw themselves as the guardians of Chinese traditions in Singapore, and the reformists who saw it as an affront to their preeminence in the local Chinese community. They demonized the duo as traitors and denounced the newspaper as evil, warning the young not to read it. As a result of these negative pronouncements, the paper's circulation suffered. Some of the staff became disheartened and gave up their posts. The chief editor resigned and Teo Eng Hock had to take over the post despite his lack of qualifications and experience in running a newspaper. After barely two years in circulation, the newspaper ceased operation towards the end of 1905.

It was around this time that Sun arrived in Singapore from Saigon where he had just set up a Tongmenghui branch in Cholon.[9] At a meeting with Tan Chor Nam, Teo Eng Hock and Li Chu Chih, the decision was made to establish a branch of the Tongmenghui in the British colony.[10] After a two-week stay during which he was accommodated at Wanqingyuan, the villa that Teo had purchased for his mother and then renovated for Sun, Sun left for Europe, where he spent the winter and early spring.

Returning to Singapore in late March or early April 1906, Sun gathered 15 of his supporters on April 6 to inaugurate the founding of the Singapore office of the Tongmenghui. During the ceremony at Wanqingyuan, the 15 founding members swore and signed an oath in the presence of Sun undertaking to "work for the expulsion of the Manchus, the restoration of Chinese sovereignty, the establishment of the Republic and the equalization of land rights." Tan Chor Nam was elected chairman, with Teo Eng Hock as his deputy while Teo's nephew Lim Nee Soon was placed in charge of the propaganda department. Of the 15 founding members, ten were wealthy

Sun Yat-sen with members of the Tongmenghui's Singapore branch, at Wanqingyuan villa, circa 1906: *(seated, left to right)* Lin Ganting, Teo Eng Hock, Tan Chor Nam, Sun Yat-sen, You Lie, Lau Kam Seng, Lim Nee Soon; *(standing, left to right)* Goh Ngo Sow, Teo Bah Tan, Zhang Ji, Chan Lui Ho, Deng Ziyu, Wong Yew Ting, and Teo Peng Kay.

or well-to-do merchants. Conspicuously absent from the leadership of the branch were members of the working classes – workers, shop assistants, rickshaw puller, hawkers. This pattern was to persist until the fall of the Qing regime, and conformed to Sun's idea of the roles that various groups would play in the revolution. As he repeatedly spelt out to his supporters, the role of the *huaqiao* was to bankroll the revolution. This led him to focus on the wealthy merchants in the overseas Chinese communities, who were obviously in the best position to provide funds and help in the sale of bonds, a major source of funds for the uprising.

Sun departed Singapore on the *Polynesien* bound for Yokohama on April 9.[11] During his absence, the newly minted members of Tongmenghui Singapore laid the groundwork for setting up branches in peninsular Malaya. Aside from its geographical proximity, there were strong economic, social and kinship ties between the Chinese communities on both sides of the Johor Strait, and across which there were no immigrations formalities to impede the free flow of goods or human traffic. The discovery of tin ore in a few Malayan states in the 19th century had enriched a considerable number of Chinese and more than a few had gone on to amass immense economic power and influence with the Malay rulers and their British overseers. The peninsula was thus the logical next step for the Tongmenghui to extend its footprint.

Sun was accompanied by Hu Hanmin on his return visit to Singapore in July 1906. While Hu stayed on in Singapore to help draft the constitution for the Singapore office, Sun departed on a tour of Seremban, Kuala Lumpur, Ipoh and Penang in peninsular Malaya, with Tan Chor Nam, Lim Nee Soon, Li Chu Chih and others in his entourage.[12] Penang was a port while the others were important mining centers. The predominantly Chinese population in these towns were quite well informed about China's precarious state. Like *huaqiao* elsewhere, they desired a strong and modern China if for no other reason than to enhance their own social standing in their host countries. This would hopefully end the discrimination against them due to perceptions of China as a weak and backward nation. In this regard, the influence of the reformists was clearly evident as many appeared more comfortable with the reformists' gradualism than with Sun's call for radical change.

The first stop was Seremban, the capital of the state of Negeri Sembilan. Arriving on July 17, Sun and his entourage found little enthusiasm for revolution among the Chinese. Yet Sun could not organize a public meeting without alerting the authorities, something they worked assiduously to avoid. Instead they held an informal meeting with a small group of mostly merchants in the Mining Association. While they would have liked to see a resurgent China, their main philosophical difficulty with revolution was the fear of increased foreign aggression and the partition of China. They found Kang Youwei's reform agenda more reassuring. Sun failed to convince these men to establish a Tongmenghui branch but the meeting laid the groundwork for one the following year and another at Kuala Pilah, a small town about 25 miles (40 km) east of the capital.

The Chinese in Kuala Lumpur, the capital of the state of Selangor and of the Federated Malay States[13], were more welcoming, perhaps because of Sun's celebrity status. His abortive Guangzhou uprising in 1895 had been widely reported in the local press, and his kidnap in London made him virtually a household name among the local *huaqiao* community. The favorable reception may also have been due to the remarkable work done by You Lie and Too Nam in proselytizing revolution through the Kuala Lumpur branch of the Zhonghetang. Too Nam, Sun's Chinese tutor in Hawaii, had returned to Malaya and was now giving Chinese tuition to the Protector of the Chinese of the Federated Malay States. Through Too Nam's influence with this British official, Sun was able to obtain a permit to hold a public meeting at the Grand Theatre. In a speech to a packed audience, Sun explained why he sought to overthrow the Manchu regime and replace it with a republic. This was the first time he addressed an audience made up mostly of merchants, traders, shopkeepers and workers with little or no education, a sharp contrast to the kind of audience that he was accustomed to in Japan. He spoke in simple language and made liberal use of analogies to get his points across. A similar meeting was held at the Youth League.

Sun's presentations at both locations showed little of the fiery anti-Manchu rhetoric that had characterized his speeches in Hawaii and the United States. He had been able to speak freely in those places without fear of reprisals from the authorities because he had acquired certification attesting to his Hawaiian birth and permanent resident status. No such latitude was available to him in British territories. Any verbal attack on the Manchus would have antagonized his British host and compromised his mission. If his audience in Kuala Lumpur had expected a hardened criminal, his eloquence and gentlemanly demeanor would have come as a pleasant surprise. This may partly explain his success in setting up a branch in Kuala Lumpur on August 7. Sixteen men signed up on the spot, joined a few days later by another 14. Sun met separately with the legendary tin mining magnate Loke Yew, rumored to be the richest man in British Malaya at the time. Sun's hope of financial contribution to the uprising in southern China that was already in the works fell on deaf ears for the astute businessman showed not the slightest interest in Sun's enterprise.

In Ipoh, Sun and his entourage were threatened with violence. There was a Zhonghetang branch in the town but the influence of its members was no match against the reformists led by Foo Choo Choon, the man the local Chinese called the "Tin King." A corporate raider in the mold of

Andrew Carnegie, Foo had built up a formidable business empire through acquisitions of weaker mines and other businesses. He had close relations with the Qing government. When he found out that Sun and his entourage were staying at the Commercial Bureau of Perak, he sent men to harass them, forcing them to move to a local hotel and backtrack to Kuala Lumpur the next day.

After the harrowing experience in Ipoh, Sun decided to cut short his tour and returned to Singapore. Tan Chor Nam and Teo Eng Hock continued on to Penang with a letter of introduction to Goh Say Eng, a wealthy rice merchant. Goh gave them a hospitable reception and with 21 other merchants formed a Tongmenghui branch in the port town.

In spite of the relative success of the Malayan tour, Loke Yew's lack of interest in the revolution and the reformists' threats in Ipoh disenchanted Sun of his hopes with the wealthy merchants. He realized from the experience that the backbone of the revolution in the *huaqiao* communities would not be the wealthy but people from the lower classes. Most members in the latter groups, however, were illiterate, with only a vague understanding of republicanism. Thus the immediate task ahead, as Sun had foreseen, was to spread the message of revolution to the middle and lower social classes.

Given the Tongmenghui's seditious intent towards the Qing government, with whom the British hoped to maintain cordial relations, the revolutionaries would never have been allowed to operate openly. This left the Tongmenghui with only one option: to operate as a clandestine organization with several types of entities to front its subversive activities. The most important of these were the "reading clubs," which provided reading materials to the public and venues to hold talks and recruit new blood into the Tongmenghui.[14]

The prototype of the reading clubs was the Sin Chew Reading Club in Singapore, co-founded in March 1903 by a Chinese missionary, Cheng Ping Ting. His objective was to provide free newspapers, magazines, books and other materials for young people to improve their literary standards, to arouse their interest in learning, to promote their patriotism toward China, and to win them over to Christianity. The Sin Chew Reading Club had no affiliation with either the reformists or revolutionaries but following Cheng's recruitment, the Tongmenghui gained the use of the Club to front its recruitment drives, proselytize its cause, make newspapers, books and periodicals available, and support other revolutionary activities. The idea proved so successful that reading clubs were established all over the world. Of the more than 100 clubs that were eventually formed, more than half were in Nanyang.

Important as the reading clubs were in spreading propaganda, they did not have the geographical reach of newspapers. After the *Thoe Lam Jit Poh* ceased operations, Tan Chor Nam, Teo Eng Hock and a few merchants started the *Union Times* as a new revolutionary newspaper. This soon fell into the hands of the reformists, who turned it into the organ of the Baohuanghui. At this point, the revolutionary duo started the *Chong Shing Yit Pao*. The inaugural issue was published on August 20, 1907, and until its demise in February 1910, the *Chong Shing Yit Pao* imported revolutionary writings published in Japan, Shanghai and Hong Kong, which were then distributed by Tongmenghui branches in other parts of Nanyang. Zou Rong's *Revolutionary Army* was the perennial favorite but a close second was Chen Tianhua's *Harsh Awakening*. The *Sun Pao*, launched in 1909, became the main revolutionary newspaper in Nanyang after the *Chong Shing Yit Pao*.[15]

Public talks and mass rallies were two important links in the revolutionary propaganda chain in British Malaya due to the low literacy rates in the *huaqiao* communities in Nanyang. They had long been used in Japan, where the overseas Chinese community included a high proportion of students. When the center of revolutionary activity shifted to Nanyang after 1907, public talks and mass rallies became important additions to the Tongmenghui's arsenal. Public talks typically attracted crowds in the hundreds and were usually sponsored by reading clubs. Mass rallies on the other hand, because of the sheer size of the audience and organizational complexity, were usually organized by Tongmenghui branches or the *Chong Shing Yit Pao*. Sun's Three Principles of the People was frequently the subject at public talks and mass rallies, but the only principle preached in British Malaya was nationalism. There were good reasons for this. The majority of the *huaqiao* were illiterate and even the middle-class merchants who had received some private tuition would have found democracy and the concept of people's livelihood somewhat foreign. Moreover, it was easier to find historical examples and simple analogies for nationalism.[16] Another propaganda channel that proved popular with the illiterate masses was drama troupe performances, one of the oldest forms of literary expression and social entertainment since the Song dynasty. During periods under conquest dynasties, it was a means of keeping Han Chinese nationalism alive.[17]

In the two years following Sun's tour of peninsular Malaya, more than ten Tongmenghui branches were established throughout British Malaya. In addition, seven revolutionary newspapers and more than 50 reading clubs were formed between 1907 and 1911. During the same period, branches were also set up throughout Nanyang, a region that had been colonized by one imperialist power or another.[18]

The exception was Siam (now Thailand), which remained an absolute monarchy under an indigenous dynasty until 1932. At the turn of the 20th century, she had the largest overseas Chinese population in the world. Sun first visited Bangkok in 1903. He met with some Chinese tycoons who, like their counterparts in Malaya, were not ready to embrace revolution. On his second visit in 1906, Sun went beyond making personal contact with wealthy Chinese in Bangkok. He established a branch of the Tongmenghui and appointed Seow Hoodseng as branch chairman and put him in charge of fundraising. These were roles for which the Hokkien activist was particularly well suited.[19]

Seow's ancestors were Ming loyalists who retreated to Taiwan after the collapse of the Ming dynasty. When the Zheng Chenggong regime fell and the Manchus gained control of Taiwan, the Seow family fled to Malacca. Five generations later, Seow Hoodseng's father moved to Bangkok, where Seow grew up. His proficiency in classical Chinese gained him the respect of the Chinese community while his facility in the Thai language enabled him to communicate with officialdom. More significantly, as a British subject born in the Straits Settlements, Seow enjoyed extraterritoriality rights in Siam and this gave him much freedom and security. He worked for a time in a distillery after completing his schooling before embarking on a successful career as an attorney. He did not meet Sun in May 1903 but was sufficiently fired up by Sun's ideals to start a Chinese revolutionary newspaper in partnership with a Cantonese intellectual, which soon flopped, however, due to funding difficulties.

Under Seow, Tongmenghui Bangkok adopted a broad-based appeal to the *huaqiao* community for support through *Huaxian Ribao*, a bilingual newspaper, in Chinese and vernacular Thai, which he launched in 1907. His anti-Manchu editorials and articles emphasizing the oppression, corruption and ineffectiveness of Manchu rule gained him a wide readership in the Chinese community and among progressive Thais, but also made enemies of some Chinese and Thais in high places. His tirades were intended not only to rally support from the Chinese community but also to discredit the Baohuanghui's reform movement and to counteract the work of Qing agents who were rallying support for their own modernization projects throughout Nanyang. Seow's aim was to drive home the point that no reform could occur so long as the Qing dynasty remained in power and that all reforms propagandized by the imperial court or Kang Youwei were lies to pacify the Chinese people and forestall the inevitable revolution.

Seow's criticism of absolute monarchy and implication that republicanism was a more modern and rational form of government was problematic in the context of Siam's own political system. In spite of his vehement denials that his comments were not directed at Siam's absolute monarchy, many in high places were not convinced that such a fervent supporter of Chinese republicanism could pay wholehearted allegiance to the Siamese throne. Moreover, much of his writing had also started to influence some Chinese in Siam in a subversive way.

In the same year that he launched the *Huaxian Ribao*, Seow also founded the Bangkok Chinese Club as a front for the Tongmenghui. By late 1908, when Sun made his final visit to Bangkok, the Tongmenghui was already well known for its anti-monarchist agenda among Thai authorities. On December 1, a large crowd turned up to hear Sun speak at the opening of the Chinese Association in Bangkok, another front organization that Seow had set up. In his keynote address Sun made some very critical remarks about absolute monarchy. That speech sent shockwaves through Bangkok. Seow had to apologize to the outraged metropolitan minister who officiated at the grand opening of the Association's new clubhouse. Fearing reprisals by the Qing government, a number of members withdrew from the Association.

Sun delivered an even more aggressive and rousing speech to another large gathering in Bangkok's Chinatown. Calling for the overthrow of the

Manchu dynasty and the establishment of a republic in China, he concluded it with the usual appeal for financial contributions. The speech succeeded in fanning Chinese public opinion against the Qing regime. Many cut off their queues to renounce their allegiance to the Manchus. Many more donated generously to the cause. These two speeches finally breached the limit of the Siamese authorities' patience, and Sun was politely asked to leave the kingdom for good. Seow Hoodseng and the revolutionary movement in Siam were seriously compromised by the incident.

In the two years following Sun's expulsion from Siam, strikes and protests became a popular expression of discontent in Bangkok's Chinatown. In 1910, Chinese secret societies organized a labor strike to protest a tax increase on the *huaqiao* in Siam. This was the biggest and most serious labor unrest in the history of modern Thailand and brought Bangkok and every major city in the country to a standstill for three days. It failed to attain its goal but revealed the power of the *huaqiao* over the Siamese economy and their ability to express their demands in a way never before experienced in Siam. Barely two years after the Chinese Strike of 1910, a revolutionary plot to assassinate the Thai king and establish a republic was foiled. Some of the ringleaders were found to have been heavily influenced by the Chinese revolutionary movement and Seow's writings on republicanism. In the end, Sun's visits to Bangkok, the establishment of the Tongmenghui branch, Seow's journalistic propaganda and the proliferation of local Chinese-language revolutionary newspapers may have done less in promoting the cause of the Chinese revolution than in provoking political unrest in Siam.[20]

It was because of this fear of the Chinese revolutionaries' potential to provoke political unrest that the colonial authorities in the Dutch East Indies never granted Sun a permit to visit. Kang Youwei, on the other hand, was allowed to travel freely throughout the Indies in 1903. He got in touch with the Chinese communities and set up a number of Chinese schools. This was not because the Dutch were partial towards the reformists, whom they tolerated, but because the colonial government was fearful that the spread of revolutionary propaganda would lead to Chinese nationalism and its destabilizing effect among the Indies Chinese. A number of Chinese revolutionary journalists, for instance, were deported for writing seditious articles. Sun's contacts with the *huaqiao* in the Dutch colony were thus made through the branch in Batavia (now Jakarta), which was set up in the spring of 1907 by two Tongmenghui members from Singapore. To avoid alerting the Dutch colonial government to its existence and activities, the branch adopted the name Jinan She, or Southern Sojourner's Club.[21]

Following the Singapore model, the Jinan She established reading clubs throughout the Dutch East Indies. They were typically located in Chinese schools and adopted the name of the host school. This was a necessary precaution; the Jinan She was a clandestine organization and conducting its activities openly would only invite intervention by the Dutch colonial authorities. The first reading room was in Batavia but most of the others were located in Surabaya and the Outer Islands. These were the centers of the *totok*, the new Chinese immigrants, who found revolution more appealing than the Chinese *peranakan*, who could no longer speak Chinese. At least 52 reading clubs were established by 1911, most of which were under the charge of revolutionaries from Singapore rather than local *huaqiao* communities. Newspapers were widely used by the Indies revolutionaries to proselytize their cause but more importantly to raise funds for the various uprisings in China. There were at least five newspapers, though all were short-lived due to the low literacy rate among the Chinese and the negative attitude of the Dutch towards the revolutionaries and their activities.

The attitude of the Dutch only partially explains the early success of the reformists vis-à-vis the revolutionaries. The other reason was the nature of Chinese society in the Indies. Until towards the end of the 19th century, most of the Chinese in the Indies were *peranakan*, families that had settled for generations. They tended to be more concerned with local affairs. Many of their elites were officers appointed by the colonial government and so were loyal to the Dutch. Their main concern was their own prestige and power in the local community. They were wooed by the Qing regime, bestowed imperial titles and encouraged to invest in China. In turn, their association with the Qing government gained them more respect in the *peranakan* community. The *peranakan* were also sympathetic to the reformists. There was at the time a pan-Chinese reform movement in Java initiated by the *peranakan* elites to improve the local Chinese condition and the education of their children. Initially this reform movement took the form of Confucian revivalism. They had contacts with the Confucianists in Singapore, mainly through Dr. Lim Boon Keng, who also advocated the teaching of Confucianism. The *totok* on the other hand were sojourners rather than settlers. They regarded the Indies as a place to make money before returning home to China. They spoke Chinese, observed Chinese customs and tended to be more China-oriented. Chinese nationalism thus meant more to them than to the *peranakan*, and so they were more sympathetic to the revolutionaries.

The Chinese revolutionary movement developed rapidly with the support of the *totok* Chinese. The preferred destination of new Chinese immigrants was the Outer Islands, and it was there that revolutionary activities were particularly active. Another center of unusual revolutionary activity was Surabaya. Confucian revivalism in China began around 1895 as an integral part of the reform movement led by Kang Youwei. At the height of the Hundred Day Reform in 1898, Kang wrote a memorial to the Guangxu Emperor to make Confucianism the state creed, establish Confucian temples and base the national calendar on Confucius' birthday. Kang failed to convince the emperor, who in any event did not have the political power to implement the proposal.[22] There were similar attempts in Batavia and British Malaya to revive Confucianism but the use of the Confucian calendar did not take root before the establishment of the Chinese republic in 1911. In Surabaya, on the other hand, some Chinese scholars and merchants had initiated the use of the Confucian calendar in the early 1880s. In 1889, they converted an existing temple into one dedicated to Confucius, taking the name Wen Miao, Temple of Confucius.[23]

The erection of the Wen Miao was the result of a long process of re-sinicization that began in Surabaya in the mid-19th century. In the first phase, the reformers tried to reverse the trend towards "peranakanization," or the acculturation of the Chinese into local society, by reviving Chinese customs at the family level. The second phase was the revival of Confucianism to spread Chinese education and culture, and to strengthen their ties to the fatherland at a time when the empire was crumbling. The third and last phase was the dissemination of revolutionary ideas to overthrow the Manchus. Beyond the cult dedicated to Confucius, the Wen Miao was the venue of an intense political life animated by reformers as well as revolutionaries who found it convenient to work with the Confucian cult.

The list of Wen Miao donors engraved on a tablet shows a number of merchants. Many were reformers but there were also those who supported the Tongmenghui, Guangfuhui and Zhonghetang. Tao Chengzhang, who led the smear campaign against Sun, fled to the Dutch East Indies in 1907, first to Bangka and then to Surabaya. With the help of the Hongmen secret society, he recruited several brothers from the Tjio family to join the Guangfuhui. The Tjios were a large family in Surabaya that originated in the village of Shudou in Quanzhou, Fujian province. They owned a dozen businesses located in the Kapasan quarter with names all starting with "Hup," meaning "united." But the family was anything but united where politics was concerned. An eminent member of the family, Tjio Poo Liauw, was known as a reformer but he was also the treasurer of the Tongmenghui. Another family member, Tjio Poo Tjhat, the principal of the firm of Hup Thye, supported Sun's movement but did not join the Tongmenghui or any political organizations.[24]

The revolutionaries in Surabaya were different from their Singapore counterparts in one respect. In Singapore, the revolutionaries started as a covert operation but emerged into the open with the launch of the *Thoe Lam Jit Poh* in 1904. In Surabaya, government suppression obliged the revolutionaries to remain underground. They associated with the reformists using the Wen Miao as a cover to promote revolution. It is not known if the reformists were aware of the revolutionaries in their midst.

With a Chinese population less than a fifth of British Malaya, Burma (now Myanmar), under British rule since 1886, does not appear to have been a priority for Sun. There is no evidence that he ever visited the country or indeed expressed any plan to do so. Nevertheless, a branch was established in the Burmese capital of Rangoon (now Yangon) when Lim Nee Soon and another Tongmenghui member from Singapore visited in December 1908 to raise funds for the *Chong Shing Yit Pao*.[25]

By the end of 1908, the Tongmenghui had a presence in every country in Nanyang except the Philippines. It was only on the eve of the 1911 Revolution that a branch was finally set up in Manila. This is ironic considering that the Philippines was the first country in Nanyang that Sun had any contacts. We already know that in 1899 he had volunteered to intermediate an arms deal between Japanese pan-Asianists and the Filipino independence movement in the hope of using the Philippines as a staging point for uprisings in China. When this failed, the head of the Philippines independence movement, Emilio Aguinaldo, gave Sun 100,000 yen through Mario Ponce as a gesture of gratitude and support to the Chinese revolutionary cause. What is less well publicized is the offer that Aguinaldo made to send soldiers to help Sun's armed struggle after the Philippines gained its independence. So in the case of the Philippines, it was not just ethnic Chinese but native Filipinos, too, who found common cause with the Chinese revolutionaries. Interestingly, one of Sun's professors at the College of Medicine in Hong Kong was a Filipino, Dr. Lorenzo Pereira Marques. His next-door neighbor at Rednaxela Terrace[26] was Dr. Jose Rizal, the Filipino revolutionary leader who had practiced medicine in Hong Kong in 1891 and 1892. There is no evidence that Sun ever met Rizal, but he would have been familiar with the latter's work and ideals.[27]

Why did the revolutionaries wait until 1911 to set up a Tongmenghui branch in the Philippines in view of her special place in Sun's orbit? There are several plausible reasons. A Baohuanghui branch had been established in the Philippines in 1899 followed by the launching of two local Chinese newspapers to serve as its organ. Close on the heels of the reformists were the Qing emissaries who began visiting the Philippines at the turn of the century. Through their propaganda machineries, they warned the local Chinese of reprisals against family members in China if they supported the revolution against the dynasty. The Filipino *huaqiao* took these warnings seriously and consequently were reluctant to support the revolutionary movement. Another possible reason was the strict enforcement of the U.S. Chinese Exclusion Law prohibiting ethnic Chinese from entering the United States and her territories, of which the Philippines was one. This made it difficult for Chinese revolutionaries to travel to the Philippines.

This is not to say that there was no Chinese revolutionary activity in the Philippines before the establishment of a Tongmenghui branch. Indeed, a nascent movement had begun to develop a decade earlier with the arrival of Dr. Tee Han Kee to take up an appointment as medical inspector with the Philippines Health Service in 1901. A native of Fujian province, Tee was a contemporary and friend of Sun at the College of Medicine in Hong Kong. Regarded as one of the early modernizers among the Chinese in the Philippines, his criticisms of the Manchu dynasty and the imperial institution laid the groundwork for the revolutionary movement in the American territory. As early as 1903, Chinese revolutionary publications such as Zou Rong's *Revolutionary Army* were already being distributed among the Chinese communities in the Philippines. Later, other revolutionary publications from Hong Kong and the Tongmenghui's own *Minbao* also found their way among the Filipino Chinese. The Chinese revolutionary movement took a further step forward in 1909 with the establishment of a reading club in Cavite, which was later moved to Manila. Other branches followed suit in various parts of the islands. Books, magazines and newspapers were made available to disseminate revolutionary ideas to members.

The support for Sun's movement by the Filipino *huaqiao* did not go unnoticed. *CableNews-American* reported on March 12, 1908: "The Manila Chinese ... are in rebellion against the constituted authorities of China ... spending thousands on the rifles and ammunitions which equip the troops now in the field against the government ... It was their money that brought the guns seized on the *Tatsu Maru* ... for attempting to smuggle a quantity of arms and ammunitions into the hands of Chinese revolutionists ... and which paid for a dozen similar cargoes brought in Japan with the connivance of the Japanese government."[28] Three more years would pass before Li Zhi from Tongmenghui Hong Kong arrived in Manila in the spring of 1911 to set up the party structure and launch a newspaper, *Kong Li Pao*, to serve its propaganda needs. In recognition of his pioneering role in the local revolutionary movement, Tee Han Kee was elected chairman of the Manila chapter of the Tongmenghui.

SUN YAT-SEN HAD very definite ideas about the roles that particular social groups would play in his revolution. Just as he depended on the secret societies to provide the muscles for armed uprisings, and on the intellectuals to set up the republic, the part he assigned to the Chinese overseas was to bankroll the revolution. In this regard, he considered it natural to target the wealthiest of them. Indeed, fundraising was Sun's principal occupation and preoccupation for most of his revolutionary career. He was constantly on the move during his 16 years of exile from 1895 until 1911, in search of money and exercising the utmost ingenuity in acquiring it. It was discouraging work, however. Often he would acquire only enough money to cover the expense of his travel to the next stop.

The most important sources of funds were donations, loans and proceeds from the sale of "patriotic bonds." The distinction between them was somewhat artificial. The Chinese often make gifts in the guise of loans with no expectation of repayment as a way to save the face of the beneficiary. The bonds were essentially promissory notes to repay the purchaser many times his investment after the establishment of a republican government. Most of the purchasers of these bonds probably knew of their speculative nature, but the Chinese, well-known for their risk-taking capacity, were apparently willing to bet on the long shot.

During the Xingzhonghui period, the main sources of funds were the Chinese in Hawaii, Hong Kong and Japan. After the formation of the Tongmenghui in 1905, Sun's financial targets became more ambitious. He and his associates established offices throughout Nanyang to cultivate the *huaqiao* in the region and tap their wealth. However, until 1909 they faced stiff competition from the more respectable Baohuanghui. With its stronger network of newspapers and more solid support among the wealthy in the Chinese communities, the Baohuanghui probably raised more money than the Tongmenghui ever did in Nanyang and elsewhere.

Sun's initial targets in Nanyang were the wealthy merchants. He soon discovered that they were not an easy lot to convince, especially those with businesses or investments in China. Few among them were willing to compromise their businesses by engaging in activities against the interests of the Qing regime, from whom some wealthy merchants had also purchased titles and official posts. These honors allowed them to claim legitimacy for their leadership positions in the local Chinese community. It was in their interests to maintain the status quo and it made more sense for them to support reform and constitutional monarchy. A few wealthy individuals helped, but for the most part they were not a significant source of funds until the outbreak of the Wuchang Uprising.

The main contributors in Nanyang to Sun's cause were people from the middle and laboring classes. These were people with little or no formal education, who had left their homeland in search of opportunities in Nanyang to better themselves and support their families back home. With no political or economic links with the Qing regime, these simple and humble folk were less inhibited in giving full expression to their anti-Manchu sentiments. From their meager income, they gave Sun his strongest financial support. This partly explains why the Tongmenghui branches in Nanyang placed so much emphasis on the establishment of reading clubs, the organization of public talks and the staging of drama performances.

Sun used much the same arguments to convince the common folk of Nanyang to part with their hard-earned money as he had with *huaqiao* elsewhere. He appealed to their patriotism and their sense of being Chinese. His call to drive out the Manchu barbarians resonated well with the men from Fujian and Guangdong, where there was a long tradition of hatred and resistance against the Manchus. Another appeal to patriotism was the promise of a glorious and modern China. To migrants who had tried to escape poverty in China, prosperity and modernity were strongly appealing. In Siam, they saw a modernizing Asian country. Elsewhere in Nanyang, they saw Western colonial administrations making material improvements and creating a climate conducive to business. To these Chinese, Sun held out the hope that with the establishment of a republic and the elimination of corrupt and antiquated bureaucrats, China would enter the modern world of the Western powers. Sun also played on the wounded pride of the migrant Chinese, emphasizing the humiliation of being second-class subjects in Western colonies. He reminded them that the Manchu government could not protect them and promised that a new republican Chinese government would. No less important was Sun's charisma and his ability to identify himself with his audiences. By most accounts, he is said to have had a magnetic personality and his manner exuded sincerity and commitment. He spoke as one who had the inside track on the life of an overseas Chinese, who had acquired both a Western as well as a Chinese education.[29]

If the appeal to patriotism was not sufficient, sweeteners were sometimes used to add allure. A common incentive was the promise of special privileges or honors after the establishment of the republic: guaranteed citizenship, business preferences and the naming of public landmarks after the donor.

Following his abortive appeal in 1906 to Loke Yew, the tin mining magnate from Kuala Lumpur, Sun made several more attempts. In 1908, after his exile from Indochina and in desperate need of funds for another uprising in Yunnan, he urged his friend Teng Tse Ju to persuade Loke to save the situation. In exchange for a donation of S$100,000, Loke would be given monopoly rights to all the mineral resources of Yunnan for ten years. This, too, failed to move the multimillionaire.[30] There was also a plan to establish a Chinese industrial company in San Francisco. It was to be capitalized at US$1 million through the issue of 10,000 shares at US$100 each. Sun held out the prospect that the company would enjoy monopoly rights in China for ten years. It does not appear that there were any takers.[31]

While much is known about Sun's modus operandi and the people he worked with, the Tongmenghui's records are too fragmentary to allow more than an episodic snapshot of the financial contributions of the *huaqiao*. Inevitably many records were lost, others deliberately destroyed, and not all benefactors wished to have their names associated with a clandestine organization. Moreover, funds were raised by various individuals in different countries and there was no central organization responsible for record-keeping. Nevertheless, a number of studies exist which attempt to bring some coherence to the Tongmenghui's financial efforts.

Between May 1907 and April 1908, the Tongmenghui staged six uprisings in Guangdong, Guangxi and Yunnan. One study estimates that of the HK$300,000 raised for these revolts from the overseas Chinese, a third came from British Malaya. Another study shows that the first of these revolts, the Huanggang Uprising in May 1907, was entirely planned in Singapore. The cost of this operation and the aborted second uprising in Chaozhou, to the tune of about S$50,000, was raised entirely from the *huaqiao* in the British colony.[32] The last and most significant uprising under the Tongmenghui banner was the Huanghuagang Uprising in Guangzhou in April 1911. Over 20 percent of the HK$200,000 raised for it was from British Malaya, with another 30 percent from Dutch East Indies, French Indochina and Siam. In other words, more than half came from Nanyang.[33]

In the months following the Wuchang Uprising in 1911, HK$2.4 million is estimated to have poured in from *huaqiao* communities in many parts of the world. Over a third was from British Malaya, and two-thirds of this was remitted to the revolutionary provincial governments that had been set up in Guangdong, Fujian and Shanghai. These governments were in dire need of funds to consolidate their positions and to maintain law and order. It was particularly crucial in the case of Shanghai. With the fall of this global city, the revolutionaries gained control of the telecommunications network for all China, encouraged the Qing navy to defect to the revolutionary camp and paved the way for the capture of the strategic city of Nanjing. These events possibly changed the course of the revolution.[34]

Incomplete as these numbers are, they show nevertheless that the overseas Chinese in Nanyang, British Malaya in particular, played an important role in the success of the 1911 Revolution. The importance of the Nanyang *huaqiao* can also be gleaned from the fact that of the 102 Tongmenghui branches established worldwide, 59 were in Nanyang, and of the more than 100 reading clubs, more than half were in British Malaya.[35]

What the numbers do not show are the expenses incurred by the Chinese in Singapore as the regional headquarters and center of revolutionary activities in Nanyang. A good deal of money was spent on headquarters administrative expenses and the dispatch of missions to set up and visit the various branches in Nanyang. Settling the refugees, accommodating them and providing them with jobs incurred a good deal of money too. Singapore also had to contribute towards the maintenance of the *Chong Shing Yit Pao* and other newspapers. If these sums are included, the paramount position of Singapore within the Nanyang region becomes obvious.

Sun's principal source of funds during the Xingzhonghui period had been his brother Sun Mei and the *huaqiao* in Hawaii and Japan. In 1906, Sun Mei lost his wealth as a result of new American land regulations and could no longer act as the movement's main financial benefactor. In August 1906, he was finally adjudicated a bankrupt. With Sun Mei's move to Hong Kong the following year, Sun also lost his principal fundraiser in the Islands. The establishment of the Tongmenghui Singapore office in April 1906 was fortuitous. Just how fortuitous would be revealed as Sun embarked on a new chapter in his revolutionary career.

Chapter 8

BATTLE CRIES FOR A REPUBLIC

JAPAN'S VICTORY in the Russo-Japanese War launched her into the major league of the global political order. Now that she belonged to the imperialist camp and could use her great power status to join in the slicing of the Chinese melon, Japan no longer felt the need to support intrigues in China, whose revolutionaries' ties to Japan's own anarchists were in any event already beginning to prove vexatious. Moreover, Japan's own military and conservative factions were starting to fear that Chinese republicanism might infect the Japanese spirit and their reverence for the emperor. The Japanese government, which had been hounding Chinese student activists since late 1905, took more drastic steps in 1907. In February, it expelled 39 Chinese students from Waseda University, a pioneer in the spreading of modern liberal ideas, and other institutions. Under pressure from the Qing government, it gave Sun the same treatment later in the month.

The pretext for Sun's expulsion was a speech that he had given in Tokyo the previous month. According to Kokuryukai sources, Sun hinted that since the anti-Manchu revolution was to secure China's revival, he would have no objection if Japan, in return for her help, felt that she deserved territory north of Changchun in Manchuria. The Qing government claimed otherwise, that Sun's speech was a particularly aggressive presentation of the Three Principles of the People with strong anti-Manchu overtones. Whichever the case, Sun's speech attracted sufficient attention for the Qing government to press its Japanese counterpart for Sun's expulsion.

Sun's friend Uchida Ryohei convinced Prince Ito Hirobumi, Japan's first prime minister and now a senior statesman, to allow Sun to leave with dignity and to keep on good terms with the Chinese revolutionary. The Foreign Ministry was in complete agreement with Uchida and also concurred that Sun should be allowed to return in three or four years. An elaborate farewell dinner was held in Sun's honor and he was presented with 60,000 yen as a farewell gift from the Foreign Ministry through Uchida. Miyazaki Torazo and his group were indignant at their government's myopia in evicting Sun, while a Tokyo broker felt so strongly about the action that he gave Sun another 10,000 yen from his own resources.

The Japanese banishment order against Sun was published in the *Singapore Free Press* of March 6, 1907, which also reported that he was on his way to the colony. It was a brief stopover, however. His final destination was Hanoi, where through the connivance of certain French interests, he was to operate for about a year. His plan was to launch a series of revolts across the Indochinese border into Yunnan, Guangxi and western Guangdong. These planned uprisings were tied in to a minor peasant revolt that had broken out in the spring in Qinzhou, close to the Indochinese border and easily accessible from Hanoi. The revolt grew out of local sugar growers' protests against the imposition of an additional tax on their production.[1] Two military commanders, reportedly sympathetic to the revolutionaries, were dispatched by the Guangdong provincial government to suppress it. General Guo Renzhang, a personal friend of Huang Xing, commanded two infantry battalions in Qinzhou. He seemed quite receptive to Huang Xing's suggestion to revolt against the Manchus but was reluctant to act on his own. Guo's colleague Colonel Zhao Sheng was in command of one infantry battalion and one battery of artillery in neighboring Lianzhou. Zhao had joined the Guangdong New Army after his discharge from the Jiangsu New Army for promoting revolution among his troops, and joined the Tongmenghui shortly after he was promoted to the rank of regimental commander.[2] Sun would position himself to take advantage of this unstable situation. In western Guangdong, he would form an alliance of revolutionaries, peasant rebels and the two military commanders to take over the area. He would simultaneously launch coordinated revolts in other parts of the province. Once all of Guangdong was under the control of the revolutionaries, sympathetic uprisings would follow in the rest of the country. That at least was what Sun hoped would happen.

Arriving in Singapore on March 18, Sun met with his Teochew supporters to discuss the final details of two proposed uprisings in Chaozhou, the origins of which predated the founding of the Tongmenghui. The idea had begun in 1904 with a proposal from Lin Shouzhi (Lim Shou Chih). A key member of Tongmenghui Singapore, Lin grew up in China and developed revolutionary sympathies probably after meeting Chen Shaobai in Hong Kong in 1894. The following year, Lin joined his father in Singapore, and when the latter died in 1904, he was left with a considerable fortune. In escorting his father's coffin back to China for burial, he proposed to Tan Chor Nam and Teo Eng Hock that he set up a clandestine revolutionary cell in his home prefecture of Chaozhou.

Accompanying Lin on the journey to Chaozhou was Huang Naishang, who was tasked with distributing copies of Zou Rong's *Revolutionary Army*. The father-in-law of Dr. Lim Boon Keng, who had helped Sun to secure the release of his Japanese friends in 1900, Huang was born in Fujian province, converted to Christianity at the age of 18, and obtained his *juren* degree at the relatively late age of 46. His attention was then diverted to the political unrest and foreign invasion of China. A classmate of Khoo Seok Wan, who was rumored to have contributed S$250,000 to the Baohuanghui, Huang became involved with the reform movement. But after meeting Sun in 1900, he began to waver in his conviction. The Boxer Uprising and the bitter experience he had with the British colonial government over the sale of opium in Sibu, which he founded between 1900 and 1902, may have caused him to turn toward revolution. When he returned to Singapore from Sibu in 1902, he was firmly in the revolutionary camp.[3]

With the help of another friend, Xu Xueqiu (Koh Soh Chew), who would later play a key role in the two Chaozhou uprisings, Lin and Huang set up an organization pledging itself to the overthrow of the Manchus and the restoration of Chinese rule. Centered in Hongan village in Haiyang county (now Chao'an district), branches were formed throughout the county. The local secret societies responded positively to their call, and it was then that Lin began planning the two Chaozhou uprisings with Xu, who had attempted an uprising in Chaozhou in April 1905. When that was aborted, he went to Singapore, where in June 1906 he met Sun and was persuaded to join the Tongmenghui and to make another attempt in eastern Guangdong. Xu had originally planned an armed attack on Chaozhou with a secret society force on February 19, 1907, during the Chinese New

Year holidays. It was postponed at the last minute, either because of bad weather or indecision. Sun urged him to coordinate it with the uprisings being planned in other parts of Guangdong. Xu accordingly went to Hong Kong to await instruction from Sun in Hanoi.[4]

Sun's master plan for a series of coordinated uprisings soon began misfiring one after another. On May 12, while Sun's agent from the Haiphong branch of the Tongmenghui was negotiating with the Qinzhou tax rebels, troops led by Guo Renzhang and Zhao Sheng, unaware of Sun's intentions with respect to the tax rebels, attacked and captured the rebel stronghold. The death of the rebel leader and the suppression of the tax rebels dashed Sun's hopes for an immediate takeover of Qinzhou.[5]

Meanwhile, the secret society members recruited by Xu Xueqiu for the Chaozhou revolt had gathered in the vicinity of Huanggang, a walled town on the coastal road to Fujian. Their activities aroused the suspicion of the Chaozhou brigadier-general, who sent out a patrol to investigate and detained suspects. The secret society leaders on the spot warned Xu in Hong Kong that the situation in Huanggang was becoming tense but were merely told to avoid a confrontation at all costs. Ignoring the instruction, the rebels decided to make a preemptive attack. On the night of May 22, a rebel force attacked the small garrison of government troops at Huanggang. By dawn they had captured the town and immediately issued proclamations in Sun's name urging the local people to remain calm and the merchants to go about their business as usual, while assuring the missionaries and their Chinese converts that they would not be harassed. For the next two days, the rebels stayed put in the town to await instructions and reinforcements from Hong Kong.

The Tongmenghui office in the colony did not learn of the uprising until it was too late. Xu rushed to Huanggang but got no further than Shantou. On May 25, government reinforcements landed on the coast 10 miles (16 km) away. Better armed than the rebels, who were equipped with old-fashioned rifles and muskets, they drove the insurgents to the hills. On May 27, Huanggang was recaptured by government troops. Unlike the rebels, who had maintained order and discipline, and molested neither foreign missionaries nor their converts during their five-day occupation of the town, the victorious Qing troops looted and destroyed property. Over 100 secret society members whose names appeared on a captured membership list were slaughtered.

According to Sun's master plan, Deng Ziyu, a veteran of the failed Huizhou Uprising of 1900 who had taken refuge in Singapore, was supposed to organize a revolt in his native region in the lower East River valley of central Guangdong with the support of his connections in the secret societies. When the Huanggang revolt broke out, Sun had just arrived in Hong Kong from Singapore. As soon as he learned of the uprising, he dispatched emissaries among the secret society lodges to incite them to rebel while Deng remained in Hong Kong to buy arms and ammunitions. Like Xu, Deng missed the uprising entirely but his agents managed to put together a secret society force.[6]

On June 2, six days after the revolt at Huanggang was crushed, this force overran the Qing garrison at Qinuhu, a market town less than 10 miles (16 km) from Huizhou, the site of Sun's 1900 uprising. Over the next week, they raided a number of other market towns along the East River and one of its tributaries, avoiding better defended places and refraining from attacking the prefectural capital. Like their Huanggang comrades, the rebels behaved commendably and indeed were welcomed with firecrackers by the villagers. But unlike their Huanggang counterparts, they did not publicly acknowledge their association with the Tongmenghui. The proclamation they issued was cast in traditional secret society terms, calling for the expulsion of the barbarians and the restoration of the Ming dynasty. When better equipped government troops finally arrived to reinforce the local troops, the rebels gave up the fight, particularly since there were no supporting uprisings elsewhere in the area.

On June 11, as the Qinuhu revolt was on the verge of collapse, there was a botched attempt to assassinate Brigadier-General Li Qun, who was fast becoming the dominant figure in Guangdong. The assassination was likely a revenge for his part in suppressing the Huanggang and Qinuhu uprisings. Liu Xifu, a founding member of the Tokyo Tongmenghui, volunteered for the mission. Assisting him were three other Tongmenghui members. Liu's plan was to assassinate Li Qun as he left the governor-general's compound on June 11. While assembling his bombs, one of them accidentally exploded, blowing off his hand. One of his assistants and a doctor succeeded in removing much of the incriminating evidence before he was arrested. In consequence, Liu escaped execution and was given a ten-year term in prison, which was later reduced to just two years.[7]

The Huanggang Uprising, listed in the official history as Sun's third revolutionary uprising, was the first to be initiated by overseas Chinese. Their role in the Guangzhou Uprising of 1895 and the Huizhou Uprising in 1900 had been in support of Sun's actions. In contrast, the Huanggang uprising – as well as another attempt at Chaozhou a few months later – was hatched, planned and funded entirely in Singapore. After the failed attempts, more than 100 rebels sought refuge in British Malaya. Many were put up at Wanqingyuan, Teo Eng Hock's shops and other accommodations rented by Lin Shouzhi, and given jobs in Lim Nee Soon's farms and rubber estates.[8]

The Huanggang Uprising and the preparations for the second attempt at Chaozhou completely exhausted the funds that Sun had raised, including remittances from Singapore. Fortunately, he had Zhang Renjie, the Parisian antique dealer whom he had first met in 1906 on board the *Tonking*. Zhang had promised Sun to help him financially and never let him down. Thus, when Sun cabled him from Hanoi, Zhang promptly remitted a total of HK$60,000. The money enabled Sun to proceed with his next four risings.[9]

These four insurrections were directed from his staff headquarters in Hanoi, which had been set up several years earlier. During his visit in the winter of 1902–3, Sun had met a number of officials in the colonial government and was given tacit permission to live in Hanoi and discreetly pursue his revolutionary activities. While they would not allow the transportation of arms to the frontier, neither did they deny the revolutionaries access to weaponry, a policy ambivalence that reflected the diversity of opinions among French political circles. Notwithstanding official policy that favored cooperation with the Qing government, the champions of colonial expansionism were always happy to use whatever means to bring about the downfall of the Manchus for their own economic exploitation.[10]

In Hanoi and Saigon, the seats of the colonial government, the expansionist party was the stronger among the colonial officers, entrepreneurs and adventurers. They did all they could to help Sun by providing him with money, military advisers and arms. The money was channeled to Sun through various means, including the comprador of the Banque de France, while the technical advisers were French military officers "on leave." The purchase of arms was negotiated by traffickers though deliveries were sometimes intercepted by the colonial authorities. The expansionist party could count on a measure of cooperation from the diplomatic corps and certain government circles in Paris, but it could not defy the official policy too blatantly. It was therefore hoping for a successful insurrection that it could present to the government in Paris as a fait accompli and ensure the success of its own agenda.

Sun was affected by all these contradictions, and a policy of compromise that was unstable and ambiguous. The colonial government refused to extradite Sun and compromised only to the extent of placing him under surveillance and curtailing his freedom of maneuver. Within these liberal limits, the Indochinese sanctuary offered Sun and his revolutionary comrades considerable advantage in terms of personal security, financial assistance, technical advice, and in the event of a successful insurrection, the prospect of immediate diplomatic and military aid.

The theaters of operation of the four border insurrections were in Guangxi, Yunnan and western Guangdong, close to the Indochinese border. This was a sparsely populated region that included many ethnic minorities. It was inadequately patrolled, security was virtually non-existent and every village in this frontier region was a fortified camp. The political authorities were far away and the border remained extremely porous, which made the area especially attractive to outlaws and fugitives. Opium, the main crop of this region, found a profitable market in the French colony, the trafficking of which bred greed and violence. It was among this wild bunch of brigands that Sun recruited his allies, whom he left considerable latitude to direct operations in the field. One of the boldest was a Jiangxi native named Wang Heshun. Born into a poor family, he joined the Triads after a stint fighting alongside the imperial army. He met Sun and joined the Tongmenghui in 1906, and based himself in Hanoi.

The first of the border insurrections was at Fangcheng, a market town in western Guangdong close to Guangxi and Tonking. For several months past, sugarcane growers in the area had been protesting against the imposition of an additional tax on their production. This was a situation that the revolutionaries hoped to capitalize on with the complicity of the two local military men, General Guo Renzhang and Colonel Zhao Sheng. In preparation for the revolt, Sun sent emissaries to make contact with both these officers, who agreed that if Wang Heshun was able to start a large-scale revolt, they and their troops would join it. At the same time, Sun engaged French instructors to teach his fighting men how to handle guns, and sent Wang to Qinzhou to form a new force from among the defeated tax rebels, disaffected peasants and the secret societies.[11]

Three months passed before Wang and his men saw any action. Then on September 1, the commanders of the two Guangxi companies defending Fangcheng defected to the revolutionary camp. Why they did so is not clear. In any event, with their help, Wang and several hundred fighters captured Fangcheng without a fight on September 3. The local magistrate refused to cooperate and steadfastly insisted that in serving the Qing regime he was neither a traitor to the Chinese nor a slave of the Manchus. Exasperated with the magistrate's recalcitrance, Wang ordered his execution and those of his personal secretaries. Aside from this instance of swift justice, the rebels neither looted nor harmed anyone. Wang and his band then set out for Qinzhou, expecting the support of Guo. Unimpressed by the size of Wang's following, Guo refused to open the city to the rebels, claiming that he was under suspicion by the local *daotai*, or circuit intendant. Wang gave up on Guo and headed towards Lingshan, northeast of Qinzhou. On September 9, he began a two-day siege of the city and waited for Zhao Sheng to arrive with his troops. Zhao, too, was unwilling to risk joining Wang's small and poorly armed force. Instead of helping them, he attacked the rebels and lifted the siege on Fangcheng. Guo reportedly treated his prisoners cruelly during and after the mopping-up operation. The uprising had lasted all of ten days. The defeated rebels withdrew to the mountains on the Vietnamese border while Wang returned to Hanoi to report the mission's failure to Sun.

While the Qinzhou Fangcheng Uprising was in progress, Xu Xueqiu was readying to launch his second uprising at Chaozhou. He had met with Sun in August to explain the failure of the Huanggang Uprising and to ask for Sun's support for another attempt, this time in the East River region.

Sun agreed to supply him with new arms and ammunition that his Japanese agent Kayano Chochi had just purchased in Tokyo. The shipment was to be smuggled ashore at Haifeng in southeastern Guangdong, where Xu was to make arrangements to receive the shipment. When the *Koun Maru* stopped off the coast at Haifeng on the morning of October 12, there was no one to take delivery. The ship had been expected the previous night, and when she failed to show up at dawn, the lighters that Xu had hired to take the cargo ashore dispersed. While he hurried off to try and round them up again, the *Koun Maru* waited offshore. A passing government patrol boat became suspicious and went out to investigate. Alarmed, the Japanese skipper sailed off hurriedly. In Hong Kong, the revolutionaries and their Japanese sympathizers made another attempt on the ship's homeward voyage. Before her regular cargo of coal could be unloaded, the Japanese consul ordered her to leave port at once. He had been warned that the Qing government had requested the Hong Kong authorities to seize the ship. Consequently, the smuggling attempt was abandoned, as was Xu's plan for a second uprising in Chaozhou.

The revolt that broke out in December at Zhennanguan was the only one in which Sun had a direct hand in military operations, and the first time since 1895 that he set foot on Chinese soil. It was part of a larger plan, the objectives of which were the three strongholds defending the route from Tonking to Yunnan and Guangxi. The complexity of the initial plan, the role it assigned to transport vehicles, and the choice of the strongholds close to the Tonking-Guangxi and the Tonking-Yunnan railway lines, suggest the part played by French advisers working with Sun. The Zhennanguan Uprising in December 1907 involved only one, albeit the most important, of the three strongholds.[12]

The Zhennanguan pass, situated in southwestern Guangxi, had a strategic importance, as evinced by the presence of a garrison of several thousand men and several cannons. The pass was to be traversed by the Tonking-Guangxi railway, of which only the Hanoi-Langson portion had been built. At the news that 80 local rebels, mostly coolies recruited from the Yunnan Railway Company, had seized Zhennanguan with relative ease on December 3, Sun accompanied by Huang Xing, Hu Hanmin, an opium-smoking French captain on leave and several others took the train as far as

Langson and marched the rest of the way to Zhennanguan. They reached the fort on December 4 but found no arms cache, only a Krupp cannon, which the French captain, after many efforts, used to help repel a loyalist counterattack.

With money, Sun could have bought off the local commander. Instead he and his party had to rush back to Hanoi to obtain funds with which to buy the arms and ammunitions before large Manchu reinforcements arrived. The *huaqiao* responded generously and a French bank dangled the prospect a large loan if the revolutionaries could demonstrate the viability of their enterprise by capturing Longzhou, the administrative center closest to Zhennanguan and the first important station on the line that was to extend the railway from Hanoi to Langson into Chinese territory. Somehow Sun managed to obtain the arms and ship them by train. And somehow the Hanoi authorities decided to let the shipment through after customs held it up for a day. But the rebels, already surrounded, could not receive the goods. On December 8, they crawled out of the fortress, were arrested and then released by the French authorities once they reached the Tonking border. The recapture of the fort by regular Chinese forces put an end to the Zhennanguan Uprising.

The participation of the French captain in the revolt and the active part he played in the battle is an indication of the interest taken in the operation by certain elements of the French colonial army. The location of the insurrection close to the Hanoi-Langson railway line, the bank's conditional offer of funds, the fact that most of the fleeing rebels were recruited from among coolies working for the Yunnan Railway Company all point to the involvement of French commercial interests in the revolt. The hidden hands of French opportunists did not pass unnoticed by authorities on both sides of the Sino-Indochina border. The Qing government, fearful of the consequences that French involvement would have on the development of revolutionary sentiments, lodged numerous diplomatic protests. The French government for its part was also concerned about the influence that the Chinese revolutionaries would have on the rise of Vietnamese nationalism. Under pressure from both governments, the French colonial government issued a deportation order against Sun. On January 25, he was put on a boat bound for Singapore. Huang Xing and Hu Hanmin stayed on to organize the last two insurrection attempts across the Indochinese border.

The first of these took place once again in western Guangdong, an area still troubled by anti-tax protesters. Brigadier Li Chun had been recalled to Guangzhou to help deal with the British naval intervention in the West River, leaving Guo Renzhang in charge of military operations. Zhao Sheng apparently was no longer in Lianzhou. Still hopeful of rallying Guo's supposed sympathy for the revolution, Sun and Huang Xing planned an invasion of Qinzhou by an expeditionary force. Bandits and secret society bands again participated but there was now a new element that differentiated this insurrection from previous attempts. This was the expeditionary force of about 200 *huaqiao* from Hanoi and Haiphong that Huang Xing had recruited. An emissary met with Guo at his camp in Qinzhou and, by exaggerating the revolutionaries' resources, allegedly obtained a promise of cooperation, at least to the extent of supplying arms and ammunitions to the expeditionary force once it arrived. The campaign itself was largely the work of Huang Xing, because of Sun's expulsion from Indochina.[13]

On March 27, 1908, Huang Xing and a group of more than 200 men crossed into Qinzhou and Lianzhou, unopposed by either Chinese or French border guards. Over the next two days, this expeditionary force roamed freely while its leaders tried and failed several times to establish contact with Guo. On the third day, Huang's men clashed, perhaps accidentally, with two of Guo's battalions and defeated them. All hope of aid and cooperation from Guo vanished when four days later, on April 2, the revolutionaries now grown to 600 men, routed Guo's troops once more. In truth, Guo seems to have acted purely as a mercenary, his actions oscillating according to the size of the recompense; whatever was on offer from Sun's emissary was clearly judged to be inadequate. Pursued by reinforced government troops and low on ammunition, the revolutionaries headed into the mountains on the Guangxi border. Individually and in small groups, they made their way back to Indochina. Although Huang Xing himself did not reappear in Hanoi until May 5, the Qinzhou-Lianzhou Uprising was effectively over by mid-April. It lasted a little more than two weeks. Unlike Wang Heshun, Huang Xing avoided the cities and town and operated mainly in the countryside. For the first week or so, he and his men had some success in attracting the support of the local peasantry and secret societies. Later on, when they were on the run and some of them resorted to indiscriminate plundering and killing, the popular support evaporated.

The last border insurrection, which broke out in April 1908 at the Hekou fort, was originally planned to be coordinated with the Zhennanguan Uprising, and probably had the best chance of success. The Hekou fort, with a garrison of 2,500 men, guarded one of the main routes between Tonking and Yunnan. On the Indochinese side of the border was Laokay, an important stop on the Yunnan railway line which now extended into Chinese territory as far as Mengzi. The French-owned Yunnan Railway Company, threatened with bankruptcy, was trying to extend the construction of the line into the richer regions of central Yunnan, a service that would be more profitable. A successful insurrection from Hekou to Mengzi and Kunming would have provided it with the means to complete its construction plans. Huang Xing, who had come to lead the rebels, wanted to move on Mengzi, where supplies of arms and French aid awaited them. The capture of Mengzi would have established the credibility of the revolutionaries and loosened the purse strings of the Bank of Annam. The Yunnan Railway Company had also promised the rebels the use of the railway to transport their weapons. Never had the situation been more promising.[14]

On April 30, a small secret society band captured the town of Hekou. Within days, defecting police and army units swelled rebel ranks to several thousand. French opportunists again showed interest but stood on the sidelines until there was clearer indication that the movement could seize a large chunk of the mineral-rich province. That possibility vanished when Huang Xing, who had returned to Hanoi in search of funds, was arrested and expelled on May 12. This condemned the insurrection to failure, and by the end of the month the Hekou Uprising fell apart. It also brought an end to French funding for Sun and his efforts at insurrection.

The refugees from the Zhennanguan Uprising fled mainly to French Indochina, particularly Hanoi and Haiphong, which were geographically closer to the Chinese border than British Malaya, and where Tongmenghui branches had been established. They became restless and inclined to cause trouble. Some of them became involved in a local Vietnamese plot to poison French troops. This infuriated the French colonial government, which had accommodated these refugees not because they were sympathetic to the Chinese revolution but as bargaining chips with the Qing government for more concessions. The progress of this bargaining led the French colonial government to harden its attitude towards Sun and the revolutionaries. Eventually, the Qing and the French governments reached agreement on a joint program to suppress the activities of Chinese revolutionaries in French Indochina. The French contemplated extraditing the refugees to China, which in all probability would mean death. Arguing that they were political refugees and not common criminals, Sun who was already in Singapore made a number of requests to have them sent to British Malaya. The governor of French Indochina agreed to deport them to Singapore instead. The first batch of about 60 refugees arrived in May 1908. Subsequent arrivals swelled their numbers to more than 400.[15]

The influx of so many refugees presented problems for Sun and Tongmenghui Singapore. Jobs had to be found for these refugees and they had to be housed, clothed, fed and taught to comply with local laws. Despite concerted efforts to secure jobs for them in British Malaya and the Dutch East Indies, only about a hundred were able to find employment. Frustrated by defeat, the unemployed tended to be hot-tempered and troublesome, with a number even resorting to armed robberies. The reformists capitalized on these problems to discredit the revolutionaries and blame them for the mounting unrest in Singapore. Sun decided that the only solution was to open a quarry which could absorb them. A capital sum of S$3,000 was needed and Hu Hanmin toured Malaya to raise the money. A quarry was subsequently opened at the beginning of 1909, which absorbed about 200 refugees. A number of these refugees would later serve in the Huanghuagang Uprising in April 1911.

The border insurrections in 1907–8 had little chance of success. A few hundred social outcasts rampaging through the countryside or attacking some remote fort could hardly pose much of a threat to the Qing court situated over a thousand miles away. Within the Tongmenghui, Sun's strategy with its string of failures provoked Zhang Binglin to reproach Sun for never having delivered a significant blow at the Manchus and for wasting precious resources while creating a terrorist image for the revolutionaries.

Zhang believed that a theater of operation in the Yangtze Valley closer to the political center of the empire would have a better chance of toppling the dynasty than Sun's insistence on uprisings in the coastal provinces of southern China.[16]

Realizing that Sun would not abandon his southern strategy, Zhang's Guangfuhui comrades set about implementing their own plans in the Yangtze valley. On July 6, 1907, Xu Xilin assassinated Enming, the Manchu governor of Anhui province at the provincial capital of Anqing. A native of Zhejiang, Xu became radicalized after visiting Japan in the spring of 1903 and joined the Guangfuhui. Through an older cousin who had once been Enming's superior, Xu obtained a position as superintendent of the Anhui police academy and almost immediately plotted with another cousin, a radical feminist by the name of Qiu Jin in Shaoxing, Zhejiang, to launch a coordinated revolt against the Manchus. A torchbearer for many social causes, especially women's rights, Qiu had joined the Guangfuhui while studying in Tokyo. On her return to China in 1906, she became a director of a modern girls' school in Zhejiang.[17]

The uprising at Anqing, of which the assassination of Enming was only a preview, was quickly suppressed within hours. Xu was captured and after a brief interrogation was beheaded, and his heart was cut out as an offering to the dead Manchu governor. Qiu Jin's brother was arrested and under torture divulged information that led the authorities to her school. Resistance was brief and subdued; Qiu and 17 others were captured. As leader of the revolt, she was made an example of and beheaded on July 15. Her execution at the relatively young age of 31 turned her into a martyr, a heroine and a symbol of women's independence in China.

The four insurrections across the Sino-Indochinese border raised troubling questions about the collaboration between Sun and the French. The official French response was to deny the allegations of the Qing government, attributing it to the anti-French reports of the governor-general of Yunnan and Guizhou. Such official denials are an integral part of state diplomacy but they also reflected the disapproval of those in the higher reaches of the French administrative and political hierarchy towards the cooperation. Among the French who supported Sun and his intrigues, there were undoubtedly generous spirits motivated by sincere desires to bring modernity to China. But it was the greed of the railway and mining companies of Indochina, and the ambitions of those who supported them in Paris, that were the main bases of these border intrigues. The withdrawal of French aid in 1908 was also provoked by a fear that the subversion in southern China might soon spread to Tonking, where a number of anti-French incidents had raised alarms. Sun saw no contradiction in his nationalist ideals and the imperialistic designs of his French patrons and was quite willing to compromise the resources and sovereignty of the future republic to secure foreign aid by any means, even if such aid was tainted by self-interest. But the cozy relations between Sun and the French turned the leaders of the Tongmenghui, most of whom were hostile to foreign aid, against their *zongli*. It also isolated Sun from Chinese public opinion, which was becoming increasingly aware of the dangers of imperialism in all its guises.[18]

The six failed revolts, though depressing, were not devoid of significance. Starting with small secret society and bandit gangs, Sun and Huang Xing were able to incite rebellions that drew popular support and the sympathy of some government troops. Their men fought bravely, behaved well and were able to hold their own for several weeks on a number of occasions. What was missing was the mass agitation that a better planned strategy could have achieved. But far from changing his strategy, Sun was convinced more than ever that money was the key to success. Over the next few years, as he lost control of a fragmented Tongmenghui, Sun continued to give primacy to the quest for funds, even when it meant going against the grain of Chinese nationalism.[19]

An incident that sparked a wave of nationalist indignation began off the coast of Macau a month before Sun's expulsion from Hanoi. In spite of the vigilance of the foreign-managed Imperial Maritime Customs Service, it was an open secret that immense quantities of arms and ammunition were being smuggled into China, much of it from Japan. On the evening of February 5, a Chinese gunboat, acting on information relayed from Kobe, seized a Japanese freighter, *Tatsu Maru II*, off the coast of Macau for smuggling arms. While escorting the Japanese vessel to Huangpu, the captain of the Chinese gunboat hauled down the Japanese flag and hoisted the Chinese flag. Japan reacted with indignation at the insult to her national honor. Rejecting the Chinese offer to submit the dispute to arbitration, the Japanese issued an ultimatum demanding acceptance of humiliating terms, which included an apology, punishment of the Chinese captain and an indemnity. The Qing government had no alternative but to acquiesce to the demands and release the Japanese vessel.[20]

The people of Guangdong, as in the 1905 anti-American boycott over the Chinese Exclusion laws, reacted to the Japanese bullying with equal indignation and took matters into their own hands to defend China's honor. On March 20, merchants, the gentry, students and thousands of ordinary folk declared a boycott of Japanese goods. The many women among the demonstrators urged their supporters to wear rings engraved with the words "national humiliation." The press, now a force to be reckoned with in China, spread the news. Crowds sang patriotic songs while throwing Japanese-made goods into bonfires. Within days, similar demonstrations erupted in other provinces in south China, Hong Kong and some overseas Chinese communities. In Singapore and Malaya, the movement was not confined to just Japanese goods but found expression in unusual ways, such as the boycott of Japanese prostitutes operating in the urban areas and mining centers. The more fanatic ones even guarded Japanese brothels to prevent Chinese from patronizing them.

The boycott continued until the end of the year but the economic impact was much less than that of the 1905 anti-American boycott since the agitation was confined largely to south China, Hong Kong and British Malaya. Still, it disturbed the Japanese because of their heavy dependence on the China market. Chinese businessmen took the opportunity to push native substitutes and to enhance their industrial competitiveness. Sun and his comrades were too closely involved with Japanese gunrunners to make a fuss over the *Tatsu Maru* incident. Though he was now a persona non grata in Japan, he had received financial aid and other favors from the Japanese and hoped for more in the future. Thus when Uchida Ryohei, who had interceded with his government to give Sun a generous send-off the previous year and who was now tasked with enlisting Chinese dissidents against the boycott, wanted a favor in return, Sun found it expedient to accommodate his Japanese patron. At a stormy Tongmenghui meeting in Tokyo, Sun managed to get an anti-boycott resolution passed. The

Tongmenghui's Hong Kong organ, run by one of Sun's followers, was the only paper in south China to condemn the boycott. His efforts on behalf of the Japanese did not translate into benefits, but it cost him and the Tongmenghui considerable loss of prestige among Chinese nationalists.[21] This was just the tip of the iceberg, for Sun was about to be confronted by far bigger problems.

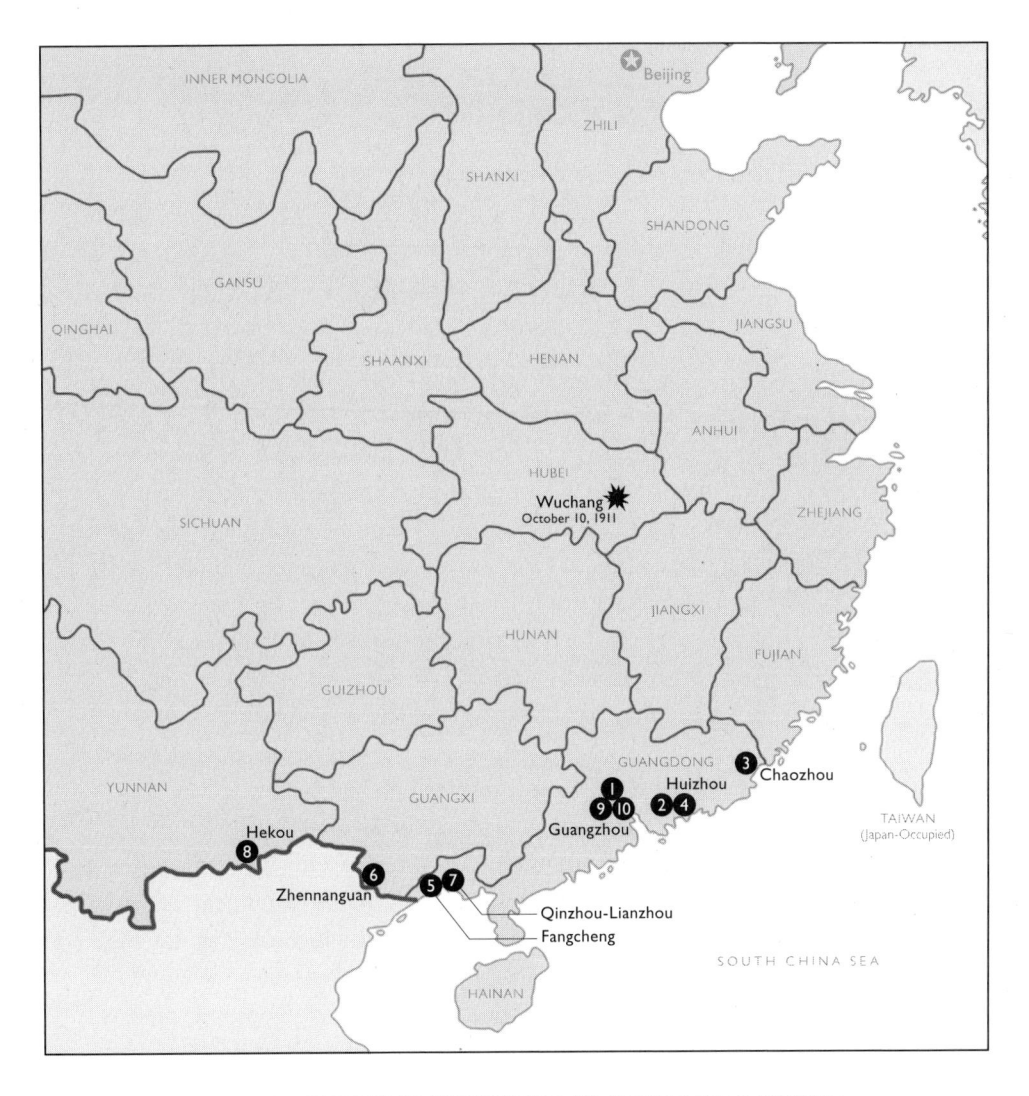

MAP 3 · THE TEN UPRISINGS PLANNED/ORGANIZED
BY SUN YAT-SEN, 1895–1911

1. Guangzhou — October 26, 1895
2. Huizhou Sanzhoutian — October 8–22, 1900
3. Chaozhou Huanggang — May 22–27, 1907
4. Huizhou Qinuhu — June 2–13, 1907
5. Fangcheng — September 1–17, 1907
6. Zhennanguan — December 1–8, 1907
7. Qinzhou-Lianzhou — March 27 to May 3, 1908
8. Hekou — April 29 to May 26, 1908
9. Guangzhou New Army — February 12, 1910
10. Guangzhou Huanghuagang — April 27, 1911

Chapter 9

THE WINTER OF DISCONTENT

SUN'S BANISHMENT from Japan in February 1907 was the beginning of one of the darkest periods of his life. Four failed insurrections followed fast on the heels of his deportation. Then came his expulsion from Indochina, followed later by two more failed uprisings. When he returned to Singapore in March 1908, the energy and enthusiasm that had greeted him barely a year earlier had all but dissipated. Even his staunchest supporters were no longer as helpful and his efforts to raise money for the Hekou uprising scheduled for April 1908 proved extremely disappointing. The economic depression in 1907–1908 may have been part of the reason but the series of failed uprisings must have weighed heavily on the minds and pocketbooks of his supporters. There were more troubles on the horizon. Since 1895, when Sun first embarked on his career as a professional revolutionary, he had been involved in eight rebellions, and in every instance, he was on the offensive. His role was about to be reversed in a revolt where the instruments of combat were not guns but words, and in which he was not the hunter but the prey.

The Tongmenghui, it may be recalled, was a marriage of convenience contracted for the sole purpose of overthrowing the Qing dynasty and restoring Chinese rule. In the urgency to consummate the matrimony, little attention was paid to its organizational weakness and the potential for conflicts. Given the haste with which the merger was put together, it was inevitable that members continued to pledge their allegiance to their respective provincial organization and leaders. In the conflicts that were soon to tear the Tongmenghui apart and severely test Sun's authority, people took sides according to such provincial solidarities.

The first clash was in February 1907. Huang Xing wanted a new flag for the Tongmenghui, one with a Chinese character that would symbolize the policy of the equalization of land rights. Sun insisted on retaining the old Xingzhonghui flag designed by his childhood friend Lu Haodong. The ferocity of the argument over such a minor matter shocked everyone. Huang Xing was reportedly very bitter about Sun's overbearing and dictatorial style in handling the disagreement. Another dispute occurred the following month. It was over a far more serious matter and it was not just with Huang Xing. Sun did not disclose to the other Tongmenghui leaders the 60,000 yen that he had received from the Japanese as a farewell gift. When the matter came to light, his peers construed it as a bribe for Sun to leave Japan without creating a scene. They criticized Sun for his arrogance and cast aspersions on his integrity. Zhang Binglin was so exasperated that he took down Sun's portrait hanging in the *Minbao* office and threatened to remove him as *zongli*.

Another uproar broke out in June, after Sun's deportation, when the Yangtze leaders found out about the arms that Sun had contracted to purchase with a view to organizing an uprising in Guangdong. They had opposed Sun's strategy of southern risings and were aghast that he had gone ahead over their objections. They accused him of buying obsolete weapons, implying that he had personally profited from the transaction. The Cantonese entourage tried to mediate but Sun rejected any attempt at conciliation. In turn, he accused Zhang Binglin of revealing the party's military secrets by sending an uncoded message to try to stop the arms purchase. Henceforth, Sun excluded the other Tongmenghui leaders from all military secrets. In October, he appointed Miyazaki as his attorney to make financial arrangements and negotiate the purchase of arms in Tokyo.[1]

The straw that finally broke the proverbial camel's back was a conflict over the *Minbao*. Funding had become increasingly uncertain after the paper was banned in China. In the winter of 1907, Tao Chengzhang traveled to Singapore to ask Sun for S$3,000 to help with the *Minbao*'s finances, and for a letter of recommendation for him to raise funds among the Nanyang *huaqiao* for a proposed uprising in Zhejiang, a strategy that Sun had categorically rejected. Sun was so infuriated by the challenge to his authority that not only did he reject both of Tao's requests, he absolutely forbade Tao to solicit funds from the Nanyang *huaqiao*.[2] In truth, Sun had lost interest in the *Minbao* once it came under the exclusive direction of Zhang

Binglin. This was inevitable following his deportation from Japan and the subsequent departure of his loyal lieutenants Hu Hanmin and Wang Jingwei, both of whom had played such important roles in the early issues of the *Minbao*. Thereafter, Sun pinned his hopes on the *Chong Shing Yit Pao*, which had begun publishing in Singapore in August 1907.[3]

Tao ignored Sun's admonishment and embarked on a fundraising tour of Nanyang in 1908, taking the opportunity to denigrate Sun to anyone willing to lend a sympathetic ear. In the Dutch East Indies, he seemed to have found sufficient support to set up Guangfuhui branches in Banka and Surabaya. In Singapore, Xu Xueqiu and Chen Yunsheng, the main figures in the two Chaozhou uprisings, helped Tao to garner support from the Teochew community. The two men had their own grievance against Sun, whom they blamed for failing to complete the shipment of arms and ammunitions from Japan, which had forced them to abort the second Chaozhou uprising.

Henceforth, Tao and his partisans openly competed with Sun for funds from the *huaqiao*. In 1908, they embarked on an aggressive campaign to raise funds for the uprising in Zhejiang. Though their efforts were conducted in the name of the Guangfuhui, they requested that monies be remitted to the Tongmenghui in Tokyo or Singapore. Indeed, Tao and his associates maintained their association with the Tongmenghui, which with its longer history enjoyed greater credibility among the *huaqiao* in Nanyang.[4]

In July 1908, Sun reorganized the Singapore branch of the Tongmenghui as the Nanyang Regional Headquarters and appointed Hu Hanmin as director. Until this time, the Singapore branch had been performing the functions of a regional office in all but name. The new status did not confer any new authority but increased its administrative burden, as all Nanyang branches were now required to file bimonthly reports to Singapore. The purported aim was to facilitate communication among the rapidly growing number of branches, and between the branch network and the Tokyo headquarters. But the timing of its implementation suggests it had as much to do with keeping a tighter rein on the activities of the branches and their members in light of Tao's smear campaign against Sun.[5]

Relations between Sun and the Guangfuhui went from bad to worse after the Japanese government suspended the *Minbao* in October 1908. Sun did not offer to help when Zhang Binglin stood trial as the paper's editor.[6] In fact, Sun took such a cavalier attitude toward the whole affair that he set out on a tour of the Tongmenghui branches in peninsular Malaya on his usual quest for money as well as to recruit members. It does not seem that he achieved his financial objective, but a bit of welcome news greeted Sun a few days after his return to Singapore. The Guangxu Emperor passed away unexpectedly on November 14, followed the very next day by the demise of the Empress Dowager Cixi. The 2-year-old Puyi, who had been anointed by Cixi on her deathbed, was installed as the new Son of Heaven, with his father Zaifeng as regent. Zaifeng, whose formal title was Prince Chun, was a grandson of the Daoguang Emperor.

The Qing consulate-general in Singapore and the Chinese Chamber of Commerce published notices in the local press calling on the Chinese to close their shops on November 19 to mourn the deaths of the two Manchu royals. Chinese schools were to close for three days and the leaders of the various dialect groups were invited to attend a mourning ceremony at the consulate. Sun and Hu Hanmin, who were both in Singapore, decided to turn the occasion into a parody by selling a tear-inducing ointment on the day of mourning with appropriately wide publicity given in the *Chong Shing Yit Pao* the day before. The attempt at mockery was not lost on the reformists, who hired secret society toughs to guard against the disruption of the ceremony. On the day of mourning, the revolutionaries were on hand with their ointment to ridicule the merchants who turned up at the consulate in official gowns and feathers. There was no violence at the consulate but elsewhere there was sporadic fighting throughout the day. Calm was restored only after Sun's intercession at the request of the colonial authorities.[7]

With the death of the Guangxu Emperor, the Baohuanghui lost its raison d'être, and the Chinese reform movement was significantly weakened. Instead of seizing the opportunity to go on the offensive, the Tongmenghui continued to be mired in internal dissent. In 1909, Sun tried to resume publication of the *Minbao* but now entrusting its editorship to his faithful lieutenant Wang Jingwei. While Zhang was lambasting Sun for hijacking the *Minbao* name and calling on the *huaqiao* to stop sending him funds, Tao was circulating an open letter denouncing Sun's high-handedness, questioning his integrity, and calling for his expulsion from the Tongmenghui. He stopped short of calling for the Guangfuhui to secede from the Alliance. As Zhejiang natives, Tao and Zhang realized that they could not hope to compete with Sun and his Cantonese entourage for the support of the Nanyang *huaqiao*, most of whom were from southern provinces like Guangdong and Fujian. They needed the Tongmenghui, which had already established a track record in Nanyang, which the Guangfuhui lacked.[8]

Tao's letter and Zhang's statement were widely circulated among the *huaqiao* communities in Nanyang and America. Those in America began to lose faith in Sun and the Tongmenghui, but the anti-Sun campaign made little headway in British Malaya. In April 1909, Tao toured peninsular Malaya to campaign against Sun but without much success and in fact provoked the opposite reaction. A group of revolutionaries from the smaller branches issued a public statement on November 1909 castigating Zhang and his fellow dissidents for their disgraceful behavior as intellectuals. The following month, a reading club in Kuala Pilah issued a statement in the *Chong Shing Yit Pao* refuting the allegations against Sun as mere fabrications. The paper itself came out in Sun's defense and in several editorials accused Zhang of treating the *Minbao* as his personal mouthpiece. Significantly, the Nanyang Regional Office in Singapore and the larger Tongmenghui branches in peninsular Malaya did not join in the fray.

The anti-Sun campaign did not result in the breakup of the Tongmenghui, but it badly concussed the revolutionary movement in British Malaya and crippled the operations of the Singapore regional office. A number of its leaders left the revolutionary movement and withdrew their financial support. The Regional Office's activities were badly disrupted and several programs were terminated. The *Chong Shing Yit Pao* ceased operations in early 1910, and one of the largest reading clubs in the island closed down at the end of the year. The strife within the Tongmenghui was too good an opportunity to pass up for the reformists and the *Union Times* made hay of the situation and gave it full publicity.

The disarray within the Tongmenghui and its loss of momentum did not translate to relief for the Qing dynasty. The growing nationalism and the modernization to which it had finally pledged its commitment continued to work against the regime. In 1908, the court outlined a plan for constitutional reforms to be implemented in nine years. The provincial assemblies created the following year demanded a shorter timetable. With the death of Cixi, the dynasty had lost its strongest personality. Her demise also marked a temporary halt to the meteoric rise of the regime's ablest military leader, Yuan Shikai, who was relieved of all his posts by the regent in January 1909. That October, death had also overtaken Zhang Zhidong, the last of the four old guards who had steered the dynasty through crisis after crisis since the mid-19th-century rebellions.[9] Thus at a time of heightened tension, an infant boy not quite four years old sat on the Dragon Throne under the regency of his father, a weak Manchu prince. These unmistakable signs of dynastic decay prompted Sun to consider another stab at his favorite target, Guangzhou. The obstacle as always was the funds to make it happen.

In the spring of 1908, a French businessman had intimated to Sun that he might be able to help secure a 10-million-franc (about US$2 million) loan in Europe. Such a loan, if it could be arranged, would not only solve Sun's short-term need for funds for the planned uprisings, it would also solve the longer-term needs of the revolution. With little prospect of raising the money in Nanyang, Sun decided to follow up on the lead. On May 19, 1909, he departed Singapore for Europe and spent the entire summer pursuing the deal. The Frenchman turned out to be just an intermediary and was unable to deliver. Sun now turned to Paul Doumer to work for the loan. The former governor-general of Indochina seemed to be making some headway when a cabinet change in July put a halt to all fundraising activities for the Chinese revolution. Sun received the bad news in October while he was in London working on another loan. This, too, ended in disappointment.[10] Before his departure from the British Isles, he wrote to the American adventurer, author and military strategist Homer Lea suggesting a meeting on his forthcoming visit to the United States. Sun had met Lea in 1904, most probably when Sun was calling for "American Lafayettes," but did not continue the relationship as Lea at the time was a trusted confidante of Kang Youwei. Sun had read Lea's recently published book, *The Valor of Ignorance*, and was impressed by the American's analysis of the Japanese military threat to the United States.

In New York, where Sun arrived in November, an American broker tried to interest him in a scheme to corner the Malayan tin market. If successful, the deal would have earned Sun a tidy commission. Chinese tin miners, whose cooperation was essential, refused to be involved and nothing came out of the proposal.[11] More significant was a meeting Sun had with Yung Wing, the progenitor of the Chinese Education Mission. For a time, Yung had harbored monarchical ambitions of his own but now at 80 years old and living in retirement in Hartford, Connecticut, he had significantly lowered his sights. Yung was acquainted with Homer Lea through a conspiratorial scheme known as the Red Dragon, and he convinced Sun that this could benefit his revolutionary movement. Yung had wanted Lea and his partner Charles Boothe to travel to New York to meet Sun, but Lea was in such poor health that he could not do so. Boothe suggested Sun should meet with him and Lea in California. Meanwhile, Yung introduced Sun to Walter W. Allen, another interested party in the Red Dragon who had good connections to powerful Wall Street houses.[12]

For the next three months, Sun traveled the length and breadth of North America setting up branches under the name Zhongguo Gemingdang, or the Chinese Revolutionary Party, and pleading for financial support in the Chinatowns of the continent. The reception was substantially better this time as there was comparatively little competition from the Baohuanghui. The death of the Guangxu Emperor had left the organization without a cause while Kang's questionable handling of its funds had taken the luster off the founder's sterling image. Kang had allowed the society to be turned into a commercial enterprise with investments on several continents. A number of these investments had turned sour but more troubling were questions about how these investments were made. One concerned a US$800,000 investment of the Baohuanghui's funds in Mexican streetcars which was alleged to have been registered in the name of his daughter, a student at Barnard College in New York. Kang was also spending an inordinate amount of time with a 17-year-old female consort on cruises to exotic destinations, all on the Baohuanghui's account.[13] Still, Sun only managed to raise HK$8,000, a far cry from the HK$20,000 he had promised his people in Hong Kong and far less than the amount deemed necessary to ensure the success of the next uprising in Guangzhou.[14]

This rebellion, which Sun had been planning for the past year, finally broke out on February 12, 1910, two days after his arrival in San Francisco. What was different about this attempt, apart from its meager financing, was that for the first time the main strike force was made up of mutinous soldiers from the two regiments of the Guangdong New Army. The first regiment was under the command of Colonel Zhao Sheng, who had helped to put down the rebellion at Fangcheng in 1907. After the mopping-up operation, he was transferred to Guangzhou and eventually dismissed from the New Army for his revolutionary sympathies. His successor Ni Yingdian also became a revolutionary convert and joined the Tongmenghui. Over the course of several months, he created a cadre of revolutionary sympathizers in the first regiment, but was less successful with the second regiment. The revolutionaries' activities within the New Army did not escape the attention of military brass who in late 1909 discharged several soldiers on suspicion of engaging in subversive activities. Among them was Ni himself, who then joined the ranks of professional conspirators in the Tongmenghui.[15]

In preparation for the revolt, the Tongmenghui had opened a South China Regional Office in Hong Kong under the charge of Hu Hanmin. Huang Xing, Zhao Sheng, Ni Yingdian and other revolutionary leaders began converging in Hong Kong toward the end of January 1910. Early the following month, they joined Hu Hanmin to finalize the battle plan and set the date for the revolt. The consensus was to launch it during the Lunar New Year holidays beginning on February 10, a time when it would be more difficult than usual to maintain tight security. But they could not agree on a specific date. Hu Hanmin preferred a date close to the end of the month in order to await further deliveries of funds and military supplies. Huang Xing and Zhao Sheng on the other hand favored a date within the first week of the New Year to minimize the risk of discovery by the authorities.

While the Tongmenghui leaders deliberated the date, a minor dispute between an infantryman from the second regiment of the New Army and a shopkeeper broke out on New Year's Eve in Guangzhou. The detention of the soldier by the police led to a brawl between his regimental comrades and the police during which two police stations were burnt down. Fearing further disturbances, Guangzhou officials disarmed the soldiers and canceled all military leave, and docked the pay and confined to barracks the entire Guangdong New Army. The soldiers of the first regiment who were garrisoned outside Guangzhou mutinied when they learned on February 11 that they were being penalized for something they did not do. Seizing arms that had not been confiscated, they marched on Guangzhou.

In Hong Kong, the revolutionary leaders looked on helplessly as the violence in Guangzhou escalated. Ni Yingdian, the first to arrive in the provincial capital, concluded that the plan for a coordinated revolt was no longer feasible. The only possibility of success now was to gain control of the mutiny and redirect it to serve revolutionary ends. On the following morning, Ni appeared before his ex-comrades to urge them to revolt, assuring them that reinforcement was on the way. With Ni leading the charge, the soldiers marched once more toward Guangzhou and straight into a clash with loyalist forces. The under-armed mutineers were no match for the Reserve Forces and were easily defeated. Ni was among the first to be killed. Demoralized, most of the mutinous soldiers discarded their uniforms and weapons and fled in confusion. Three ringleaders were executed; another 33 soldiers were given prison sentences and more than 1,000 were discharged. The first regiment was disbanded, but the second regiment, which had refused to join in the mutiny, was left intact.

The subversion of modern army recruits, many from better backgrounds and better educated than the traditional soldiers of the Green Standard, opened up a whole new line of strategy for the revolutionaries. It was also a sign of the times and spelled danger for the dynasty. The discontent with the government had now crossed class barriers. Not only peasants, but the gentry and merchants had now developed sympathies for the revolutionaries. For the militants in the Tongmenghui, the failure of the Guangzhou New Army Uprising, Sun's ninth revolutionary attempt, was a terrible disappointment. Many left the revolutionary movement. The membership in Hong Kong fell from 2,000 in 1909 to less than 200. Feng Ziyou, who had held the fort in Hong Kong for the past four years, set off for Vancouver to pursue a career in journalism. Wang Jingwei opted for individual terrorism. In April, he made an assassination attempt on the regent, an act of folly that earned him a prison sentence. If Sun was disheartened by the latest setback, it did not slow him down.[16]

In mid-March, Sun finally met with Homer Lea and Charles Boothe in Long Beach, California. A short, frail hunchback who suffered from poor health, Lea was a racist, an amateur military strategist and a militarist of the fiercest Social Darwinist kind. Though lacking formal military training, he had dreamed of leading armies as a student at Stanford from 1897 to 1899. He published *The Valor of Ignorance* in 1909, a book that earned him high praise in professional military circles. In it he predicted a Japanese attack on the United States, which proved prescient 32 years later when Japan bombed Pearl Harbor. His distaste for the Japanese was matched by a passionate interest in China and the Chinese, which he romanticized in a novel, *The Vermilion Pencil*, published in 1908. He studied the Chinese language and history and befriended many Chinese in the Bay Area.[17]

Homer Lea

Lea became involved in Chinese affairs and joined the Baohuanghui while still at Stanford. In the summer of 1900, he dropped out of college and traveled to China, where he received a commission as a lieutenant-general in the embryonic Baohuanghui army. His role was to train its soldiers in Guangdong and Guangxi, and lead an attack on Guangzhou from Macau with a "coolie army of 25,000" to restore the Guangxu Emperor to the throne. The plan failed and Lea returned home to the United States. In 1904, he masterminded a plan to covertly train a cadre of Chinese soldiers in America, which eventually grew into a network of military schools in more than 20 cities across the continental United States. The idea was to send these soldiers to China to take part in a coordinated coup to restore the Guangxu Emperor. Lea hired former U.S. Army soldiers as instructors and commissioned them into the Baohuanghui army. His clandestine program nearly collapsed in 1905 when the U.S. Secret Service and several states investigated it for possible violation of neutrality laws. Lea's affiliation with the Baohuanghui ended in late 1908 after the death of the Guangxu Emperor.

Lea then tried to become a U.S. trade representative to China but failed. It was at this time that he put together the military conspiracy known as the Red Dragon. The plan called for organizing a revolutionary plot to conquer several provinces in China that would later extend throughout the empire. It was a scheme that bordered on fantasy and was doomed from the outset yet was so potentially lucrative as to prove irresistible to some. His co-conspirator in this enterprise was Charles Boothe, a retired New York banker living in South Pasadena. Yung Wing was their adviser on Chinese affairs. In the fall of 1908, Boothe enlisted the aid of his childhood friend Walter W. Allen. A hardheaded businessman, Allen was less optimistic about the project than the two Californians, but agreed nevertheless to act as their link with the eastern financial establishment. He suggested raising a little more than half of the projected US$9 million cost of the venture from American investors and the balance from Chinese sympathizers. Both groups would have formal control and share the profits proportionately. Voting control, however, would be vested exclusively with the Americans. Investors would be paid ten percent annual interest with the pay dirt to come from concessions granted to the syndicate by the revolutionary government. These included a 99-year franchise to build and operate all Chinese railways and a monopoly of China's mineral resources. They needed a Chinese figurehead and had considered Kang Youwei for the post but Allen took him off the list when he learned of Kang's financial improprieties. Yuan Shikai was also on the list but there was no way of getting in touch with him. Allen had mentioned Sun to his conspiracy partners but after meeting him in New York with Yung Wing, he had strong reservations about Sun's capacity and credibility for leadership. He advised against relying on Sun, whose organization he felt was only capable of mounting sporadic and easily quashed uprisings, not the sustained revolution that the three Americans had in mind.

Allen's reservations did not dampen Lea and Boothe's enthusiasm for Sun. Satisfied that they had found their man, they struck a deal with Sun. The plan was simple. American mercenary officers would be sent to southern China to train the revolutionary forces. Arms brought in from the United States would be stockpiled in western Guangdong until they were needed. Lea would be the commander-in-chief while Boothe would be

Sun's "sole foreign financial agent," with full powers to negotiate loans with New York bankers, receive and disburse the money. Lea as Commanding General could also requisition funds from Boothe. But there were never any funds. Earlier Allen found that Wall Street was cool toward China investments in general, let alone a speculative venture such as the Red Dragon. J.P. Morgan, Allen's preferred investment banker for the scheme, showed no interest and neither did its less illustrious peers. Allen's role in the conspiracy ended when Morgan gave its final refusal in the summer of 1910. Though aware of Allen's failure to excite Wall Street, Lea and Boothe continued to feed Sun with optimistic reports even after Allen's exit. Sun on his part was not completely taken in and had his own doubts whether American capitalists would commit financial suicide by participating in a venture as speculative as the one being put on the table, but he saw no harm in trying to lure them with attractive baits. He had no doubt in his mind that a strong China could easily abrogate any demeaning relationships with foreigners, with whom he had no hesitation to walk both sides of the street in the meantime. On March 24, while sailing from San Francisco to Honolulu, Sun wrote asking Lea to negotiate with the U.S. War Department for the sale of certain secret diplomatic documents in his possession that concerned a plan for a possible Japanese attack on the United States.

Following a two-month stay in Hawaii setting up branches in the Islands, Sun returned to Japan for the first time since his deportation. His arrival in Yokohama in mid-June 1910 under his Hawaiian identity, Dr. Alaha, was not kept a secret but the Japanese nonetheless responded evasively to enquiries from the Chinese minister in Japan. Probably through Miyazaki's intercession with the Japanese generals not to write Sun off completely, the war minister's view prevailed at a cabinet meeting and Sun was allowed to remain in Japan. Sun's relationship with the Tokyo Tongmenghui leaders, however, took a turn for the worse. At a stormy meeting, he told them that "the Alliance has long since been dissolved," and challenged them to set up their own independent organization if they were strong enough to do so. That was what Sun himself had been doing. During his recent American tour, he had formed new branches under the banner of the Zhongguo Gemingdang, or Chinese Revolutionary Party. He had also modified the membership oath and started using the slogan "Three

Principles of the People." The Alliance did not break up but Sun's Yangtze rivals began planning independent actions in their home region. Huang Xing was the exception; he still backed Sun. He was one of the 17 provincial leaders who signed the power of attorney for Boothe to carry out his functions under the Red Dragon scheme. But he dismissed the idea of having American officers lead the revolutionary army. After a stay of barely ten days, Sun departed for Singapore in early July, apparently to spare the Japanese government's uneasiness due to pressure from the Chinese Legation.[18]

In contrast to his previous visits, Sun was given a languid welcome when he returned to Singapore on July 11. Even his most ardent supporters were visibly less hospitable and helpful because of his string of failed uprisings and the alleged embezzlement that Tao Chengzhang had leveled against him. The Nanyang Regional Office was in complete disarray and its organ *Chong Shing Yit Pao* had ceased publication. Sun chose not to stay at Wanqingyuan but at Deng Ziyu's Kuang I Chang Hotel in Chinatown, where he gathered his remaining supporters for a series of meetings. It soon became apparent that the situation was hopeless and it would be futile for Sun to continue operating out of Singapore. On July 19, he boarded the German steamer *Roon* bound for Penang. He had intended to stay a week or two but several days of meeting with Goh Say Eng was all it took for Sun to decide on Penang as the new location for the Nanyang Regional Office. He instructed Zhou Hua, the secretary of the Nanyang Regional Office, to gather all the party papers and bring them with him to Penang, where he was to retain his old job.[19]

Sun's choice of Penang to relocate the Nanyang Regional Office was no capricious decision. The island came into Britain's orbit in 1786, much earlier than Singapore, with which she shared many similarities. She was part of the Straits Settlements and as such was administered very similarly to Singapore. Her well-developed infrastructure was second only to Singapore in British Malaya. The large number of foreign banks operating in the island and the excellent telecommunications facilities would enable the Nanyang Regional Office to continue moving money and information efficiently throughout Nanyang. Like Singapore, too, Penang's population was predominantly Chinese, a similarity that cut across all social classes down to the underworld. The crucial consideration for Sun was the unwavering loyalty of the Penang leaders and their unswerving commitment to his revolutionary agenda. They ran a tight ship and the branch's front organization, the Penang Philomathic Society, had been a model for all the reading clubs in Nanyang.

In October 1910, Sun invited his closest supporters to Penang for a meeting. This crucial assembly, known to history as the Penang Conference, was held on November 13 in his Penang residence at 400 Dato' Kramat Road. Determined to show his adversaries that he did not need their help, Sun did not inform the Tokyo militants, nor the leaders of branches that had failed to rally to him in the character assassination campaigns against him. Many of the delegates were disheartened by the setbacks: Wang Jingwei's imprisonment, the failure of the New Army Uprising, and the party's financial difficulties. Vowing that this would be his last attempt to overthrow the Manchu dynasty, Sun waged an ingenious fundraising drive that offered something for everyone. He put up for sale, in the name of the future republic, rights of citizenship, business concessions, terms of office in parliament and, for the highest donors, statues and parks named in their honor. Appealing to their emotions as well as their dreams of wealth and honor, Sun declared that revolution was in accord with the teachings of China's ancient sages, who approved of the overthrow of despotic rulers. Other countries had found prosperity through revolution and this was the way for China to gain an equal footing with powerful nations. Under the Manchus, he warned, China faced partition or conquest and the overseas Chinese, even if wealthy, would continue to suffer indignities. To drive home this point, Sun recounted an experience that a Chinese millionaire from Java had shared with him. This millionaire had stayed late visiting a friend and had forgotten to bring his pass, without which, according to Dutch regulations, a Chinese could not stray far from his home after dark. But a Japanese could. So the millionaire hired a Japanese prostitute who was living next door to take him home. A Chinese millionaire, Sun concluded in disgust, was regarded in Java as lower than a Japanese prostitute because the Chinese government was too weak to protect Chinese living in foreign lands. The *huaqiao*, Sun averred, were missing the boat by pursuing wealth through trade. A revolution in China would provide fantastic opportunities. The tycoons who built America did not amass their wealth from trade but from funding revolutions in foreign lands. Given China's incomparable natural resources, the *huaqiao* could earn "100 times more than they could get from trading" if they helped the revolutionaries.[20]

Sun's rhetoric carried the day and the conference agreed on Guangzhou as the target for the next uprising. They planned to raise S$130,000 (S$50,000 from each of British Malaya and the Dutch East Indies, and S$30,000 from Siam and Indochina), with a minimum of S$100,000. The Guangdong New Army was to be the backbone of the uprising, and 500 volunteers would be recruited to guide it. Following the capture of Guangzhou, Huang Xing was to launch an attack on Hunan and Hubei while Zhao Sheng would lead the attack on Jiangxi and Nanjing.

The Penang Conference was a personal victory for Sun; he had prevailed in his strategy of attacking the coastal instead of the inland provinces. Two days later, he held another meeting at the Penang Philomathic Society for the local stalwarts. Imploring them to do their part to save China, he again invoked his favorite theme, that the overseas Chinese should sacrifice their money by donating to revolutionary funds, while the comrades in China sacrificed their lives. Putting his reputation on the line, he vowed that he would either die or retire and would not trouble them again if the revolt should fail. His emotional appeal produced another S$8,000.

The amount raised fell far short of even the minimum target of S$100,000. Since September 1910, Sun had been pressing Boothe for interim funding but the latter was unable to deliver even the US$50,000 that Sun had asked for as a private loan, leave alone the half million dollars that was promised. In November, Sun wrote to Boothe that unless he received some money within three months, his forces would take independent steps. If successful, the terms of their agreement would have to be changed. Further pleadings failed to produce a penny and in March 1911 Sun asked Boothe to return the power of attorney. The following month, Boothe admitted that Red Dragon was history.[21]

With his credibility on the line and the prospect of obtaining millions from America now all but dead, Sun and his partisans decided to double up their effort on the *huaqiao* in Nanyang. This was still work in progress when Sun was politely told to leave Penang. The reason was a public speech he made on October 30 at the Ching Fang Ko Club on Macalister Road in

Sun Yat-sen, with his son Sun Ke, May 1910.

which he had collected money in the name of a Chinese education fund and made an oblique attack on British colonial rule in Malaya. Apprised of the speech, Sir John Anderson, the governor of the Straits Settlements, now decided that Sun's activities could no longer be regarded as educational. He had a subordinate intimate to Sun that "his further presence in the colony was no longer considered desirable."[22]

The deportation was a devastating blow to Sun's revolutionary future. Barred from China, Hong Kong, Japan and now virtually all of Nanyang, there was nowhere in Asia that he could carry out his operations. He had to abandon his plan to go to Singapore to help with the fundraising efforts there and entrusted a few of his faithful lieutenants to take charge of all preparations for the uprising. The most important task was to raise the S$100,000, without which the entire operation had to be aborted. In this, the campaign in British Malaya was particularly important. Penang was the regional office and failure there would discourage the other branches and jeopardize the entire campaign. Consequently, Sun delegated the party's top leaders to direct the campaign – Hu Hanmin and Teng Tse Ju in British Malaya, and Huang Xing in Siam and Indochina.

In spite of a less than happy ending, Sun's five-month sojourn in Penang was one of the rare moments that he spent some quality time with his family. His constant companion Chen Cuifen had joined him in early August. His brother Sun Mei arrived in early November together with Sun's wife Lu Muzhen and their two daughters. Only his son, Sun Ke, was absent as he was studying in Honolulu. Sun departed Penang for Europe and America on December 6, 1910. A week in Paris proved fruitless and after brief stopovers in New York and San Francisco, he arrived in Vancouver in February 1911. For four days, he packed in audiences of over a thousand and sold S$63,000 worth of bonds. This money plus the S$14,000 he had raised in the United States far surpassed the sum to be raised in British Malaya and was immediately remitted to Hong Kong, the operational center for the Guangzhou uprising. This was to be the alliance's supreme effort.[23]

The S$50,000 to be raised in the rest of British Malaya got off to a bad start in Singapore. Only about a hundred attended a meeting on Christmas Day at Wanqingyuan. The local leaders, including the branch chairman Teo Eng Hock, were conspicuous by their absence. No surprises there: none of them were invited to the Penang Conference. At the end of the day, only about S$3,000 was raised. Teng Tse Ju's effort in Malacca was equally dismal. In all, only S$12,000 was raised, a far cry from the target of S$50,000. At the second round of fundraising, on New Year's Day in Seremban, where Teng Tse Ju had considerable sway, Huang Xing made an emotional pledge to sacrifice his life for the success of the revolt. This would undoubtedly have reminded his audience of Wang Jingwei's sacrifice in his assassination attempt and Sun's oft-used reminder that "comrades overseas sacrifice their money, comrades in China sacrifice their lives." The response was astounding; a local leader upped his original donation of S$1,000 to S$6,000. Similar meetings were held in Perak, with equally satisfying results. Within a week, the money raised added to the amount from the first round of fundraising was just a little short of the target of S$50,000.

Huang Xing departed Singapore for Hong Kong on January 13, 1911, to take charge of operations with Zhao Sheng as his deputy. The battle plan was reminiscent of the Guangzhou Uprising of 1895. The assault by a commando force from Hong Kong was to be coordinated with simultaneous uprisings by secret society gangs, this time augmented by units of the New Army. Huang Xing assembled an 800-strong commando force and set up his general headquarters in Happy Valley. Unlike in the 1895 uprising, these daredevils were not bandits and secret society members but Cantonese, a few extra-provincials and Nanyang *huaqiao*. An ordnance was set up at Lyndhurst Terrace to make bombs, which were to be the rebels' chief weapons as they were powerful and cost-effective. By March *huaqiao* donations from all over the world had reached Hong Kong and these were used to purchase arms in Hong Kong, Japan, Vietnam and other sources. These were first shipped to Hong Kong and then clandestinely transported to Guangzhou, where 40 secret cells working independently were set up to facilitate the transfer. Two rice shops were opened specifically for the mission to serve as safe houses. Accommodation for the combatants were rented by "couples" organizing their weddings and the arms transported in the sedan chairs of the brides-to-be.[24]

Five days before the date scheduled for the revolt, a volunteer from Singapore, Wen Sheng Tsai, went on a frolic of his own and assassinated the new Manchu general in Guangzhou. Captured by the police, he admitted his association with Sun. On the way to the execution ground, he called on the throngs of spectators lining the street to follow his lead. In truth, the plan for the revolt was well above Wen's pay grade and he knew absolutely nothing about it. Nevertheless, the assassination confirmed in officials' minds an earlier report in the *Hong Kong Telegraph* of February 25, 1911, about the presence in Guangzhou of a revolutionary group led by a graduate from Japan named Wong (Huang), quite obviously a reference to Huang Xing. Security measures were stepped up, with house-to-house searches conducted throughout the city. Arms belonging to the Guangdong New Army, whose loyalty was still in doubt because of the mutiny the year before, had their firing pins removed. Several battalions of the more trusted Reserve Forces were summoned from outlying districts to reinforce the defense of the provincial capital.

The assassination forced the revolutionary leaders to go back to the drawing board. At an emergency meeting in Hong Kong, they decided to proceed with the revolt but to delay it a couple of weeks. It was also determined that the uprising would now consist of ten separate but simultaneous attacks on various government offices in Guangzhou, with each attack force consisting of 50 to 100 volunteers, and with Huang Xing and Zhao Sheng in overall joint command. Since Zhao was a familiar figure in Guangzhou from his recent stint as regimental commander of the New Army, Huang was to arrive ahead of him and decide the new date for the uprising. Huang chose April 27, a Thursday.

Almost immediately after Huang Xing's arrival in Guangzhou on April 23, a number of the revolutionary leaders advised him to postpone the uprising indefinitely on the grounds that the security measures taken by the authorities would make it that much more difficult for the revolt to succeed. On April 26, Huang told the volunteers who had arrived in Guangzhou to return to Hong Kong and those still in the colony to stay put until further notice. No sooner had this been done, other leaders pressed Huang to launch the attack without further delay. Insisting that a postponement was tantamount to abandonment, they argued that it would disappoint the *huaqiao* who had given so generously to the revolt and would undermine their confidence in the revolutionary movement. As Huang wavered, an informant brought news that some of the Reserve Forces units that had been brought in as reinforcements were revolutionary sympathizers and would support an uprising. Huang now decided to revert to his original plan to launch the uprising on April 27. He wired Zhao Sheng again to send the volunteers to Guangzhou. The quickest way to Guangzhou was still by ferry, which operated only twice a day on New Year's Day. Zhao and Hu Hanmin decided to dispatch half the volunteer force on that evening's service and the rest the following day. They asked Huang to delay the revolt by a day.

The first contingent arrived on the morning of April 27 but Huang Xing was now against any delay and would not wait for the second contingent. Not unexpectedly, the last-minute changes in plans thoroughly confused the various attack forces scattered in different parts of the city. A force of 100 and 60 volunteers armed with pistols and homemade bombs led by Huang attacked and easily captured the governor-general's mansion. Unable to locate the governor-general, they set the compound ablaze. They then divided into four groups, each group attacking a different target in the city. The group headed by Huang headed for the city's south gate, where it clashed with a unit of the Reserve Forces. The commander of this unit, who was killed in the encounter, was apparently one of the revolutionary sympathizers. He and his troops were on their way to take part in the attack. To avoid a premature clash with loyalist troops, they had postponed putting on the identifying white armband, which Huang and his men were obviously unaware of. The fiasco killed whatever chance the revolt had of succeeding.

When Zhao Sheng and Hu Hanmin arrived in Guangzhou with the second contingent of volunteers, the revolt had been suppressed and the city sealed up. They returned to Hong Kong on board the same ferry. Some of the defeated rebels trapped inside the city, including Huang Xing, who was wounded, managed to get out with the help of sympathizers. Others were captured and executed, all 86 of them. Only the bodies of 72 were recovered by their comrades and buried together. At least 13 are believed to have been from British Malaya. A memorial service was held at the Penang headquarters of the Tongmenghui to mourn the death of the martyrs. In 1918, a memorial was erected at Huanghuagang in the northern suburbs of Guangzhou in memory of the "72 Martyrs" of the Guangzhou March 29 Uprising[25].

Few of the planned supporting uprisings outside the city took place due to the changes in the battle plan and the speed with which the revolt was put down. Revolutionaries in the New Army were not informed of the final plan and were caught completely off-guard. Only one unit of the Reserve Forces sympathetic to the rebels made it to the revolt, and Huang Xing had unknowingly neutralized it. One of the bandit bands did rise up the day after the uprising. They seized a market town and proceeded toward Guangzhou. En route they were quickly put down by a detachment of the Reserve Forces.

Sun was in Chicago when telegrams from Hong Kong brought the sad news and an urgent plea for funds to help survivors. He rushed to San Francisco and sold HK$15,000 worth of bonds to the secret societies, and prevailed upon his followers in Hawaii to remit another HK$5,000 to Hong Kong. These remittances provided some relief but could not make up for the paralyzing blow to the Tongmenghui network and the morale of its members. Sun, too, had his share of gloom, but he quickly recovered from his tenth defeat and resumed his old routine. By August he was able to start sending funds again to Hong Kong.[26]

It was also in August that the Tokyo militants led by Song Jiaoren established the Tongmenghui Central China Regional Office in Shanghai to pursue their own strategy. The stated purpose was to coordinate the activities of the revolutionary groups blossoming in the Yangtze. In truth, it was a declaration of war on Sun and his Cantonese entourage. The announcement accompanying the inauguration criticized the past weakness of the Alliance and Sun's faulty leadership, all of which Song and his comrades promised to fix. Clearly, what the Tokyo leaders were hoping to achieve was to turn the Central China Regional Office into the Alliance's leading arm and to persuade the *huaqiao* to redirect their pocketbooks to the Tokyo leaders. The overthrow of the Manchu regime and the establishment of a republican regime remained part of their program but no mention was made of "people's livelihood." Eager to create an opposition front with widespread appeal, Song and the other Tokyo leaders wanted to avoid alienating the local elites, many of them landowners. They also tried to rally the constitutionalists by stressing the threat of foreign intervention and abandoning their denigration of the Manchu race and the attacks on Liang Qichao. While still claiming that revolution was necessary, Song rejected Sun's strategy of southern risings. Situated at a distance from the power center, an uprising there would have the best chance of success but would be unlikely to bring about the collapse of the Qing regime. He considered the Yangtze valley as offering the best choice as a theater of operation. Being closer to the capital, a successful insurrection there could rapidly spread northward.[27]

Sun had staked practically all the resources of the Tongmenghui on the Huanghuagang revolt and lost. It was a devastating blow to the Alliance, which was so weakened that by its own admission it would be another five years before it could organize another revolt. The defeat was especially painful to supporters in British Malaya, particularly those who had contributed so generously to the cause. For Sun, it was his last chance to deliver a fatal blow at the Qing dynasty. But the political situation in China was changing and a revolutionary situation had been rapidly developing since 1910. The loyalty of the armed forces had become suspect. The public's contempt for the dynasty grew while their faith in the government declined. The Huanghuagang Uprising and the assassination that preceded it had struck fear into the hearts of officials, who for weeks were afraid to venture out of their compounds. In the summer a British intelligence report predicted that the next anti-Manchu rising in Guangzhou would receive strong grassroots support. Perhaps the report was right and the revolutionaries erred only in their timing. Had the revolt taken place just a few months later, the outcome might have been very different. For the circumstances that would finally precipitate the fall of the dynasty were already taking shape in Guangdong and the Yangtze provinces.[28]

Chapter 10

THE SPARK THAT STARTED THE FIRE

BY THE SUMMER of 1911, Sun had spearheaded ten abortive uprisings, six in eastern Guangdong and four from across the Indochinese border into western Guangdong, Guangxi and Yunnan. Already in his mid-forties, he was no closer to realizing his dream of overthrowing the Manchu dynasty and setting China on the road to republicanism than when he first embarked on his career as a professional revolutionary 16 years earlier. The spark that finally started the fire which incinerated the 268-year-old Qing dynasty and extinguished China's two-millennia-old imperial institution began in a single city. Sympathetic risings spread throughout the realm, just as Sun had always envisioned it. In a cruel twist of fate that robbed him of his moment with history, it began by accident while he was on the other side of the world.

The second half of the 19th century was a period of rapid railroad construction worldwide, but not in China. Here railways were considered a disruptive force to the harmony between man and nature, and it was deemed disrespectful and inauspicious to relocate or build over the ancestral graves scattered throughout the countryside. Qing officials, too, were against extending China's railway network out of concerns that this would help to accelerate foreign penetration into the Chinese heartland. Thus despite the willingness of many foreign banks to lend to the Qing government for railroad construction there was little interest, so that at the end of 1896 China had only 370 miles (600 km) of track. By comparison, the United States had 182,000 miles (300,000 km) and Britain 21,000 miles (34,000 km). Even tiny Japan with a land area less than five percent of China's, had 2,300 miles (3,700 km) of track.[1] After the Sino-Japanese War and the "scramble for concessions," the Western powers began building and operating railroads in their respective spheres of influence. Some also acquired extraterritorial rights and concessions to exploit natural resources on certain segments of their railroad.

The Qing court's attitude toward railways changed after the Boxer Uprising. During the conflict, they discovered that imperial troops could use the railroads to move about rapidly and then destroy the tracks to prevent foreign troops from advancing. After the dust of battle had settled, the Chinese themselves entered the railroad business and turned to the international capital markets for financing. On top of high interest rates secured by mortgages on the railroads and liens on their future earnings, the foreign loan syndicates managed the construction, purchasing and operations of the railroads. The one railroad built entirely by Chinese engineers with indigenous capital cost about a third less per mile than those of comparable quality built under the auspices of Western banks. It was thus a hugely profitable business for the foreign syndicates. With Europe flush with surplus capital, foreign bankers tripped over one another to lend to the Chinese, often using their countries' diplomats to exert pressure on Beijing.[2]

This was happening at a time of rising nationalism in China, as evidenced by the anti-foreign boycotts, the anti-missionary protests and the proliferation of anti-Manchu tracts. One consequence of this upsurge in nationalism was the emergence of a "rights-recovery movement," and the buy-back of foreign railroad concessions was an important part of it. In a few isolated instances, the furor over foreign control of the railroads enabled provincial railroad companies to raise the funds domestically towards redemption, but there was just not enough indigenous long-term capital to redeem more than a token few.

The longest and most ambitious railroad project was the link between Beijing and Wuhan, the sprawling tri-city metropolis comprising Wuchang, the provincial capital of Hubei, the industrial city of Hanyang and the great river port of Hankou. The megalopolis was central China's industrial heartland and transportation hub, much as Chicago is in the United States. Before the completion of the Beijing-Wuhan line in 1905, negotiations were already under way to extend it from Wuhan to Guangzhou in the south and westward from Wuhan to Chengdu, the Sichuan provincial capital. The merchants and gentry prodded the Qing government into buying back the American concession to build the Wuhan-Guangzhou line, which it did with money borrowed from the Hong Kong colonial government. The provincial railway companies then undertook to build the two extensions from Wuhan. After several years, the sale of shares produced only a trickle of the required capital, and construction was held up. In 1908, Zhang Zhidong, the last of the four great Confucian statesmen, was put in charge of railroad matters. Seeing no alternative to foreign funding, he recommended the nationalization of the lines and bringing them under central government control.

The gentry and merchants who had hoped to profit from the railroad development were outraged. They charged that the move was a conspiracy to sell out China to the foreign powers. These entrepreneurs were the most influential people in the provinces and along with returned students dominated the newly created provincial assemblies. The government's hesitation to proceed in the face of the protests did not prevent massive demonstrations from sprouting up all over the country. Zhang Zhidong's sterling reputation might have been sufficient to defuse the agitation. On his death in 1909, the court made the fateful decision of appointing Sheng Xuanhuai, another of Li Hongzhang's protégés, to head the Ministry of Communications; railway matters came under his purview. In spite of his distinguished career in the bureaucracy, Sheng had a reputation as the empire's most notorious wheeler-dealer. Those opposing the loan immediately focused their attacks on him and raised charges of corruption.

In spite of the unrest, there was no immediate threat to the Qing dynasty. The Tongmenghui was in disarray and the revolutionary movement was going through a crisis of relevance. The dynasty had also managed to defuse the threat of revolution through reforms and concessions to public opinion. Too frightened to share real political power, yet too weak to resist demands for political reforms, the regent Zaifeng, father of the boy emperor Xuantong (Puyi), had created elected provincial assemblies in 1909. These were to serve as consultative bodies but he hoped that they would also serve as checks on provincial administration. The outcome was dramatically different. In the absence of a National Assembly, the provincial leaders became all the more active at the provincial level. Far from being content with their consultative function, they governed their provinces in virtual autonomy. They put so much pressure on the court that Zaifeng was forced to convene a National Assembly in June 1910, with half its members elected, and the other half appointed by the imperial court. Shortly after its formation, the National Assembly also exceeded its consultative role and demanded a shorter timetable for a parliamentary government.

In response to the demand, the Qing court agreed on November 4 to advance the date from 1916 to 1913. While most reformists were satisfied with the court's partial concession to their demands, others were reportedly so unhappy that they returned to their respective provinces to organize a revolution. Then in December, the court issued its decision on the sensitive question of the detested *towchang*, which opponents of the custom saw not only as a reminder of the dynasty's alien origin but also as a symbol of China's backwardness in the modern world. In anticipation of a favorable ruling from the court, many Chinese, especially students, began cutting off their queues in the latter half of 1910. The court's negative decision was taken by some reformists as another indication of the court's unresponsiveness to public opinion.

Liang Qichao's followers, who had abandoned the revolutionary route after the post-Boxer reforms, informed him in March that they were returning to the revolutionary path. Liang himself published an article in the same month renouncing his previous warning of the threat of partition by the foreign powers in the event of a revolution. He now declared that it was possible for China to go through a revolution without necessarily inviting foreign intervention. Ignoring these danger signals, the Qing court sounded its own death knell with three fatal decisions within a span of two weeks in May 1911.[3]

It had made compliant noises in response to the National Assembly's demand for a cabinet to replace the Manchu-dominated Grand Council. On May 8, the court unveiled a cabinet with eight Manchu members, one Mongolian and just four Han Chinese. This was a jab at Chinese ethnic pride and a blow to the dynasty's fast-diminishing legitimacy. The reformists were upset by the court's disregard of their desire for a greater sharing of power with their Manchu overlords. When they failed to secure the immediate summoning of a parliament, they had accepted in good faith the Qing court's promise to name a cabinet soon. By unveiling a cabinet dominated by incompetent Manchus, the court only succeeded in alienating its gentry constituency throughout the country. On May 10, the court announced that it would proceed with the nationalization of the Wuhan-Guangzhou and Wuhan-Chengdu rail lines. Ten days later, on May 20, Sheng Xuanhuai signed a loan agreement with the Four-Power banking consortium to float a £10 million loan for the project. As usual, the rail lines were to be put up as collateral and there were also the usual provisions for the syndicate's control over construction, purchasing and operation.

The Qing regime had by now totally exhausted its credibility and political capital. In the prevailing atmosphere of mutual suspicion and distrust, the deal with the foreign banks seemed to fulfill the long-standing belief that the Manchus were conspiring with the Western powers against China's interests. Emotional mass rallies and demonstrations organized by the Railway Protection Movement followed. Instead of appeasing the railway investors, the foreign powers instigated the Qing government into taking a tough stance. The popular anger was particularly strident in Sichuan, where the railroad investors were to be compensated entirely in government bonds. Leaders of the Sichuan provincial assembly and prominent railroad investors in the province vowed not to pay further taxes and to continue fighting for their demands. The government moved to suppress the volatile situation, resulting in 32 deaths in the provincial capital. Conditions in Sichuan quickly deteriorated and the government was compelled to transport New Army troops from nearby Wuhan to suppress the unrest.

This was a god-sent opportunity for the Tongmenghui to deliver its coup de grâce but China's premier anti-Manchu organization was not ready to capitalize on the developing mayhem. Song Jiaoren had been planning to set up the Tongmenghui's Central China Headquarters to rally the various revolutionary groups in the Yangtze Valley, which so far had only paid lip service to the Alliance. This did not happen until July 1911 and Song estimated that it would take at least two years to complete the preparations. The storm clouds broke much too soon and Song decided to sit out. But if the Tongmenghui was not ready to act, other anti-dynastic groups were not ready to wait. For more than a decade, the small revolutionary groups of Hubei province had been continuously active. Pursued by the authorities, they had dissolved time and again, only to reincarnate under different guises.

In 1911, they were gathered together in two principal societies. The Gongjinhui, or Progressive Society, an offshoot of the Tongmenghui, had been recruiting members from the local secret societies. The second group hid behind the innocuous name Wenxueshe, or Literary Institute. It had in its membership register several thousand soldiers of New Army units stationed in Wuchang. Like the Tongmenghui, students led these groups, but unlike the Alliance, they were self-sufficient and did not have to rely on foreign allies or funding. More importantly, their fighting forces were stationed in China, ready for action. These revolutionary groups had a vague commitment to republicanism but the force that bound them together was the common objective to overthrow the Qing dynasty. They also maintained a loose liaison with the non-Cantonese leaders of the Tongmenghui, in particular Huang Xing and Song Jiaoren. In September, the two Hubei revolutionary groups worked out an agreement to schedule their respective uprisings in October.[4]

The New Army, which was destined to play a key role in the collapse of the Manchu dynasty, was a relatively new element in the Qing military organization. After China's defeat in the Sino-Japanese War in 1895, the Qing government resolved to rebuild China's military strength by creating new armies from scratch. The first of these armies were sponsored by Zhang Zhidong in Hubei and Yuan Shikai in the North. In 1901, in the aftermath of the Boxer Uprising, Empress Dowager Cixi launched the New Policy reforms, a thorough overhaul of Qing policy in government, education and the military. Yuan Shikai's army was expanded to form the Beiyang Army, which later emerged as the strongest military force in China. In 1904, the government formulated a long-term plan to reorganize the newly created armies into 36 divisions reporting directly to the capital. This was the New Army. Initially expected to be completed by 1922, the deadline was later brought forward to 1912. By 1906, there were ten divisions: five were part of Yuan's Beiyang Army in the North, the sixth was made up of Zhang Zhidong's troops in Hubei, and the remaining divisions and some independent brigades were spread elsewhere throughout the country.[5]

The New Policy reforms made dramatic progress in many areas but the Qing government was facing a crisis of legitimacy. The refusal of the leading provincial officials to support Cixi's pro-Boxer stance suggested that the throne could not always count on the compliance of its Chinese officials. To ensure that the military's final authority rested with the Manchus in Beijing rather than the Chinese in the provinces, the Ministry of War was reorganized under the direction of a senior Manchu officer. The following year, another Manchu was appointed to the newly created post of Comptroller of the Army. Both Zhang Zhidong and Yuan Shikai were kicked upstairs to the Grand Council so as to wean their troops away from them. A new system was put in place to station divisions of the New Army at strategic locations across China, including cities where there were garrisons of the Eight Banners, which were slowly being phased out.

But the Qing's control over the military remained problematic. The command structure was fragmented, especially in the North, where the Beiyang Army remained loyal to Yuan Shikai. The court's response to his prestige and popularity was to retire him altogether in 1909. This left him angry and his loyal senior officers disgruntled. Since the abolition of the civil examinations in 1905, many ambitious young men had embarked on military careers, which offered a swift channel for upward social mobility. Restless and idealistic, many of these men were nationalistic and were actively involved in the agitations of the provincial assemblies. A number of them had also joined the anti-dynastic societies, and those stationed in Wuchang had been apprised of the preparations for an uprising. Originally scheduled for October 6, the day of the Mid-Autumn Festival, it was postponed to the end of the month when rumors started circulating of an impending uprising on the earlier date.[6]

On the evening of October 9, a group of Hubei revolutionaries accidentally exploded a bomb while assembling explosives at their hideout in the Russian concession of Wuchang. While comrades rushed the injured to hospital, police officers who had responded to the explosion discovered the membership register of people enrolled in the revolutionary societies. Alarmed at the large number of Hubei New Army soldiers on the list, the police began rounding up suspects. As tensions rose, an altercation broke out between Sergeant Xiong Bingkun and his company commanders in the

8th Engineer Battalion on the evening of October 10, the date subsequently celebrated as the "Double Tenth Day" marking the start of the 1911 Revolution. The officers suspected that materials from the Wuhan ammunition dump, which their battalion was detailed to guard, had been smuggled to the revolutionaries. With the police indiscriminately rounding up soldiers suspected of revolutionary sympathies and tensions running high, Sergeant Xiong shot the officers and persuaded his men to mutiny. Under Xiong's command, the engineering unit stormed and seized the arsenal, which contained domestically produced as well as foreign-made arms. Using their captured booty, they launched a successful attack on the city's main fort. With loyal troops in short supply, the Manchu governor-general and his Chinese military commander abandoned the city. By noon the following day, the New Army rebels had taken control of the city of Wuchang. Many accounts later suggested that Qing forces would have prevailed had the governor-general held his ground – similar outbreaks in Guangzhou and Sichuan had been easily suppressed through prompt action.[7]

News of the fall of Wuchang quickly spread. By the evening of October 11, revolutionaries had captured the city of Hanyang, and on the following morning seized control of Hankou. The revolutionaries then formed a military government in Hubei under Tang Hualong, the president of the local provincial assembly, as civil governor, and drafted, allegedly at gunpoint, Li Yuanhong as military governor. Popular with the troops and well-liked by the provincial leaders, Li was an ideal candidate. As the former commander of the 21st Mixed Brigade who had advocated the modernization of China's military, the Qing court would find it difficult to brand him a rebel or a bandit. The revolutionaries then sent telegrams bearing Li's name to urge other provincial governments to join the revolution, warning them that the Han Chinese might never have another chance to overthrow the Manchus. Meanwhile, Tang Hualong persuaded the foreign consuls in Hankou to remain neutral.

Li Yuanhong

Skeptical at first that the uprising would succeed, Huang Xing and Song Jiaoren did not arrive in Wuchang until late October. By that time, the New Army insurgents had obtained the support of the gentry and their representatives in the provincial assembly, as well as the neutrality of the foreign powers. All Huang and Song could do was to integrate themselves into the revolution but their presence did not change anything. Huang, who became commander-in-chief of the revolutionary forces, was subordinate to Li Yuanhong, who retained his overall leadership, while Song returned to the lower Yangtze to create a second revolutionary center.

Consequently, the Tongmenghui played a significant role in only a few places. Chen Qimei, an ardent supporter of Sun with strong links to businesses and the secret societies in Shanghai, became military commander after leading a successful attack on the local arsenal. To maintain the momentum, he sent his young associate Chiang Kai-shek to storm the government *yamen* in the historic city of Hangzhou, which he won over to the revolution. In Guangdong, Hu Hanmin took over after the imperial governor fled when merchants in Guangzhou turned against the dynasty.[8]

The Qing government responded to the unfolding crisis by ordering a coordinated counterattack on Wuhan by two Beiyang Army divisions while summoning Yuan Shikai back from his enforced retirement. With his long history of leadership over the Beiyang Army and strong personal ties to its senior officers, the court believed that he would be able to rally the Beiyang troops in the service of the dynasty. Chastened by his unceremonious retirement, Yuan was too shrewd to accept the appointment as military commander of the empire before he had a chance to size up the situation. While Yuan was buying time, events moved quickly. On October 22, the New Army in both Shaanxi and Hunan provinces mutinied and obtained the support of leaders of the provincial assemblies. During the last week of October, three more provinces rose against the Manchus. At the end of the month, a senior Northern general ignored a Qing order to lead his troops south. Instead he joined with a number of other field commanders in issuing 12 demands to the Qing court.[9]

The key elements of the demands were to establish a parliament within the year, to have this legislative body promulgate a constitution, to elect a prime minister, and to declare an amnesty for all political prisoners. The demands also sought to deny the emperor all rights of summary execution and to prohibit members of the Qing imperial clan from serving in the cabinet. The Manchu court complied with most of these demands within a week. Three days after the National Assembly elected Yuan Shikai premier, the court issued a decree on November 11 confirming his appointment and ordering him to form a cabinet, which Yuan promptly filled with his partisans. Throughout November, Yuan performed a delicate balancing act, using his influence over the Beiyang Army to play the Qing against the revolutionaries. Qing forces managed to recapture Hankou and Hanyang but this was of little comfort to the court as one province after another declared support for the revolution.

The Qing's position was considerably weakened when loyalist forces after several weeks of fighting were defeated at Nanjing in early December. The city had been the imperial capital in the early years of the Ming dynasty and since that time held a symbolic significance. By early December, 14 provinces had declared their independence from the Qing regime. The formation of a unified revolutionary government became a matter of some urgency to prevent regional rivalries as well as to present an appearance of unity for the benefit of the dynasty and the foreign presence. It was the historic city of Nanjing that the revolutionaries chose as the seat of the provisional government. Meeting on December 14, the Wuchang and the Shanghai factions clashed over the choice of a provisional head of government. The Wuchang faction supported Li Yuanhong while the Shanghai group favored Huang Xing. The assembly could not agree on this nor on the powers of the future leader. Some headed by Song Jiaoren demanded that those powers be limited by a cabinet while others pleaded for a regime of the presidential type.[10]

Sun was on the other side of the globe in his usual quest for funds from the *huaqiao* communities as the revolution he had tirelessly promoted for the past 16 years was unfolding. On October 11, the day after the Wuchang revolt, he was in Denver, Colorado, reading a week-old coded telegram from Huang Xing requesting funds for a prospective uprising in Wuchang. Sun was thus taken aback when the next morning's paper carried the headline: "Wuchang occupied by the Revolutionaries." An even greater surprise awaited him on October 14 when his train passed through St. Louis en route to Chicago. An article in a newspaper he picked up reported that there were plans to have "Dr. Sun Yat-sen" serve as the first president of the republic if the unfolding revolution were to succeed.

With his dream rapidly coming true, Sun did the unexpected: he decided against returning to China right away. Was he concerned for his own safety? If the rebellion failed, he would be heading straight into the hands of the Qing government, and his execution would be a virtual certainty. Was he buying time to see how the chips would fall? Or was he acting in the belief, as he later explained in his autobiography, that the neutrality of the foreign powers was crucial to the outcome of the revolution, so "at that point the diplomatic front was more important than the firing line"? Whatever his motive was, it turned out in retrospect to be a shrewd decision.[11]

His first stop was Washington, D.C., but his request for a meeting with Secretary of State Philander Knox conveyed through an intermediary was refused because the Taft administration was already committed to a policy of neutrality in the Chinese revolution. Unfazed by the rebuff, Sun set sail for London, where he arrived on October 20. He checked into the Savoy Hotel under his Japanese pseudonym Nakayama and had a reunion with Dr. Cantlie and his wife.[12] He also met with Homer Lea, who was in London putting the finishing touches to his latest and final book, *The Day of the Saxon*, in which he predicted the breakup of the British Empire. In this and his earlier book *The Valor of Ignorance*, Lea viewed the American and British contest for dominance as the Anglo-Saxon aspect of a larger Social Darwinist struggle between the races, which he believed was inevitable. In this impending clash, Lea's ultimate goal was to forge an alliance between the Anglo-Saxons and the Chinese to counterbalance other regional and global competitors.[13]

In spite of his failed plan to subvert the Chinese imperial regime, the American adventurer now decided to be the Lafayette that Sun had often dreamt about. Sun appointed him his military adviser with the rank of lieutenant-general in the Chinese army. Acting as a spokesman for Sun, Lea proposed to the Four-Power banking consortium that they divert funds intended for the Qing government to the future Chinese republic. Lea's friend Sir Trevor Dawson, hopeful that his armament company Vickers, Sons & Maxim would receive orders for weapons once Sun became the

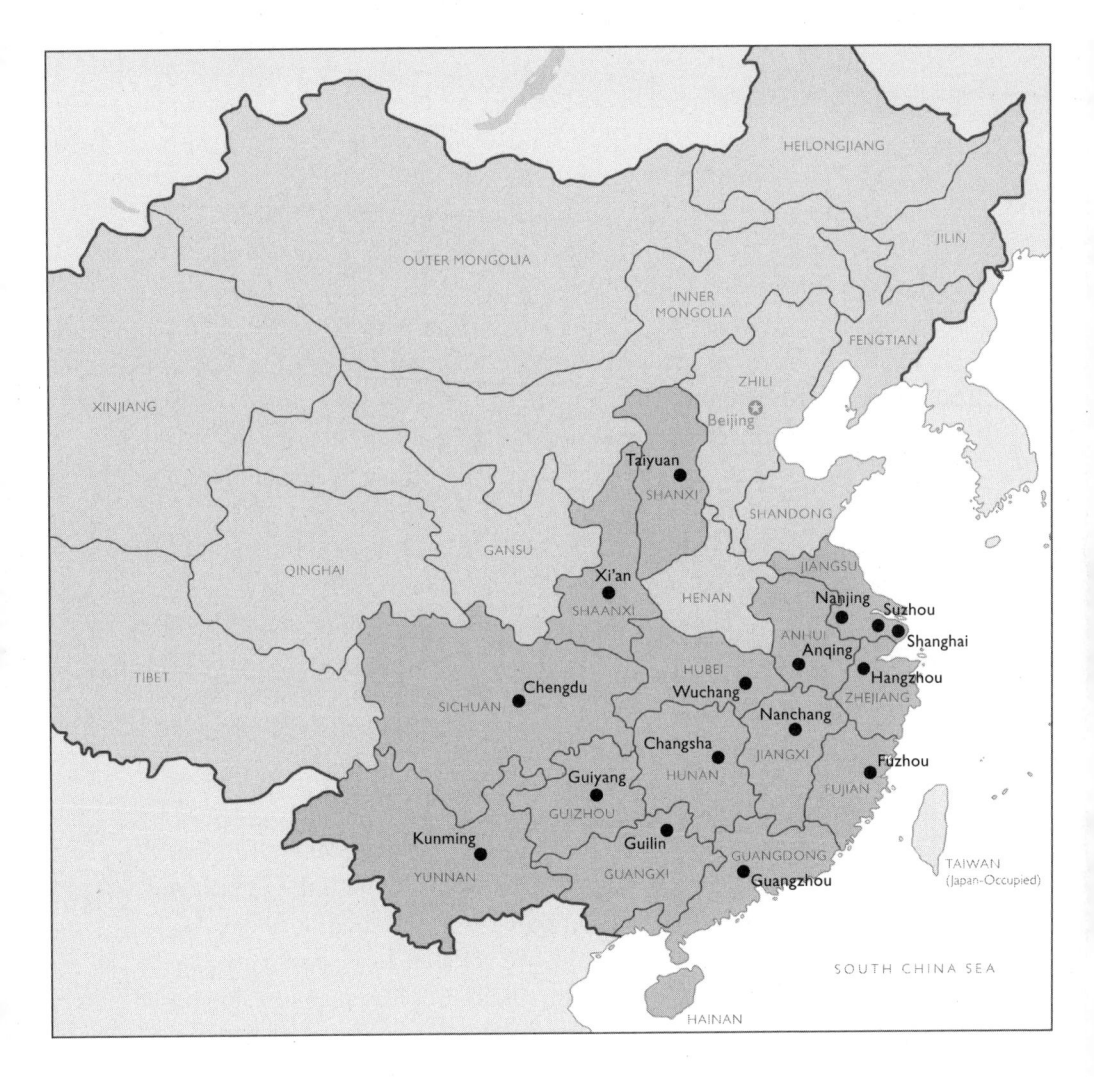

MAP 4 · THE 1911 REVOLUTION:
INDEPENDENT PROVINCES AS OF DECEMBER 1911

Province/City	Provincial capital	Date declared	Province/City	Provincial capital	Date declared
Hubei	Wuchang	October 11	Zhejiang	Hangzhou	November 4
Hunan	Changsha	October 22	Jiangsu	Suzhou	November 5
Shaanxi	Xi'an	October 22	Guangxi	Guilin	November 7
Shanxi	Taiyuan	October 29	Anhui	Anqing	November 8
Jiangxi	Nanchang	October 31	Guangdong	Guangzhou	November 9
Yunnan	Kunming	October 31	Fujian	Fuzhou	November 10
Shanghai	-	November 4	Sichuan	Chengdu	November 27
Guizhou	Guiyang	November 4	Nanjing	-	December 2

president of Chinese republic, submitted on November 14 a memorandum co-signed by Sun and Lea to the British Foreign Secretary Edward Gray. The memorandum declared that once Sun became president, he would grant special privileges to Britain and the United States. And in return for their support and friendship, he would place the Chinese navy under the command of British officers and seek the advice of the British in regard to any agreement that China might make with Japan. Sun and Lea also wanted Gray's assistance to arrange financial backing for their revolutionary government; to block loans to the Qing government that the Four-Power banking consortium was arranging; and to instruct the British colonial authorities in British Malaya and Hong Kong to rescind the travel ban on Sun.

Gray did not bite. The Foreign Secretary had made up his mind and was betting on Yuan Shikai as the leader who would emerge the commanding figure in China. The banking consortium needed no prompting; it had already decided as early as November 8 not to advance any further loans to China until the political situation had cleared and a responsible government took office in Beijing. In the end, all that Sun managed to obtain from the Foreign Office was the lifting of his travel ban in British territories.

Sun saw little point remaining in London after failing to arrange a US$5 million loan through the Hongkong & Shanghai Bank. Still desperate for money, he decided to stop in Paris to confer with the French government and to solicit financial support before heading home to China. The possibility of a Sino-French alliance violated Lea's worldview but he acquiesced because of Sun's desperate situation. Their four-day sojourn in Paris was equally disappointing. Though Sun met with some important political figures, including Georges Clemenceau, who had been prime minister from October 1906 to July 1909, all that Sun obtained was confirmation of French diplomatic neutrality, which was forthcoming in any event by reasons of political expediency. Sun also met with Stanislas Simon, the director of the Banque de l'Indochine on November 23, but Simon merely repeated what Sun had known all along, that there would be no loan to China until the dust had cleared. This was not exactly what Sun had hoped to hear but at least the enemy would not get any funding either. While in Paris, Sun learnt that Li Yuanhong and Yuan Shikai were both being considered as presidential candidates. Without the foreign financial backing that he had hoped for, Sun doubted that he would be a contender for the presidency, and promptly wired the revolutionary leaders in Shanghai that either man would be acceptable to him.

Nothing concrete came out of Sun's grand European diplomatic tour but it was not all for nothing. His contacts with Western political and business leaders had given him an "aura of prestige." On November 24, Sun and his entourage, comprising his son and secretary Sun Ke, Homer Lea and his wife, and several Chinese comrades left Marseille on board the British steamer SS *Devanha* bound for China. He declined to speak to the press when the ship made an overnight stop in Penang on December 14. Lea, granting an interview, explained why it was important for Britain and the United States to support the establishment of a strong government in post-Qing China. He asserted that China could help protect British interests in the Pacific and India against possible Russian expansionism, as well as counterbalancing Japanese dominance in the Pacific to help protect America's commercial interests in the region. The rest of Sun's family – his wife Lu Muzhen, his two daughters and his constant companion Chen Cuifen, who had remained behind in Penang when he was deported in December 1910 – joined him for the journey to Singapore.

The Chinese in Singapore were skeptical when they first learned of the Wuchang Uprising. Few had expected another insurgency so soon after the disastrous Huanghuagang revolt. The skepticism soon turned into jubilation as news continued to report sympathetic risings elsewhere in the empire and the increasing number of provinces declaring independence from the crumbling Qing dynasty. With prospects increasing with each passing day that the revolution had a fair chance of overthrowing the Manchu dynasty, many jumped on the revolutionary bandwagon. A group of revolutionaries got together in October to launch the *Nam Kew Poo* (Straits Chinese Morning Post) to report on the progress of the uprising in China. Within two weeks of its launch, the circulation of this newspaper reached 2,000, the highest ever achieved by a Chinese newspaper in British Malaya during this period.[14]

By early November, when reports reached Singapore that the Forbidden City and its royal residents were in the hands of revolutionaries, many in the Chinese community were in a state of virtual ecstasy. Never mind that the reports had not been confirmed, the good tidings spread like wild fire through fliers and newspapers, by word of mouth and speeches in public parks, as well as by an enterprising young man cycling around the town with the news painted on the back of his white shirt and a revolutionary flag flapping from his straw hat. In the early morning of November 6, Singapore's Chinatown was the scene of "pandemoniacal noise," its streets mired ankle-deep in the debris of thousands of dollars' worth of spent firecrackers. Shops were open but no business was transacted; bosses were too busy celebrating along with the sea of Chinese swarming the streets. Buildings were adorned with red buntings and revolutionary flags were hoisted on many Chinese shops and houses. The only imperial dragon flag still flying in front of a Chinese bank on Kling Street was hauled down and ceremoniously burned. Hundreds of Chinese severed their *towchangs*, the detested symbol of their subjugation to the Manchus. In the western part of the town, some zealots waylaid fellow Chinese still sporting pigtails and gave them a free coiffure. Special performances were staged at the Chinese theater on Wayang Street to raise funds for the revolution. Photographs of Sun Yat-sen along with those of Li Yuanhong, offered for sale, fetched unheard-of prices.[15]

Tongmenghui members who had been lukewarm toward the Huanghuagang Uprising were prompt in their response. On November 10, they organized a public meeting at which over a thousand Chinese jostled their way in. While representatives from the various *bangs*, or dialect groups, were delivering speeches, people from the audience were thrusting donations large and small into the collection boxes marked "Relief Fund for Chinese Martyrs" to avoid rankling the British authorities. Several thousand dollars were reported to have been collected that day.[16]

Responding to an appeal for financial aid from the revolutionary government in Fujian, two Tongmenghui leaders, Tan Boo Liat and Tan Kah Kee, took the lead in convening a public meeting at the Thian Hock Keng (Tian Fu Gong) Temple on November 13. Twenty members were elected to serve on the committee of the "Fujian Security Fund," which raised S$129,000 from the Hokkien *bang* during a nine-month campaign. A week later, on November 20, the Cantonese, Teochew, Hakka and Hainan *bangs* held a similar meeting at the Thong Chai Medical Institution on Wayang Street. Teo Eng Hock, Tan Chor Nam and Lim Nee Soon were among the most enthusiastic promoters of the "Guangdong Security and Relief Fund," which collected S$200,000 from fellow provincials by the following August. Meanwhile, the womenfolk from the Cantonese community went door to door and collected more than S$20,000.

Sun's arrival had been widely expected ever since his ship departed from Penang. He was no longer the rebel who sought "sympathetic faces and generous purses" among the Chinese. It was now the people who turned up in large numbers to greet him at the pier when the *Devanha* docked at Singapore on December 15. Sun looked "remarkably well" in spite of his heavy travel schedule over the past two and a half months. Attired in a simple white suit, he was described by the *Straits Times* as "the picture of anything but the inspirer of a great world-striking movement." To the Chinese at the pier, that hardly mattered; he was their Man of the Hour.

Sun and his entourage spent the night as guests of Tan Boo Liat at his splendid Golden Bell Mansion on the slope of Mount Faber, the highest point along the southern ridges of Singapore with a commanding view of the harbor. During his overnight sojourn, Sun met with his Singapore partisans to discuss the situation in China. A clear and present danger he highlighted to his interlocutors was the untenable situation where there were two centers of revolutionary activities, one in Shanghai and a second in Wuchang. He refused to be drawn into the debate on who the eventual leader might be, except to say that his immediate task on returning to China was to consolidate the two revolutionary centers and concentrate the power at Shanghai. Once this was done, the next step would be to submit the revolutionaries' demands to the Qing court, and if these were not accepted, the revolutionary forces would march on Beijing. He specifically ruled out any role for the Manchus in the new republican government except as private citizens. On this there could be no compromise, Sun insisted, and the Tongmenghui was ready to stand or fail by their demand for absolute power.[17]

Many of his supporters, including several Japanese, turned up to greet Sun and his entourage when the *Devanha* berthed in Hong Kong on December 21. The Japanese adventurers, so active over the past decade, had taken little part in the revolution. Their initiatives had been frustrated by their government's ambiguous and often conflicting policy toward the revolution as well as by Sun's absence. His return now gave them hope of regaining a toehold in the revolution. Homer Lea, who was not particularly fond of the Japanese, made no effort to hide his feelings, but there was little he could do to prevent them from accompanying Sun on his journey to Shanghai.[18]

Sun also had a reunion with his Cantonese supporters in the Tongmenghui. Appointed military governor of Guangdong in November, Hu Hanmin's presence in Hong Kong was not a matter of courtesy; he had a specific agenda. Concerned that Yuan's military strength would eventually reduce Sun's possible presidency to a nominal position, his aim was to prevent Sun from proceeding to the Yangtze provinces and having himself elected provisional president by the Nanjing assembly. He wanted Sun to set up a provisional government in Guangzhou, consolidate the Tongmenghui's Cantonese base and prepare for a showdown with Yuan. But Sun saw things differently. His priority was to remove the Manchus, and that would require the foreign powers to remain neutral, which would not be possible if there was renewed fighting. While sharing Hu's suspicion of Yuan, Sun believed that by rallying Yuan to the revolution, they could use him to obtain the abdication of the Qing dynasty and put an end to the civil war. Conceding that Yuan might eventually pose a problem, Sun believed he had the support of the masses and appeared not to be overly concerned about Yuan. Most of the Tongmenghui leaders also favored negotiation over confrontation with Yuan. Their viewpoint was reinforced by the opinion of no less an authority than G.E. Morrison, the London *Times* correspondent. He warned that it would be futile to expect early recognition by the foreign powers if the leader was anyone other than Yuan Shikai, who alone had the confidence of the powers. Hu Hanmin rallied to Sun's plan after a long debate and the two men then traveled together to Shanghai.

In contrast to the enthusiastic reception in Singapore and Hong Kong, nobody was at the Huangpu wharf to greet Sun when he arrived in Shanghai on a cold and gray Christmas morning. Most of the Alliance leaders were huddled together with provincial delegates in Nanjing haggling over the leadership of the provisional government. They were still deadlocked

Official portrait of Sun Yat-sen as provisional president of the Republic of China, January 1, 1912.

on the choice of a provisional head of government. With Sun's arrival in China, a movement quickly emerged to nominate him as a candidate. This succeeded but the debate over the form that the new republic would take was far less consensual. Song Jiaoren, who probably distrusted both Sun and Yuan, favored a parliamentary system with ministerial responsibility to put a cap on the powers of the president. Sun prevailed with his argument that "at this time of emergency, we cannot adopt a political system which restricts the power of the man we trust."[19]

It was therefore as a president endowed with extensive powers that provincial delegates elected him by 16 votes to one on December 29. Li Yuanhong became the vice president and Huang Xing was given the crucial war portfolio. The Republic of China came into being on January 1, 1912, and Sun arrived in Nanjing from Shanghai to inaugurate his mandate. Aside from the oath of investiture, the only sign of ostentation was the official ceremony at the tomb of the first Ming emperor just outside the city. Here Sun paid homage to the long-departed Hongwu Emperor and vowed that he would evict the Manchus just as Hongwu had reclaimed Heaven's Mandate from the Mongols more than 500 years earlier.

Sun's cabinet was a constellation of talented and remarkable individuals that surpassed, in terms of the quality of its members, those put together in later decades. Serving alongside Huang Xing, who was the de facto prime minister, was Wang Zhonghui as minister for foreign affairs. A brilliant, multilingual scholar, he had authored an English translation and annotation of the German Civil Code. Wu Tingfang, brother-in-law of Sir Ho Kai, became minister of justice. The first Chinese to be admitted to the English bar, Wu had formerly served as secretary to Li Hongzhang. Cai Yuanpei, the man of letters, was given the education portfolio.

The stream of *huaqiao* who visited Nanjing to collect on the promises Sun had made to them during his fundraising days was a constant source of irritation to his partisans. But it was the presence of so many foreign advisers that caused the most alarm. The Japanese especially were not popular with the revolutionaries and they were absolutely feared by the Shanghai business fraternity. Adventurers like Miyazaki Torazo were now joined by businessmen, in particular representatives of Mitsui & Co., which was pursuing an active policy of economic expansion in China. Their presence also bothered William H. Donald, who had become an adviser to Sun. But having returned empty-handed from his U.S. and European tour, Sun needed funds to pay the revolutionary troops in the lower Yangtze valley and it was the Japanese who provided the funds.

China was now in an anomalous situation of having a republican president in Nanjing and a Manchu emperor on the throne in Beijing. Indeed, the process toward a resolution was already set in motion in early November. When it became evident that the revolution would not easily succeed or be defeated, the two sides held preliminary talks that culminated in the convening of a formal conference in mid-December at Shanghai. Meanwhile, Yuan Shikai continued his meteoric rise in the capital. He arrived in Beijing on November 13 to take up his new post as prime minister, and once installed in the capital began to extend his power. First, he persuaded the court to grant him the authority to make decisions in all matters except those involving the imperial household. Then with the support of Empress Dowager Longyu, widow of the Guangxu Emperor, he engineered the resignation of the prince regent Zaifeng, who was blamed for all the problems of the past three years. No new regent was appointed and she took over the conduct of court affairs. In December, Yuan succeeded in removing the Palace Guards from the court's control and appointed a former protégé,

Feng Guozhang, as the unit's new commander, and another former protégé, Duan Qirui, to take over from Feng at the Hubei front. Not only had Yuan regained control over his Beiyang divisions, he had reversed the court's recent attempts to reassert its authority over the military.[20]

With his power entrenched, Yuan wrote to Li Yuanhong concerning a ceasefire and a negotiated political settlement. He appointed a close ally, Tang Shaoyi, as his emissary to negotiate with Wu Tingfang, the revolutionaries' chief negotiator. Yuan also enlisted the help of Wang Jingwei, who had chosen to remain in Beijing after his release from prison for the attempted assassination of Zaifeng, the prince regent. On December 1, the revolutionaries at Wuchang agreed to a local ceasefire. The military phase of the revolution was virtually over when on December 7 the court consented to a formal conference with the revolutionaries.

Before the formal talks began at Shanghai in mid-December, each side had begun to stake out its negotiating position. The choice was between monarchical or republican constitutionalism. In preliminary talks with Li Yuanhong in early November, Yuan's emissary contended that the Qing court had met most of the revolutionaries' demands by transforming itself from an autocratic to a constitutional regime. To bolster its case for a constitutional monarchy, the court issued two edicts denying the revolutionaries' accusations of racial discrimination. To back up the court's claim of racial impartiality, Yuan's ten-member cabinet had only one Manchu minister on board. On December 7, the cabinet, which had now replaced the court as the decision-maker on matters of governmental policy, agreed to do away with the *towchang* requirement, but without making it mandatory. Many Qing officials quickly shed their queues but Yuan kept his until the end of the dynasty.

What the revolutionaries demanded was republican constitutionalism, which was not negotiable. The talks between Tang Shaoyi and Wu Tingfang thus centered on the future of the Qing imperial household, the Manchu aristocracy and the bannermen population at large. To bring the revolution to a quick and successful conclusion, the more moderate elements in the Nanjing government and the revolutionaries were willing to make significant concessions to all these interested parties if the Qing regime would step aside in favor of a republic. As early as November 11, Li Yuanhong had also informed Yuan that his Nanjing government was prepared to recognize Yuan as president if the latter would defect from the Qing.

By the end of December, the Qing court had all but agreed to abdicate. Only the holding of a convention to formalize the transition from monarchy to republic remained. The abdication did not happen, however, for another six weeks. The agreement negotiated by Tang Shaoyi and Wu Tingfang to which the Qing court had reluctantly given its assent aroused considerable opposition from elements on both ends. Sun and the more radical among the revolutionaries were outraged that Wu had yielded too much, in particular a national convention to decide China's future polity. In the Qing camp, some diehard conservatives were upset that Tang had not fought hard enough for the dynasty. On January 2, Yuan Shikai abruptly repudiated the Tang-Wu agreement, asserting that the establishment of the republic violated the provision that China's future polity be decided by a national convention. He probably wondered, too, if the revolutionaries' promise to make him president was still good in light of Sun's election. Sun assured Yuan that he would step down if Yuan could get the Qing to abdicate.

With his future assured, Yuan changed his tune. Instead of waiting for a national convention to decide the fate of China's polity, he pressed the Qing court to accept the revolutionaries' offer and abdicate at once to avoid the fate of Louis XVI in the French Revolution. On January 16, he personally delivered to Empress Dowager Longyu a secret memorial asserting that popular opinion had turned irretrievably against the dynasty. Coincidentally, Yuan was nearly killed in an assassination attempt as he left the Forbidden City. Three local members of the Tongmenghui were seized and executed to take the blame for the plot.

On January 26, more than 40 Qing generals and military officers joined Duan Qirui in sending a telegram to Yuan's cabinet as well as several imperial princes imploring the dynasty to abdicate immediately and thus save the country from turmoil. What finally took the wind out of the Manchu resistance was the assassination of the most vocal opponent of abdication among the Manchu nobles. His death coupled with the warning telegram from Duan finally convinced the intransigents that their cause was lost.

On February 12, the Empress Dowager Longyu issued three edicts to proclaim the abdication of the Qing dynasty. She admitted in the abdication edict that the Qing had lost Heaven's Mandate and she was therefore transferring the emperor's sovereignty to the entire nation to establish a constitutional polity. With those few simple words, China's 25th and last dynasty came to an end. Under the Articles of Favorable Treatment which formed part of the abdication agreement, the deposed Xuantong Emperor (Puyi) was accorded the same courtesy as a foreign sovereign; subsidized to the tune of 4 million taels annually; permitted temporarily to reside in the Forbidden City but to move at a later date to Yiheyuan, the Summer Palace; and provided with the usual number of guards and attendants. The agreement also stated that the republic would pay for the Guangxu Emperor's tomb and for his funeral. It was an extraordinarily generous severance pay, in contrast to the last Russian monarch, Tsar Nicholas II, who was brutally murdered along with his entire family in the aftermath of the 1917 Bolshevik Revolution.

The abdication edict contained a statement authorizing Yuan to form a provisional republican government and to negotiate for national unification with the revolutionaries. This was not in the version prepared by the Nanjing government and accepted by Yuan. It was secretly inserted by Yuan to show that he derived his authority not from the Nanjing regime but from the abdicated Qing emperor. Sun and the revolutionaries were incensed but could do nothing about it.

Nevertheless, in spite of their suspicions about Yuan's intentions, the revolutionaries kept their word. The day after the abdication, Sun resigned his post and recommended that Yuan be named his successor conditional on the latter assuming his post in Nanjing as the seat of government. On February 15, the provisional parliament duly elected Yuan the provisional president, with Li Yuanhong retaining the provisional vice presidency. On the same day, Sun and a large entourage traveled to the tomb of the founder of the Ming dynasty and announced to the spirit of the departed Hongwu Emperor that the Manchu conquest of Ming China had been avenged and that finally the occupation of China by the "eastern barbarians" had come to an end.

On February 18, a delegation was dispatched to Beijing to escort Yuan to Nanjing. But Yuan was not about to trade his power base in the North for the revolutionaries' stronghold in the South. To justify the need for his continued presence in Beijing, he instigated his own soldiers to riot. This left the revolutionaries no choice but to allow him to be inaugurated in Beijing, which took place on March 1. The next day, Sun promulgated the provisional constitution, and on April 1 formally relinquished his duties as provisional president. Four days later, parliament voted to make Beijing the national capital. The United States was the first to recognize the new republic.

An article that Sun wrote and published in the March 1912 issue of the *Strand Magazine* summed up his attitude toward his resignation and his hopes for the future of China:

> Whether I am to be the titular head of all China, or to work in conjunction with another, and that other Yuan Shih-Kai, is of no importance to me. I have done my work; the wave of enlightenment and progress cannot now be stayed, and China – the country in the world most fitted to be a republic, because of the industrious and docile character of the people – will, in a short time, take her place amongst the civilized and liberty-loving nations of the world.[21]

Sun's presidency lasted a little over six weeks. During his brief tenure, he launched two important initiatives: the replacement of the traditional Chinese calendar with its 10-day periods by the 7-day week, and the adoption of the Gregorian calendar, with January 1, 1912, as the first day of the republic; and the substitution of the imperial Qing dragon by a flag with five horizontal colored stripes representing China's five major ethnic groups.[22] Sun had pushed for an American-style president-centered system but when it became clear that Yuan would become president, he and the other revolutionaries shifted to a British-style cabinet-centered system that would place greater limits on presidential power. The provisional constitution that the parliament eventually drafted and promulgated was an awkward compromise between these two systems, which left the relationship between the president and the cabinet dangerously ambiguous. This debate on presidential power versus ministerial responsibility, although settled for the moment, was to continue for the first few years of the republic.

Chapter 11

BETRAYAL OF THE REVOLUTION

THE YEARS FOLLOWING his resignation from the presidency were some of Sun's saddest and most disappointing. Though the script was not his, he did his best to play the role that fate had dealt him. He relinquished the presidency to Yuan Shikai believing that the military strongman was the only man who could obtain the abdication of the Manchu dynasty, avert a civil war, and lead China down the road to constitutional government. Having double-crossed the Guangxu Emperor during the Hundred Day Reform and abandoned the Qing imperial house in 1912, Yuan now betrayed the revolution and observed republicanism only in name. The revolutionaries' attempt to reassert parliamentary government was mercilessly suppressed and their leader brutally murdered. With his republican dream hijacked and in tatters, Sun turned on his successor with a vengeance and opposed Yuan in every way possible until the latter's death in 1916.

Sun disappeared almost completely from the political scene after resigning the presidency. He handed political power to Yuan and before long also turned over control of the Tongmenghui to the party's number three, Song Jiaoren. These two men now dominated the course of events. Yuan favored authoritarian means of modernization and was prepared to use all the political tricks he had picked up in the imperial court. Song, one of the few Chinese to understand the meaning and practice of parliamentary institutions, wanted to rely on those institutions to chart China's path to modernity.[1] The difference in their characters and ideologies set them on an inevitable collision course.

Under the provisional constitution that was adopted in March 1912, the president was supposed to govern in accordance with the wishes of a cabinet headed by a prime minister. As head of government, the prime minister's task was to promote consensus within the cabinet and to ensure that the president's actions stayed within the bounds of the law. In the absence of an elected parliament, Yuan was able to choose his close ally Tang Shaoyi as his prime minister. A Cantonese from Xiangshan, Sun's home county, Tang had attended the Government Central School in Hong Kong before continuing his studies at Columbia University as a member of the Chinese Education Mission. He served as Yuan's principal private secretary when the latter was governor-general of Zhili and later as Yuan's chief negotiator in the North-South dialogue that paved the way for the peaceful transition of power from the Qing dynasty to the new republic. On a visit to Nanjing at the end of March 1912, Tang negotiated the formation of a coalition cabinet that included four Tongmenghui leaders, one of whom was Song Jiaoren. Huang Xing was denied the crucial War portfolio, and the ministries assigned to the four Tongmenghui members (Justice, Education, Agriculture and Industry) made their participation merely symbolic. Factional squabbles soon paralyzed parliament and friction also developed between Yuan Shikai and Tang Shaoyi, who had recently joined the Tongmenghui. Tang resigned the cabinet in June, and the four Tongmenghui members followed suit a few weeks later. This played right into Yuan's hands for he could now appoint even closer associates to the cabinet, which soon came completely under his control.

Sun Yat-sen with Tang Shaoyi, the first prime minister of the Republic of China, in front of the Presidential Mansion, Nanjing, March 25, 1912.

In accordance with the provisional constitution, a parliament was to be elected within six months of the formation of the government. Election laws and regulations, including the adoption of a bicameral system, were promulgated by the provisional government in August 1912. In preparation for the historic event, the Tongmenghui reorganized itself and absorbed several smaller parties to form the Guomindang, or Nationalist Party. Rallied against the Guomindang were a number of smaller parties, in particular the Gonghedang (Republican Party) led by Li Yuanhong, the Minzhudang (Democratic Party) under Liang Qichao, and the Unity Party.[2]

Meanwhile, Yuan Shikai invited his predecessor to Beijing for talks to help heal the rift with parliament following the fall of the Tang Shaoyi cabinet. A grand official reception, complete with a guard of honor, welcomed Sun on his arrival in the capital on August 24. The next day, he attended a meeting of the Guomindang. Sun remained its titular head but delegated to Song Jiaoren the responsibility for navigating the party's foray into the new game of parliamentary politics. But while Song was devising means of taming Yuan's authoritarian tendencies, Sun was playing the role of an elder statesman singing praises of his successor. No mean schemer himself, Yuan responded by laying out the red carpet for Sun and extending to the former president all the courtesies befitting a visiting head of state. A palace designed for the reception of visiting royals and aristocrats served as Sun's residence during his stay. He took part in many public meetings at which thousands flocked to see and hear him. Together with Huang Xing, who had joined him in Beijing, they held huge banquets prepared by the presidential kitchen and to which princes of the Qing imperial family were invited.[3]

In the course of his stay until September 20, Sun held numerous meetings with Yuan to discuss industrial development, defense, foreign affairs and even agrarian reforms. Convinced that the railroad was the key to China's economic development and her path to world power status, Sun expressed a desire to devote himself to this field. Yuan readily obliged and appointed him Director of Railways, a post of little consequence except the illusion of leading a grand enterprise. To make sure that he continued to stay out of politics, Sun was provided with a handsome stipend and given full powers to set up plans for a national railway network and to negotiate with foreign banks for financing.

A week later, Sun left Beijing in a special train to visit the northern provinces and promote his vision of a China crisscrossed by networks of railways. He was accompanied by a group of fundraisers, government officials and others. Among them was Charlie Soong, his old friend from Shanghai whom Sun had appointed as Treasurer for Railways, and his eldest daughter, Song Ailing, who headed Sun's English secretariat. Also in the group was the Australian journalist William H. Donald, who had attached himself to Sun's entourage since the 1911 Revolution. The United States, Sun informed his audiences, had been as poor as China, but with money borrowed from abroad she built a 200,000-mile (320,000 km) railway system and became the richest country in the world. Since China was five times as large, she would need a million miles (1,600,000 km), a goal that Sun was confident could be achieved within ten years! Later, he reduced his target by 30 percent but this would still require billions of dollars, money which China did not have and could not borrow from abroad. All his exhortations fell on deaf ears, however, except in good old Japan where people in high places were still ready to listen to his grandiose plans.

When Sun arrived in Japan for a month-long state visit on February 13, 1913, his Japanese hosts treated him almost like a head of state. He was given the use of a special railway coach, accommodated at the best hotels and feted at lavish banquets attended by the cream of Japan's political, financial and military fraternities. Sun was deeply touched when Acting Prime Minister Katsura Taro revived the old pan-Asian theme and proposed that China and Japan work together to liberate India and awaken the non-white peoples of the world so that Japan would "never have to worry about land for colonization and commerce, and would never pursue the crude policy of conquest." Katsura also warned Sun about Yuan Shikai and advised him not to challenge the president until Sun was in a stronger position. This was strange talk for a prime minister whose government adopted a policy of support for Yuan. In truth, Japan had only fallen into line with the Western powers on the advice of her British allies.[4]

In speeches to Chinese and Japanese audiences, Sun claimed that China, a continental power, and Japan, a maritime power, were mutually dependent. He warned that a leaning toward Russia could only spell trouble for China, citing Russia's role in Outer Mongolia's declaration of independence from China in 1911. Because of the Americans' policy of isolation, Sun discounted the likelihood of help from them. In any event, he saw the U.S. along with the Europeans as imperialist powers against whom China needed Japan's help. Such talk was music to the ears of the Japanese, who in turn gave Sun the impression that he had bought himself some personal insurance in case of trouble with Yuan.

Discussions on February 24 at the headquarters of Mitsui & Co. led to a plan to form the Industrial Company of China to exploit China's mineral wealth with funds provided by Mitsui, Mitsubishi and other *zaibatsu* (Japanese conglomerates). Sun was to be chairman while a Japanese diplomat and entrepreneur was to manage the company as chief executive officer. But before this could be announced, a conflict between Yuan Shikai and the Guomindang escalated to crisis proportions. Sun could not reap the fruits of his efforts, nor the Japanese the opportunity to recover their position in China.

An outstanding reformer in the waning days of the Qing dynasty, Yuan enjoyed popular support. Many believed he was the only man who could hold China together, a belief that Yuan did nothing to discourage. But Yuan considered republicanism an inconvenience, and refused to be constrained by constitutional or other means. To him political opponents were a nuisance and he did not hesitate to use whatever means necessary to eliminate the annoyance, including murder. This was exactly what happened in the crisis that began with the Guomindang's landslide victory in the parliamentary elections, in which it took 269 out of a total of 596 seats in the lower house and 123 seats out of 274 in the upper house. The Guomindang secured more votes than the Republican, Democratic and Unity parties combined, which now merged to form the Jinbudang (Progressive Party) in support of Yuan.[5]

Under the provisional constitution, Song Jiaoren was virtually assured of the premiership and he would have the dominant role in forming the cabinet. By making it obvious that he intended to use parliament to place Yuan in a straitjacket, or even to replace him, Song put himself up as a target for elimination. On March 20, while waiting at Shanghai's railway station to board the train for Beijing to cash in on the Guomindang's stunning victory, Song was killed by an assassin's bullet. The prime minister,

Yuan's henchman, and a cabinet secretary were directly implicated and it was widely believed that Yuan himself had put out the contract on Song.[6]

Sun returned to Shanghai on March 25, five days after Song Jiaoren was gunned down. He urged the central and southern provinces to declare their independence and prepare for an armed confrontation with Yuan Shikai. But Sun did not control the Guomindang. He was nominally president but the leadership of the party was exercised by a group among whom Sun was simply *primus inter pares*. Some of these men, Sun and Huang Xing among them, owed their authority to their prestige and their revolutionary credentials. Others, like Hu Hanmin and Li Liejun, respectively military governor of Guangdong and of Jiangxi, derived their power through their control of a territorial base or military force. To take on Yuan Shikai militarily required the active collaboration of all these men. With the exception of Li Liejun, the others were reluctant. Though aware of the threat that Yuan posed to the republic, they were averse to taking on his vastly superior military forces. Moreover, to declare independence and take up arms would be a strike against national unity and the republic. Violence was justified in 1911 but in the spring of 1913 it might appear to be a struggle for power and dishonor those who resorted to it.[7]

On April 26, the day after the complicity of Yuan's people in Song's murder was publicly confirmed, a British-led consortium of foreign banks gave Yuan the thumbs-up by extending to his government a £25 million Reorganization Loan. Given China's financial straits, the loan was probably unavoidable but his detractors suspected that Yuan intended to use the proceeds to consolidate his own power. More importantly, he failed to obtain parliamentary approval for the loan. It was on this violation of the constitution that the Guomindang, still reluctant to take up arms, challenged him though it left the door open for compromise. In May, Sun appealed to the foreign powers not to sponsor the demise of parliamentary democracy in China but this deterred neither Yuan nor the consortium, and Yuan got the money anyway. In preparation for the inevitable showdown with the parliamentarians, in June Yuan dismissed Hu Hanmin, Li Liejun and Bo Wenwei, the Guomindang military governor of Anhui, from their posts.[8]

Until this time, the Guomindang had hoped to avoid open confrontation. They were even ready to vote in favor of the loan if Yuan would only submit it to parliament for ratification. But Yuan, confident of his own position, was in no mood for compromises. In early July, the governors dismissed by Yuan declared the independence of their provinces, and were soon joined by Fujian, Hunan and Sichuan. Sun, still grieving over the death of his elder daughter, left it largely to Huang Xing to conduct the military response.[9]

Hostilities finally broke out on July 12 in Jiangxi and quickly spread to Shanghai and northern Jiangsu, where Huang Xing's crack troops in Nanjing were routed by Yuan's forces. Huang's decision to evacuate Nanjing at the end of the month effectively brought the Second Revolution to a close. Fighting continued, but even with covert Japanese assistance the Second Revolution never really had a chance and collapsed altogether in early September. Sun had already left for Japan in August and he was soon joined by Huang Xing and other revolutionary leaders. This left the field wide open for Yuan to employ increasingly brazen methods to consolidate his power over the government.

On October 6, Yuan cowed an already intimidated parliament into electing him president, the office that he had been occupying on a provisional basis. The next day, the foreign powers rewarded him with recognition of his regime, following the lead of the United States, which had done so in May. On the second anniversary of the 1911 Revolution on October 10, Yuan inaugurated his mandate at a spectacular ceremony. On November 4, he outlawed the Guomindang and expelled its legislators from parliament, which he dissolved altogether in January 1914. By May, when he promulgated a new constitution that would permit him to rule indefinitely, Yuan had already assumed full dictatorial powers.

Sun's arrival in Japan on August 9, 1913, was a low-key affair compared to his triumphant visit just six months earlier. The Japanese government had little use for him for they could now obtain concessions in China by simply exerting pressure on Yuan Shikai. For a while it was even doubtful whether Sun would be allowed to land. Fortunately, he still had powerful friends among the ultranationalists like Toyama Mitsuru who with Inukai Ki helped to secure permission for Sun to enter Japan. Toyama even accommodated Sun in his Tokyo home for a time. Japanese public opinion was sympathetic toward Sun but the Europeans, who just the previous year had hailed Sun as a patriot, now accused him of provoking instability in the pursuit of personal ambition. Contrastingly, Yuan emerged from the Second Revolution with even more solid support from the West, especially Britain.

Sun was deeply affected by the Guomindang's defeat in the Second Revolution and was desperate to overthrow Yuan. Just how desperate is shown in two letters he wrote in 1914. On May 11, Sun penned a letter to Japanese Prime Minister Okuma Shigenobu proposing an alliance between China and Japan to drive Yuan Shikai from office. As a quid pro quo, he offered unrestricted residence for Japanese in China, a customs union and Japanese commercial dominance in China. Britain's greatness, he pointed out in his letter, depended on India, for which she had had to fight. He was offering Japan a potential India, for which all Japan had to do was to arm and help the Guomindang forces against Yuan. The letter barely moved the Japanese, who, as their foreign minister said, were still waiting for the right "psychological moment" to realize its aims in China.[10]

In August, Sun turned to an American acquaintance, James Deitrick, a self-made man who started working as a telegraph operator at the age of 12 and by 35 was president of a railway company. They had met in London, probably in 1911. The next year, Deitrick wrote to Sun to secure contracts for financing and building railways in China, and to persuade Sun to develop a nationwide Boy Scout and Girl Scout movement in China. Nothing came of these proposals but Deitrick's claim in 1912 that he could raise vast sums of money for both enterprises prompted Sun in 1914 to write to him for help. He asked Deitrick to try to raise at least US$10 million from various capitalists with the promise of franchises to operate department stores in China after Sun had overthrown Yuan and set up his own government. There followed a series of correspondence which showed early promise but in the end was no more successful that his earlier attempt with the Japanese.[11]

The several thousand revolutionaries who took refuge in Tokyo in 1913 were sadly disillusioned and discouraged, believing that Yuan was now firmly in control. Some decided to take a break. Li Liejun left for Paris and Huang Xing for the United States shortly after. Before outlawing the Guomindang in November 1913, Yuan Shikai had demanded that the party expel the militants responsible for the Second Revolution. Huang Xing, Li

Liejun, Chen Jiongming and a number of others were all named, but Sun's name was not on the list. Yuan offered a reward of C$10,000 for Huang Xing's head, but nothing for Sun's. Deserted by his comrades and now ignored by his enemies, a lesser person would have thrown in the towel and called it a day.[12] But Sun was made of sterner stuff.

To prove that the years he had devoted to the revolution had not been in vain, Sun created a new secret organization in Tokyo on September 1, 1914. The Zhongguo Gemingdang, or Chinese Revolutionary Party, as the new party was called, had been in the works since late 1913. Sun seems to have lost faith at this point in parliamentary institutions and decided that China was not ready to adopt them. His criticisms were directed mainly against his own party, not so much its plan for government but rather its absorption of several smaller parties into its fold. This had attracted a group of opportunists who bogged down the Guomindang in compromises and abandoned his Three Principles of the People, the Three Stages of Revolution and the Five-Power Constitution. What Sun had in mind was a return to a more centralized and disciplined party with absolute loyalty and obedience to the leader à la the secret societies. To safeguard his own authority against rival ambitions that had led to the failure of the Tongmenghui, every member of the new party was required to take and sign an oath of personal allegiance to Sun and to "sacrifice his life and liberty to the salvation of China." The status of each member and his membership privileges were to be determined according to when they joined, that is to say, before, during or after the success of the revolution. The program of the new party was a return to the Three Principles of the People, minus the nationalism, which Sun reckoned had already been achieved with the demise of the Qing dynasty. Sun planned to seize power through a small group of committed revolutionaries, financed by overseas funds, but without the involvement of the secret societies. With the benefit of the experience in 1912, Sun was careful to specify the conditions in which power was to be exercised after the victory of the revolution. Although the schema of the Three Stages of Revolution devised in 1905 was maintained, Sun now envisioned stage two as a tutelage by the party.[13]

Many revolutionaries, in particular Huang Xing, opposed these proposals. Their main objection was the swearing of the oath of personal allegiance to Sun, which they found to be incompatible with the party's democratic agenda. They seemed prepared to swear loyalty to the "president" but Sun's intransigence on this point was a deal-breaker. Huang Xing's refusal to join the new Revolutionary Party was followed by those of Wang Jingwei, Chen Jiongming and the former southern military governors Li Liejun and Bo Wenwei. All these men preferred to continue the struggle outside the framework of the new party. The Gemingdang thus attracted only a fraction of Sun's former partisans and very few of the leaders, and only eight of the Chinese provinces were represented. At its foundation meeting, Sun was elected *zongli*, endowed with considerably greater power than he had in either the Tongmenghui or Guomindang. The post of vice president, originally reserved for Huang Xing, was left vacant as no one with the prestige could be found. The only two intellectuals who remained faithful to Sun were Dai Jitao, his personal secretary and Japanese interpreter, and Zhu Zhixin, one of the protagonists in the polemics against Liang Qichao in the *Minbao*.

Without his old revolutionary comrades, Sun turned to a new group led by a few adventurers very different from the intellectuals who had dominated the Tongmenghui. Their leader was Chen Qimei, a native of Zhejiang. He had joined the Tongmenghui while studying at the Tokyo Police Academy in 1905–6, and continued his revolutionary activities in Zhejiang and Jiangsu. In 1911, he led the attack on the Jiangnan arsenal, captured the Manchu garrison in Shanghai and later became the city's military governor. In 1913, he failed in his attack against Yuan's troops holed up in the same arsenal. He was among those who had taken refuge in Tokyo after the failure of the Second Revolution, and shared Sun's bitterness and impatience to resume the struggle. It was under the influence of Chen, who favored an insurrection in Jiangsu and provinces further north, that Sun abandoned his old strategy of southern risings. Shanghai's foreign concessions became the hub of Sun's new partisans, who enjoyed the protection of the Japanese consulate and powerful underworld organizations such as the Green Gang and the Red Gang.[14]

Chen Qimei counted among his friends the antique dealer Zhang Renjie, Sun's secret benefactor in Paris during the Tongmenghui period. Zhang wielded considerable power in Shanghai through his relations with the underworld and with "Big-ear" Du Yuesheng, the leader of the Green Gang, the city's most-feared criminal organization. Also in Chen's entourage was a young infantry lieutenant named Chiang Kai-shek, who spent an inordinate amount of time in the brothels of Shanghai in the company of Zhang and other notorious underworld figures. A native of Zhejiang, Chiang had studied at the famous Japanese military academy Shimbu Gakko between 1908 and 1911, and may have been brought into the Tongmenghui by his fellow provincial Chen Qimei. Though a military officer, Chiang's tactics were closer to banditry than traditional military art. The International Concession police apparently had several warrants for his arrest on armed robbery charges. Chiang was never prosecuted but there seems little doubt that it was he who fired at Tao Chengzhang at point-blank range in his sick-bed at the Sainte-Marie Hospital in February 1912. Tao was head of the Guangfuhui, which had split from the Tongmenghui, but he was also one of Chen's principal rivals. It is not known if Chiang was given the assassination order by his patron Chen Qimei, as some assumed, or if he acted on his own volition, which is quite possible since Chiang was known to have a violent and uncontrollable temper.

The Gemingdang did not completely replace the Guomindang. The overseas branches of the Guomindang, particularly those in Nanyang, preferred to remain under the established Guomindang brand. The discord between the two organizations was moderate at first and mainly centered around contributions from *huaqiao* sympathizers. All that changed when the "psychological moment" that the Japanese had been waiting for finally arrived.

The "psychological moment" was the start of World War I, which broke out in Europe on July 28, 1914. China had no direct stake in the conflict but a number of the belligerents possessed spheres of influence in China. Invoking the Anglo-Japanese Alliance of 1902, Japan joined the Allies and declared war on Germany on August 23. In November Japanese troops captured Germany's leased territory in Shandong, which Britain could not stop since she needed Japanese naval help in the East. In December, Japan made it clear that she had no intention of returning the former German holdings to China. Taking advantage of the West's preoccupation with the war in Europe, Japan now made a bid for the preeminent position among imperialist powers in China. On January 18, 1915, she presented Yuan's government with the infamous Twenty-One Demands. On the whole, the demands were not much more than what the foreign powers including Japan had already extracted. But the ultimatum also contained a fifth group of demands which if acceded to would have turned China into a Japanese protectorate. In early March, Japan flexed her muscles and landed additional troops to augment their existing garrisons in China.[15]

The demands were ominous enough but Japan's overbearing and bullying tactics magnified the sense of danger and the insult to Chinese nationalism. The news provoked a violent patriotic reaction in China, the likes of which had never been seen before in modern China, and rallied a number of political forces behind Yuan. Newspapers and mass rallies called for firm resistance, and a boycott against Japan was declared in late March. For many revolutionaries and republicans, Yuan's dictatorship ceased to be a factor. Encouraged by Yuan's offers of amnesty, many returned from exile to join the chorus of protests and defend their country. Even some of Sun's close associates now gave primacy to opposing Japan. Sun continued with his policy of cooperation with the Japanese, and only he, Chen Qimei and some of their closest comrades gave precedence to dislodging Yuan from the presidency. This obsession isolated Sun from the mainstream of Chinese nationalism, which was now intensely anti-Japanese, and it exposed Sun to charges of treachery by his former comrades as well as his enemy.

Militarily, China was at a disadvantage, but Japan's diplomats were no match for the Chinese. By keeping the other foreign powers informed and highlighting the threat to their own political and economic spheres of interest, they managed to get even the British to oppose the fifth set of demands, which threatened her own privileges in China. Yuan stalled for time until the Japanese, frustrated by the delay, issued an ultimatum on May 7 to agree to the demands within two days or else. By this time, Japan had rescinded the fifth group of demands. On May 9, Yuan's government accepted most of the other demands.

Japan could have obtained her demands without the saber-rattling. Western capital was tied up and in any event was less competitive. By resorting to her old imperialist tactics in the most blatant manner, Japan provoked a "new, volatile and uncompromising phase" of Chinese nationalism targeted primarily at Japan, which was to retain the honor for the next 30 years until the end of World War II.[16]

In August, barely three months after defusing the crisis provoked by Japan's Twenty-One Demands, Yuan Shikai raised his ambition to a new level. As Sun had previously warned, Yuan began orchestrating a campaign to make himself emperor. Yuan had never accepted republicanism, which he also believed the people never really understood. He might have been encouraged to restore the monarchy by Dr. F.J. Goodnow, his political adviser from Columbia University who argued that China's history and traditions made her more suited to a monarchy than a republic. It was not just Sun who balked at the betrayal of the republic but a wide segment of public opinion. As rumblings of anger over Yuan's imperial ambition gathered momentum, on October 25 Sun shocked both the Christian community and the Chinese elite by eloping and tying the knot with a beautiful young lady less than half his age.

Such stories are not uncommon but in this case the lady in question and her siblings had always regarded Sun as an "uncle." Song Qingling (Rosamonde) was the daughter of one of Sun's oldest and dearest friends, Charlie Soong. Their friendship went all the way back to 1894 when Sun was in Shanghai en route to Tianjin to present his petition to Li Hongzhang. In 1913 Soong and his family, compromised by their association with Sun, had taken refuge together with him in Japan after the failure of the Second Revolution. The following year Qingling, a recent graduate from Wesleyan College in Georgia, replaced her elder sister Ailing as Sun's English-language secretary. Qingling worshiped Sun and gave him the companionship and intellectual stimulation that his first wife Lu Muzhen never could. She was constantly by his side and helped him in his political career. However, her marriage without parental consent was frowned upon in Chinese circles while his marriage without first divorcing Lu Muzhen upset the Christian community. It cost Sun his friendship with Charlie Soong and it would be many years before the two old friends made up.[17]

Yuan made his fateful move in November 1915. A "Representative Assembly" voted, with an amazing but improbable 1,993 votes to zero, begging Yuan to take on the emperorship. On December 12, Yuan made a show of bowing to popular demand and "humbly" agreed to assume Heaven's

Sun Yat-sen and Song Qingling after their wedding in Tokyo, October 1915.

Mandate. This proclamation united against Yuan all the forces that until then had either accepted or resigned themselves to his dictatorship. The southwestern province of Yunnan greeted the proclamation with a revolt at the end of the month, led by General Cai E. A native of Hunan, Cai had studied at the famous Shikan Gakko military academy in Tokyo. Back in China he rose quickly in his military career, was made a general by the age of 29 and put in command of New Army units in Yunnan. On the outbreak of the 1911 Revolution, he declared the independence of the province and headed an authoritarian government there. After the 1911 Revolution, he rallied to Yuan, believing that China needed a strong leader at the helm. Cai did not take part in the Second Revolution but Yuan feared his independent character and assigned him to an honorific post in the capital. He was replaced by Tang Jiyao, who shared his predecessor's opposition to Yuan's imperial ambition. Backed by New Army units in Yunnan, Tang launched an anti-monarchial movement and was soon joined by Cai and Li Liejun, the former Guomindang governor. On December 15, they appealed to the other provinces to join the fight against Yuan. Calling themselves the Army for the Protection of the Country, their immediate objective was to integrate the various opposition forces and reestablish a strong and united republic.[18]

In principle, Japanese leaders preferred a monarchy in China, for Japan herself was one. But Yuan's emperorship at this time would have been tantamount to an endorsement of his anti-Japanese stand. The Japanese Army in collaboration with the Foreign Office sent several high-ranking officers to China to fund and arm rebel movements. Sun's group received 1.4 million yen, and more was promised if he could produce results. Learning from his mistake in 1912, Sun refused to ally himself with others who were not willing to recognize his leadership. He declined to join the Movement for the Protection of the Country and decided to pursue an independent course.[19]

Ignoring these ominous signs, Yuan proceeded with his enthronement as the Hongxian Emperor on New Year's Day 1916. He had seriously misjudged the ground. His imperial ambition shattered the solidarity of his clique of Beiyang generals, and his political allies abandoned him in droves. Southern provinces declared their independence one after another and mass protests erupted all over China. In March, the Japanese started doling out money to any and all rebel groups in an all-out effort to topple Yuan, who was in any event already in the last stage of his journey toward extinction. He abolished the monarchy on March 22 but the deadline for compromise had long passed; the opposition wanted him out completely. In April, the Japanese delivered their coup de grâce by persuading the foreign-run Chinese Maritime Customs Service to withhold the excess tax revenue payable to Yuan's government. Choked of funds, Yuan could not stem the tidal wave.

Accompanied by Qingling, Sun left Tokyo for Shanghai on April 27 to direct his anti-Yuan campaign. He used the Japanese money to organize insurrections in Shanghai and Shandong. These were regions of immense interest to the Japanese, and Sun hoped that their capture would further loosen Japanese purse strings. Chen Qimei's assassination on May 18 by Yuan's henchmen cut short a failing operation in Shanghai while Sun's people had no more than a fleeting success in Shandong. Recognizing that his rivals had once again beaten him to the draw, Sun ended his isolation and called for unity of all anti-Yuan forces.

As pressure mounted for Yuan to resign the presidency, he was ready to flee but died suddenly from uremia on June 6, bringing an abrupt end to the monarchical tragicomedy. Commenting on Yuan's life before his death, Liang Qichao denounced Yuan for thinking that everyone could be bought with gold or intimidated by force. Making a mockery of the constitution, Yuan's method of governance through bribery and terror had corrupted the elite.[20] Indeed, Yuan's governance and his authoritarian presidency laid the groundwork for the lawlessness that was to run wild in the following decade.

Chapter 12

CHAOS UNDER HEAVEN

Yuan Shikai's death did not realign China back on the road to constitutional government. It plunged her into the abyss of warlordism starring Yuan's former Beiyang Army protégés and a whole cast of other wannabes. While alive, Yuan was able to hold the Beiyang Army together and impose some semblance of unity. Once he passed from the scene, it fragmented into smaller units under his former commanders, who fought each other for regional and national power. The collapse of Beiyang unity encouraged other militarists as well as local thugs to seek their own goals. From that point on, militarists throughout the realm acted without restraint to torture China and the Chinese with incessant wars and naked exploitation. All under heaven was again in chaos.

During the period from 1916 to 1928, the Chinese polity was fragmented and ruled by a host of warlords. Some controlled one or two districts and financed their armies with "taxes" collected at gunpoint or through confiscation. Others dominated entire provinces and funded their operations with local taxes collected by their own bureaucracies, while the most powerful controlled two or three provinces. Some drew their revenues from rail services and commercial activities in the cities; others revived opium growing in their domains and depended on the drug trade for revenues. A number of warlords held on to the idea of a legitimate republic, hoping that they would one day be reintegrated into a constitutional state; others worked solely for personal wealth or power; and there were also those who believed that Sun and the Guomindang were China's legitimate government. Warlords differed greatly as well in character. A few indulged in extreme sensual pleasures or barbaric cruelty but there were also good men of character who tried to instill in their troops their own brand of morality.[1]

A national government continued to exist in Beijing. It was recognized by foreign nations as the legitimate government of China and regarded by most Chinese as such. But the national government itself was also a warlord government, the trophy of whichever warlord or warlord clique controlled the capital. In practical terms, "the national government's writ extended no further than the guns of the Peking warlord." Warlords fought dozens of wars against each other. Most were short-lived and limited in scope, but a few involved whole army divisions pitted against one another. The military power relationship among the warlords changed constantly. As victors assumed the role of political leaders and losers lost their posts or their heads, national and provincial positions changed hands frequently. During the dozen years of the warlord period, China had more than half a dozen heads of state, two short-lived imperial restorations, 25 cabinets that tumbled one after the other, and several brief periods of caretaker government.[2]

Two of Yuan Shikai's protégés emerged as the most important warlords in the immediate post-Yuan years: Feng Guozhang and Duan Qirui. Both began their military careers in the Tianjin Military Academy, a school founded by Li Hongzhang in 1885 to train modern army officers. Yuan enlisted them to help him establish the Beiyang Army after China's defeat in the Sino-Japanese War. For Duan, it was a natural progression. Both his grandfather and father had served in Li Hongzhang's army; there was never any doubt that he would follow in their footsteps. Feng, contrastingly, was from a family of landowners who had seen better days. He embarked on a military career only after failing to obtain the *juren* degree, which dashed his hopes of a post in the civilian bureaucracy. Both men rose quickly through the ranks and soon joined Yuan's inner circle. They remained loyal to Yuan after he was forced into early retirement following the death of his patron Cixi. During Yuan's presidency, Feng and Duan were his principal lieutenants and served in high positions in the central government as well as stints as provincial governors. However, they disapproved of Yuan's attempt to make himself emperor, perhaps because the hereditary nature of the monarchy would in time make them subordinates of Yuan's eldest son, a prospect which neither Feng nor Duan savored. Although they did not engage in active and overt opposition, their obvious disapproval encouraged others to come out openly against Yuan's monarchical ambition.

Vice President Li Yuanhong formally assumed the presidency on June 7, 1916. Disagreement emerged almost immediately as to whether he succeeded to the presidency in accordance with the 1912 constitution, or acted for the dead president according to Yuan's 1914 constitution. In other words, which of the two constitutions was in force. The revolutionaries in the south called for the reinstatement of the 1912 constitution. This was a problem because Duan favored the 1914 constitution that had given Yuan Shikai almost absolute power, and Duan was determined to have his way. The constitutional crisis was only resolved after the naval commander in Shanghai and Feng Guozhang, who feared losing his power base in Shanghai, gave their support to the revolutionaries and pressured Beijing to restore the 1912 constitution. Li weathered the crisis and on August 1 reconvened the old parliament that Yuan had dissolved in January 1914. With no military power of his own, the president carried little weight among the Beiyang generals. As a result, real power flowed to Feng Guozhang and Duan Qirui, who were respectively appointed vice president and prime minister. Each tried to install his own supporters in central government and provincial governorships. The intrigues and maneuvers between the two groups dominated the early warlord years.[3]

It was against the chaotic backdrop of the warlord period that Sun lived out his last decade as he desperately struggled to save the revolution that he had devoted his life. Without an army or a territorial base of his own, he was forced to watch the march of events from the sidelines in the immediate post-Yuan years. This was for Sun a time for reflection, lecturing and writing. Assuming once more the mantle of a senior statesman, he wanted to influence Chinese thinking on democratic government in China. In a speech on "Self-Government as the Basis of Reconstruction" before parliamentarians and leaders of various occupational groups at the Arcadia Forum at Shanghai in July 1916, he argued that the foundation for China's national reconstruction should be local self-government. Sun shared how in 1913 the people of Cleveland, Ohio, had elected 26 representatives to its district legislative assembly, and a magistrate whose function was to direct six bureaus, each concerned with a specific aspect of public administration. Under the city's system of self-government, the people exercised considerable power. They had the power of recall in addition to the power of electing city officials, and could change the actions of the district assembly. In the past, assemblymen could be bribed to act contrary to public interest. Now the people of Cleveland could nullify those deemed to be contrary to public interest, and this made it more difficult for assemblymen to be bribed. Sun believed Cleveland's system to be the most appropriate model for China.[4] The idea of local democracy was elaborated in *First Steps in Democracy*, which was later incorporated into a larger work, *Plan for National Reconstruction*. In this primer on parliamentary procedures that he completed in February 1917, Sun shelved the idea of political tutelage and looked toward the establishment of a republic within ten years. Taking Cleveland and Switzerland as his models, he advocated a system of self-government based upon the rights of election, recall, initiative and referendum.[5]

From his retreat in Shanghai, Sun gave moral support to the beleaguered Li Yuanhong as the hapless president tried to retain some semblance of republicanism in Beijing. His prime minister Duan Qirui was a scaled-down version of his late mentor Yuan Shikai and was determined to use military power to achieve his goals. The president and his prime minister seldom saw eye-to-eye and clashed constantly. The conflict between the two men went up several bars in the spring of 1917 when they took opposite positions on the question of China's entry into World War I.

When the war in Europe broke out in late July 1914, it pitted the Allies comprising France, Britain, Russia, Japan and Italy against the Central Powers of Germany, Austria-Hungary and the Ottoman Empire. The United States, having pursued a policy of non-intervention from the outset, maintained her neutrality for the first two years while she tried to broker a peace. This changed on January 31, 1917, when Germany announced a policy of unrestricted submarine warfare against any vessels approaching British waters in an attempt to starve Britain into surrendering. President Woodrow Wilson severed diplomatic relations with Germany on February 3 and called on neutral states to take similar action. The American minister in China, acting beyond his instructions, pressed the Beijing government to follow the American lead, to which China responded on February 10 by sending a protest note to Germany.

The question of China's entry into the war quickly became a highly contentious one in Chinese official circles and public opinion. The political question was which of the parties on each side of the divide would benefit from China's participation. Duan hoped to obtain financial and military aid from Japan to consolidate his own power by advocating for China to throw her hat into the ring. The new Japanese cabinet certainly believed this to be more favorable to Japanese interests than the naked aggression pursued with the Twenty-One Demands in 1915. Duan and his faction thus stood to benefit most from China's entry into the war. On the other hand, Li Yuanhong, his partisans and the Guomindang, still the majority party in parliament, had nothing to gain and everything to lose.

At this point Sun returned to the political arena and joined the debate to champion the case for China's neutrality. In March, he sent an open telegram to Britain's wartime prime minister Lloyd George protesting British pressure on China to join the war. Arguing that most Chinese could not distinguish a German from other Europeans, he warned that China's participation in the war could fan anti-foreignism in the country and that Chinese Muslims were liable to become restive if they had to fight the Islamic Ottoman Empire. Sun had a more practical reason for opposing China's entry: he suspected that Duan would use extraordinary war powers to strangle what little was left of constitutional government. Nonetheless, Duan exerted so much pressure on Li Yuanhong that the latter had no choice but to sever diplomatic relations with Germany on March 14. Sun's anti-war rhetoric did not escape the attention of German diplomats, who were now prepared to subsidize any group committed to China's neutrality. Before leaving, they paid Sun a visit and reportedly gave him US$1 million to neutralize Duan's efforts. Sun vehemently denied the allegation.[6]

Sun published his anti-war arguments in a booklet, *The Question of China's Survival*, some time in the summer of 1917. Written in collaboration with the gifted polemicist Zhu Zhixin, it was later translated into English as *The Vital Problem of China*. Never before had Sun expressed so forcefully his antagonism towards imperialism, especially the British variety. Although Japan was the main lobbyist for China to join the war, Sun built his case almost entirely on hostility towards Britain. This was possibly a swipe at the British for supporting his old nemesis Yuan Shikai. Britain, Sun argued, had done nothing to deserve China's help. He believed that once victorious, Britain would sacrifice China to divert the Russians from India, but if forced into a stalemate would sell China out to Germany. Denouncing Russia as far more dangerous to China than Germany, he declared that China would have less to lose from a victorious Central Powers than an Allied victory. The message that Sun tried to get across was clear enough, that there is nothing for China to gain by performing coolie service for the Allies. China should thus stay neutral, put her own house in order and work for better relations with Japan, which he considered China's "natural friend, unnatural enemy."[7]

On April 6, the United States finally declared war on Germany after several U.S. merchant ships were sunk by German U-boats in the North Atlantic. Not that China could contribute militarily to the war effort, but she was an invaluable source of manpower. Her men could be deployed in non-combat jobs and free up more European men to fight at the front. On May 14, Duan declared war on Germany without the approval of President Li or parliament. To preempt possible parliamentary opposition, Duan sent thousands of "petitioners" to lay siege on parliament and demand its ratification of the war declaration, while the generals and military governors of the Beiyang clique demanded the president to dissolve parliament. In retaliation, parliament pressured Li Yuanhong to relieve Duan Qirui of the premiership. Li took the fateful step on May 23, only to have a number of Duan's partisans declare the independence of their provinces.

Despite their own entry into the war, the Americans were ambivalent about involving China in the conflict. On June 4, 1917, U.S. Secretary of State Robert Lansing wrote to the American minister in Beijing that China's unity was more important than her participation in the war. He also sent similar telegrams to American ambassadors in Britain, France and Japan inviting these countries to make similar representations to China. President Woodrow Wilson, in response to a telegram from Sun dated June 8 requesting his help to keep China from being dragged into the conflict, wrote to Lansing expressing his reservations about China's entry into the war as "we may be leading China to risk her doom."[8]

Meanwhile, in his desperation to resolve his feud with Duan Qirui, Li Yuanhong turned to Zhang Xun, the military governor of Anhui, to mediate the dispute. A reactionary general who had remained a Qing loyalist after the 1911 Revolution, Zhang marched into Beijing on June 7 with his band of soldiers still sporting their Manchu queues. He forced Li to dissolve parliament and for almost two weeks in July celebrated the restoration of Puyi to the Dragon Throne. As foreign diplomats wondered how to deal with this new development, a small group of former Qing officials and scholars, Kang Youwei among them, hurried to the Forbidden City in official Manchu robes to kowtow and serve "Emperor" Puyi. But the restoration never really got off the ground. On July 12, troops led by Duan Qirui and Cao Kun stormed the palace and drove Zhang Xun and his troops from Beijing. Puyi was deposed once again, though he was allowed to continue living in stately opulence in the Forbidden City.[9] Duan regained control of the government but Li Yuanhong was forced to hand over the presidency to Vice President Feng Guozhang.

Capitalizing on the mayhem in the capital, Sun finally made his move in early July to create a rival "national" government that he had been planning for a while. He persuaded some 130 members of the 1912 parliament from Beijing to convene in Guangzhou. On his arrival on July 17, Sun delivered a speech reiterating the need to resort to force to save the republic and to preserve China's unity. Guangzhou, he said, would serve as a refuge for the legitimate government ejected by the militarists in the North and as a military base for the re-conquest of the country. The Minister of the Navy Cheng Biguang arrived in Guangzhou on July 21 with a fleet of about 15 ships to support Sun. There were not enough parliamentarians to form a quorum but an extraordinary session approved the formation of a military government with the aim of organizing a Constitution Protection Movement to restore the 1912 constitution and to launch an expedition against the Northern warlords. Sun assumed the title of Grand Marshal, and in September appointed his ministers and commanders of the armed forces. But his orders never made it beyond the cement factory where his office was located, for Sun was no more than a figurehead: he had no armed forces under his direct control.[10]

Military power was vested in the hands of Lu Rongting, head of the Guangxi clique who controlled Guangdong, and Tang Jiyao, who exercised authority over the Greater Yunnan region incorporating Guizhou and part of Sichuan. These militarists were not prepared to submit to Sun, even in the name of the Constitution Protection Movement. In their eyes, Sun's military government served not so much the Movement but his personal ambition. In any case, the political sympathies of these generals were not with Sun but with former Guomindang governors with whom they had previously collaborated in the National Protection Movement in 1916. Moreover, their antagonism was towards Duan Qirui, not the Beijing government which they continued to recognize and hoped to extricate from the influence of the Beiyang clique through a punitive expedition. Zhang Binglin, who had reconciled with Sun after a decade of conflict, traveled to Kunming in Yunnan to try to win over Tang Jiyao, but to no avail.

Nor could Sun count on the support of the rump parliament. The most powerful clique consisting of former Guomindang deputies was immune to Sun's influence. Besides, many had gone their own way and those who remained had ambitions of their own. Among the armed forces, Sun could only count on the Guangzhou garrison under Chen Jiongming. A Cantonese born into a family of literati, Chen entered the prestigious academy of law and political science in Guangzhou, where an instructor introduced him into local revolutionary circles. He was elected to the provincial assembly in 1910 and joined the Tongmenghui the following year. In 1911, he won the only battle fought in Guangdong and was made military governor of the province after the revolution. He was dismissed by Yuan in 1913 and went into exile after the failure of the Second Revolution. He refused to join the Gemingdang, but now decided to support Sun's Constitution Protection Movement. Unfortunately, his 20 or so battalions were no match against Lu Rongting's 100,000 troops stationed in Guangdong, with which clashes were frequent. To protect Chen's garrison troops from these bloody encounters, Sun sent them off to fight in Fujian. The Yunnan contingents, about 20,000 men stranded in Guangdong after the decline of the National Protection Movement, were Sun's staunchest supporters. But their territorial base was not large enough to sustain their needs and they had to depend on handouts from Lu Rongting. So, in spite

Chen Jiongming

of their sympathy for Sun, they did not have the means to support him. The Minister of the Navy Cheng Biguang soon distanced himself from Sun, whose appeal to the *huaqiao* for funds went unanswered.

For his declaration of war against Germany, Duan was rewarded with the so-called Nishihara loans from Japan in August. With his coffers replenished, Duan set out to destroy Sun's government in the South by sending troops to Hunan and Sichuan. Feng Guozhang, however, preferred a peaceful resolution to the domestic feud. The clash between the two men split the Beiyang clique in two. Though the Beijing government continued to receive the recognition of foreign powers, it ceased to have effective control over the whole country. Initially, north and central China was divided between Duan Qirui and his supporters in the Anhui clique, and Feng Guozhang and his followers in the Zhili clique. Feng's partisans sabotaged Duan's campaign against the Constitution Protection army, causing Duan's military policy to fail and his resignation from the premiership on November 22, 1917.[11]

In the hope of gaining support and loans from the United States, Sun did a volte-face on his anti-war stand. On September 26, his Guangzhou government "acknowledged" a state of war with Germany and Austria. The extraordinary parliament authorized the Guangzhou government to raise US$50 million for military purposes through a bond sale. In offering the Americans investment opportunities in exchange for loans, Sun tried to plant the idea that Japan was in the pipeline for a deal, but professed preference for the U.S. The Americans, who had heard rumors of his German connections, neither granted him loans nor recognized his government. In fact, the State Department went so far as to block the sale of the bonds in the United States and the Philippines. It is not known how successful the bond issue was but there was a steady flow of funds from the *huaqiao*, including those in U.S. jurisdictions. The following year, despite his government's declaration of war, Sun sent an agent to Germany with a proposal that Germany, in return for Chinese raw materials, combine with Russia to help him against the northern warlords, Britain and Japan. The war ended before Berlin could respond.[12]

By then, the Southern militarists were no longer as hospitable and began making moves to clip Sun's wings. In early 1918, they assassinated his bodyguards and his former principal ally Cheng Biguang. The failure of Sun's government was assured when in April Lu Rongting, with the support of the navy and a majority in the rump parliament, reorganized the Guangzhou military government. The post of Grand Marshal was abolished and replaced by a seven-member directorate. Sun was appointed one of the seven but he refused to take up the post. He departed Guangzhou, leaving the city in the hands of the Guangxi clique. Trading in his Grand Marshal's uniform for a scholar's robe, he settled down at his residence on Rue Moliere in the French Concession of Shanghai.

The next two years were for Sun a time for making the most of his new life with Qingling, playing croquet with her for relaxation, and entertaining friends and sympathizers at their little villa. It was also a time for deep reflection and setting his thoughts to paper. Most of the works he wrote during this period were as articles in the new magazine, *Reconstruction*, founded in August 1919.

His first writing of this period, *The Doctrine of Sun Wen*, probably completed in May 1919, was later incorporated as "Part I: Psychological Reconstruction" in a larger work, *Plan for National Reconstruction*.[13] It was

Sun Yat-sen's former residence on Rue Moliere in the French Concession of Shanghai.

translated into English in 1927 as *Memoirs of a Chinese Revolutionary*.[14] The aim of this essay was to correct his comrades' fallacious thinking that had led to the republican failure following the 1911 Revolution. Had they not considered his ideals "too elevated and unattainable," he could have very easily given "effect to the program of the revolutionary party, i.e., nationalism, democracy, socialism and the Five-Power Constitution." While accepting some responsibility for the republican failure, the root cause was his comrades' lack of conviction, which he attributed to the ancient axiom that "actions are difficult, but knowledge is easy." Conceding that he, too, had once believed this, several years of study had led him to the realization that the reverse was true, that "to understand is difficult, but to achieve is easy." To demonstrate his point, Sun drew on a number of analogies from everyday life.[15] Claiming that he had already surmounted the real obstacle to China's progress – knowledge – if his comrades would only have faith in him, the work of reconstruction, as he remarked in the preface, would be "as easy as the turning of a hand or the breaking of a twig." Man's evolution fell into three periods, according to Sun: "action without understanding, understanding after action, and understanding before action." He added:

> If we divide people according to their individualities, we shall find three groups: the first those who create and invent (they are called pioneers and inventors), the second, those who transmit or disseminate new ideas and inventions (these are called disciples), and the third are those who carry out what they receive from the people of the first two groups, without doubting and without hesitating (these are called unconscious performers and people of action).[16]

In expounding the knowledge-action dualism, Sun's aim was to provide the philosophical justification for the concept of single-party tutelage under a visionary leader.

This essay was directed at the Guomindang, which had ceased to be a unified party. Sun had no intention of reviving it; he did not have the patience nor had he forgotten the desertion of his comrades when he formed the Gemingdang. He preferred to wait for "opportunities to work through the power holders," and the end of World War I seemed to offer just such an opportunity. In the summer of 1918, shortly after his departure from Guangzhou, Sun sent a telegram congratulating Lenin on the success of the Bolshevik Revolution of October 1917 and conveying the hope that revolutionaries in China and Russia could "join forces for a common struggle." Georgi Chicerin, the Soviet commissar for foreign affairs, sent a friendly reply, agreeing that "the great proletariat of Russia and China" shared common interests. But what Sun had in mind was military assistance, not Soviet ideology. As always, Sun also pursued other options.[17]

Capitalizing on Japanese fears of a postwar world dominated by the Anglo-Saxon race, Sun played the pan-Asian card once again and called for East Asian solidarity. He is said to have offered Manchuria and Mongolia to the Japanese in return for help against the warlords in the North. The Japanese turned him down. Nonetheless, inspired by Woodrow Wilson's vision of a new era of global peace and cooperation, Sun thought that the victorious Western powers could be persuaded to invest in China. He began drawing up one of the most ambitious modernization schemes ever committed to paper.

The International Development of China, in which Sun set out his plan for China's rapid modernization, was originally written in English for a Western audience. It was later incorporated as "Part II: Material Reconstruction" in *Plan for National Reconstruction*. Much of the text was devoted to his plans to integrate China's many cities and towns through a network of railways, roads and dredged rivers. He envisaged an infrastructural development program that would include the construction of 100,000 miles of railways, 1 million miles of paved roads, and a multitude of other projects involving China's rivers, canals, ports, public utilities, agriculture, and so forth. A key part of the plan was the construction of two new ports, one near Tianjin and the other near Shanghai. Each city, he predicted, would grow to the size of New York. As for the mighty Yangtze River, Sun proposed that its rapids be dammed up to form locks, to enable crafts to ascend the river as well as to generate hydroelectric power.[18]

How would his enormously ambitious projects be financed? Sun believed that unless "good will and cooperation replaced competition and the scrambling for territories, the world was headed for another war." With the end of the war, he reasoned that the vast war industry in the West would need to be converted to peaceful use. If these powers would invest just a quarter of the estimated US$60 million a day in their final-year budget, it would be sufficient to bankroll his programs. Foreign investors would earn a reasonable return on their capital, and domestic private enterprises would be encouraged, except for industries possessing monopolistic characteristics, which would be nationalized.[19]

The International Development of China was published in 1920 but Sun had already started sending outlines of his plans to foreign officials in early 1919. It evoked little enthusiasm among the foreign powers, who understandably were not overly excited about lending vast sums of money to a China already heavily saddled with debt. Moreover, with Europe struggling to get back on her feet, it would be nearly impossible to raise the billions of dollars required for just a few of the projects. The American minister in Beijing, Dr. Paul S. Reinsch, who showed the greatest interest, advised Sun to scale everything down and focus on agriculture, which engaged 80 percent of China's population.[20]

While Sun was calling for a new international order based on cooperation and mutual assistance, delegates at the Paris Peace Conference in Versailles were engaged in the usual game of power politics. In 1898 Germany had leased the naval base of Jiaozhou in Shandong for 99 years from the Qing government. When World War I broke out, Japan joined the Allies, ousted the Germans from Jiaozhou and subsequently took over most of Shandong province. With the defeat of Germany, the Chinese expected that Shandong, now under Japanese occupation, would be returned to China. On November 17, 1918, thousands of Chinese staged a parade to celebrate the victory of the Allies, of which China was a member. It was in this state of high expectations that the Chinese delegates had headed off for Versailles.[21]

As it turned out, in early 1917 Russia, Britain, France and Italy had all concluded secret quid pro quo pacts with Japan agreeing to support the latter's claim to Shandong. It also emerged that in September 1918 Duan Qirui's government, too, had concluded secret agreements granting Japan the right to build two railways in Shandong and to station troops at various key points in return for the Nishihara loans. These secret agreements left

Woodrow Wilson as the lone champion of China's cause. Japan threatened to withdraw from the conference if her demands were not met. The Allied delegates and Wilson's own advisers persuaded him that it was important to first establish the League of Nations with Japan in it, and then secure justice for China later. On April 28, 1919, the peace conference resolved to allow Japan to retain her sovereignty in Shandong.

In endorsing Japan's seizure of the German concessions in Shandong, delegates at Versailles unleashed the greatest display of national furor that China had ever seen in modern times. Indignation against Japan had been seething since the Twenty-One Demands of 1915. Now on May 4, 1919, more than 3,000 student protesters gathered at Tiananmen Square and marched on the foreign legations. Finding their way blocked by police, the students set ablaze the home of Cao Rulin, the minister who had negotiated the Twenty-One Demands and the Nishihara loans. Over 30 students were arrested and the incident rapidly developed into a nationwide movement, with demonstrations in many cities and a boycott of Japanese goods. Businesses were paralyzed as merchants and workers joined in the anger. Chinese students in Paris organized a round-the-clock vigil to ensure that no delegates left their quarters lest they yield to foreign pressure. Consequently, there were no Chinese delegates at the signing ceremony on June 28.

Wilson, who was awarded the Nobel Peace Prize in 1919 for his efforts in establishing and promoting the League of Nations, sacrificed China to lure Japan into the international organization. Ironically, his own country did not join the League due to opposition in the U.S. Senate, and Japan was among the first to withdraw from the organization in 1933. Although China did not sign the peace treaty with Germany, she signed a treaty with Austria, and by virtue of that act automatically became a member of the League of Nations. The Shandong question remained unresolved until 1922 when Japan agreed to relinquish sovereignty over the province at the Washington Naval Conference.

The May 4 incident was the high point of a broader cultural phenomenon known as the New Culture Movement, which after the patriotic demonstration in 1919 became known as the May Fourth Movement. It was the revolutionary intellectual Chen Duxiu who had fired the opening salvo of the movement when he launched the *New Youth* monthly magazine in 1915. In a lead article, he contrasted the vitality of the West with the sterility of the East. Contending that Chinese thought was a millennium behind the West, he warned that China might suffer the fate of ancient Babylon unless revitalized by a new spirit. Science and democracy, he argued, epitomized the modern, creative spirit of the West. Confucian morality and the entire structure of traditional culture and beliefs were antithetical to these modern values.

Many of the students who participated in the May Fourth protest were from Peking National University (now Peking University, or Beida), which was founded in 1898 as the Imperial University of Beijing to train officials. It was transformed from a bastion of conservative learning into a thriving home for the pursuit of liberal ideas when Cai Yuanpei was appointed chancellor in January 1917. Among the youngest to be admitted to the prestigious Hanlin Academy, Cai co-founded the Guangfuhui with Zhang Binglin in 1904 and joined the Tongmenghui the following year. Disillusioned with revolutionary politics, he embarked on a four-year study course at Germany's Leipzig University in 1907. In 1912, he was appointed minister of education by Sun but resigned from Yuan Shikai's cabinet together with three other cabinet members in solidarity with Tang Shaoyi when he resigned as prime minister. Cai brought to Beida an intellectually diverse faculty.

Chen Duxiu, progenitor of the New Culture Movement, was appointed to head the School of Letters. In 1919, he spent several years in jail for supporting the May Fourth student demonstrators. Two years later, he co-founded the Chinese Communist Party with Li Dazhao, the university's librarian. In this position, Li influenced a number of students in the May Fourth Movement, including Mao Zedong, who worked in the library's reading room. Li was among the first Chinese intellectuals to look to China's villages as a basis for a political movement and among the earliest to explore Soviet Russia's Bolshevik government as a possible model for China.

Another intellectual giant who joined Beida's faculty was Hu Shi. He had studied under the philosopher John Dewey at Columbia University and was Chen Duxiu's ideological opposite. Hu stressed the need to apply the critical methods of science to the study of history, philosophy and literature. What made him famous was his promotion of the vernacular language (*baihua*) as the written language, a development that was as radical as the replacement of Latin by French and English after the Renaissance. New periodicals were written in *baihua* while new study groups and other student organizations disseminated modern ideas. Thousands of students became involved in educational and social activities among the urban masses, as well as in political agitation against imperialism and warlordism.

Sun was no more than a spectator in the initial phase of the May Fourth Movement. Even with his young wife Qingling and his son Sun Ke at his side, he had little contact with the new youth of China. Sun was skeptical about the effectiveness of mass movements and still hoped to gain power by exploiting warlord politics and launching a Northern Expedition against the militarists in Beijing. Indeed, he even went so far as to oppose young intellectuals such as Hu Shi and Chen Duxiu. While the *New Youth* magazine was advocating the substitution of *baihua* for the literary language in written texts, Sun rejected it. In his view, the classical literary language was an integral part of Chinese culture that would ensure its continuity and that of the Chinese state.

Sun's attitude marginalized him in the social development and cultural revolution that were causing such a storm in Chinese political life. But as the movement picked up steam, he saw how he could use students and intellectuals to revitalize his own party and revive his own political fortunes. He hailed the May Fourth Movement as an important contribution to the success of the revolution. Having lost his patience with Japan, Sun began speaking out bluntly against Japanese imperialism. On June 13, he told a Japanese reporter that Japan's policy toward China since 1915 had irreparably damaged Sino-Japanese relations. Asked why he singled out Japan to vent his anger, Sun responded with a sarcastic analogy, comparing Japan with a younger brother who joins a gang of thieves to rob his elder brother and then complains that his brother hates him more than the other thieves.[22]

The launch of the monthly *Reconstruction* magazine in August 1919 provided Sun with a channel to publicize his views and for his more intellectually inspired comrades to contribute to the intellectual foment of the May Fourth Movement. The magazine featured translations and interpretations of Western political writings, particularly those dealing with socialist thought. But what was uppermost on Sun's mind in the fall of 1919 was not a new culture founded on science and democracy, but the reorganization of his revolutionary organization, which had been moribund since his return to Shanghai in May 1916.[23]

On October 10, 1919, the eighth anniversary of the Wuchang Uprising, Sun announced the formation of the Zhongguo Guomindang, the Chinese Nationalist Party (the old party was simply Guomindang, Nationalist Party) in place of the Guomindang abroad; the domestic party was not reorganized until the following year. The new party was a more open organization that did away with the two issues that had alienated his old comrades: the oath of loyalty to Sun, and the categorization of members according to the length of their party membership. But Sun still claimed supreme power for himself as *zongli*. Obedience to him, Sun said, simply meant pledging allegiance to his political ideologies, pointing out that it was common practice to identify individuals with the doctrines they originated. A new constitution, promulgated on November 9, 1920, included his plan for single-party tutelage and the Five-Power Constitution as well as the Three Principles of the People, now with nationalism restored. No longer claiming that this had been achieved with the fall of the Qing dynasty, Sun touched on China's low international status. Warning that extraterritoriality gave the foreign powers coercive powers in China, he urged resistance to foreign attempts at domination. Sun also called for the integration of the five ethnic groups – Han, Manchu, Mongol, Tibetan and Muslim – into one great Chinese nation. He later qualified that what he had in mind was the assimilation of the four minorities into the Han majority. However, before organization plans could be put in place, Sun was sidetracked when Chen Jiongming's forces captured Guangzhou. This revived his dream of establishing the South as a base for the military unification of China.[24]

The Guangxi clique that had forced Sun out of Guangzhou in the summer of 1918 crumbled due to internal strife. Taking advantage of the situation, Chen Jiongming, who had been running a reformist government in southern Fujian, led the Guangdong Army to reclaim the province. In 1917 he had supported Sun's Constitution Protection Movement and first military government in Guangzhou. Now Chen wanted to rehabilitate Guangdong into a model province, an idea that was incompatible with Sun's plan to use Guangzhou as a base to unify China by force. Thus after reclaiming the city, he implored Sun to stay put in Shanghai, but Sun could not be dissuaded.[25]

With the support of Wang Jingwei and Liao Zhongkai, a few local troops and the navy, Sun was back in Guangzhou on November 28, 1920. His very first idea was to revive the military government that he had presided over two years earlier. Realizing how little support there was for the project, he threw constitutionalism to the wind and on April 7, 1921, persuaded over 200 members of the parliament that had been dissolved in 1917 to elect him president. In the absence of a quorum, he settled for the title of Extraordinary President, and placed his partisans Wang Jingwei, Hu Hanmin, Liao Zhongkai and other party members in important administrative posts. Chen Jiongming along with much of public opinion, local trade unions and members of the provincial assembly protested against these moves. Sun was forced to recognize the autonomy of the provincial government and the power that Chen Jiongming already exercised over local affairs as provincial governor and commander-in-chief of the Guangdong army.

Forming a national government was not just for domestic consumption; it was also a bid for foreign recognition, especially the Americans'. If successful, this would give Sun a share of the surplus customs revenue now being remitted exclusively to the Beijing government. To secure such recognition, Sun bent over backward to placate Western concerns. He pledged to respect all treaty obligations and to encourage foreign investments. He spoke of nationalism in Wilsonian terms as "an absolutely unmolested opportunity of autonomous development,"[26] and limited his attacks to Japan and her stooges, the warlords.

Not only did the Americans ignore his appeal for recognition, they seemed intent on humiliating him. The White House ignored Sun's congratulatory message to the newly inaugurated President Warren Harding, and the U.S. State Department refused to acknowledge receipt of his *International Development of China*, or for that matter any of his other messages. Nor would the State Department accede to Sun's request that his government be represented at the Washington Naval Conference, later held in Washington, D.C., from November 12, 1921 to February 6, 1922. The State Department even stopped American investors from dealing with Sun's Guangzhou government while the British forbade the Chinese in Hong Kong to celebrate Sun's inauguration.[27]

But Sun's popularity was growing on his home turf. No one could match his oratorical skills on a podium or his record for honesty. Unlike most politicians of the day, he had made no money out of politics. His long struggle for democracy and great-power status for China took on heroic proportions at a time when there were few national protagonists that the Chinese could look up to. Sun had his assembly of sympathizers, too, among certain Western opinion-shapers.

When Sun took office in April 1921, a U.S. vice-consul in Guangzhou tried to persuade the American Legation in Beijing and Washington not to insult Sun but to "extend real sympathy" to a government that represented China's best hope for democracy. The American philosopher and education reformer John Dewey on a visit to China in June 1921 advised a policy of "benevolent neutrality" toward Sun's Guangzhou government. Bertrand Russell, the British mathematician and philosopher who was in China at about the same time, spoke favorably of Sun and considered his government to be the best in China. In September, a *New York Times* editorial advocated that both the Beijing and Guangzhou governments should be represented at the Washington Naval Conference. It even contended that Sun had a better claim to attend the conference than "the creatures of the warlords in the North." Such glowing endorsements fell on deaf ears in Washington, however.

In October 1921, over the objection of Chen Jiongming, Sun obtained approval from the rump parliament for a Northern Expedition. Leading a weak force of men, he marched toward Guilin near the Guangxi-Hunan border where he planned to attack the autonomists of Hunan. The campaign created tension between him and Chen, who opposed any recourse to military force and was still counting on federalism to achieve national unity. Chen refused to use provincial funds to finance Sun's expedition.[28]

After a fruitless winter in Guilin, Sun brought his troops back to Guangdong in April 1922. Furious with Chen for refusing to fund his Northern Expedition, Sun dismissed him as provincial governor and commander of the Guangdong Army. This had little effect on Chen, who having returned in glory from his victories in Guangxi now had the support of the local gentry, merchants and trade unions. He was also being courted by the Northern warlords and by Comintern agents. Most importantly, Chen's lieutenant Ye Ju was in control of Guangzhou. Meanwhile, warlord politics entered a more convoluted phase.[29]

Having jointly controlled the Beijing government since 1920, the Fengtian and Zhili cliques were soon at loggerheads. In December 1921, the Fengtian clique replaced the prime minister without the prior consent of its coalition partner. The conflict intensified when the new cabinet refused to remit the military budget previously allocated to the Zhili clique, which then forced the new prime minister to resign. In response, the Manchurian warlord Zhang Zuolin threatened to resolve the conflict by force and began mobilizing his troops for a showdown.

From this time on, central power became strictly nominal and the provinces fell victim more than ever to mercenaries. Sun was maneuvering to impose his authority not only among the warlords fighting for control of Beijing but also among the military leaders in the central and southern provinces who were organizing themselves to protect their own independence. With the warlords, Sun engaged both the Zhili and Fengtian cliques; he was ready to ally himself with whichever of the two would agree to reserve for him the presidency of a new national government. Since Wu Peifu of Zhili had his eyes on the same post, Sun struck a deal with Zhang Zuolin of Fengtian in April 1922. It was an unfortunate choice. The Fengtian clique was almost immediately defeated by the Zhili clique in the First Zhili-Fengtian War. To pave the way for a pacific reunification of China, Wu Peifu called on the two "national presidents" to resign their posts. Xu Shichang in Beijing complied but Sun refused to yield.[30]

On May 6, Sun set out on another Northern Expedition from northern Guangdong. In his absence Ye Ju's troops occupied Guangzhou and demanded Chen Jiongming's restoration to his former offices. Now allied with Wu Peifu, Chen joined the chorus calling for Sun's resignation. Sun rushed back to Guangzhou and ordered Ye Ju and his troops to withdraw from Guangzhou within ten days, or face an attack of poisonous shells. His threat backfired.

In the early morning of June 16, troops led by Ye Ju attacked Sun's residence. He and Qingling escaped separately[31] and later rendezvoused on the gunboat *Yongfeng*.[32] Chiang Kai-shek answered Sun's call for help and joined him on the gunboat on June 29. This was for Chiang the turning point in his career. For several weeks Sun tried to negotiate but found that public opinion in Guangdong was with Chen Jiongming, whose achievements in the provincial capital towered over Sun's democracy rhetoric. Sun requested the American consulate for safe passage to Shanghai but the consul, under strict orders to stay out of internal Chinese affairs, turned him down. The British, anxious to get Sun out of the area, transported him to Hong Kong on August 9. The next day, Sun and Qingling boarded the *Empress of Russia* for Shanghai.[33]

The narrow escape ended Sun's second Guangzhou regime, but the extraordinary presidency was not all he lost. Ye Ju's troops burnt down Sun's Guangzhou residence and destroyed all his manuscripts, except for a few indiscreet papers revealing that Sun had been planning a Sino-Soviet-German alliance. When these papers were discovered, the *Hong Kong Telegraph* published them on September 22 under the headline, "Proposed Triple Bolshevik Alliance." The German government promptly denied the story, as did Sun, who tried to explain it away by insisting that he was merely seeking normal diplomatic relations with the two countries. He denied any sympathy for communist ideology and referred to his *International Development of China* and his still-standing offer to Western capitalists.

One of Sun's most important acts during his second Guangzhou government from December 1920 to June 1922 was to appoint his son Sun Ke as mayor of Guangzhou, a position he would hold for most of the period from 1921 to late 1924. A graduate of Berkeley with a Masters degree from Columbia, Sun Ke's attempt to implement a policy of modernization and urban renovation along Western lines was unprecedented for a Chinese city of the time. He created an elected municipal council, expanded the city's public works and introduced new programs in public health and coeducational schooling. Guangzhou became a model for other coastal cities and a mecca for educated radicals from all corners of China. Sun Ke's municipal administration produced large amounts of money for Sun's war chest. However, in order to obtain these funds, extra taxes were levied, which created strong resentment.[34]

With the Zhili clique's position in Beijing firmly entrenched, Wu Peifu restored the 1912 constitution, reconvened what was left of the old parliament and installed Li Yuanhong as president. Though warlords still dominated the political landscape, the constitutionalism that Sun had been advocating now seemed at last within reach – but without him. He had lost his legitimacy and even old comrades were advising him to retire so as not to stand in the way of the nation's hope for unity. He regretted giving in to such well-meaning advice ten years earlier. This time he decided to stick to his guns.[35]

Chapter 13

DANCES WITH BEARS

TREATED AS A political outcast by the foreign powers and now dismissed by his own comrades as a political dinosaur, Sun began turning to the pariahs of the international community. On the British gunboat journey to Hong Kong, he was already rethinking his foreign policy options. As he explained to Chiang Kai-shek, China should not ignore the other foreign powers or refrain from adopting some of their institutions and values. Sun wanted China to pay particular attention to Germany and Soviet Russia. Both countries were unhappy with the postwar settlements, which had left them weak and vulnerable. The Treaty of Versailles required Germany to disarm and to cede territories. Russia withdrew from the war in 1917 because of the Bolshevik revolution. She ceded to Germany many of her territories, which after the war were transformed into a number of new independent states. Both Germany and Russia were diplomatically isolated – in the case of Germany, because she had lost the war, in Russia's case because of the desertion by Western allies after her transition to communism. The two pariahs of the Western world were now building cordial relations, formalized by the Treaty of Rapallo signed on April 16, 1922. Under this treaty, each renounced all territorial and financial claims against the other arising out of the war and committed to cooperating in economic development. Both countries had also ceased to be imperialist powers in China.

Germany was Sun's first choice because of her superior armament industry and capacity for economic aid. She was also the first European power to treat China on the basis of equality and relinquish extraterritorial and other privileges when she signed a peace treaty with China in May 1921. In 1918, in the last year of the war, Sun had toyed with the idea of a triple alliance with Germany and Soviet Russia. After his return to Guangzhou in December 1920, Sun pressed the German consul for diplomatic recognition and economic aid. Concurrently, he had an agent in Berlin submit proposals for economic cooperation to German industrialists and foreign ministry officials. Skeptical about the stability of Sun's position in Guangzhou and reluctant to pursue an independent course in China, the Germans turned down his proposals.[1]

Soviet Russia was a different kettle of fish. Unconstrained by conventional methods of diplomacy, she was more suited organizationally for direct involvement in Chinese politics. Moreover, while delegates at the Washington Naval Conference hesitated to restore Chinese sovereignty, Lev Karakhan, the Soviet deputy commissar for foreign affairs, had as early as mid-1919 announced the repudiation of the unequal treaties forced on China by the tsarist government. This was subsequently qualified but the Soviets' voluntary abandonment contrasted with the West's insistence that China comply with every demeaning letter of the 19th-century treaties obtained through gunboat diplomacy. Although less developed than Germany and yet to fully recover from the Bolshevik Revolution, the Soviet government was looking for ways to undermine Western capitalist regimes by promoting nationalist revolutions in subjugated countries.

For the first three years after the Bolshevik revolution in 1917, the new Communist government under Vladimir Lenin was engaged in a prolonged civil war to root out supporters of the previous tsarist regime. Lenin had hoped that the peoples of Europe would join his Communist revolution and raise the world to a new stage of development. But his success in Russia was not matched by similar successes beyond her borders. In 1919, Lenin created the Communist International, or Comintern, to spread the Communist revolution throughout the world by undermining existing governments, starting in Europe. By the Comintern's second congress in July 1920, however, it had become apparent that Western governments were too entrenched to be overthrown. It was at this juncture that Lenin in his *Theses on the National and Colonial Questions* underscored the need for the Comintern to ally itself with national independence movements in colonized countries, even if they were not inspired by socialist or communist ideology. His strategy was to infiltrate these movements and take them over as they approached success. In pursuit of these objectives, the Comintern's strategy in China was to negotiate with the Beijing government, assist in the formation of the Communist Party of China (CPC), and to search out a "bourgeois" revolutionary partner for a united front.[2]

In the early 1920s, Comintern agents traveled the length and breadth of China contacting all power-holders perceived to be influential. They held talks with the Beijing government, met with warlords as well as Sun. His first meeting with a Comintern agent appears to have been in Shanghai in November 1920 with Grigori Voitinsky, who had been in China since April to encourage Chinese intellectuals to form a Communist group. Voitinsky had lived for many years in the United States and was fluent in English, which enabled him to communicate directly with Sun. According to Voitinsky's account, Sun was eager for information about Soviet Russia and her revolution, and was extremely interested in how the "struggle in southern China could be joined with the struggle in faraway Russia." Sun also asked repeatedly whether Russia could establish a powerful radio station in Vladivostok or Manchuria so that "the Canton government could keep informed about what the Russians were doing and draw on their experience." Sun left shortly after to set up his second government in Guangzhou, where he was to make several contacts with Russian agents.[3]

In June 1921, not long after being elected extraordinary president, Sun received a letter from Georgi Chicherin in which the Soviet commissar for foreign affairs complimented China for beginning the struggle against imperialism. Chicherin proposed that China begin trade with Russia at once, and establish good relations with Soviet Russia. In his reply on August 28, Sun cautioned Moscow against attempting to establish relations with the Beijing government until he was firmly in control. In a brutally frank reply the following February, Chicherin replied that the current Beijing government was the official government of the Chinese state and "we are striving to establish normal relations with it."[4]

Sun's discussions with Maring (J.F.M. Sneevliet) at Guilin, where Sun was directing the Northern Expedition in late December 1921, was his first substantive meeting with a Comintern agent. Maring was a Dutch communist with years of experience in the Dutch East Indies guiding the forerunner of the Indonesian Communist Party. He had participated in the founding congress of the CPC in July and was scouting the field for a suitable bourgeois-nationalist ally. During their meeting, Maring proposed that Sun reorganize the Guomindang to include peasants and workers; establish a military academy to create a revolutionary army; and cooperate with the CPC. Sun rejected the idea of an alliance with Soviet Russia for the moment. He was preparing to launch a military campaign into the Yangtze valley. This was within the British sphere of influence, and Sun was concerned that such an alliance might invite British intervention. He assured Maring that they could plan for complete cooperation once he gained control of Beijing.[5]

The Beijing presidency was on Sun's mind when he returned to Shanghai on August 14, 1922, after his eviction from Guangzhou by Ye Ju's troops. Later, as his prospects for seizing power in Beijing dimmed, Sun pinned his hopes on making a triumphant return to Guangzhou. To repair his tarnished reputation, he issued two manifestos to explain and defend his rationale for a Southern regime. It was a constitutional regime, he claimed, that should have opened the way to reunification. Blaming Chen Jiongming for the failure, Sun set forth ideas for national reunification and reconstruction: restoring the authority of parliament, to whose decision he pledged to abide regarding his own constitutional status; a general demilitarization by disbanding armies and converting troops to labor corps; developing the country's resources for the benefit of the people as outlined in his *International Development of China*; and a reorganization of China's political system that would allow a large measure of local autonomy.[6]

Despite his recent setbacks and little prospect of achieving power on his own, Sun's growing personal popularity made him an extremely useful asset to warlords of all shades, as well as the Communists. The American consul in Shanghai noted that Sun "has become an even greater national character than when head of the Southern Republic. His support is sought by a large number of prominent and well known military and civilian officials in the North."[7] Delegates sent by acting president Li Yuanhong to invite Sun to Beijing returned to the capital with a cordial reply expressing Sun's willingness to advise and to aid in the reconstruction and unification of China. Even Wu Peifu, the leader of the Zhili clique whose control extended to most of the Northern provinces and as far south as the Yangtze valley, was courting Sun. Wu enjoyed British support and a large segment of Chinese public opinion. Cooperation between the two men would have served national unity well and negotiations for Sun's return to Beijing through intermediaries went on for several months. While parleying with the Zhili clique, Sun did not neglect the other warlords. He sent emissaries to negotiate with the leaders of the Anhui clique as well as with Zhang Zuolin, the head of the Fengtian clique. Sun also began a series of exchanges with militarists in the Southwest to enlist them for a drive on Guangzhou.[8]

The CPC had declared its formal affiliation with the Comintern and its acceptance of the latter's discipline at the party's Second Congress in July 1922. In accord with Moscow's strategy, the Congress called for a "united front of democratic revolution" with the Guomindang, though neither the Comintern nor the CPC was proposing anything more than a loose affiliation. The Chinese Communists did not hold Sun and the Guomindang in particularly high regard, and there were skeptics who doubted whether cooperation was even worthy of consideration. They recognized, however, that a united front with the Guomindang held the promise of a wider constituency and the benefit of the latter's reputation and greater respectability. Moreover, the Guomindang was the only party with some revolutionary spirit. Its organizational weakness made it all the more attractive as a united front partner. It suited the Comintern strategy, which called for manipulating bourgeois allies within a united front, and discarding them at the appropriate time. Sun, to the Communists, seemed to fit the bill to a tee. They would soon learn that he was anything but a pliable ally.[9]

The Guomindang was not a large party; it had several thousand members, and many more supporters and sympathizers among students and labor unions. Even so, the CPC with just 300 members was puny by comparison. There was no danger of Sun or the Guomindang being overwhelmed by the Communists. What Sun feared most was the CPC competing with him for Soviet aid. Worse, if he did not cooperate with the Comintern, they would choose another candidate, perhaps his archenemy Chen Jiongming. A monopoly on Soviet arms, money and advisers was as important to Sun as the Guomindang playing the role of China's sole caretaker government during the projected period of political tutelage. And the more he learned about the success of the Soviet model, the more determined he was to carry out his plan for a single-party dictatorship.[10]

Thus when Maring visited Sun in Shanghai, probably in the last week of August 1922, to talk about a united front, Sun was ready to accept an alliance with the Chinese Communists on condition that they joined the Guomindang as individual members. Sun could not see an alliance on an equal basis with a tiny party that he judged to be less important than the Guomindang. It was also to ensure that his party would have a monopoly on Soviet aid and that the Russians did not independently arm the Communists. This was of course not what the Communists had in mind. But with Moscow's backing, Maring overcame the objection of the Communists, who insisted, however, that they be allowed to maintain their separate party organization. Sun agreed, thinking that this was a small price to pay for Soviet aid. He was so sure that the Soviets would keep a tight rein on the Communists that he appointed the leading Communist Chen Duxiu to a nine-man committee to revise the Guomindang's statutes and devise a new program.[11]

It was around the time of Maring's visit that Sun began communicating with Adolph Joffe, a Soviet diplomat who was in Beijing to negotiate the normalization of diplomatic relations with China and a settlement on the thorny Chinese Eastern Railway issue.[12] Notwithstanding Karakhan's declaration of July 1919 renouncing all privileges obtained by the tsarist government in China, the Soviets made it clear that they intended to keep the choicest parts, specifically control of the Chinese Eastern Railway in Manchuria and suzerainty over Outer Mongolia. Beijing refused to recognize Soviet Russia on these terms, but the Russians hoped that their flirtation with Sun would soften Beijing, just as their courtship of Beijing had made Sun less demanding. Moreover, the Kremlin had high hopes that Wu Peifu, who had just won the latest warlord contest and was now cooperating with the Communists, would make negotiations easier.[13]

In the fall of 1922, Sun and Joffe exchanged about half a dozen letters in which Sun requested for Soviet advisers to be sent to China and explored the idea of sending Chiang Kai-shek to Moscow to negotiate aid. In his letters, Sun did not hide his irritation with Joffe's conversations with the Beijing regime and the Soviets' impatience in not holding off negotiations normalizing Chinese-Soviet relations until after he had resumed power in the South and devised a new strategy to take Beijing. Nor did Sun hide his concerns about rumors of a Soviet plan to invade northern Manchuria and about an alliance between Moscow and Wu Peifu to drive Zhang Zuolin from Manchuria.[14] It was not just the Soviets who held Wu in high esteem. Both the British and the Americans welcomed his return to power, with Nathaniel Peffer, who later became a professor of international relations at Columbia University, declaring him as "the best man that has forged his way to the top in China since the establishment of the Republic."[15] Wu's anti-Japanese stance and steps towards restoring parliamentary government also impressed many Chinese elites, including a number of Guomindang sympathizers. It was natural that Sun should want to make peace with his erstwhile nemesis. Indeed, a number of Russian and Comintern agents as well as Chinese Communists had been advocating an alliance between Sun and Wu. With Wu's military power and resources, and the Guomindang's potential, such a coalition could become the formidable bourgeois-nationalist front that the Comintern had been seeking.[16]

The rapprochement led to the inclusion of four Guomindang members or sympathizers in the new cabinet in Beijing. Wu even helped to ease Sun's financial straits. But the entente came apart within a few months. Wu was keen to pursue Sun's proposal for national unification and disbandment of troops, but balked when Sun demanded the presidency. In common with other warlord cliques, the Zhili clique was not a solid bloc and the warlords who constituted the clique were never more animated than when their interests were at stake. So even if Wu agreed, the other warlords in the Zhili clique were unlikely to. In November, Wu could not stop his fellow Zhili warlords from wrecking the new cabinet. The following month, he dismissed his emissary and ended his discussions with Sun.

Adolph Joffe, still unable to reach agreement with the Beijing government, which remained stubbornly uncompromising on the sensitive Manchurian and Mongolian issues, decided to take a break and accepted Sun's invitation to visit him. He arrived in Shanghai on the evening of January 17, 1923, two days after forces "friendly" to Sun had driven Chen Jiongming out of Guangzhou. Sun must have been in a triumphant mood. He had just reorganized the Guomindang and was in the process of selecting candidates for his new government in Guangzhou, to which he planned to return very soon. He entertained Joffe at a dinner on January 18, and thereafter they conferred on several occasions at Sun's residence on Rue Moliere. On January 23, Joffe gave a dinner for Sun and his close associates at the Great

Eastern Hotel. The series of talks between February 17 and 26 resulted in the Sun-Joffe Declaration. Significantly, this joint statement took the form of a formal agreement between a Chinese official responsible for foreign policy and a foreign envoy. This was an important marker in Sun's political career, being the first time that a foreign power acknowledged his claim to represent China.

What this agreement essentially amounted to was Sun's acceptance of an alliance with Soviet Russia, with two reservations. First, that communism and the Soviet system could not be introduced into China, and Russia would be content to support China, that is to say Sun, in her struggle for national reunification and independence. The second was Joffe's confirmation of the 1919 Karakhan declaration renouncing all privileges secured by the tsarist government, including those relating to the Chinese Eastern Railway. In return, Sun accepted the modus vivendi that left the management of this railway to the Soviets and authorized the occupation of Outer Mongolia by Soviet troops. The joint statement made no mention of Soviet aid for Sun. This might have been negotiated by Liao Zhongkai, a close associate of Sun's, who caught up with Joffe in Japan. It was after this meeting that the Kremlin decided in March 1823 to send advisers and allocate US$2 million to Sun.[17]

The "friendly" forces that drove Chen Jiongming from Guangzhou and made possible Sun's return to that city were the remnants of the army from Yunnan that had established itself in Guangdong in 1916 in connection with the National Protection Movement aimed at Yuan Shikai. Gradually this army severed its link with its native province, which thereupon ceased to finance it. It then had to ensure its own survival by exploiting territories that it occupied and by negotiating with the surrounding powers. Its command became fragmented, but by virtue of its size it was still the major military and hence political power in Guangdong. It constituted the core of the coalition that was formed there and that overcame the power of Chen Jiongming. Sun had purchased their loyalty to the tune of C$400,000. The continuation of this alliance would have to be paid for and Sun was counting on Hong Kong to provide the funds. Sun also realized that the use of Guangzhou as his base for national agitation with international implications required at least the neutrality if not the cooperation of the British colonial government of nearby Hong Kong. In January 1923, Sun began making attempts to mend fences with the British.[18]

Sun was encouraged to make these overtures by the group of young men gathered around his son Sun Ke. These Western-educated men were committed to the economic and administrative development of Guangzhou. They had won the respect of the Cantonese merchants and were similarly held in high esteem by the Chinese elites of Hong Kong, an attitude that was strengthened by family links. Two of their foremost members had married daughters of Ho Kai, the reform-minded civic leader who had inspired Sun at the start of his career. Sun Ke and his clique preferred cooperation with the West and were opposed to an alliance with the Soviets. They worked hard to establish a liaison between Sun and the Hong Kong colonial government.

On January 11, 1923, Sun sent his foreign secretary, the Trinidad-born barrister Eugene Chen, to meet and convey to Sir Sidney Barton, the British consul-general in Shanghai, that Sun wanted improved relations with Britain. This was accompanied by an intimation that lack of sympathy from Britain and other great powers, "with whom Dr. Sun had really more in common," might lead to a rapprochement with Japan, Russia and Germany. In his second meeting with Barton, on January 19, Chen dropped the hint that a meeting between Sun and the governor of Hong Kong would be desirable.[19] In February, Sun met with the British minister, Sir Ronald Macleay, who was passing through Shanghai. Aware of Sun's influence in southern China and among *huaqiao* communities in Nanyang, as well as his imminent return to Guangzhou, Macleay advised the Foreign Office to deal tactfully with Sun.[20]

But no one could have anticipated the enthusiastic reception that Sun received when he arrived in Hong Kong on February 17, 1923, on board the SS *President Jefferson* en route to Guangzhou. Many of the colony's notables called on Sun, who was also entertained to lunch by Governor Sir Edward Reginald Stubbs the day after his arrival. The same afternoon, Sun had tea with Sir Robert Hotung, a prominent civic leader, with whom Sun shared his plan to reorganize the Guangzhou government and his need for funds to disband half the soldiers in the province. The day before his departure from Hong Kong, Sun had tea with the general manager of the

Hongkong & Shanghai Bank, and visited the University of Hong Kong, his alma mater, where he gave a much-publicized address to students. Evoking the good old days as a student in the colony, Sun revealed to his youthful audience that he had developed his revolutionary ideas upon noting the difference between the colony's good governance and the corruption of the Chinese bureaucracy. He concluded his speech with a flattering assessment of the English parliamentary system: "We must take England as a model and extend England's example of good government to the whole of China."[21]

If Sun's hope was to mend fences with the British and keep open his options with them, he had obviously succeeded. Governor Stubbs, who in early January had called him "a danger to civilization," filed a very favorable report of Sun to London as someone he could do business with. On the morning of February 21, Sun took the SS *Heungshan* to Guangzhou. At this time, he was still not sure if he would have Bolsheviks or imperialists as allies, or if at all. All he knew was that without outside help, it seemed doubtful that he would be able to hold on to Guangzhou for long.

On March 2, Sun became generalissimo of a military government that was dependent on the goodwill of the Yunnanese mercenaries who had driven Chen Jiongming out of Guangzhou. They were now bleeding Guangdong province for all they could. Only in Guangzhou, where Sun Ke was mayor, did Sun and the Guomindang hold any sway. But the city was under constant threat from Chen's forces and other warlord armies, forcing Sun to shelve his plan for the Guomindang's reorganization and to focus on more pressing issues. Meanwhile, squeezed by the Yunnan mercenaries, Sun milked the city for extra taxes and then dipped into salt revenues that had been mortgaged to foreigners.[22]

While Sun was desperately scrounging around for money to finance his government, the Western powers who collected customs and salt tax revenues in Guangzhou continued to remit all surplus funds to the Beijing government. This was a sore point with Sun. In May, the *Far Eastern Review* published "Dr. Sun's Message to the World," in which he blamed the chaos in China on the support and encouragement that "the liberal powers" had extended to "the hirelings of the military oligarchy posing as the government at Beijing." Sun proposed that the funds should be held in trust for a future unified government, and if the powers could not openly support the liberal movement in China, meaning his government, they should at least "stand aside in strict neutrality by withholding financial support to Beijing while the Chinese settle their own problems in their own way."[23]

Nothing came out of Sun's plea but the idea of British officers assisting Sun in reorganizing his government's finances briefly survived. Governor Stubbs reported to his superiors at the Foreign Office that Sun wished to enlist British experts and wondered if His Majesty's Government would approve "any of my officers being lent to him." Foreign Office officials were opposed but wired Sir Ronald Macleay for his opinion. The British minister in Beijing argued that Britain should not assist Sun in that way because such help would be construed both in China and in the United States as intervening on Sun's behalf. Furthermore, Sun had infringed reorganization loan agreements by tampering with British salt administration, and had in any event "probably reached some understanding with Bolsheviks" and "coquetted with communism and Indian sedition." The Foreign Office thus informed the Colonial Office that it would be best not to accede to Sun's request but to continue a policy of friendly neutrality.[24]

Angered at this latest rebuff, Sun delivered a blistering attack on the imperialist powers, the United States in particular, in an interview with a YMCA official. These powers collected taxes in the South, Sun complained bitterly, but remitted them to the Beijing government which then used these Southern tax receipts to attack the South. "We have lost hope of help from America … or any other of the great powers," he said. "The only country that shows any sign of helping us … is the Soviet Government of Russia."[25]

In July, when this interview was reported in the *New York Times*, help from Russia was no longer just a sign. The Soviet government had telegraphed Sun on May 1 expressing readiness to "render necessary assistance to China." Soviet military officers began arriving in China on June 21. By the fall of that year, Sun had swung to the Soviet camp, though not without some reservations. He may have been swayed in his decision by the precariousness of his position in Guangzhou. Since returning to the city in February, the coalition on which he had been banking for his reconquest rapidly fragmented. In mid-April, the Guangxi unit turned against him and tried to seize Guangzhou. This was followed by an offensive by Chen Jiongming, who still occupied the eastern part of Guangdong. In the north, the borders with Hunan and Guangxi were held by forces hostile to Sun. Only central Guangdong was controlled by the Guomindang. The Yunnanese mercenaries who constituted the core of the coalition simply refused to follow Sun's orders when it came to setting out on any campaign. He had to negotiate each and every offensive, and pay cash on the spot for the service. Sun could neither eject them from Guangzhou nor disband them, for these men were his regime's only protection.

Maintaining them was expensive business, to the tune of about C$1 million per month. Sun's government resorted to increasing taxes, extracting contributions from merchants, and confiscating properties. These raised the municipal revenues significantly but discredited his government. Sun had no choice; he had to find the money to retain control of the contingents. It was the urgency of his financial needs that forced Sun to seize Guangzhou's share of the maritime customs surplus though this inevitably brought him into open conflict with the foreign diplomatic corps.[26]

The administration of the maritime customs, under international management, used most of its revenues for the repayment of foreign loans. After World War I, a steep rise in those revenues made it possible to set aside a surplus, which the foreign powers returned to the Beijing government. In 1919, the Southern generals had laid claim to and obtained payment of a portion of this surplus but this stopped in March 1920 when the Guangzhou government disintegrated. In memoranda that Sun wrote to the diplomatic corps in September and October 1923, he asked that those payments be resumed, with arrears that he calculated to be in the ballpark of C$12.6 million. The foreign powers did not even bother to respond.[27]

Ignored by the powers and desperate for funds, Sun was all the more inclined to listen to the Soviet proposals, now delivered to him by the persuasive new Soviet emissary Mikhail Borodin (his real family name was Grusenberg) who arrived in Guangzhou on October 6, 1923. A Bolshevik veteran with close links to Lenin and other Soviet leaders, Borodin was the official representative of the Soviet government charged with carrying out Leninist strategy in China. The first phase was to remold the Guomindang into the disciplined mass organization that Sun had wanted.

Although he took Borodin's advice seriously, Sun himself remained the final arbiter of his party's policies. He did not need Borodin to tutor him in political philosophy or ideology. What he wanted were the party propaganda and organizational techniques and, above all, the methods and means for building a party army. Sun was most impressed by the role of the Soviet revolutionary army, which had not only defeated domestic counterrevolutionaries but had also repelled the invading armies of the major capitalist powers. Given his own party's dependence on guest armies and the recurrent fear of foreign intervention, there was nothing Sun wanted more than to emulate the Bolsheviks' military achievement. Just how vulnerable he was to the foreign military threat was illustrated in the latter part of the year when the controversy over customs receipts sparked a crisis.

Mikhail Borodin

Meanwhile, Sun's hold on Guangzhou was in jeopardy. For three months, his forces had been besieging Chen Jiongming's stronghold at Huizhou without making any headway. In the third week of October, Sun's Yunnan and Guangxi mercenaries lost their fight, and the tide of battle shifted against Sun. On November 5, Chen's troops began moving on Guangzhou and a week later, Sun's troops began retreating to Guangzhou. The next day, Borodin proposed a radical policy to win the support of Guangdong peasants and Guangzhou labor. He urged that a decree be issued to confiscate and distribute landlord holdings to peasants and a second decree to promise labor an eight-hour day, a minimum wage and other rights. An accompanying manifesto would explain to the city's petty bourgeoisie how they would benefit from the higher living standard of the masses. Borodin argued that if these promises were directly publicized to the peasants and workers, they would rally to the support of the troops fighting Chen's forces. According to Borodin's recollection, a propaganda apparatus was set in motion, with immediate favorable effect at the front. Then some Guomindang began to waver and put pressure on Sun. After considerable bargaining, Sun agreed to a decree providing for the establishment of a peasant union, and another decree reducing rent by 25 percent, though it would be another three years before this was implemented by the Guomindang. Borodin's strategy worked, and Sun's third government was saved. From this time forward, Sun began to call Borodin his "Lafayette" and put a good deal of faith in the Russian.[28]

The two months preceding the First National Congress of the Guomindang scheduled to be convened in January 1924 were dominated by clashes between Borodin and party moderates, and Sun's deteriorating relations with the foreign powers. In late November 1923, Teng Tse Ju leading a group of Cantonese members presented Sun with a petition denouncing "a plot to borrow the body of the Guomindang but to infuse it with the soul of the Communist Party." They condemned the new organizational principles inspired by the Soviet model, which they averred were really those of Chen Duxiu, the CPC general secretary. By including anti-imperialism in its program, the party would forgo any hope of Western aid and by advocating a struggle against militarism would isolate the warlords who held real power. As a Tongmenghui veteran who had stood by Sun through good times and bad, Teng's loyalty was beyond doubt. His criticism of Sun's new political orientation was his first against Sun, yet the latter dismissed it with a few notes scribbled in the margins of the petition. The drafting of the party's new statutes was the work of Borodin, Sun wrote, and Chen Duxiu had no part in it. To set their minds at ease, Sun declared that "there is really no difference between the principle of people's livelihood and communism," so it was pointless to worry about the substitution of the Guomindang's ideal.[29]

In December, the foreign powers sent a fleet of gunboats when Sun, frustrated in his various efforts to get a fair share of the customs revenue, threatened to seize Guangzhou Customs by force. The threat was accompanied by demonstrations, press campaigns and appeals to the Chinese in the United States. The foreign gunboats forced Sun to back down but his threat paid handsome propaganda dividends. His reputation among the Chinese soared as a consequence. Nevertheless, in spite of the acrimonious dispute over customs receipts, Western favors to the Beijing warlords and Borodin's anti-imperialist exhortations, Sun told the U.S. minister Jacob G. Schurman that the United States was the only nation that China could trust and renewed his plea for U.S. mediation to help unify China. Schurman apparently did not even bother to send a full report to Washington. What did get back to the State Department was Sun's anti-imperialist diatribe and Schurman's impression of an unbalanced mind.[30]

After this latest snub by the West, Sun was even more receptive to Borodin's urgings to commit the Guomindang to a more radical stance at the party's First National Congress held in Guangzhou from January 20 to 30, 1924. Singing praises of the Soviet model, Sun spoke of the superiority of their party organization. Bothered by Sun's conversation with Schurman, Borodin wanted an unequivocal commitment from Sun to tie the Guomindang to the Soviets' global anti-imperialist agenda. But Sun did not want to antagonize the British and the French more than he needed to and resisted Borodin's attempts. What eventually emerged was a denunciation of foreign imperialists, the warlords who were in league with them and the Chinese capitalists who shared the "spoils" with them. The first limb of the party's foreign policy platform called for the abolition of unequal treaties and an end to leased concessions, extraterritoriality, and foreign control of the maritime customs. Here, too, Sun refused to endorse Borodin's plea for radical land redistribution. The party's manifesto, however, attacked monopolistic landownership and promised land to the landless and support for workers. It also called for state management of natural monopolies and large-scale enterprises – banks, railways and shipping lines – regardless whether native or foreign-owned. The keynote of the manifesto was its direct appeal to the masses. Peasants and workers were told that the nationalist revolution would liberate them because the Guomindang opposed "imperialists, warlords and privileged classes." The Guomindang adopted a Bolshevik type of organizational form, and its constitution, drafted by Borodin, incorporated the principle of democratic centralism. All in all, Borodin could claim to have achieved a notable success during his first three months.[31]

The Congress adjourned for three days on January 25 when it received word of Lenin's death. It was during this recess that Sun began his series of lectures on his *Sanmin Zhuyi*, the Three Principles of the People. First enunciated in 1905, Sun's ideas had not changed much in 20 years, except for the redefinition of nationalism as anti-imperialism instead of anti-Manchuism. While writing the treatise on the principles, Sun's reference books and notes were destroyed when Ye Ju's troops shelled his residence in 1921. Engaged constantly in political battles, he never found time to rewrite it though he continued to refine his explanations of the concepts. The series of lectures he delivered in 1924 was his most in-depth exposition. Several thousand party members, officials and students congregated at the Guangzhou Higher Normal School to hear the lectures.[32]

The first six lectures, on the Principle of Nationalism (*minzu zhuyi*), were delivered every Sunday from January 27 through March 2. Sun's aim in these lectures was to rekindle the national pride of the Chinese, and to inspire them to join him in remolding China into a great nation on par with the foreign powers. The *Sanmin Zhuyi*, as Sun asserted, were the principles that would enable China to achieve this. The Chinese, he said, were too rooted in their family and clan structures, and enjoyed so much freedom that they were like "a sheet of loose sand." The disunity had caused China to be poor and weak in spite of her huge population and four-millennia-old civilization. And China's stagnant population was now in danger of being swallowed up by the rapidly increasing population of the West. Another danger was the powers' economic subjugation. China had lost territories under the Manchus, but since the 1911 Revolution the powers realized that they could not divide up China and turned to economic exploitation. This was even more dangerous and had turned China into a "hypo-colony" – a colony of many nations but the responsibility of none. The Chinese must be rescued quickly, Sun exhorted, or face extinction, like the American Indians. The way for China to escape her weakness was to promote nationalism, "that precious thing" that enabled a nation to survive and progress. China had lost it because of the Manchu policy of promoting cosmopolitanism, which Sun was not against per se, except it must come after national unity had been achieved.

The Anglo-Saxons, Sun asserted, were swallowing up other races – the blacks in Africa and the browns of India – and the yellow race was now in danger. There was a moment of hope when Woodrow Wilson enunciated his policy of self-determination in World War I. Many oppressed countries, including China, joined the Allies in the hope of future nationhood. But at the Paris Peace Conference, the victorious Allies realized that Wilson's policy was in conflict with their imperialist agenda, and they therefore came up with an unjust peace treaty. An unexpected silver lining of the war was the Russian Revolution. The Russians since then were determined to crush imperialism and capitalism, and to champion the poor and weak against the rich and powerful. This would inevitably lead to a Darwinian struggle for survival, not between races, but between the oppressed and the oppressors. The powers with their superior military hardware could easily destroy China, which had been preserved because of mutual suspicion among the powers. The Washington Conference had done no more than to divide up the rights and privileges of the powers in China to minimize conflict among them. But China could just as easily be eliminated by diplomacy or economic oppression, which Sun urged the Chinese to fight against by adopting Gandhi's passive resistance and developing China's economic self-sufficiency.

Sun believed that the Chinese had survived other races because of their ancient virtues; only by recovering them would China regain her former glory. Pleading with his compatriots not to reject the old morality because of Western influences, Sun urged them to recover their ancient learning as well. Lamenting that the Chinese had lost the art of personal cultivation, which he felt justified foreigners' discrimination, he exhorted his countrymen to show more concern for their personal culture. And in learning from the West, China should learn the West's most recent scientific developments. In this way China could expedite her modernization which with a revival of her national spirit would enable her to be a great world power. Only then would China be able to unify the world on the basis of her morality and love of peace. Sun concluded his lectures on the Principle of Nationalism with an inspirational summation:

> Let us today, before China's development begins, pledge ourselves to lift up the fallen and to aid the weak; then when we become strong and look back upon our own sufferings under the political and economic domination of the Powers and see weaker and smaller peoples undergoing similar treatment, we will rise and smite that imperialism. Then will we be truly "governing the state and pacifying the world." If we want to be able to reach this ideal

in the future, we must now revive our national spirit, recover our national standing, unify the world upon the foundation of our ancient morality and love of peace, and bring about a universal rule of equality and fraternity. This is the great responsibility which devolves upon our four hundred millions. You, gentlemen, are a part of our four hundred millions; you must all shoulder this responsibility and manifest the true spirit of our nation.[33]

Sun's considerable knowledge of Western political institutions was on full display in the six lectures on the Principle of Democracy (*minquan zhuyi*) held between March 9 and April 26. Democracy, he said, gave ordinary citizens a sense of participation in the affairs of their country and made them more willing to make sacrifices for their nation. In adopting democratic institutions, China would not be importing a totally alien concept. Although dynastic governments did not hold elections for public offices, the concern for the welfare of the people that characterized democracies also characterized ancient China. Indeed, Confucius had preached the "people's right" more than 2,000 years ago. But Sun was not impressed with the record of Western parliamentary government, which he said had progressed less rapidly than autocratic states such as Germany and Japan. This, he said, was because Western democracies had fostered an unfortunate attitude of "opposition to government." To avoid repeating the mistakes of the West, Sun distinguished between "sovereignty" and "ability." Sovereignty, he said, belonged to the people, but the government must be run by experts. To preserve the people's sovereignty and their ability to restrain the excesses of public officials, he proposed giving citizens the rights of suffrage, recall, initiative and referendum. Thus, if voters supported a particular candidate, they could *elect* that person into office. If they became dissatisfied with an incumbent's performance, they could *recall* him from office before the end of his term. If citizens supported the creation of a new law, they could *initiate* the process, and if they supported the abrogation of an existing law, they could vote to amend or repeal it in a *referendum*. To achieve this, Sun proposed that the government be composed of five *yuan*: executive, judicial, legislative, censorate, and examination. The first three were as articulated by Montesquieu and implemented in the United

States. In imperial China, these powers were vested in the person of the emperor. In spite of the concentration of power, China had its own system of checks and balances. The censorate had the power to impeach corrupt officials and remonstrate with the emperor when he violated customary laws, while the examination *yuan* through the civil service examinations rather than the emperor selected talents for the government bureaucracy.

On April 12, the day before he delivered his fourth lecture on Democracy, Sun released his *Fundamentals of National Reconstruction*. This collection of 25 essays summarizing his political philosophy was in essence Sun's prescription on the three stages through which national reconstruction was to proceed. First, there would be a period of military rule during which the government would suppress counterrevolutionary forces. Once this was complete, a period of political tutelage conducted by the military government would follow. During this stage, experts qualified by examination would instruct the people on how to carry out their civic rights and obligations, beginning at the level of the *xian* (county or district), the lowest level of politics and administration in China. Each *xian*, after achieving autonomy, would elect a delegate to a provincial assembly. When all the *xian* in a province were autonomous, constitutional government would begin in that province, and its assembly would then elect a governor to supervise the affairs of the province and to act under the direction of the national government in matters of national import. The process of electing a central government would begin with the drafting of a constitution when more than half the provinces had achieved autonomy. The constitution would be promulgated by a people's congress and a national election would then be held. At this point, the military government would turn its functions over to the newly elected central government, and the final stage of constitutional government would begin.[34]

Long dependent on mercenaries, Sun finally got the party army that he wanted. On June 16, 1924, he presided at a ceremony marking the inauguration of the Huangpu Military Academy, located on an island south of Guangzhou, where earlier provincial military schools had stood. Constructed with money from the Soviet Union, which also supplied the instruction, the purpose of the military school was to train a corps of disciplined officers to form the core of a party army. The Soviets' organization

Sun Yat-sen at the inauguration ceremony of the Huangpu Military Academy, May 1924, flanked by his wife Song Qingling and Commandant Chiang Kai-shek.

and training methods were to have a lasting impact on the Guomindang armies. It was at the Huangpu Academy that the system of attaching commissars to army units was first adopted. Chiang Kai-shek, who had returned from Moscow the previous December, was appointed the Academy's commandant. The first cohort of 500 cadets had been admitted to the six-month course on May 1.

When Sun resumed his lectures on August 3, on the Principle of People's Livelihood (*minsheng zhuyi*), it was at the height of the crisis provoked by the Guomindang faction opposed to cooperation with the Soviet Union and the Communists. To appease this group, Sun refuted Marx's theory on class struggle and surplus value, relying heavily on Maurice William's *Social Interpretation of History* to supply the ammunition.[35] William's thesis that social and not economic forces shaped history dovetailed with Sun's idea that harmonizing the interests of workers and capitalists, rather than class struggle, was the key to social progress. The West had developed to such an oppressive state that she was forced to adopt the Marxist method of class struggle. China was not yet so highly industrialized and class struggle was therefore not inevitable. These assertions and his remark that Communism was inappropriate for China earned him a rebuke from Borodin. Under pressure from the Comintern agent and in order to bring together the extremists in the Guomindang and the CPC, Sun presented in his second lecture an ideological justification for the collaboration:

> We cannot say, then, that the theory of communism is different from our *Min-sheng* Principle. Our Three Principles of the People mean government "of the people, by the people, and for the people" – that is, a state belonging to all the people, a government controlled by all the people, and rights and benefits for the enjoyment of all the people. If this is true, the people will not only have a communistic share in state production, but they will have a share in everything. When the people share everything in the state, then will we truly reach the goal of the *Min-sheng* Principle, which is Confucius' hope of a "great commonwealth."[36]

While the West had not able to solve the problem of livelihood, Sun boasted that the Guomindang could – through the equalization of landownership. This was an idea based on the "single tax" proposed by Henry George. In *Progress and Poverty* (1879), George argued that the state should collect the entire price increase on unimproved land as tax. This would discourage land speculation while providing the state with enough revenue to abolish all other taxes. Sun's proposal was a lot more moderate. He would allow landowners to assess the value of their own land and pay the state a one percent tax on the declared value. The state would reserve the right to buy the land back at the declared value. If a landowner under-declared the value of his landholdings, he ran the risk of the government buying his lands back at their declared price. This ingenious method to guard against undervaluation by owners may have been Sun's own idea, or he may have read about self-assessment in 19th-century New Zealand.

Food, declared Sun, was the main problem of livelihood in China. Tens of thousands died every year from starvation because China did not produce enough and had to import food. To help solve this problem, Sun wanted China to follow France's example of intensive agriculture. Peasants should be incentivized and given their own land to till, and agriculture improved through the use of machinery, fertilizers and other means. Reforestation should be practiced on a national scale to minimize droughts, and rivers deepened to prevent floods. The aim of the Principle of People's Livelihood, Sun said, was not just to provide nutrition for all the people but cheap clothing, shelter and transportation as well. The problem of clothing was taken up in his fourth lecture. China, implored Sun, needed to improve her sericulture to catch up with the silk industries of other countries. She exported cotton but bought it back as cotton goods. The Chinese wore foreign cloth which profited foreigners who controlled the Maritime Customs. Whereas foreign cloth attracted just one payment of the *lijin* transit tax, Chinese cloth was subjected to tax at every *lijin* station when transported in the interior of China. Sun urged the Chinese to buy native products and boycott foreign goods. The state should also establish clothing factories on a large scale to provide everyone with clothing.

The lecture on clothing on August 24 was Sun's last. The remaining lectures on shelter and transportation were never delivered, as Sun was forced to turn his attention to more pressing matters, beginning with a dangerous situation brewing in Guangzhou. Fed up with the high taxes imposed by Sun's government and the growing menace of organized labor, merchants in Guangzhou had organized themselves into a Merchants' Volunteer Corps and raised a powerful private militia with the intention of seizing the city. They conspired with two British to smuggle a vast quantity of arms. When the arms arrived in Guangzhou on August 9 on board a Norwegian cargo ship, the *Hav*, Sun had them seized and stored at the Huangpu Academy. The merchants retaliated by calling a general strike that brought business to a standstill. Sun threatened to bombard the business section of the city but was forced to back down when the British threatened naval intervention. Agitated, Sun published on September 1 a blistering denunciation of British hypocrisy, charging them with atrocities in their own dominions. The merchants ended their strike and a crisis was averted, but the arms issue continued to fester.

Not long after the conflict with the Merchants' Corps was defused, Sun decided to launch a Northern Expedition against the Zhili clique. On September 12, he departed for the northern border of Guangdong province and set up his headquarters in the little town of Shaoguan. The campaign took everyone by surprise, and drew criticisms and protests, even from within his own entourage. Sun Ke resigned as mayor, Liao Zhongkai left his post as civil governor, and Chiang Kai-shek refused to allow Huangpu cadets to take part in the expedition. The Communists protested that the campaign had nothing to do with the revolution and forbade the trade unions and peasant associations to be involved.

Sun had achieved much in the ten months since his return to Guangzhou – the reorganization of the Guomindang, his new Soviet allies, and the Huangpu Academy. Why did he turn his back on all that? In a letter to Chiang Kai-shek on September 9, he explained why he saw it necessary to launch a Northern Expedition at the earliest opportunity:

> During this strike, if we had delayed a day longer, a conflict would surely have emerged, and the objectives of the English gunboats would have been my headquarters, the gunboat Yung Feng and Whampoa, which could be pulverized in a few minutes. We absolutely do not have the power to resist them. Although this time we fortunately escaped, later we may again take up the issue at a suitable time. This is the first reason why we cannot but evade death here and pursue life elsewhere.
>
> Second, the attack by our enemies in the East River is right now on the point of being incited, and if another situation like that at Shi-p'ai should occur, it is very difficult to conjecture who would get the benefit.
>
> Third is the greed and tyranny of the guest armies which produced all sort of evil consequences. This is also a vital reason. For these three vital reasons we cannot continue to stay in this place another moment; therefore, it is best to relinquish it quickly, leave completely, and plan a different road to life.
>
> The very best road to life now is through a Northern Expedition. Furthermore, the Fengtien Army has gone through the pass,

Chekiang may stand firm, men's hearts are all set upon overthrowing Ts'ao [Cao Kun] and Wu [Peifu], and in the vicinity of Wu-han there are troops under my influence. If we take advantage of this situation and struggle with determination, increasingly urge on and advance straight ahead, taking the battlefield as our school, then the outcome is sure to be good.[37]

Clearly, Sun was not simply escaping from a difficult situation in Guangzhou; he was reverting to an earlier strategy of alliance with various warlords opposed to the Zhili clique as a path to the presidency in Beijing. This was an ambition that Sun had been nursing since 1922, which his support for the United Front had not dispelled. The Comintern strategy of a gradual buildup and mass-based nationalist movement was too cumbersome and slow for the impatient Sun. Nothing could distract him from his planned expedition, not even the lack of cooperation from his Soviet military advisers, which simply forced him to turn to the mercenaries of Yunnan and Guangxi. He was content to manage the crisis of the Merchants' Corps from a distance.

While Sun was holed up in Shaoguan, the Guangzhou merchants negotiated with his emissaries for the return of the arms seized from the steamer *Hav*. Desperately in need of cash for his Northern Expedition, Sun authorized the return of the weapons to the merchants for a price. October 10, the day that the merchants were supposed to get their arms back, was the 13th anniversary of the 1911 Revolution. That afternoon a Nationalist parade marched along the bund. Their path was blocked by the Merchants' Corps who were unloading their weapons in the port of Guangzhou and refused to let the parade through. A melee broke out. The merchants again called for an immediate general strike, Sun's overthrow and the return of Chen Jiongming.

In response, the Guomindang formed a committee endowed with full powers to deal with the merchants. Borodin, with Sun's backing, was clearly in the driver's seat. On October 14, the order was given to attack the business quarter. In the process, the whole area was set ablaze. The burning, plus the looting and the civilian casualties that followed, tarnished Sun's reputation and that of the Guomindang. The Guangzhou merchants immediately sent telegrams to Chinese communities at home and abroad blaming Sun specifically for the devastation. The government organized relief efforts but had difficulty persuading the Cantonese to channel relief funds through its hands.

A week later, another warlord contest was to shift the balance of power in the North and once again alter the military and political landscape of China.

Chapter 14

THE FINAL JOURNEY

WHEN IN 1922 the Zhili clique emerged victorious in the Zhili-Fengtian War, Wu Peifu became China's indisputable strongman. By mid-1924, he was in control of large swaths of China proper. He had given up hope of unifying China by political means and adopted a policy of unification through military force. Although Zhang Zuolin's Fengtian armies were defeated, his base in Manchuria was not invaded. He began to reorganize and strengthen his armed forces in preparation for an attack on Zhili. All that was needed to spark renewed hostilities was an incident.

That catalyst was a battle that began in early September 1924 for control of Shanghai between the warlord of Jiangsu, an ally of Wu Peifu, and the Zhejiang warlord, who was allied with Zhang Zuolin.[1] Wu sent troops to aid his ally and Zhang responded by invading Zhili, thus precipitating a second war between the Zhili and Fengtian cliques. To block Zhang and his troops from crossing the Great Wall into China Proper, Wu ordered his "adopted son" Feng Yuxiang to lead his crack troops north to the Great Wall while other Zhili troops marched on Shanhaiguan, the main gateway to Manchuria from northern China. On September 21, the first of Feng's units began marching northward. In a classic double-cross, Feng marched his troops back towards Beijing and seized the capital in a pre-dawn raid on October 23. The next day, he forced President Cao Kun to issue proclamations calling for the cessation of hostilities and dismissing Wu from his posts. The armies that had taken part in the coup were formally reorganized as the Guominjun, the National People's Army, with Feng as commander-in-chief.[2]

Wu rushed back to Tianjin with a small contingent when he learned of Feng's betrayal, leaving his armies to hold the Fengtian forces at bay. Unable to obtain aid from his associates in central China, Wu and a few thousand of his troops fled to their ships and sailed to the Yangtze after just a few engagements with Guominjun troops near Tianjin. In the course of a few weeks, Wu had been toppled from his position as the leading warlord in China to the status of a fugitive with a price on his head, a catastrophe from which he never fully recovered. On November 2, Feng forced Cao Kun to tender his resignation. A caretaker government, established under Feng's sponsorship, administered state affairs while Feng, Zhang Zuolin and other leaders discussed the future of northern China. Three days later, on November 5, Feng sent a small contingent of troops with an order to evict Puyi from the Forbidden City, where he had been living in relative opulence since his abdication in February 1912.

The Zhili clique's defeat in the Second Zhili-Fengtian War created a vacuum in the capital. Feng Yuxiang had driven out the man who had dominated northern China militarily since early 1922. In that time, Wu had acquired the stature of a statesman devoted to the public interest and a reputation to rival Sun's, which neither Feng nor Zhang Zuolin had to stake their claim to the presidency. As an ally of the Fengtian clique, Sun was theoretically on the winning side. Feng's successful coup rendered it superfluous for Sun to continue with the Northern Expedition that he was preparing to launch against the Zhili clique's Southern allies. On October 27, Sun sent two telegrams to the Northern generals expressing his interest to visit the capital for reunification talks. Three days later he abandoned his general headquarters at Shaoguan to return to Guangzhou. He had decided to go to Beijing to promote his candidacy for the presidency of a united China.

That decision rested, however, with the Northern warlords, and the man they had in mind was Duan Qirui, not Sun. Like the Northern generals, Duan was a product of the Beiyang Army. As prime minister in 1917, he had used his position to put the Anhui clique in power. Since the defeat of his group in 1920, Duan no longer possessed any military strength. This in itself qualified him eminently for a symbolic presidency in the eyes of the northern warlords. Moreover, Duan had the patronage of the Japanese.

Sun's proposed journey to Beijing was thus fraught with risk. The Communists expressed concern that it was a political trap set by the imperialists and militarists, while the moderates in his own party were anxious for Sun's personal safety. By presenting his journey to the capital as essential for the triumph of "a central revolution," Sun won approval from the various stakeholders. In bidding farewell to Huangpu Academy cadets on November 3, Sun told them that his purpose in going to Beijing was to launch "a great revolution." For the past quarter-century, he said, the revolution "had been confined to the provinces and that is why it had had only a weak influence ... But if it roots itself in the capital, then its influence will be very great." Feng Yuxiang's victory, according to Sun, opened the way to this great central revolution. Once "militant action" was carried to the North, the militarists and bureaucrats would be forced to hand over power to the Guomindang. This was a plan for which Sun claimed to have the support not only of the party but of anti-imperialist forces across the country. The next day, he reassured officers at a farewell reception that he was not going to Beijing to seize power but to "develop propaganda, organize groups, and create a movement in favor of the application of the Three Principles of the People."[3]

Sun's journey to Beijing did not mean a break with the policy of the United Front. Indeed, the seventh anniversary of the Bolshevik revolution on November 7 was commemorated with much fanfare in Guangzhou. Sailors from a Russian cargo ship which had brought in arms for the Huangpu Academy paraded alongside Chinese workers and soldiers. Sun himself joined with Soviet diplomats and advisers in celebrating the success of the Russian Revolution. On November 12, various workers' and students' associations organized a grand parade to celebrate Sun's 58th birthday, in which 20,000 people were said to have participated. The following day, Sun made his triumphant departure for Beijing, leaving behind a reorganized party that for the first time in its history commanded extensive popular support. He also left behind a government in the process of consolidation, controlled by moderates under Hu Hanmin. Sun made several stops on his way to the capital: Shanghai, Kobe and Tianjin. He was accompanied by his wife Qingling and an entourage of 18 supporters that included his Soviet advisor Mikhail Borodin, Eugene Chen, and Wang Jingwei. Negotiations with the Northern generals and the Yangtze warlords continued throughout the several weeks of traveling.

Sun played to the crowd by exalting anti-imperialistic incantations en route to Shanghai, calling in particular for the immediate abolition of extraterritoriality and the abrogation of the unequal treaties. Thus when he arrived at his adopted city on November 17 and let it be known that he intended to stay at his own residence on Rue Moliere in the French Concession, it provoked a hostile reaction from the expatriate community. An article in a leading British newspaper, the *North China Daily News*, denounced him as an undesirable person whose presence in Shanghai would destroy the neutrality of the city; it urged that he not be allowed to remain. Sun retorted with a sharp rebuke, reminding the British that as foreigners they were guests of China and that they had better behave accordingly:

> If, therefore, foreigners should dare to oppose or obstruct my presence in Shanghai, I, with the support of my countrymen, am determined to take some drastic steps to deal with them. Be it remembered that we, Chinese people, are not to be trifled with so long as we dwell in our own territory.

To make sure that his warning was taken seriously, Sun also called for the abolition of the foreign settlements. Irritated by Sun's defiance, the American consul-general joined the chorus calling for his expulsion from foreign concessions. If Westerners saw Sun as a dangerous agitator, the Chinese cheered him as a great patriot. A large crowd turned out to welcome him to their city.[4]

The purpose of Sun's visit to Shanghai was to size up the situation in the North, and to determine when and under what circumstances he would go to Tianjin to confer with Duan Qirui, Feng Yuxiang and Zhang Zuolin. On November 20, the day before Sun's departure for Japan, Duan announced that he was going to Beijing as provisional chief executive to organize a provisional government. Within a month, he would convene a reconstruction conference of provincial delegates as a prelude to a National Assembly. The details were left vague enough to accommodate Sun's formula, which was to convene a preliminary conference, and then have them elect a National Assembly.

In an interview with a Japanese correspondent on the sea journey to Kobe, Sun said that his purpose in going to the capital was to create an atmosphere conducive to the convening of a broadly representative people's assembly:

> Although there is a rumor that I am to assume the Presidency in Peking, I have no idea, at least for the present, of taking up that position. I would rather remain as I am, because of my belief that China today badly wants a man who is capable of creating and unifying strong public opinion and I think I am just the man she wants.

He added that his main hope was to persuade the powers to give up their concessions and other unjust privileges.

Sun continued to vent his anger with anti-Western and in particular anti-British pronouncements during his stay in Kobe from November 24 to 30. These outbursts seemed not so much an emotional reaction but a strategy with the purpose of obtaining the support of the Japanese in his negotiations with the Northern militarists. The Japanese had stopped dealing with Sun since the death of Yuan Shikai in 1916, for they could now extract concessions and privileges from the succession of weak governments in Beijing through a combination of threats and financial aid. To try to win back Japanese support, Sun had sent Li Liejun, the former Guomindang military governor of Jiangxi, to Japan in October to test out Japanese reaction to the old pan-Asian theme. The Japanese government was evasive, for the Guomindang's position on the unequal treaties was incompatible with their idea of Sino-Japanese solidarity. Li was welcomed by Sun's old cronies in the Kokuryukai, the Black Dragon Society, but only because Zhang Zuolin, to whom the Japanese army had contributed, seemed to reassure them regarding Japanese interests in Manchuria and Mongolia.[5]

The Japanese public gave Sun and his group an enthusiastic welcome. Hopeful of eliciting further Japanese public opinion in his favor, Sun delivered his famous pan-Asian speech to a large audience at a Kobe school on November 28. Calling on Japan to renounce Western-style imperialism and to return to her East Asian heritage based upon "benevolence and justice," Sun declared that Asians could now count on the support of the Soviet Union, who was "attempting to separate herself from the white peoples of Europe." The choice facing their country, Sun challenged his audience, was "whether Japan will be the hawk of the Western civilization, of the rule of Might, or the tower of strength of the Orient."

Displeased by the Guomindang's pact with the Soviets, whom Sun praised for having magnanimously given up all special rights acquired by tsarist Russia, the Japanese government gave Sun a cold reception and refused to invite him to Tokyo. Adding insult to injury, Japanese Prime Minister Kato Takaaki and other dignitaries laid out the red carpet for Duan Qirui's emissaries. Nonetheless, a group from the House of Peers and several officers from the Ministry of War visited Sun, who also met with Toyama Mitsuru, the ultranationalist kingpin of the Kokuryukai and Sun's one-time secret benefactor. Sun's old friend Inukai Ki, now communications minister, did not accept Sun's invitation to visit him in Kobe but sent a vice-minister in his place. In all these private conversations, Sun was seeking official Japanese help for the abolition of the unequal treaties, financial assistance, and perhaps also for help in his bid for the presidency. He left Japan empty-handed.

Sun was in severe pain when he sailed for Tianjin. The day after his arrival on December 4, he had to be confined to his bed. Even so, the foreigners continued to hurl insults at him and the French refused him entry to their concession. Sun's political hopes were also slipping fast. Pressured by foreign diplomats, the ruling triumvirate went ahead with the conference without Sun. Duan was told that his government would be recognized if it acknowledged all existing treaties. This was their price for recognition of his government, a practice which had become commonplace with each regime change in Beijing. Sun was furious when Duan agreed but the decision was inevitable given the dependency of Duan's government on foreign financial aid.

Sun's pro-Soviet and anti-West speech in Kobe had caused considerable concern among his Guomindang colleagues. In mid-December leading party members issued a statement clarifying that neither Sun nor the Guomindang were Bolshevik or Communist sympathizers, and that their friendly relations with the Soviet Union were due solely to her repudiation of tsarist aggression, and the conclusion of new treaties with China on the basis of equality. At about the same time, Zhang Zuolin had an emissary convey to the British minister in Beijing that Zhang had warned Sun on the latter's arrival in Tianjin against associating with the Bolshevists, and that this could lead to a break between them if Sun persisted. According to the emissary, Sun took the point. On December 19, Eugene Chen, Sun's foreign secretary, called on the British minister to claim that Sun's Kobe speech had been distorted through double translation. Chen explained that while Sun and his party believed in friendship with the Soviet Union, he was not anti-West. These attempts to soften Sun's sharp messages to the West occurred before the severity of his illness was known and were intended to allay Western concerns about Sun's intentions in the event he became part of a new government.[6]

Sun's condition deteriorated rapidly. On New Year's Eve, he was rushed in a special train to Beijing, where a large throng was at the Qianmen Station to welcome him. Too ill to address them, he was whisked away to the Hotel de Pekin where he gave a brief press conference. This was his last public appearance. On January 26, he was admitted to the Peking Union Medical College, a missionary-established hospital funded by the Rockefeller Foundation. A surgical procedure confirmed the diagnosis of terminal-stage cancer of the liver. It was too far advanced for treatment. Thereafter daily bulletins reported his condition. Sun stayed in the hospital for almost three weeks, but realizing that his days were numbered he accepted an invitation to spend his remaining days at the residence of Wellington Koo, China's leading diplomat who had led the negotiations at Versailles.

As news of Sun's terminal illness spread, many of his closest associates rushed to Beijing, but three of his most important lieutenants, Hu Hanmin, Liao Zhongkai and Chiang Kai-shek, had to remain in Guangzhou, where the party's hold on the city was still precarious. An Extraordinary Political Council was formed around Wang Jingwei with five others coopted, among them Eugene Chen and Mikhail Borodin, who were the only two non-family members allowed into the sick room.

On February 24, when Sun's condition appeared critical, Wang Jingwei in the presence of Song Qingling, Sun Ke and Sun's brothers-in-law, Song Ziwen (T.V. Soong) and Kong Xiangxi (H.H. Kung), asked the *zongli* to leave his final instructions. But Sun merely listened and approved a text composed by Wang Jingwei in consultation with the other members of the Extraordinary Political Council. The Guomindang would later aver, for reasons of propriety, that Sun was the author of the testament and Wang

Jingwei was merely the scribe. The latter then produced another draft of a private will. Sun approved this draft too, but at Qingling's request the signing of the testament was deferred.

Not until March 11, on the eve of his death, did Sun, with his wife guiding his trembling hand, sign the Political Testament that would later assume a quasi-sacred character and serve as the charter of the Guomindang:

> For forty years, I have devoted myself to the cause of the people's revolution with but one end in view, the elevation of China to a position of freedom and equality among the nations. My experiences during these forty years have firmly convinced me that to attain this goal we must bring about a thorough awakening of our own people and ally ourselves in a common struggle with those peoples of the world who treat us on the basis of equality.
>
> The work of the Revolution is not done. Let all our comrades follow my *Plans for National Reconstruction*, *Fundamentals of National Reconstruction*, *Three Principles of the People* and the *Manifesto* issued by the First National Convention of our Party, and strive on earnestly for their consummation. Above all, our recent declaration in favor of the convocation of a National Convention and the abolition of unequal treaties should be carried into effect with the least possible delay. This is my heartfelt charge to you.[7]

The private will bequeathed Sun's worldly possessions to his wife Qingling – his books, papers, personal effects, and the house on Rue Moliere, the only possession of any significant monetary value. The man who had handled vast sums of money for the revolution died with little to his name. At a time of rampant corruption, his integrity added to his luster and raised his stature way above those of his rivals, the warlords.

There was a third text, a farewell letter addressed to the Central Committee of the Soviet Union:

> My dear comrades
>   As I lie here, with a malady that is beyond men's skill, my thoughts turn to you and to the future of my party and my country.

> You are the head of a Union of free republics which is the real heritage that the immortal Lenin has left to the world of the oppressed peoples. Through this heritage, the victims of imperialism are destined to secure their freedom and deliverance from an international system whose foundations lie in ancient slaveries and wars and injustices.
>
> I am leaving behind me a party which I hoped would be associated with you in the historic work of completely liberating China and other exploited countries from this imperialist system... I have therefore enjoined the Kuomintang to carry on the work of the national revolutionary movement... To this end I have charged the party to keep in constant touch with you; and I look with confidence to the continuance of the support that your Government has heretofore extended to my country.
>
> In bidding farewell to you, dear comrades, I wish to express my fervent hope that the day may soon dawn when the USSR will greet, as a friend and ally, a strong and independent China and the two allies may together advance to victory in the great struggle for the liberation of the oppressed peoples of the world.[8]

This was in English, supposedly prepared by Eugene Chen in consultation with Borodin, and read by Song Ziwen to the dying Sun. It was not signed by anyone as witness and was not given to the press along with the other two wills. It was first published in *Pravda* on March 14 and released in China three days later. Given these circumstances, the principal leaders of the Guomindang never held it in the same high regard as they did the Political Testament.[9]

Sun drew his last breath on March 12, 1925, leaving unfinished the revolution that he had inspired. Until the last few years of his life, Sun was not particularly well regarded by his countrymen. But a poll conducted by the *Weekly Review of the Far East* shortly before his death showed him leading by a wide margin the group of men most admired by educated Chinese. After his death, there was spontaneous outpouring of grief across China, Nanyang and other Chinese communities abroad that could not have been induced by any propaganda machinery. His followers wanted to honor his memory in the greatest possible way and to obtain the maximum possible advantage for the revolutionary cause he had espoused. They demanded official holidays to mourn his passing; the assignment of public funds for memorial expenses; and the renaming of public parks in his honor. Some of their demands, however, were tempered by the family's wishes.

Sun had been baptized as a Christian, and according to some among his relatives and followers, he had clearly stated before his death that he wished to die a Christian. His widow Qingling and his son Sun Ke were determined that he should have a Christian funeral. But some of his influential followers were fiercely anti-Christian; they saw Christianity in China as the religious arm of Western imperialism. Naturally they rebelled at this idea and were planning to turn the funeral service into a political demonstration. In the end a compromise was worked out. Two separate funeral ceremonies were held on March 19. A Protestant service for family and their guests was held at the great hall of the Peking Union Medical College. After hymns and readings from the Bible, Kong Xiangxi evoked his late brother-in-law's deep Christian convictions in his address to the congregation.

After the Christian service, Sun's casket was escorted by crowds of students who tussled for the honor of marching beside the bier to Central Park (now Zhongshan Park), adjacent to the imperial palace buildings. Here a second service was held, presided over by the Guomindang and its Soviet allies, with Soviet Ambassador Lev Karakhan assuming the role of chief mourner. In a pavilion inside Central Park, Sun's coffin was draped with the Guomindang flag while loudspeakers blared a recording of his speeches. Over the next three weeks, thousands filed past the bier to pay their last respects to the revolutionary hero. Memorial services were held throughout China and abroad as the Chinese mourned the loss of the man who had come to symbolize their motherland's struggle for modernity and equality among nations, while newspapers throughout China were printing his eulogies. One of the most insightful was from Tang Shaoyi, the first premier of the Republic:

> We were not only fellow-provincials, but natives of the same district, our homes being but eight miles apart in Heung-shan [Xiangshan]. For some 40 years we have known of one another

and since the founding of the Republic, we have often been associated in public service.

To Dr. Sun will have to go the credit of having made the revolution an effective force and of having crystallized public opinion behind a democratic movement, which has survived all the mistakes and the reactions of the past thirteen years ...

At the moment of mourning, we shall forget everything about him but one outstanding fact and that is that he was the champion of democracy in China. Everything else will be forgotten. Every personal whim, every personal dissension, every difference of opinion will be forgotten, only the large fact of his life will remain, his struggle against despotism, his struggle against corruption, his struggle for the right of the governed to a say in the government. And throughout the country as this thought sweeps the minds of the people, as this thought becomes the cry of the suffering millions, as men speak it and write it and read it, a spirit will be abroad in the lands which will make itself felt and which in the end will shake Peking to its very foundations.[10]

On April 2, a military detail escorted the heavy Chinese wooden casket to the beautiful Temple of Azure Clouds in the Western Hills a few miles outside of Beijing. There in a lofty chamber in the old temple splendidly oriental in its design and mellow with tradition, Sun was laid to rest. He could not have found a more beautiful or auspicious final resting place, but it had been his wish that he be buried in Nanjing near the tomb of the first Ming emperor. So in the Temple of Azure Clouds he rested for the next four years while a permanent resting place was constructed for him on Purple Mountain just outside Nanjing.

Chapter 15

THE ROAD TO PURGATORY

For most of his political career, Sun was not held in particularly high esteem by his compatriots. This changed in the last years of his life after he began speaking out against the foreign powers and their interference in China's domestic affairs. Indeed, at a ceremony to mark the 25th anniversary of the founding of Beida (Peking University) in December 1924, about a thousand people, largely intellectuals, were asked whom they considered the greatest Chinese of the time. Sun took first place with 473 votes, more than twice the number secured by second-placed Chen Duxiu, the leading Communist.[1]

Modern Chinese nationalism had risen in tandem with Sun's prestige, as evidenced by the May Thirtieth Incident in 1925. The background to this episode was a series of labor unrests in Shanghai. At the many foreign-owned plants in the city, wages were low and working conditions were atrocious. In Japanese-owned factories, it was not uncommon for workers to suffer beatings by their Japanese supervisors. In February 1925, Chinese workers went on strike to protest low wages at a Japanese cotton mill. Mediation resulted in a settlement, but the Japanese subsequently rejected it, resulting in a second strike. On May 15, an altercation broke out between Chinese workers and their Japanese supervisors. A Japanese drew his gun and fired on the Chinese, killing one worker and wounding several others. The British-dominated Shanghai Municipal Council did not prosecute the guilty Japanese. Instead they arrested a number of Chinese workers for disturbing the peace. On May 30, students staged a mass demonstration to protest the British action. A Municipal Council police lieutenant ordered his men to fire into the crowd, killing ten and wounding several dozens. Fifty students were arrested.

Not only in Shanghai but all over China, indeed throughout the world, Chinese reacted to the shooting with fury and indignation. The next day, a general strike and boycott of foreign goods engulfed Shanghai. Banks and businesses were closed, students boycotted classes and workers went on strike. By mid-June more than 150,000 people were on strike in Shanghai and some two dozen cities throughout China. Not until December, after the British inspector-general and his lieutenant were sacked and the Municipal Council paid an indemnity to the deceased and the injured, did the public outrage subside. Although the labor unrest was initially instigated by economic demands, the strike was political when it finally came about. It was a protest against imperialism in China, which by the end of the decade would be dealt a severe blow.

Impressed by the rising tide of Chinese nationalism, the Comintern decided to increase its investment in the Chinese revolution. On October 7, 1925, Borodin announced the establishment of the Moscow Sun Yat-sen Communist University of the Toilers of China to honor the fallen hero. The goal of the university was to train Chinese revolutionaries to be highly skilled political workers "capable of wielding a pen to sway the masses and of wielding a sword to direct a campaign." Classes began on November 7, 1925, on the eighth anniversary of the Russian October Revolution. In spite of its name, the university's curriculum did not include the works of Sun Yat-sen.[2]

Few Chinese students pursued their advanced studies in Soviet Russia because she was considered rather backward. After its establishment, the Moscow Sun Yat-sen University became a highly desirable destination and hundreds of students flocked to study there. It was closed down in the fall of 1930 after the collapse of the Guomindang-Soviet Alliance. Notwithstanding its short lifespan, the university's influence extended well beyond 1949. Many of its graduates went on to important government positions, two of the most well-known being Deng Xiaoping and Chiang Ching-kuo. An early attempt to reform the Chinese language was undertaken by a group of Chinese students at the university, which also undertook a monumental translation project to render Western texts by Marx, Engels, Lenin and others into Chinese. A number of its graduates continued to translate such works after their return to China, which contributed significantly to the thinking of a great many Chinese.

Out of reverence for its departed leader, the Guomindang resolved at its Second National Congress in January 1926 to reserve the position of

Sun's burial at the Sun Yat-sen Mausoleum on Purple Mountain, outside Nanjing, on June 1, 1929. Sun died on March 12, 1925, and his coffin was housed at the Temple of Azure Clouds outside Beijing while the mausoleum was being constructed.

zongli for Sun in perpetuity. The first anniversary of his death was observed with great fanfare in many places. Memorial services were held in Beijing on March 12, and for several days following. Giant lanterns inscribed with slogans such as "Abolish the unequal treaties" were hung in public places while a lantern parade wound its way through the capital. There were ceremonies, too, for laying the cornerstone of the mausoleum being constructed for Sun in the countryside near Nanjing. A committee formed shortly after his death to plan for his final interment selected the burial site on the south slope of Purple Mountain, east of the tomb of the first Ming emperor. Lying on a foothill embraced by two ranges and facing another distant hill, it was an auspicious site according to the Chinese art of *fengshui*. An international competition to select the design for the Sun Yat-sen Mausoleum attracted over 40 proposals from domestic and foreign architects. The winning design was by Lu Yanzhi, a well-known Chinese architect who graduated from Cornell University in 1918. Construction began in 1926 and was completed in 1929 at a cost that was about four-fifths of the Shanghai municipal government's revenue in 1928. The style of the mausoleum has been described as a fusion of classical Chinese architecture and modern technology and materials. It is one of the most prominent and significant buildings in the architectural history of republican China and stands as one of the most sacred sites in modern Chinese history.[3]

THE GUOMINDANG HAD no succession road map in place and Sun never named a successor. His death unleashed the demons and gave free rein to the battle for party leadership. The struggle became entangled with the conflict between the right and left wings of the party over the policy of the United Front with the Communists. There were three contenders for the party leadership, all of whom had been closely associated with Sun since the founding of the Tongmenghui in 1905. Wang Jingwei was the best known by virtue of his assassination attempt on the prince regent in 1910. Politically left of center, he was popular with both the right and left wings of the party. The conservative Hu Hanmin was one of Sun's closest lieutenants. As head of the right wing of the Guomindang, he wanted to see an immediate end to the relations with the Communists and the Soviet Union. The third candidate was Liao Zhongkai, the party's money man. More inclined to the left than most of his associates, he was generally considered the leader of the party's left wing. Liao favored developing China along socialist lines and collaboration with the Communists.

On July 1, 1925, the Guangzhou revolutionary government was transformed into a "national" government – the Nationalist government – to challenge the warlord government in Beijing. As no one was deemed capable of immediately replacing Sun, a 16-man Political Council was formed to lead the party and the new government. Wang Jingwei was elected chairman of the Council, a position that effectively made him head of government. Hu Hanmin was sidelined as foreign minister, an exalted title with little substance as no foreign nation had as yet recognized the Nationalist government. Liao Zhongkai was named finance minister. Chiang Kai-shek declined to join the Political Council; he felt it was inappropriate for a military man to participate in the operation of a civilian government. Instead he was appointed to the new Military Council. At his suggestion, all military units including those of the allied warlords were now integrated into the National Revolutionary Army (NRA). Among party leaders, he was the most forceful in calling for an early launch of a Northern Expedition to unite the country.[4] Wang Jingwei, the Communists and the Comintern on the other hand preferred to continue with the strikes and boycotts that were hurting British interests in Hong Kong and Guangzhou.

In August, Liao Zhongkai was gunned down by assassins while alighting from his car to attend a meeting of the Guomindang Central Standing Committee in Guangzhou. The murder was never solved but an inquiry committee that included Chiang Kai-shek identified the culprit as Hu Hanmin's cousin, who fled Guangzhou before he could be hauled in for questioning. The same inquiry committee also uncovered a plot by a group of Guomindang Right members to exterminate the leftists in Guangzhou. Several senior officers under Xu Chongxi, the top Guomindang general and a key member of the Political Council, were executed. General Xu himself was not directly implicated, but he was charged on suspicion of having secret contacts with the late *zongli*'s archenemy Chen Jiongming. On the morning of September 20, Chiang Kai-shek with a small cohort of soldiers surrounded Xu's residence and demanded that he leave Guangzhou for three months. With the Political Council's approval, Chiang and Wang Jingwei shipped the anti-Communist Hu Hanmin to Moscow to serve as the official Guomindang representative to the Comintern.[5]

With Liao Zhongkai and Hu Hanmin eliminated from the succession equation, Wang Jingwei was the obvious choice to take over the *zongli*'s mantle. He became by default heir presumptive and de facto leader of the Guomindang. Because of his inclination toward the left, the party's right wing became increasingly disgruntled with him. In November, a group of Guomindang Right members met in the Western Hills just outside Beijing in a rump session of the Central Executive Committee. They voted to fire Borodin, expel the Communists and dissolve the Political Council. However, the Western Hills meeting was declared ultra vires at the party's Second National Congress in January 1926. Not only did it confirm Wang's leadership and elect more Communists to the party's top committees, the Congress also reaffirmed the policy of cooperation with the Soviet Union and collaboration with the Communists. Thus when Borodin departed for the north shortly after the Congress, the party's left wing was clearly in control, and Communist power and influence were dominant in party affairs. But Borodin had gravely underestimated one man: Chiang Kai-shek.[6]

On March 20, 1926, Chiang declared martial law in Guangzhou, alleging discovery of a Communist plot to kidnap him on board the gunboat *Zhongshan* and ship him off to Russia. Soviet advisers in the city and Communist political advisers in the NRA were arrested; trade unions were shut down and their activities suppressed. The incident signaled a dramatic turn to the right. As leader of the party's left wing, Wang Jingwei felt threatened and went into hiding, departing for France shortly after.

The Central Executive Committee meeting adopted Chiang's proposals to limit the influence of the Communists in the Guomindang. But Chiang was not yet ready for a complete break with the Communists; he still needed Soviet military assistance and the cooperation of the Communists for the Northern Expedition that he was planning to launch. Thus while taking steps to constrain the Communists in the party, Chiang also apologized for the March 20 coup, which he blamed on a misunderstanding by his subordinates. He reaffirmed his support for the United Front and requested Soviet advisers to continue their work. Chiang's apology did not quite placate the Communists. Some wanted to seize control of the Guomindang while others wanted to withdraw completely. In the end the matter was resolved by the Comintern in Moscow, which ruled that they should remain in the Guomindang.

On June 5, 1926, Chiang was named commander-in-chief of the NRA and the Northern Expedition. A month later, he assumed office as Supreme Commander, with the Western media henceforth referring to him as "Generalissimo." Chiang was now more determined than ever to launch the Northern Expedition at an early date. The timing was certainly opportune. The warlords in the North were once again fighting among themselves. In the aftermath of the Second Zhili-Fengtian War, authority in the North was divided between the Fengtian and Guominjun cliques but tension soon arose between them. Zhang Zuolin, supported by the Japanese, began building up a military alliance of the northeastern provinces. Feng Yuxiang, well aware of what his erstwhile rival was up to, formed his own northwestern alliance with help from his new Soviet supporter.

Fighting between the two cliques broke out in November 1925 when one of Zhang Zuolin's generals, Guo Songling, mutinied and defected to Feng Yuxiang's Guominjun clique. Feng and Guo prevailed initially but the latter was killed in a battle with Zhang's cavalry forces and his army destroyed. Wu Peifu now returned to the scene and allied himself once again with Zhang Zuolin. Overwhelmed by the combined forces of the two warlords, Feng retreated to his base in northwest China. To end the conflict, he agreed to retire from politics and soon afterward left for the Soviet Union. This was not sufficient to satisfy Zhang Zuolin, who in alliance with Wu Peifu attacked the Guominjun in January 1926. At this point Feng, who had returned from the Soviet Union, forged an alliance with the Guomindang.[7]

The Northern Expedition was officially launched on July 9. The NRA marched swiftly northward and by the end of the month had captured Hunan. After the NRA gained control of the Wuhan tri-city metropolis in mid-October, Guomindang leaders including Chiang Kai-shek decided that a seat in central rather than southern China would be more appropriate for a government that purported to govern the whole country. Not long after the Nationalist government made the move to Wuhan on January 1, 1927, anti-British sentiment in the city flared up, demanding the return of the British concession at Hankou. The British who had abandoned gunboat diplomacy two years earlier opted to return their concessions at Hankou and Jiujiang in Jiangxi province to the Chinese in March. This was the first stage of British imperial retreat from China.

The government in Wuhan was dominated by Borodin and the Guomindang Left, with the two important ministries of workers and farmers placed under Communists. They religiously carried out Stalin's order to intensify the mass movements, and arm and mobilize them to embarrass the Guomindang Right. Chiang was simultaneously building a power base of his own. Deliberately ignoring Borodin's advice to bypass Shanghai and continue on his northward march, Chiang moved immediately against Sun Chuanfang (no relation to Sun Yat-sen), who controlled five rich provinces around the lower Yangtze. By late March 1927, Sun Chuanfang had been driven out of the region and the great cities of Nanjing and Shanghai lay at Chiang's feet. By then, Wuhan and Nanjing had formed two separate power centers within the Guomindang hierarchy. A split appeared imminent and Chiang was determined to purge the Communists from the party.

At dawn on April 12, 1927, contingents of troops and gangsters attacked working-class quarters in all parts of Shanghai, executing many of those captured. The slaughter continued the following day and soon spread to other cities under Chiang's control. Hundreds, perhaps even thousands, of workers lost their lives. The working-class movements were shattered in many cities and the CPC was decimated and in disarray. The Wuhan government promptly branded Chiang a counterrevolutionary and dismissed him as commander-in-chief of the NRA. This hardly affected or bothered Chiang. The very next day, April 18, he set up his own Nationalist government at Nanjing and continued with the Northern Expedition.

To counter Chiang's success, Borodin proposed that Wuhan collaborate with Feng Yuxiang and Yan Xishan to launch its own Northern Expedition. In early May, Wuhan troops began advancing northward to meet Feng at Zhengzhou, inflicting heavy casualties on the Fengtian army along the way. Once they reached their destination, Feng and Yan refused to cooperate on the grounds that Wuhan represented the Communist regime whereas Nanjing was the true Nationalist government. Feng then proposed a joint Northern Expedition by Chiang, Wuhan and himself. When Borodin and Wang Jingwei rejected it, Feng publicly demanded that Wuhan expel Borodin and the Communists from the Guomindang.

Wuhan's predicament was compounded by the power struggle between Stalin and Trotsky. In the wake of Chiang's string of successes, Trotsky criticized Stalin's flawed strategy in China. To vindicate his China policy, Stalin badly needed a victory. On June 1, he sent a telegram to Borodin and the CPC ordering them to raise a separate army and to transform Wuhan into a Communist regime with Wang Jingwei as a puppet. The telegram was leaked by a Comintern agent M.N. Roy to Wang. Wang took no retaliatory action immediately but began distancing himself from the Communists and limiting the CPC's membership and leadership within the party. His patience was breached when on August 1, 1927, the Communists launched the Nanchang Uprising using the name of the Guomindang Left. This prompted Wang to order an immediate crackdown on the Communists and the reorganization of the front organizations such as the

General Labor Union. Borodin and other Soviet advisers were sent home to Russia.

Chiang immediately sent emissaries proposing reconciliation but Wang refused to consider it until Chiang resigned. On August 12, Chiang handed in his resignation, calling on the Guomindang to unite and complete the capture of Beijing and north China.[8] In December, he married Song Meiling, the younger sister of Sun's widow Song Qingling, which made him Sun's brother-in-law. Not only had Chiang gained a young, educated and beautiful wife, his prestige and standing rose as a result of his new relationship with the late *zongli*.

Without Chiang at the helm, the Nanjing government faced many difficulties, particularly financial ones. Bankers and the wealthy capitalists of Shanghai were no longer pressured by Chiang's underworld patron, the Green Gang, to lend or contribute funds. While Chiang was on his honeymoon, a flurry of cables from warlords and Huangpu officers called on him to resume his office. The Wuhan government was officially dissolved in February 1928. Wang Jingwei finally admitted his mistake and joined the chorus calling for Chiang's return. The following month, Chiang arrived in Nanjing with his new bride and resumed his duties as chairman of the Military Council and commander-in-chief of the Northern Expedition.

Chiang resumed the Northern Expedition in April 1928 with the objective of taking Beijing, which was then occupied by the Fengtian clique under Zhang Zuolin. While Chiang's own forces attacked Shandong, his allies Feng Yuxiang and Yan Xishan led their armies toward Beijing from the west across Hebei. At the urging of his Japanese patrons and many of his own supporters, Zhang Zuolin decided to withdraw from North China on June 3. As Zhang's train neared Mukden (Shenyang) the following morning, soldiers from the Japanese Guandong Army bombed his train, killing him. His son Zhang Xueliang, who inherited his authority in Manchuria, immediately recalled all the Manchurian troops in North China, and subsequently pledged his allegiance to the Nationalist government. On June 6, Yan Xishan's 7th Division triumphantly entered Beijing and occupied the capital in a bloodless coup.

By the end of 1928, all the major warlords had accepted the national leadership of the Guomindang, and the greater part of China was unified after 13 years of civil anarchy. On December 31, 1928, the Nationalist government officially declared a unified China. Nanjing was made the new national capital and Beijing was renamed Beiping, "Northern Peace." To legitimize his regime, Chiang Kai-shek presented himself as the "zealot disciple and faithful guardian" of the *zongli*'s thought and dedicated his new government to the fulfillment of Sun Yat-sen's Three Principles of the People, the Five-Power Constitution, and the Fundamentals of National Reconstruction. The Nationalist government received prompt recognition as the sole legitimate government of China. Proclaiming that China had reached the end of the military phase of Sun's formula for the three stages of revolution, it announced that the country would now embark on the second phase, under the tutelage of the Guomindang.

Sun's dream of a China unified through a Northern Expedition had finally been fulfilled and he became the "uncrowned king of New China"[9] during the Nanjing Decade that followed. In government offices, party meetings, factories, barracks and schools in areas where the Nationalists held sway, a ceremony was held every Monday according to a set ritual. After bowing three times before a portrait of Sun, those present listened to a reading of his Political Testament and thereafter observed three minutes of silence. Sometimes a patriotic address followed, or the Nationalist song was sung. The Three Principles of the People became compulsory study in all educational institutions, and students were expected to have a good grasp of its doctrines.[10] The purpose of these exercises was to establish that the history of the revolution rested solely on Sun and the Guomindang and its ideology based on the Three Principles of the People, as formulated in 1924.

Meanwhile, the Nationalist government was also building the cult of Sun. His entombment on June 1, 1929, was as symbolic as it was grandiose. In line with the new image of Sun that the Guomindang wanted to promote, he was now attired in a Confucian scholar's gown rather than the Western suit he had worn when he lay in state. A luxuriously appointed special train transferred Sun's coffin 600 miles (1,000 km) from Beijing to the Sun Yat-sen Mausoleum on Purple Mountain outside of Nanjing. As the train neared Nanjing, airplanes circled overhead and Chiang Kai-shek arrived with an armed escort to meet the funeral coach. Diplomats from dozens of countries and thousands of ordinary citizens attended the ceremony. In a national funeral led by Chiang and key Nationalist leaders, Sun was installed in his final resting place. The majestic monument reclining on a mountain slope, fronted by a huge flight of steps, the beauty of the countryside and the proximity of the Ming tombs, all combined to enhance the solemnity of the spot and encourage reverence.[11]

To commemorate the occasion, Umeya Shokichi, Sun's faithful Japanese supporter, ordered four full-length bronze statues and 100 bronze busts of his old friend. One of the statues was presented to the Sun Yat-sen University in November 1933 at the ceremony for the laying of the foundation stone for its new campus.[12]

IN TRUTH, the Northern Expedition had not quite unified China, and warlord power remained an important feature of the Chinese political landscape. In the early years of the Nanjing Decade, five military factions each having suzerainty over a cluster of provinces and about half a dozen autonomous regions controlled more territories in China than did Nanjing. Several armed conflicts broke out between the regional militarists and the national government in the first few years of the Nanjing Decade. Thereafter, Nanjing and the warlords settled down to mutual tolerance in an uneasy peace. The warlords pledged nominal allegiance to Nanjing, and the Nationalist government used force only in times of crisis. This was in accord with the government's decision not to try and unify the country by force, a policy dictated by military realities. From the beginning of the 1930s, Chiang was engaged in a difficult war with the Communists and could ill afford another major struggle with the warlords as any such conflict might encourage foreign aggression.

The seriousness of the foreign threat was demonstrated by Japan's military action in Manchuria in the early morning of September 18, 1931. Soldiers of the Japanese Guandong Army set off a bomb on a stretch of railway track owned by Japan's South Manchuria Railway near Shenyang. Blaming Chinese soldiers for the explosion and for firing on them, the Guandong Army attacked Shenyang. The incident led to a full-scale invasion of Manchuria. In 1932 the territory was organized as a Japanese puppet state, Manzhouguo (Manchukuo), with Puyi, the last Qing emperor, as head of state. The Japanese continued to nibble away at north China. Few informed Chinese were in any doubt as to what Japan's intention was.

Chiang made no attempt to resist the Japanese aggression militarily. He believed that effective resistance could only come with national unity. This in turn required the destruction of the CPC, which had made a comeback after it was almost exterminated in 1927. The two men responsible for its rejuvenation were Mao Zedong and Zhu De. From their hideout in the Jinggang mountains on the Hunan-Jiangxi border, they developed political and military concepts that marked the beginning of the Red Army and its adoption of guerrilla tactics. Throughout 1929 and 1930, Mao and Zhu strengthened their army and expanded their territory, while other Communist commanders were also forming armed forces and establishing political control in their respective territorial bases. These non-contiguous areas were called rural soviets, a name derived from the councils of workers, peasant and soldiers set up in Russia during the 1905 and 1917 revolutions. In November 1931, delegates from a number of Chinese soviets met in Ruijin, Jiangxi, and proclaimed the establishment of the Chinese Soviet Republic.

When Feng Yuxiang and Yan Xishan's offensive against the Nationalist government finally collapsed in the fall of 1930, Chiang turned his attention to the destruction of the resurgent Communists. Between late 1930 and the spring of 1933, Chiang launched four "encirclement campaigns" against the Chinese soviets. None of these campaigns achieved its objective, but on his fifth attempt in late 1933 Chiang came very close to exterminating his enemies. But the Red Army and the CPC's administrative and political personnel, perhaps 100,000 in all, broke through the Nationalist cordon in late 1934 and set out on the epic Long March, a journey of about 7,500 miles (12,000 km) through some extraordinarily difficult terrain. It ended a year later in Shaanxi in northwestern China, with less than 10 percent of those who had begun making it to the finish line. En route, party leaders held a crucial meeting in the town of Zunyi in Guizhou in January 1935. It was at this meeting that Mao began his meteoric rise in the party hierarchy. In late 1936, a year after the Long March ended, the small Shaanxi town of Yan'an became the Communists' capital.

Chiang Kai-shek's army pursued the Communists throughout the Long March. Once they had reached Shaanxi, Chiang began planning extermination campaigns to destroy the Communists once and for all. His preoccupation with domestic enemies in the face of the Japanese threat increasingly alienated Chinese intellectuals and a number of army officers, who pressured him to change his policy. It included the officers and troops of warlords Zhang Xueliang, who commanded the Northeast Army, and Yang Hucheng, the commander of the Northwest Army. These armies were ordered by Chiang to mount an offensive against the Communists. Weary of a civil war, the officers and men became susceptible to the United Front propaganda. By the summer of 1936, both Zhang and Yang were won over. Chiang became suspicious at the lack of results and in December flew to Xi'an, the provincial capital of Shaanxi, to personally monitor the progress of the campaign against the Communists.

At daybreak on December 12, Zhang Xueliang's bodyguards battled their way into the compound where Chiang was spending the night and held him hostage. Zhang made a deal with Chiang that he could gain his freedom on condition that he relieve the pressure on the Communists and take a stronger stand against the Japanese incursion into Chinese territory. The agreement concluded, Chiang was released on Christmas Day.[13] In early 1937, the Guomindang and the CPC negotiated a truce and formed a second United Front against the Japanese. The Communist armed forces were placed under the overall command of Chiang as the New Fourth Army and the Eighth Route Army.

The suspension of the Civil War and the formation of the second United Front could not have occurred at a more opportune moment. Six months later, on July 7, 1937, Japanese troops from the Guandong Army used the pretext of a "missing" Japanese soldier near Lugouqiao (Marco Polo Bridge) outside Beiping to clash with Chinese troops. This skirmish not only marked the beginning of the open but undeclared Second Sino-Japanese War, it also hastened the formal announcement of the second United Front against Japan. In August, Japanese troops captured Shanghai. The following month they bombed Nanjing, forcing Chiang to flee to Wuhan. The Japanese completed their capture of Nanjing in December and immediately unleashed an orgy of rape and murder that has gone down in history as the Nanjing Massacre or the Rape of Nanjing. At least 100,000 people, and possibly as many as 300,000, were brutally killed over a period of several weeks. The effect of the Nanjing Massacre was to galvanize the Chinese to more intensive resistance. Despite the vigor of the Chinese defense, however, their troops continued to lose ground. In October, the Japanese attacked Wuhan and Chiang was forced once more to flee and relocate his capital, this time to the interior city of Chongqing.

On November 3, 1938, Japanese Prime Minister Konoe Fumimaro issued a statement on "the new order in East Asia," which was effectively a manifesto for the domination of China. Senior members of the Guomindang were split over how to respond. Some like Wang Jingwei believed that there was hope for peace by accepting Japan's terms. In June 1939 he traveled to Tokyo to discuss the formation of a Japanese-sponsored government, and in March the following year installed himself as head of such a government.

The Second Sino-Japanese War postponed the adoption of a draft constitution that the Nationalist government had promulgated on May 5, 1936. Based on Sun's five branches of government, it gave the National Assembly the powers of election, recall, initiative and referendum. The Assembly that had the power to adopt it was scheduled to convene in November 1937 but was postponed indefinitely due to the Japanese invasion.[14] Nevertheless, Sun who up until this time was known by his title of *zongli*, was canonized as *Guofu*, "Father of the Nation," in 1940. Because of the war with Japan, the Guomindang sought to downplay the close ties that had existed between Sun and his Japanese friends, patrons and supporters. The Japanese and Wang Jingwei, on the other hand, invoked the same relations to rationalize their policies under the guise of the Greater East Asian Co-Prosperity Sphere as a manifestation of the pan-Asianism advocated by Sun.[15] In 1941, Wang Jingwei published a collection of pro-Japanese texts by Sun, *China and Japan: Natural Friends, Unnatural Enemies*.[16]

Despite Japan's steady territorial gains in north China, the coastal regions, and the rich Yangtze valley, the alliance between the Communists and the Nationalists began to break down after late 1938. The distrust between the two parties was scarcely veiled and conflicts between them became more frequent after 1940 in areas not under Japanese control. The

Communists expanded their influence wherever opportunities presented themselves – through mass organizations, administrative reforms, and the land- and tax-reform measures favoring the peasants – while the Nationalists attempted to neutralize the spread of Communist influence.

Japan's sneak attack on Pearl Harbor on December 7, 1941, drew the U.S. into World War II and changed the complexion of the war in China. The Second Sino-Japanese War became part of the Pacific theater of war, and the U.S. emerged as a major player in Chinese affairs. Now an ally in the war against Japan, the U.S. began a program of massive military and financial aid to the beleaguered Nationalist government. In January 1943, the U.S. and Britain led the way in revising the unequal treaties. Shortly after, the U.S. signed a new agreement with China for the stationing of American troops on Chinese soil for the common war effort against Japan. In December, the Chinese Exclusion Act of 1882 and similar laws enacted by the U.S. Congress to restrict Chinese immigration into the U.S. were repealed. The wartime policy of the U.S. was to help China become a strong ally and a stabilizing force in postwar East Asia. As the conflict between the Nationalists and the Communists intensified, the U.S. sought unsuccessfully to reconcile the rival forces for a more effective response against Japanese aggression.

The U.S. explosion of two atomic bombs over Hiroshima and Nagasaki in August 1945 brought World War II to an end. China emerged from the war nominally a great military power but in reality was a nation economically crippled by the war and plagued by internal chaos, spiraling inflation, profiteering, speculation and hoarding. Millions were rendered homeless by natural disasters and the unsettled conditions in many parts of the country; starvation was evident everywhere.

Following Japan's surrender, government and Communist troops rushed into occupied territories to receive the Japanese surrender and seize the vast stash of enemy arms and equipment. The Communists were at a slight geographical advantage as they were in control of north, south and central China whereas government forces were concentrated in south and southwestern China. Determined to win the race, Chiang ordered the Japanese to hold out against non-government forces and appealed for American help to airlift his troops to occupied territories.

With U.S. assistance and Japanese cooperation, government troops regained control of nearly all the important cities in central, east and south China, forcing the Communists to retreat to the countryside. Meanwhile, Soviet troops had swept into Manchuria on August 8. Their advance did not stop even after the Japanese surrender on August 14. Their presence facilitated the entry of Communist forces into Manchuria. While they handed over to the Communists vast quantities of Japanese arms and equipment, they hung on to Manchuria.

To resolve these issues, Chiang invited Mao to a conference at Chongqing. Mao accepted the invitation only after U.S. envoy Patrick Hurley flew to Yan'an and vouched for his safety. Little progress was made at the conference, largely because Chiang and Mao distrusted each other and refused to compromise on important issues. The only significant agreement to emerge from the conference was a joint communiqué on October 10 agreeing to the convocation of a Political Consultative Conference (PCC).

In line with a new policy of non-military assistance to the Nationalist government, President Harry Truman dispatched General George C. Marshall as his special envoy to China to help bring about political unification. Arriving in China in mid-December 1945, Marshall found both parties receptive to his mediation and seemingly ready to endorse his programs. Beneath the veneer of cordiality, however, the two sides were still deeply distrustful of each other. The Communists wanted a coalition government in which they and other political parties would share political power with the Guomindang. They refused to give up their army or surrender territories under their control until the national government ceased to be a mere extension of the Guomindang. Chiang Kai-shek, who feared that a coalition government would be allowing the Communist nose into the Guomindang tent, promised that political liberalization would come but the Communists would first have to give up their army. The Communists rejected the condition as it would leave them vulnerable.

Marshall's mediation nevertheless produced impressive results. In January 1946, he committed both parties to a ceasefire, the immediate convening of a PCC to discuss the formation of a coalition government, and the integration of Communist and government forces into a national army. In March, Marshall left China for the U.S. to arrange a loan. During his absence, the extremists in both parties stirred up local clashes which soon turned into large-scale fighting in April 1946. Fighting would have been worse but for the return of Marshall, who arranged for a 15-day truce on June 6. By now war fever had gripped both the Communists and the Nationalists and by mid-1946 both sides had decided once again to turn to the battlefield to settle their differences.

Buoyed by their string of victories, the Nationalist government announced on July 4 that they would convene the National Assembly in November in disregard of the PCC resolution that such an Assembly would only be called after the formation of a coalition government. The Communists announced that they would boycott the Assembly and Mao called for a war of self-defense. In spite of repeated warnings from the United States that they would not underwrite his war, Chiang could not believe that the Americans would not come to the aid of the Nationalists if the situation became desperate.

In the early stage of the war, government troops scored wins at almost every encounter. Encouraged by the Nationalists' victories, Chiang convened the National Assembly on November 15, 1946, in spite of the Communist boycott. The Assembly adopted a new constitution which reaffirmed the Three Principles of the People as the state ideology, the five-branch government and the people's four rights of suffrage, recall, initiation and referendum. Chiang Kai-shek's speech to the Assembly showed how much he had been influenced by Sun's elitist belief that "the people exercising political powers must possess the ability and habits to maintain and safeguard the five powers...." Echoing Sun's argument that the people were not then able to protect their political powers under a fully fledged Five-Power Constitution, Chiang argued that the National Assembly would only be given the right to elect and recall the president and vice president of the republic, but not the other high-ranking officials. The powers of initiative and referendum could only be exercised after these two powers had been successfully employed in half the counties in the country and after the National Assembly had instituted regulations and implemented them.[17]

Unswayed by the Communists' charge that the constitution was illegal, the Nationalist government proceeded with the election of a new National Assembly in November 1947. Convened on March 29, 1948, the Assembly elected Chiang president, with Li Zongren as vice president. With this election, the 21-year political tutelage of the Guomindang, which Sun had originally envisaged to last only six years, came to an end. But even as Chiang assumed his office, the tide of war was starting to shift against the Nationalists.

Beginning in mid-1947, the Nationalist advance began to run out of steam as more government troops were being assigned to garrison duties in newly reconquered areas, thus reducing the troop strength at the front. In contrast, the Communist army had been expanding rapidly and in the second half of 1947 embarked on a general offensive. The severest loss to the Nationalists was in Manchuria, where it cost Chiang 470,000 of his best troops. It was a devastating blow to the morale of the government forces. From this point on, Communist forces scored one victory after another. In January 1949 they took Tianjin and Beiping without any resistance when the defending Nationalist commander General Fu Zuoyi surrendered to Lin Biao's overwhelming forces.[18]

Between September 1948 and January 1949, the government lost 1.5 million men. With such staggering losses, the Nationalist forces simply collapsed. Chiang was forced to resign by the Guomindang on January 21, 1949, and Vice President Li Zongren took over as acting president. Li tried to persuade Mao to compromise on his eight-point program for Guomindang surrender.[19] But there was no reason for Mao to compromise with victory now within grasp. On April 21, Communist forces crossed the mighty Yangtze and three days later captured Nanjing, forcing the Nationalists to seek asylum in Guangzhou. Shanghai fell in late May. In the following months, Communist forces moved quickly to consolidate their hold across the country.[20]

With final victory in sight, Mao Zedong assembled a PCC in Beiping in late September. The Communist Party dominated the body but 14 other political parties were also represented. Mao was elected chairman and Beiping, now renamed back to Beijing, was designated the nation's capital. The new regime adopted a new national flag as well as the Gregorian calendar.[21] The civil war was effectively over when on October 1, 1949, Chairman Mao proclaimed the establishment of the People's Republic of China (PRC) from a reviewing stand atop Tiananmen, the Gate of Heavenly

Peace, which was once the main entrance to the Forbidden City. Conspicuously present by his side was Sun's widow, Song Qingling, who later held several prominent positions in the new Communist government and represented China at a number of international events. Just before her death in May 1981, she was given the special title of Honorary President of the People's Republic of China.

Meanwhile, Chiang had gone back to Chongqing in August 1949, planning to make a last stand. The People's Liberation Army (PLA) – the new name of the Red Army after World War II – took the city at the end of November, however, and Chiang was forced to flee to nearby Chengdu in Sichuan province. From there he departed from the Chinese mainland for the last time on December 10, bound for Taipei, which he proclaimed as the temporary capital of China. By then an estimated 2 million Chinese from the mainland had already settled on the island. Chiang vowed to retake the Chinese mainland, just as Zheng Chenggong the Ming loyalist had vowed in the 17th century. Chiang died in April 1975, and like Zheng, never set foot on the mainland again.

War is an awful business and civil war is the most horrible of all. The enemy is not some alien being but fellow countrymen, often one's own kith and kin. For the Chinese, the civil war was especially painful: it split their country into two Chinas. Large numbers of families were divided and separated, and for many years were prevented from making contact. While relations across the Taiwan Strait have substantially improved in recent years, tension is not altogether absent. The PRC insists there is only one China and so did Taiwan for a time. But the ultimate goal of the present government of Taiwan is independence for the island. On her part, Beijing has consistently made clear that the reunification of Taiwan is a core issue and not negotiable. And while China prefers a peaceful resolution, she has unequivocally warned that Taiwan's independence would be a *casus belli* justifying a military response.

Chapter 16

THE MAN AND HIS LEGACY

SUN'S CHARACTER WAS as complex as his maneuvers against the Qing dynasty, militarists and imperialist powers to establish a strong, united, modern and republican Chinese nation. Much of what has been written about him was colored by bonds of friendship or the enmity of foes, while the sanctification that began after his death has created a mythical figure that obscures the real man. Evaluating his character thus presents a special challenge. Nevertheless, from his own writings and the observations of others, it is possible to draw a reasonable sketch of this larger-than-life Chinese patriot.

One of the first things most people noticed about Sun was his calm temperament, pleasant manner and reticent composure. He spoke softly and rarely raised his voice, but he was quite capable of showing his wrath, as Inukai Ki wrote of his friend in 1930: "whenever the corruption and rottenness of the Manchu court was raised, he immediately became very fluent in criticizing and attacking them. His words were so sharp and no longer in good temper."[1] This side of Sun was on display when the foreign community in Shanghai objected to him staying at his own home in the French Concession on his way to Beijing in 1924. Sun angrily reminded them that they were guests of China and should behave accordingly. Sun was also capable of stronger measures when his position was threatened, as for instance when he allowed Chiang Kai-shek to set ablaze a business center in Guangzhou during the Merchants' Corps revolt.

Another strong impression is his personal integrity. Sun raised large sums of money from diverse *huaqiao* communities around the world, but kept for himself only so much as was needed for his own sustenance. Money meant little to him. His modest accommodation and simple lifestyle are testaments to his attitude towards wealth. At his death, his entire estate comprised only his books, some personal effects and a small house. The man who had raised and disbursed vast sums departed with so little to his name. Such integrity at a time of generalized corruption set him head and shoulders above his rivals.

The handling of large sums of money occasionally embroiled Sun in allegations of misappropriation. In 1909, Zhang Binglin and Tao Chengzhang accused him of mismanaging Tongmenghui funds and challenged his leadership of the party. There is no evidence that Sun profited from his revolutionary activities, but these charges proved highly damaging to his fundraising efforts and his cause. Nevertheless, Sun forgave them both. In 1917 he invited Zhang to be the secretary general of his first Guangzhou government. As Sun later explained to Cai Yuanpei, his quarrel with Zhang was a quarrel between friends and he never considered Zhang an enemy. Similarly, despite his estranged relations with Huang Xing, Sun continued to consult his old comrade and delivered a moving eulogy at his funeral.[2]

Sun's kindness was not just to people he knew. His bodyguard Morris "Two-Gun" Cohen, a 200-pound Polish-born Jewish adventurer, recounted several examples of Sun's compassion for complete strangers. Not only did he spare the life of a spy on death row, Sun took him into his employment. Cohen also recalled how Sun would stroll among the coolies in Guangzhou to listen to their woes and offer alms whenever he came across a beggar. Sometimes Sun would even financially arrange for a child's schooling. Towards the end of his life, Sun asked Eugene Chen to trace George Cole, the porter at the Chinese Legation who had helped him to escape. When Sun found out that Cole's widow was still alive, he left an instruction to pay the old lady a pension for life. This was one of the last orders issued by Sun.[3]

Sun's compassion made him seem quite "quixotic and strangely unrevolutionary."[4] While dedicated to the cause of revolution, he was strenuously opposed to killing. In a 1906 speech, he stressed that there would be no revenge killing against the Manchus. In his sixth lecture on Nationalism in 1924, he highlighted the ancient Chinese saying, "He who delights not in killing a man can unify all men." In difficult situations, he preferred peaceful solutions to violent measures, compromise rather than prolonged struggle. Harold Schiffrin called Sun a "reluctant" revolutionary because "for all his audacity, he lacked the ruthlessness that marks the true revolutionary."[5] Indeed, Sun has been called the "kindest of all revolutionaries."[6]

Sun had many warm friends among his classmates, revolutionary comrades, the *huaqiao* and Christian communities, Japanese *ronin* and American adventurers. He also knew a great number of people from all walks and stations in life: wealthy Hong Kong compradors, secret society leaders, humble workmen, *huaqiao* merchants, labor union leaders, foreign politicians, and a whole generation of young Chinese intellectuals. Many of these people stuck by him through thick and thin to serve him and his cause. Others came in and out of his life as he needed their help. They were all attracted by his sincerity, his persuasiveness and his selfless commitment to his cause. Dr. Cantlie wrote of his former student: "his [Sun's] friends ... are willing to devote their energies, their time, their very lives to forward his aims, but also for the man himself ... The secret of his success is unselfishness – seeking only his country's good, not his own advancement; a patriot indeed with no axe to grind, no place seeker, willing to rule if called upon, ready and anxious to stand aside when the interests of his country are to be benefited thereby."[7]

Sun was a charismatic and inspirational speaker with an uncanny ability to tune in to the wavelength of his interlocutors. As Sun himself explained, "If you meet a farmer, speak to him about freeing him from his miseries. The farmer will then certainly warmly embrace what you have to say. Do the same when meeting workers, merchants, and scholars."[8] Nathaniel Peffer, a professor of history at Columbia University who had spent 25 years in China, wrote of Sun: "I have never known anybody who has been face to face with Dr. Sun who has not been impressed with him ... Nothing about him strikes you until he speaks – in a low and uninfected tone with rapid flow of words. His poise, his dignity, his enthusiasm and, above all, his utter sincerity record themselves on your memory forever."

Few people could match Sun on a podium. Li Luchao, his secretary between 1916 and 1924, wrote in 1974: "In public speaking, he [Sun] was a ready and eloquent speaker ... inspirational and stirring ... easily understood and appreciated by the masses ... he never used strong and abusive language and on issue of politics he never exhorted his audience to use violence."[9] J. Ellis Barker, writing in 1911 in the *Fortnightly Review*, one of the most prominent and influential magazines in England at the time, also thought that Sun was an excellent speaker – though he spoke softly and "almost monotonously with hardly any gestures," he "captivated his audiences with his convincing arguments."[10]

Sun read extensively. His bibliographical interests ranged from Chinese classics and history to contemporary works but he is known to have favored Western works on economics and politics. The knowledge he gained from his wide reading as well as his extensive travels made him a political thinker who sought to synthesize East and West, traditional Chinese values with modern Western concepts. He was "in all probability a more assiduous and widely read student of political science than any other world leader of his day except [Woodrow] Wilson; he studied innumerable treatises on government, and was surprisingly familiar with the general background of Western politics and theory," wrote Paul M.A. Linebarger.[11]

"He [Sun] dreamed of Utopia, of establishing a sane and orderly government," recalled Li Luchao, "For his dreams of such high ideals, which were hardly possible, he was dubbed by the Cantonese as 'Big Gun,' a synonym for being idealistic and impractical." He was not always practical, sometimes leading himself and others in idealistic and unrealistic directions. But Sun was no mere Don Quixote; he was, par excellence, a man ahead of his time. His insistence that China adopt republicanism at a time when the world's major nations were still monarchies was visionary. He realized earlier than most thinkers and leaders of his day the need for a new international order based on cooperation rather than competition. He was also among the first to advocate international integration through the exchange of views and ideas, and the free flow of products, services and capital – the process we know today as globalization. His appeal for such cooperation and integration was extremely bold; it ran counter to the diplomatic practices of the Western nations at the time, which aimed to make China the dumping ground for their overproduction. Not until the second half of the 20th century would international economic cooperation between industrialized and developing nations find a place at the heart of political debate.[12]

Sun may have oversimplified and underestimated the challenges of modernizing China but he was a harbinger of the future China. The basic concept underlying his scheme to "make capitalism create socialism" was at the root of many of the policies later put in place by Deng Xiaoping in pursuit of China's Four Modernizations: China's opening to the West, the use of foreign technological and financial expertise, a special role to the coastal regions, the co-existence of private enterprise with a public sector, and social stability.[13]

Sun's plan to integrate China's numerous cities and towns through a network of railways, roads and dredged rivers was neither technologically possible nor financially viable at the time. Similarly, his plan to dam up the rapids of the mighty Yangtze and the other infrastructural projects in his *International Development of China* – all of them were ridiculed as unrealistic and far-fetched. Fast-forward to the 21st century and we see that many of them have in fact been realized. In 2015, Shanghai handled more than two and a half times the tonnage that passed through America's largest port of South Louisiana, and more than five and a half times her third largest, the Port of New York and New Jersey.[14] China has the second longest rail network on earth, over 191,270 km (120,000 miles) as of 2014, but its high-speed rail network of over 20,000 km (12,000 miles) is more than all the high-speed rail networks in the rest of the world combined. There are plans to lay a further 15,000 km (9,000 miles) by 2025.[15] China's road network exceeds 4.1 million km (2.5 million miles) as of 2011 and is the third longest in the world after the United States' 6.6 million km (4 million miles) and India's 4.7 million km (2.9 million miles).[16] The most ambitious of Sun's visions was the damming of the Yangtze to generate hydroelectricity. This, too, has been realized in the form of the Three Gorges Dam, which comprises the largest hydroelectric project on earth. This has a generating capacity of 22,500 megawatts compared to the 14,000 megawatts of the Itaipu Dam in Brazil and Paraguay, the second largest hydroelectric dam in the world.[17]

Nathaniel Peffer, in trying to unravel "the enigma of Sun Yat-sen" – that is to say his prestige as a revolutionary and the disdain for him as a political figure – had some harsh words for Sun: "Dr. Sun is gullible beyond imagining and credulous past understanding ... his two most pronounced weaknesses – his vanity and his hunger for flattery – subject him to imposture and betray him into squandering his energy."[18] In spite of his shrewdness, Sun could sometimes be naive. His belief that free elections would immediately enable the people to select honest and sincere officials with high moral standards was certainly quite credulous. Sometimes he was also not as astute in judging the character of people and allowed himself to be deceived. He trusted Liang Qichao and introduced him to his brother Sun Mei and others in Hawaii. Similarly, he trusted Yuan Shikai to implement constitutional government, only to be betrayed by both.

Notwithstanding his complex character, simplicity is the word that comes to mind when speaking about Sun's personal life. His residence in the French Concession in Shanghai was a modest 2-storey house with the most basic furniture. The only sign of ostentation was a book-filled study and a lawn for croquet, his only known outdoor recreation. He indulged in calligraphy but little is known of his other aesthetic interests, or if there were any. Sun was very careful about his diet, preferring fish and vegetables to meat, and consumed fruits in copious quantities. He never smoked, rarely drank alcohol and never tea or coffee.[19]

Sun may well have been one of the very first Chinese to receive a foreign education before obtaining a classical Chinese education. Views vary as to when and how Sun acquired his classical Chinese learning. The noted sinologist Yu Yingshi believes that Sun read the Confucian classics and dynastic histories while he was a student at the Boji Medical School in 1886.[20] This however contradicts Sun's own humorous admission in a speech before a group of Cantonese parliamentarians in Shanghai in July 1916: "I had mimicked the pupils of our school in reading the Four Books and Five Classics, only to forget them later on. ... So I read the English translations… And what do you know! I understood them after a while."[21] Very possibly it was at the British Museum following his release by the Chinese Legation in London that Sun read the English translations of the Chinese classics under the guidance of Professor Graham.[22]

Regardless how Sun acquired his proficiency in the ancient texts, there is little doubt that he was deeply influenced by the teachings of Confucius in his political ideology. Asked by a Russian visitor a few months before his death to identify the intellectual inspiration of his revolutionary doctrine, he replied that it was "a development and a continuation of the ancient Chinese doctrines of Confucius."[23] Sun justified his revolution against the Manchus and his crusade against imperialism in terms of the Heavenly Mandate. He exalted traditional virtues and believed in moral education rather than laws to maintain social order. Asian civilization, Sun believed, was based on *wangdao*, or the rule of right, whereas Western civilization was based on *badao*, or the rule of might. In his famous speech in Kobe on November 28, 1924, he argued for the traditional values of the Asian *wangdao*.

In his 1924 lectures on the Principle of Livelihood, Sun expressed his hope of achieving *datong*, or "Great Harmony,"[24] a classical Chinese concept that refers to a utopian world ruled by men of exceptional virtue and ability in which the helpless are cared for and people live in perfect peace and harmony. Some scholars cite this as evidence of Sun's belief in communism but his unequivocal rejection of class conflict rules this out. Moreover, *datong* is not a Marxist concept but one born of traditional Chinese thought. Sun's desire to achieve social goals through peaceful means might have been influenced by the teachings of Confucius, and just as likely by the writings of Maurice William.

Sun's interpretations of certain Confucius doctrines, for instance his ideas on democracy, were unorthodox. He displayed a similar lack of conventionality in his Christian faith. This has led some to argue that he was not a true Christian but portrayed himself as one to gain political mileage. Sun indeed occasionally emphasized his Christian faith to Western audiences to gain political mileage, as for instance after his release from the Chinese Legation in London. But he also professed his Christian faith to Chinese audiences when it was not in his interests to do so, especially as Chinese scholars had rejected Christianity as un-Chinese. To his credit, he did not disavow his Christian faith during the Boxer Uprising, which was a time of intense antipathy toward Christian missionaries and their Chinese converts. He could have capitalized on anti-clerical sentiment and garnered support from Boxer supporters. There was no need for him to draw attention to the fact that he was dying as a Christian. Yet on his deathbed he grasped the hand of his brother-in-law Kong Xiangxi and said: "You are a Christian; I, too am a Christian." Later, Sun whispered to Kong: "I want it to be known that I die a Christian." One of his deathbed injunctions to a leftist follower was: "Don't make trouble for the Christians." His family organized a Christian funeral for him in the face of opposition; there was no political capital to be gained from this.[25]

Sun did not regularly attend church, nor did he observe Christian holidays or festivities. This does not mean that he was not a Christian, only that he eschewed ecclesiastical Christianity. "I do not belong to the Christianity of the churches," he said, "but to the Christianity of Jesus who was a revolutionary."[26] He was not alone in rejecting ecclesiastical Christianity; many of his countrymen at the time perceived the church as the religious arm of Western imperialism.[27] What of Sun's visit to the tomb of the first Ming emperor to pay respects to the departed monarch after his inauguration as provisional president, when he declared: "How could we have attained this measure of victory had not your Majesty's soul in Heaven bestowed upon us your protecting influence." Did this not contradict his Christian belief? Not in the context of his time. Given that both Catholics and Protestants were divided on the matter of ancestral worship and other traditional Chinese rites, Sun's action could hardly be considered unchristian.

A missionary for secular ends was how his biographer Paul Linebarger saw Sun: "The West has sent thousands of missionaries to China. China has sent only one to the West ... [Westerners] have preached the Gospel of a life after death. Dr. Sun, as a missionary to the Western man, is preaching the gospel of a life before death." Of Sun's methods of conversion, Linebarger said: "Dr. Sun never makes the mistake of getting converts in the same manner a missionary obtains his converts to Christianity. The missionary appeals to a man's heart. Dr. Sun has more success than any missionary has ever had because, he not only appeals to his heart but to his reason as well."[28] Indeed, Sun himself is reported to have said: "God sent me to China to free her from bondage and oppression, and I have not been disobedient to the Heavenly mission." On the day before he died, he declared: "I am a Christian; God sent me to fight evil for my people. Jesus was a revolutionary; so am I."[29]

Sun was a fiery nationalist, and like many such zealots, was egotistical, at times even self-righteous, with a mystical belief in his destiny to restore China to the Chinese. According to a witness, Sun said on his deathbed: "Just as Christ was sent by God to the world, so also did God send me."[30] It was this spiritual faith that gave him the extraordinary courage in times of despair to carry on his divine mission.

If Sun was such a nationalist, his appeals to the foreign powers for help may appear perplexing. While he admired their modernity and achievements, he also harbored intense feelings against them for their imperialist aggression in China. Yet throughout his political career he was often willing to offer, in return for their help, concessions that actually tightened the foreign grip on China. This has proved embarrassing from a nationalist point of view, and has diminished Sun's right to be called a patriot. He was well aware of the problem, often seeking to keep such agreements secret. This was not hypocrisy, but expediency. Operating from a position of weakness, he had little choice but to maneuver the foreign powers into a position of rendering help. He may have been opportunistic, but his ultimate patriotism was clear. Indeed, he seems to have had no intention of keeping many of the promises he made to the foreign powers. He probably received as much as 2 million dollars from Germany in early 1917, yet his Guangzhou government declared war on Germany in September.[31]

In spite of his intense feelings against the governments of the major powers for their imperialistic policies in China, he was sufficiently pragmatic to admire their achievements. Among foreign nations, he most admired the United States, despite her hostile position in the Guangzhou customs case, and Japan, despite the encroachment of her militarists in China during and after World War I. The assistance rendered by Miyazaki Torazo and Homer Lea probably most affected his views of these two countries. He maintained a particular distaste for the British.[32]

Considering his serious and reserved nature, it may come as a surprise that Sun was somewhat of a Don Juan, carrying on two relationships while married to Lu Muzhen. He met Chen Cuifen in 1891 through Chen Shaobai in Hong Kong. It is not known when the amorous liaison with Chen started, only that she followed him to Japan after the Guangzhou Uprising in 1895. Thereafter until the eve of the 1911 Revolution, she accompanied Sun on his travels and performed housework for him and his comrades-in-arms. Lu Muzhen showed no jealousy toward Chen, who after all was merely playing the traditional role of a concubine. In fact, she regarded Chen as effectively a younger sister, and Sun's children looked up to her as an aunt. Chen never married but had an adopted daughter who later married a grandson of Sun Mei.[33]

Otsuki Kaori was the daughter of Sun's Japanese landlord while he was living undercover in Yokohama's Chinatown in 1898. He "married" Otsuki in 1902 when he was 36 years old and she just 15. Sun left for his travels shortly after and did not see Otsuki again until 1905. A daughter, born the following year, was adopted out to the Miyakawa family. Consequently, her name, Miyakawa Fumiko, bore neither the Sun nor the Otsuki family name. Apparently, Sun's family knew of the relationship but kept it a family secret for decades until Kubota Bunji, a Japanese researcher, uncovered the story.[34]

Song Qingling, Sun's second wife, was everything that Lu Muzhen could never be. Young, beautiful, sophisticated and Western-educated, she involved herself in every aspect of her husband's life and work. Not only did she continue as his secretary, she was also his sounding board. Qingling backed Sun's decision to ally with Soviet Russia, displaying for the first time her pro-Soviet sympathy. Chiang Kai-shek proposed marriage to her after Sun's death, which she saw as a crude political maneuver to appropriate his prestige and legacy. From this time onward, she was highly suspicious of Chiang. She resisted her family's entreaties to accede to Chiang's leadership and remained in Wuhan when Chiang moved his capital to Nanjing. In July 1927, she took her disdain for Chiang a step further by issuing a statement attacking Chiang's leadership and his betrayal of the revolution. The declaration burned Qingling's bridges to her well-connected family. She fled to Moscow after Chiang triumphed over the Wuhan government. Now the black sheep of the family, she denounced her sister Meiling's marriage to Chiang. While in Russia, Qingling became active in the international Left in Europe.

When Japan launched a full-scale invasion of China in 1937, the Guomindang and the CPC formed the Second United Front. This political rapprochement led to a reconciliation between Qingling and her sisters. They made several public appearances to promote the United Front against Japan but quickly returned to opposite sides of the political divide after Japan's surrender in 1945. Qingling lent her prestige to the CPC, standing with Mao Zedong when he announced the establishment of the PRC on October 1, 1949, at Tiananmen Square. She wanted to join the CPC but was advised that her voice would carry more weight if she was not a member.

Nevertheless, she held a number of ceremonial positions and kept herself occupied in other ways, editing a PRC magazine and directing a charitable organization for impoverished children. In public speeches, she invariably stressed the relevance of the Three Principles of the People to the new challenges that China faced. Qingling played the role of Sun's widow for a full 56 years and was finally inducted into the CPC a few weeks before her death from leukemia in Beijing in 1981.

Sun had three children with Lu Muzhen: a son, Sun Ke, and two daughters, Sun Yan and Sun Wan. Sun Ke and Sun Yan were born in Cuiheng village and moved with their mother in 1905 to Hawaii, where they lived with Sun Mei and his family. Sun Wan was born in Hawaii. In 1912, the three siblings continued their studies in the United States. Of the three, Sun Ke seems to have been the closest to his father. He graduated from the University of California, Berkeley, in 1916 and obtained a Master of Arts degree in economics from Columbia University in New York the following year. He returned to China and over the next several decades served in various capacities, including mayor of Guangzhou and vice president of the Nationalist government. He moved to the United States in 1953 and died from an illness in Taipei 20 years later. Sun Yan contracted an illness in 1913, returned to Macau and died at the age of 19. Sun Wan returned to Macau after her graduation. In 1921 she married Dai Ensai, foreign secretary in Sun's Guangzhou military government. After the establishment of the People's Republic in 1949, she and her husband moved to Macau, where they remained until her death in 1979.

Sun's revolutionary and political career came at a great personal cost. Before the 1911 Revolution, he hardly spent any time with his family, who were also dragged into the turmoil of the revolution and had to seek sanctuary abroad. Because of his travels and other commitments, he could not be at the deathbed of his mother, his daughter Sun Yan or his brother Sun Mei, nor attend their funerals. His sacrifices were not always appreciated. Critics complained that he talked a lot while asking for money and then did little. The plots and revolts he organized all failed in their immediate purpose. The defeats led to dissension among the revolutionaries and criticism of Sun's leadership. He worked to overthrow the Qing from the relative safety of exile while letting others do the dirty work. Colleagues like

Huang Xing, for instance, never hesitated to put himself in harm's way for the cause, and thus chalked up a more credible revolutionary record than Sun. He was late for the 1911 Revolution because he was busy talking up revolution in the U.S. He reached Shanghai in late December 1911, after the main fighting was over.[35]

Interestingly, one of the most flattering tributes paid to Sun came from one of his fiercest critics, Dr. G.E. Morrison, correspondent for the *Times* and an adviser to the Beijing government in the 1910s. Morrison considered Sun to be the main obstacle to progress in China and was bitterly opposed to his Guangzhou government. Morrison's connection to the *Times* gave him great influence to alienate British sympathy for Sun and his cause. On his deathbed, however, Morrison confided to James Cantlie: "If I had appreciated the character of Sun Yat-sen years ago as I do now, the history of China would have been different."[36]

SUN'S LEGACY SURVIVED the partition of China in 1949. After Chiang Kai-shek and his Nationalist government took refuge in Taiwan, the veneration of Sun became an integral part of their strategy to restore legitimacy. Sun's portraits, citations and calligraphy adorned all public squares and thoroughfares in Taiwan in the 1950s and 1960s. The Three Principles of the People was used to indoctrinate the new generations and to justify a social and economic policy imposed in large part by Taiwan's American ally and protector. Taiwan's opening up to the international market from 1960 and the growing role of private enterprise, both of which were instrumental in creating her economic miracle, were represented as stemming from the strategy of modernization preached by Sun.[37]

Meanwhile, a different discourse emerged in the People's Republic of China (PRC). Here Sun was assigned a more modest role as a "pioneer of the revolution," alongside the likes of Marx, Lenin and Mao, rather than "father of the nation." Like the Guomindang, the CPC recognized Sun's contribution to the 1911 Revolution that resulted in the abdication of the Qing dynasty and the collapse of the imperial regime. However, the failure of the Republic reflected not so much the wavering of Sun's disciples, as claimed by the Guomindang, but the incomplete nature of an economic revolution that had made it impossible for new social forces to assert their power and thereby condemned the "old democratic revolution" to failure. Furthermore, while the Guomindang kept silent on the anti-Western sentiments that Sun had expressed on numerous occasions, the Communists emphasized his anti-imperialist pronouncements. The Guomindang stressed Sun's concern to preserve the originality of his party and his own doctrine, even between 1923 and 1925 when he was collaborating with the Chinese Communists and the Soviet Union. Beijing laid emphasis on the relations of trust between Sun and his allies within the first United Front and upon the alignment not only of Sun's strategy but also his thinking with the Socialist model offered him by his Soviet advisers. Finally, the Communists' reverence for Sun centered not so much on the Three Principles of the People, but the Three Great Policies that he adopted toward the end of his life: alliance with the Soviet Union, collaboration with the CPC, and support for the peasants' and workers' movements. By adopting these policies, the Communists claimed that Sun proved himself to be a close friend of the Chinese Communists, and helped them to triumph over the Guomindang in 1949.[38]

In the 1950s, Zhou Enlai[39] called Sun "the great hero of China's democratic revolution," hailing him for leading the struggle to overthrow feudalism and imperialism. In 1956, Mao Zedong added his personal endorsement to this narrative in a speech on the 90th anniversary of Sun's birth by celebrating his "clear democratic revolutionary standpoint in the sharp struggle against the Chinese reformist camp," adding that Sun had "led the Chinese people to overthrow the imperial system and establish the republic."[40] The national discourse on Sun changed during the Cultural Revolution. His democratic revolution was now seen as petit-bourgeois and the 1911 Revolution cast in a rather negative light.

Deng Xiaoping's reform era saw a paradigm shift in the reading of Sun and the 1911 Revolution. Deng wanted to move away from the economic model of the Mao era and give priority to the Four Modernizations (of agriculture, industry, education, and science and technology) first set forth by Zhou Enlai in 1963. This policy gave absolute priority to economic development while the realization of socialist goals was set aside until such time when modernization had been achieved. The protected public sector was superseded by encouragement for private and collective enterprises ruled by market forces. The ideal of self-sufficiency was abandoned in favor of an open-door policy of financial and technical cooperation with foreigners, especially in the Special Economic Zones created in the southern provinces in 1979.

These radical changes provoked violent resistance from party conservatives, who deplored what looked like the revival of capitalism and the return of foreign imperialism, the abandonment of socialism, and the betrayal of China's sovereignty and national interests. Deng had to look for new sources of legitimacy that would allow China to pursue his projects within the acceptable ideological framework. He found it in Sun's Three Principles of the People, which proposed a model that closely paralleled the form of state capitalism that Deng had in mind. Sun's prestige was supposed to legitimize the reformers' open-door policy, the appeal to private capital and the priority given to the development of the coastal zones. The 1980s thus saw Deng mentioning Sun's name every time he needed to muster elite support for his reformist policies.[41] In 1984, he coined the phrase "socialism with Chinese characteristics" to promote his Four Modernizations.[42]

On the 120th anniversary of Sun's birth in 1986, Peng Zhen[43], a leading member of the CPC, announced that Sun's understanding of national unity would henceforth be the basis of the regime's new policy towards Taiwan, a rhetoric that has been employed since. In the 1990s, Jiang Zemin wanted to surpass Sun as an ideologue but still found it necessary to call on Sun's name. His aides repeatedly emphasized how Jiang's Three Represents was inspired by Sun's Three Principles but without its flaws. In a speech marking Sun's 140th birthday anniversary, Hu Jintao praised Sun as an outstanding patriot and called on China's various ethnic groups, compatriots on Taiwan, and all Chinese in the world who respected Sun to unite and strive harder for China's full reunification, the great rejuvenation of the Chinese nation, and the building of a harmonious world featuring lasting peace and common prosperity.[44]

The attention given to Sun in China was part of a bigger plan to induce Taiwan to reunify with the mainland. After decades of hostility without any contacts or exchanges, in January 1979 the Standing Committee of the National People's Congress (NPC) called for "peaceful unification" with Taiwan. In 1981, the Chairman of the NPC proposed direct party-to-party talks, direct postal, commercial and maritime links, and the creation of a special administrative region for Taiwan, within which she would have near-autonomy, an arrangement which in 1983 Deng characterized as "one country, two systems."[45]

Beijing's unexpected shift in policy toward Taiwan and her unification formula were initially viewed with skepticism by the Guomindang regime, given the contrast in political, economic and social development between the two sides. President Chiang Ching-kuo attributed this to the application of Marxism-Leninism in China and the doctrines of Sun Yat-sen in Taiwan. While reiterating his administration's policy of the "three no's" (i.e., no contact, no negotiation and no compromise), he declared that unification was only possible on the basis of the Guomindang's interpretation of Sun Yat-sen's Three Principles of the People.

The thaw in relations began in 1986. On May 3, a Taiwanese pilot landed a China Airlines cargo plane en route to Bangkok at Guangzhou's international airport, where he defected. The incident forced the Taiwan authorities to appoint official representatives to meet with PRC officials in Hong Kong, the first such meeting since 1949. The following year, Chiang lifted martial law and allowed Taiwanese residents to visit relatives on the mainland. The ban on commercial and cultural exchanges with the mainland was relaxed, though these still had to be conducted indirectly. In 1988, Chen Li-fu, a respected member of the Guomindang, proposed a formula for negotiating reunification with the mainland based on Chinese culture. To establish a "common confidence" between the Guomindang and the CPC, he proposed investing Taiwan's foreign exchange reserves on the mainland, and for the two sides to work together to implement Sun Yat-sen's economic program as outlined in *The International Development of China*.[46]

The rapprochement between the two former combatants was shattered by the Tiananmen Square protests of June 1989. Earlier concerns about PRC governance resurfaced, as did skepticism about the prospects for reunification. Nevertheless, the potential for reunification based on Sun's Three Principles of the People remained very much alive, as evidenced by the public display of Sun's portrait in China, references to his Principles by officials as a format for reunification, and the continued expansion in trade across the Strait.

In February 1991, the Nationalist government adopted the National Unification Plan, which laid out a three-stage process for developing relations with the mainland. In May, it officially ended its hostility toward the PRC. A semi-official Strait Exchange Foundation (SEF) was formed to take charge of unofficial exchange. Respecting Taiwan's desire to engage only in unofficial exchange, the PRC created the Association for Relations Across the Taiwan Strait (ARATS). A meeting between representatives of SEF and ARATS in Hong Kong in December 1991 produced the so-called 1992 Consensus, which states that there is only one China but leaves each side to define what that means. The SEF and ARATS subsequently held many meetings, the most important of which were the talks between ARATS Chairman Wang Daohan and SEF Chairman Koo Chen-fu in Singapore in April 1993.

In 1994, Taipei formally dropped its long-time policy of competing with Beijing for the right to represent China and began to adopt the concept of "two Chinas" or "one China one Taiwan." Beginning in February, Lee Teng-hui embarked on an aggressive diplomatic campaign to raise Taiwan's international visibility, visiting Southeast Asia, Africa, Central America and the Middle East. Beijing viewed his diplomacy as a prelude to independence and exerted pressure on countries that had diplomatic ties with Beijing not to treat Lee as a head of state, or extend him customary diplomatic privileges. Despite Beijing's diplomatic efforts on the Clinton administration to stop Lee from visiting the U.S., Lee made his historic visit to his alma mater Cornell in June 1995. Cross-Strait relations quickly deteriorated and the PRC conducted two missile tests off the coast of Taiwan.

Lee's intentions soon became clear. In 1999, he overturned the Guomindang's "One China policy" and proposed his "two-state theory," and declared that future negotiations would take place only on a "special state-to-state" basis. Both the PRC and a significant section of the Guomindang felt that these tacit declarations of quasi-independence betrayed Sun Yat-sen's principles, which for many were the philosophical key that bridged the gap between China and Taiwan's competing ideologies. As part of the nativization of Taiwan's national history and culture, the pro-independence camp challenged Sun's image as the father of the nation.

The election of Chen Shui-bian of the Democratic Progressive Party (DPP) to the presidency in 2000 further changed Taiwan's mainland policy. Shortly after taking office, Chen began talking about promulgating a new constitution and creating a "Taiwanese identity" through a process of de-sinicization, while his administration adopted a series of policies designed to delink Taiwan from China. Two years later, he openly described cross-Strait relations as "one state on each side." Consequently, all contact between SEF and ARATS came to a complete halt and there was rising tension and hostility across the Taiwan Strait. Chen's provocative policies led Beijing in 2005 to adopt the "Anti-secession Law" which sanctioned the use of "non-peaceful means" to counter any attempt by Taiwan to declare independence. The following year, Chen abolished the National Unification Plan and pushed for a referendum on Taiwan's admission to the United Nations, amendments to the constitution and limits on investments on the mainland. Despite rising political tensions, however, economic ties and other non-governmental exchanges across the Strait continued to expand, driven largely by market forces and globalization.[47]

In 2008 Ma Ying-jeou promised in his inauguration address that there would be "no reunification, no independence and no war" but otherwise pursued a policy of active engagement with the mainland. Mainland tourists were allowed to visit Taiwan, trade and investment were relaxed, and direct flights, shipping and postal services finally instituted. The signing of the Economic Cooperation Framework Agreement (ECFA) in June 2010 paved the way for free trade and was one of the many agreements signed by Ma's administration with China. These measures did little to create good jobs for the many young Taiwanese worried about their future. In February, a radical independence group took down a statue of Sun Yat-sen in the southern city of Tainan. The following month, frustration boiled over into the Sunflower Movement. Students and social activists occupied the legislative building to protest against the Cross-Strait Services Trade Agreement. Nonetheless, cross-Strait relations took a quantum step forward when Ma met with Xi Jinping in Singapore in November 2015, the first between the presidents of China and Taiwan.

Tsai Ing-wen's presidency got off to a confusing start in 2016. While vowing to reduce Taiwan's economic dependency on the mainland and refusing to acknowledge the 1992 Consensus, she nevertheless led senior officials in paying tribute to Sun Yat-sen at the Martyrs' Shrine four days after her inauguration amidst protests by pro-independence activists. The following day, she halted a controversial proposal by a DPP legislator to remove portraits of Sun from public buildings as required by a 1945 law.[48] Then in December 2016 she phoned President-elect Donald Trump ostensibly to congratulate him on his electoral victory. This was the first direct contact between the U.S. and Taiwanese presidents since the breaking off of diplomatic relations in 1979. After the call, Trump declared that the U.S. was not bound by the One China policy, adding that he might use it as a bargaining chip to wrest trade and other concessions from Beijing. Tsai appeared to have scored a minor diplomatic victory but her high-stakes gamble backfired. She did not get to meet Trump during her January 2017 stopovers in the U.S. en route to and from South America. In February, Trump reaffirmed the One China policy during a telephone conversation with Xi Jinping, thus ending all speculation. In April, Xi visited the U.S. and met with Trump, who emerged from the meeting declaring Xi to be a "great guy" with whom he got on "very, very" well and developed a "terrific" relationship. Trump later said that he was not going to declare China a currency manipulator, thus reversing one of his most touted campaign promises.

Tsai's brazen act undoubtedly cheered pro-independence Taiwanese as surely as it would have infuriated those in favor of maintaining the status quo or unification. But her tribute to Sun and the suppression of the DPP proposal to remove his portraits from public buildings suggest that the *Guofu* will continue to dominate cross-Strait relations for some time. But if he were alive today, Sun would have been saddened that China remains a divided country almost 90 years after the successful completion of the Northern Expedition that nominally unified China. That the possibility of war still looms large over the Chinese nation like a Sword of Damocles would have greatly distressed him, particularly since the belligerents are the heirs to the United Front that he created to unite China.

On the other hand, Sun would have been struck by China's transformation from a poor, backward and debt-ridden country into a global power with its own nuclear arsenal and space program, huge foreign exchange reserves, and an economy that will soon surpass that of the U.S. Given that all these were achieved on the back of the old Chinese entrepreneurial spirit and China's opening to the world, the *Guofu* would have been vindicated in his belief that communism was suited neither to the Chinese temperament nor to Chinese culture. He would have been especially gratified that China has replaced class struggle with nationalism, and substituted globalization for world revolution. He would have approved of Xi Jinping's creation of the Asian Infrastructure Investment Bank and his Belt and Road Initiative to promote the economic development in Asia. If Sun could see all this, he would be able to take comfort that his life's work was not in vain. For while Mao fostered national unity on the Chinese mainland and Deng Xiaoping brought hundreds of millions of Chinese out of the poverty line to the shopping line, the vision that drives modern China clearly emanates from Sun Yat-sen.

EPILOGUE

In a life of 60 years spanning a period of dramatic turmoil in China as the once-proud nation struggled to break out of her quagmire and restore her greatness, Sun Yat-sen devoted almost his entire adulthood to the salvation of his country. His life, however, is a story of frustrated hopes and shattered dreams. The uprisings against the Manchu overlords failed repeatedly. He held power for only a brief moment, relinquishing it to obtain the abdication of the Qing dynasty and avoid a prolonged civil war. The republic he created turned into a fiasco, hijacked by Yuan Shikai and corrupted by warlords and self-seeking politicians. His vision of China crisscrossed by networks of railways fell on deaf ears and nothing came out of his grandiose plans for China's economic transformation within his lifetime. No foreign government recognized any regime he headed and none paid any heed to his overtures and appeals for help. He died without achieving his dream of a modern and united China.

Sun's deep personal commitment to China never wavered even in the face of so many setbacks. Such determination could only have come from an "enduring confidence both in his cause and in himself."[1] He was not always practical, and some of his ideas and dealings might raise eyebrows even today. But whatever he did, he did for the good of China. To his fellow countrymen, he was a "patriot of unique purity," a symbol of selfless love of country. He was a prophet of Chinese nationalism whose vision extended beyond space and time. Today he is both a symbol of the unfinished Chinese revolution, as well as an icon of China's unity. No one from his chaotic age matches his reputation for integrity, courage and selfless commitment. This is why generations of ethnic Chinese all over the world continue to revere and celebrate him.

A university on each side of the Taiwan Strait bears his name.[2] His portraits adorn all public buildings and schools in Taiwan. On the Chinese mainland are numerous museums and memorial halls dedicated to his memory. Some, like the one in Nanjing, are national in character and reinforce the official discourse. Others, such as the one in Zhongshan city in Guangdong, are focused on specific interests. In virtually every city there is at least a public park, a thoroughfare, a square or other public landmark named in his honor. This is remarkable in a country where government policy eschews the naming of public landmarks after her leaders. Even more remarkable are the public facilities and other landmarks beyond Greater China that bear his name, some of them in the most unlikely places: a classical Chinese garden in Vancouver; a museum in Chicago; a memorial park in Honolulu; a street in Port Louis, Mauritius, and a road in Kolkata, India; a memorial hall in Kobe; and a relief at the Hakusan Shrine in Tokyo, to name just a few. There are probably more public landmarks dedicated to the memory of Sun Yat-sen than any other historical figure anywhere in the world.

The anniversary of his birth and death are regularly commemorated around the world, with the decade turns generally on a grander scale than other years. In 2016, the 150th anniversary of his birth, the celebrations kicked off in May with a conference at the East-West Center in Hawaii. This was followed by an all-day forum in August at the University of Hawaii Manoa campus to examine Sun's revolution. In October, a forum was held in Fukuoka, Japan, at which some 200 scholars, college students and entrepreneurs from China, Japan, Singapore and Canada, among other countries, gathered to review and study Sun's ideas and their significance. In Singapore, the Sun Yat-sen Nanyang Memorial Hall held a special exhibition, "One Night in Wuchang," while the Sun Yat-sen Museum in Penang launched a new version of the 2007 movie, "Road to Dawn," which dramatizes Sun's time in Penang in 1910. Even the Philippines, which had just resolved her differences with China over the South China Sea, issued an 18-peso stamp with a portrait of Sun Yat-sen with Mario Ponce, Sun's co-conspirator to smuggle Japanese arms to the Filipino independence movement in 1899.

A number of events were organized throughout Greater China. In Zhongshan, more than 300 people, including descendants of Sun and his followers and many from Hong Kong, Macau, Taiwan and Singapore, gathered at his former home to pay tribute. In the provincial capital,

EPILOGUE

Sun Yat-sen and Abraham Lincoln on a 1942 U.S. postage stamp. Under Sun's portrait appear the Chinese words for his Three Principles of the People – Nationalism, Democracy and People's Livelihood.

Set of four stamps issued in 2016 by the PRC to commemorate the 150th anniversary of Sun's birth. Similar stamps were issued separately by the postal authorities of Hong Kong and Macau.

Guangzhou, senior officials and grassroots leaders gathered at the Sun Yat-sen Memorial Hall to commemorate him. Local authorities in Shanghai held a conference while local officials and others gathered to pay respects at Sun's former residence. In Nanjing, nearly 200 officials and local residents visited the Sun Yat-sen Mausoleum to pay tribute. In Taipei, the chairwoman of the Guomindang unveiled a special exhibition at the Sun Yat-sen Memorial Hall. Events were also organized in other Chinese cities, as well as in Hong Kong and Macau. The postal authorities of China, Hong Kong and Macau separately issued special sets of stamps to commemorate the occasion. The People's Bank of China issued a set of three commemorative coins: a gold coin worth 100 yuan (US$14.80), a silver coin worth 10-yuan and one made of copper alloy worth 5 yuan. The last circulates as normal Chinese currency, the first one with Sun's image to do so.

China's leaders have been acknowledging Sun since the early days of the People's Republic, with official statements issued on every anniversary of his birth and death. In 2016, a conference was held on November 11 at the Great Hall of the People in Beijing to celebrate the 150th anniversary

343

of Sun's birth. At the gathering attended by senior party and government officials, President Xi Jinping underscored China's determination to safeguard her sovereignty and territorial integrity, and stamp out any attempt to divide the nation: "All activities that intend to divide the country will certainly be firmly opposed by all Chinese people. We will never allow any one, any organization, any party to split off any tract of territory from China anytime, or in any way." Holding up Sun Yat-sen as a champion of China's unity, he said: "The best way we commemorate Sun Yat-sen is to learn and carry forward his invaluable spirit, to unite all that can be united and mobilize all that can be mobilized to carry on the pursuit for a rejuvenated China that he had dreamed of." Xi was responding to the growing calls for independence in Taiwan. That he used the occasion to address it and directly invoked Sun's name to the task is significant. It is an affirmation of the CPC's continuing effort to use the "common celebration of Sun's memory" as a "useful psychological bridge"[3] for the eventual return of Taiwan to the bosom of the motherland.

Xi's speech reflected the Chinese leadership's revived concern that Taiwan under newly elected president Tsai Ing-wen might again seek independence, as her DPP predecessor Chen Shui-bian had attempted a decade earlier. Why does Taiwan, a small island with a population of less than 24 million, rank so high in the Chinese leadership's consciousness and national policy agenda? Obviously no country wants to give up territory, no matter how insignificant. But to risk war with the U.S. and give up all the economic progress made just to hold on to a small island? To understand Chinese leaders' absorption with the reunification of Taiwan, it is necessary to appreciate what it would mean for China if Taiwan were to break away.

China is encircled by U.S. military bases in countries that form an arc stretching from South Korea and Japan in the north and running southward to the Philippines, Thailand, Singapore and Australia. There are currently no U.S. bases or military installations in Taiwan but an independent Taiwan could very well be used in a de facto alliance with Japan and South Korea to contain China's rise. China is heavily dependent on imported oil from the Middle East. The Taiwan Strait is just 100 miles (160 km) wide and an independent Taiwan with foreign support would have the ability to disrupt China's supply lines, with possibly devastating consequences for China's economy and stability.

To maintain its relevance in a globalizing China, the CPC has been promoting Chinese nationalism to bolster its own legitimacy. By making reunification a core party goal, it has effectively linked the Taiwan issue with its own legitimacy. If Beijing is unable to prevent Taiwan's independence, it could be used as an excuse by dissidents and activists to oppose the party and possibly usurp power. The loss of Taiwan would also upset the integration of restive regions, which has been relatively successful to date, and set a dangerous precedent for Xinjiang and Tibet, where there are already separatist movements. No Chinese leader or leadership group could survive if Taiwan is lost under its watch.

Above all, Taiwan's critical importance to contemporary China stems from her humiliation by imperialist powers. Taiwan was Japan's trophy for her victory in the Sino-Japanese War in 1895 but was returned to Chinese sovereignty with Japan's defeat in World War II. After Chiang Kai-shek fled to Taiwan, he began launching counteroffensives to retake China, which the PRC responded to with equal vigor. Truman had effectively abandoned Chiang but the outbreak of the Korean War brought to the fore the fact that a communist Taiwan would create "an enemy salient in the very center" of a U.S. strategic perimeter.[4] Accordingly, Truman ordered the 7th Fleet to the Taiwan Strait, whose presence caused the PLA to abort its planned invasion of Taiwan and transformed the island from a Chinese domestic issue into a Sino-U.S. relations conflict.

In December 1954, the U.S. signed the Mutual Defense Treaty with Taiwan. With U.S. support, Taiwan represented China at the United Nations but under increasing pressure from Communist and developing states, was replaced by the PRC in 1971. Beijing's victory at the UN was the result of the emerging Sino-American rapprochement prompted by Washington's hope of enlisting Beijing in a global containment of the Soviet Union. During Nixon's visit to China in February 1972, he signed the Shanghai Communiqué which committed Washington to progressively reduce its military presence in Taiwan and ultimately withdraw all U.S. military troops from the island. The communiqué also acknowledged the United States' "One China" policy and left the Taiwan question to be settled by the Chinese themselves. However, it was not until January 1979, during the Carter administration, that the U.S. severed diplomatic ties with Taiwan, abrogated the Mutual Defense Treaty, withdrew her military from Taiwan, and established official relations with Beijing.

The Taiwan Relations Act enacted by the U.S. Congress in February 1979 prevented Taiwan from a possible takeover by the PRC. The Act does not bind the U.S. to come to Taiwan's defense, but it does require the U.S. president to regard any Chinese use of force against Taiwan as a "threat to the peace and security" of the region. The Act also authorizes the sale of U.S. defensive arms to enable Taiwan to defend herself. Every administration from Carter to Obama has sold arms to Taiwan over protests from Beijing. The last sale was in late 2015, during the Obama administration. In March this year, the Trump administration was reported to be crafting a new arms package for Taiwan, which however has been delayed by the president as he tries to get Beijing to do more to rein in North Korea, which has launched a dozen missile tests since February through July 2017.

With the return of Hong Kong and Macau in 1997 and 1999 respectively, Taiwan is the last significant Chinese territory that is still not under China's sovereignty. Chinese state and party declarations portray the Taiwan issue as the last vestige of the humiliations inflicted on a helpless China in the heydays of Western and Japanese imperialism. There are also those who see the continuing arms sales to Taiwan as a sign of the U.S. perpetuating the humiliation and the main obstacle to China assuming her rightful place in the world. Indeed, Taiwan is China's Achilles' heel. So long as she remains separated from China, Taiwan can be used as a pawn to pressure China into tuning her national agenda to coincide with the U.S.'s geopolitical priorities and the vagaries of her domestic politics. Thus, while China today is the second most powerful nation in the world after the U.S., she is still not the mistress of her own destiny, and the revolution inspired by Sun Yat-sen to create a modern China free from foreign interference remains a work in progress. That is why I have called Sun's revolution the Unfinished Revolution.

NOTES

PREFACE

1. The source for this story is Robert Lawrence Kuhn, *How China's Leaders Think* (Singapore: John Wiley, 2010), 382–3.
2. Yuan Xunhui, Zhang Juan and Shannon Tiezzi, "A Chinese Perspective on Obama's Asia Policy: An Interview with Zhu Feng." *The Diplomat* (November 9, 2016).
3. Odd Arne Westad, *Restless Empire: China and the World since 1750* (New York: Basic Books, 2012), 2. Westad is the ST Lee Professor of U.S.–Asia Relations, John F. Kennedy School of Government, Harvard University.
4. Ooi Kee Beng, *The Eurasian Core and its Edges: Dialogues with Wang Gungwu on the History of the World* (Singapore: ISEAS Publishing, 2015).

PROLOGUE

1. The Jurchens spoke a Tungusic language which together with the Turkic, Mongolic, Koreanic and Japonic languages form the Altaic language family, named after the Altaic Mountains in Central Asia. See Stefan Georg, et al, "Telling General Linguistics About Altaic" in *Journal of Linguistics* 35 no. 1 (March 1999), 65–98. Manchuria is a name used mainly by Japanese and Westerners to refer to a large geographical region in northeast China now occupied by Heilongjiang, Jilin and Liaoning provinces, as well as part of today's North Korea and Russia. The Chinese call the region Dongbei (Northeast), an abbreviated form of the Chinese term Dongbei Sansheng (Three Northeast Provinces).
2. "China Proper" is a term coined by Western writers to refer to the 18 historic provinces within the Great Wall. Manchuria, Mongolia, Tibet and Xinjiang were known during the Qing era as Outer China.
3. The Kangxi, Yongzheng and Qianlong emperors.
4. Opium is the dried latex of the poppy plant. Arab traders introduced its cultivation to China sometime during the Tang dynasty. The poppy was used initially as a medicinal herb and it was not until the 15th or 16th century that the making of opium from poppies began. By the mid-17th century, the Chinese were smoking a mixture of opium and tobacco, a practice introduced by Portuguese traders. It was probably at some point in the 18th century that the Chinese dropped the tobacco and started smoking pure opium. The

Portuguese and the Dutch are believed to have pioneered the opium trade in China, but it remained relatively small until the British got in on the act. See Xiaoxiong Li, *Poppies and Politics in China: Sichuan Province, 1840s to 1940s* (Newark, NJ: University of Delaware Press, 2009), 24.

5 The full text of Commissioner Lin's letter to Queen Victoria has been translated in Ssu-yu Teng and John K. Fairbank (eds.), *China's Response to the West* (Cambridge, MA: Harvard University Press, 1982), 24–27.

6 Hsin-pao Chang, *Commissioner Lin and the Opium War* (Cambridge: Harvard University Press, 1964), 192–93.

7 The five treaty ports were Guangzhou, Shanghai, Xiamen, Fuzhou and Ningbo.

8 There are numerous books on the Taiping rebellion but two that I find particularly interesting are Jonathan Spence, *God's Chinese Son: The Taiping Heavenly Kingdom of Hong Xiuquan* (London: HarperCollins, 1996) and Thomas H. Reilly, *The Taiping Heavenly Kingdom* (Seattle, WA: University of Washington Press, 2004).

9 An excellent text on the Chinese Maritime Customs Service is Hans van de Ven, *Breaking with the Past: The Maritime Customs Service and the Global Origins of Modernity in China* (New York, NY: Columbia University Press, 2014).

10 Not to be confused with Yiheyuan, the Summer Palace with the marble boat in the northwestern suburb of Beijing which was restored in 1888 on the orders of the Empress Dowager Cixi. The Yuanmingyuan (Garden of Perfect Brightness) was started by the Kangxi Emperor in 1709 and substantially reconstructed by the Qianlong Emperor. It has been left in ruins as a reminder of the damage done by British and French troops in 1860. See Carol Brown Malone, *History of the Peking Summer Palace under the Ch'ing Dynasty* (Urbana: University of Illinois Press, 1934), reprint (New York: Paragon Book Reprint, 1966).

11 Immanuel Hsu, *The Rise of Modern China*, 6th ed. (New York: Oxford University Press, 2000), 215–16.

12 Hsi-sheng Ch'i, *Warlord Politics in China, 1916–1928* (Stanford: Stanford University Press, 1976), 11-12

13 Karl Marx, "Revolution in China and in Europe," *New York Daily Tribute* (June 14, 1853).

14 See Hodong Kim, *Holy War in China: The Muslim Rebellion and State in Chinese Central Asia, 1864–1877* (Stanford: Stanford University Press, 2004) for an account of the rebellion and how Russia came to control Ili.

15 Hsu, *Modern China*, 261.

16 Ibid., 251–52.

NOTES

17 Mary Clabaugh Wright, *The Last Stand of Chinese Conservatism: The T'ung-chih Restoration, 1862–1874* (Stanford: Stanford University Press, 1957), 45.
18 Hsu, *Modern China*, 266
19 Before the Opium War, tributary affairs were conducted by the Ministry of Rites. Relations with Russia and Central Asia were governed by the Lifan Yuan (Office of Colonial Affairs). Trade with the West was under the jurisdiction of the governor-general at Guangzhou, who delegated it to the Cohong and *hong* merchants. Between the two opium wars, the governors-general at Guangzhou and Nanjing were China's de facto foreign and deputy foreign ministers.
20 Jerome B. Grieder, *Intellectuals and the State in Modern China: A Narrative History* (New York: The Free Press, 1981), 68.
21 Teng and Fairbank, *China's Response*, 30–35.
22 Timothy B. Weston, *The Power of Position* (Berkeley and Los Angeles, CA: University of California Press, 2004), 15–17.
23 Grieder, *Intellectuals*, 69.
24 An excellent text on the Chinese Education Mission is Edward J.M. Rhoads, *Stepping Forth into the World: The Chinese Education Mission to the United States, 1872–1881* (Hong Kong: Hong Kong University Press, 2011).
25 The assessments of the Self-Strengthening Movement in this and the next paragraph are from Jonathan D. Spence, *The Search for Modern China* (New York: Norton, 1990), 217–20; Hsu, *Modern China*, 287–91, and John King Fairbank, *The Great Chinese Revolution, 1800–1985* (New York: Harper & Row, 1986), 120–21.
26 Frederic Wakeman, Jr., *The Fall of Imperial China* (New York: The Free Press, 1975), 185–86.

CHAPTER 1: HOPE OF THE NATION

1 Jaeyoon Kim, "The Heaven and Earth Society and the Red Turban Rebellion in Late Qing China," *Journal of Humanities & Social Sciences* 3 no. 1 (2009), 1–35.
2 Nanyang, literally Southern Ocean, is the Chinese term for what is today's Southeast Asia, though the two terms are not exact equivalents. Nanyang used to refer to the countries immediately to the south of China. This included British Malaya, British Burma, the Dutch East Indies, French Indochina, Siam and sometimes also Ceylon and British India. Today when we speak of the Nanyang Chinese, we are referring to those Chinese settled in countries reachable by sea, i.e., Indonesia, Malaysia, Philippines and Singapore. It does not include those Chinese who migrated overland to countries on the Asian landmass from neighboring Chinese provinces. See Lynn Pan (ed.), *Encyclopedia of the Chinese Overseas* (Singapore: Chinese Heritage Centre and Editions Didier Millet, 2006), 16.

3   Helen G. Pratt, *In Hawaii: A Hundred Years* (New York, NY: Charles Scribner's Sons, 1939), 249.
4   Henry B. Restarick, *Sun Yat-sen, Liberator of China* (New Haven, CT: Yale University, 1931), 14.
5   Harold Z. Schiffrin, *Sun Yat-sen and the Origins of the Chinese Revolution* (Berkeley: University of California Press, 1968), 13.
6   Yen Ching-hwang, *Overseas Chinese and the 1911 Revolution* (Kuala Lumpur: Oxford University Press, 1976), 131n45.
7   Restarick, *Liberator*, 17.
8   Francis Tsui, *Hong Kong: Where a Future Revolutionary Leader was Nurtured* (Honolulu: Dr. Sun Yat-sen Hawaii Foundation, n.d.). http://sunyatsenhawaii.org/index.php?option=com_content&view=article&id=105%3Ahong-kong-where-a-future-revolutionary-leader-was-nurtured&catid=52%3Aa-humanities-guide&Itemid=101&lang=en
9   Harold Z. Schiffrin, *Sun Yat-sen: Reluctant Revolutionary* (Boston: Little, Brown and Co., 1980), 26.
10 Renamed Victoria College in 1889 and Queen's College in 1894.
11 Sun's baptism may have been in late 1893. See Lyon Sharman, *Sun Yat-sen, His Life and Its Meaning: A Critical Biography* (Stanford: Stanford University Press, 1934), 382–387.
12 Yuen Seng Leung, "Religion and Revolution – The Response of the Singapore Chinese to the Revolutionary Movement in China," in Lee Lai To, *The 1911 Revolution* (Singapore: Heinemann Asia, 1987), 67.
13 The principal text on the Sino-French War in this and the following four paragraphs is Immanuel Hsu, *Modern China, The Rise of Modern China*, 6th ed. (New York: Oxford University Press, 2000), 325–330.
14 Schiffrin, *Revolutionary*, 27.
15 Schiffrin, *Origins*, 17
16 Canton Hospital was renamed Boji Hospital in 1860. See Chi-chao Chan, Melissa Liu and James C. Tsai, "The First Western Style Hospital in China," *Archives of Ophthalmology* 129, no. 6 (June 2011), 793.
17 Schiffrin, *Revolutionary*, 29.
18 G.H. Choa, *The Life and Times of Sir Ho Kai: A Prominent Figure in Nineteenth-Century Hong Kong*, 2nd Ed. (Hong Kong: The Chinese University Press, 2000).
19 In 1954, Alice Memorial Hospital, Nethersole Hospital and Ho Miu Ling Hospital were merged to form the Alice Ho Miu Ling Nethersole Hospital. Ho Miu Ling was the elder sister of Ho Kai.

NOTES

20 James Cantlie and Sheridan Jones, *Sun Yat-sen and the Awakening of China* (New York, NY: Fleming H. Revell Co., 1912).
21 Marie-Claire Bergere, *Sun Yat-sen,* trans. Janet Lloyd (Stanford: Stanford University Press, 1998), 34.
22 Schiffrin, *Origins,* 27–28.
23 Guo Wu, *Zheng Guanying: Merchant Reformer of Late Qing China and His Influence on Economics, Politics and Society* (Amherst, NY: Cambria Press, 2010), 1–2.
24 Sidney H. Chang and Leonard H. Gordon, *All Under Heaven: Sun Yat-sen and His Revolutionary Thought* (Stanford, CA: Stanford University Press, 1991), 12.
25 Chang and Gordon, *All Under Heaven,* 15.
26 Schiffrin, *Origins,* 37.
27 Bergere, *Sun,* 40.

CHAPTER 2: BAPTISM BY FIRE

1 For further reading on the Sino-Japanese War, see S.C.M. Paine. *The Sino-Japanese War of 1894–1895* (Cambridge: Cambridge University Press, 2003). A shorter account is Bruce Ellerman, *Modern Chinese Warfare, 1795–1989* (London: Routledge, 2001), Chap. 7: The Sino-Japanese War and the Partitioning of China.
2 Schiffrin, *Revolutionary,* 38.
3 Bergere, *Sun,* 51.
4 See Chun-tu Hsueh, "Sun Yat-sen, Yang Ch'u-yun, and the Early Revolutionary Movement in China," *The Journal of Asian Studies,* 19, no. 3 (May 1960), 307–318, for a more detailed biography of Yang Quyun.
5 Schiffrin, *Revolutionary,* 39.
6 Bergere, *Sun,* 53–55.
7 Peter B. High, *Umeya Shokichi: The Revolutionist as Impresario* (Nagoya University, n.d.), 108–111.
8 The account of the planning for the Guangzhou Uprising in this and the next paragraph is from Schiffrin, *Origins,* 61–62. Umeya Shokichi's procurement of arms is from High, *Umeya,* 111.
9 Schiffrin, *Origins,* 63.
10 The membership composition of the Xingzhonghui is from Schiffrin, *Origins,* 54–55.
11 Ibid., 83–87.
12 High, *Umeya,* 112
13 Bergere, *Sun,* 58–59.
14 Sun Yat-sen, *Kidnapped in London* (Bristol: J.W. Arrowsmith, 1897), 32–37.

15 Schiffrin, *Origins*, 119.
16 Sun, *Kidnapped,* 133–134.
17 Sharman, *Critical Biography*, 47–48.
18 Sun Yat-sen, "China's Present and Future: The Reform Party's Plea for British Benevolent Neutrality," *Fortnightly Review*, 61 no. 363 (March 1, 1897), 424–425 and 440.
19 Schiffrin, *Origins*, 138–139.

CHAPTER 3: MAN OF HIGH PURPOSE

1 The main text for the discussion on pan-Asianism in this and the following four paragraphs is Bergere, *Sun,* 71–73. The Kokuryukai derived its name from the translation of the Amur River, which the Chinese call Heilongjiang, or the Black Dragon River, which in Japanese is Kokuryuko. See also Eri Hotta, *Pan-Asianism and Japan's War 1931–1945* (New York: Palgrave Macmillan, 2007), which traces the evolution of the Pan-Asianist ideal, and how it was later used to justify Japanese aggression in China and other Asian countries.
2 Schiffrin, *Origins*, 141.
3 The meeting between Sun and Miyazaki in this and the next two paragraphs, including the quotations, is from the latter's account in his autobiography, *My Thirty-Three Year's Dream: The Autobiography of Miyazaki Toten,* trans. Eto Shinkichi and Marius B. Jansen (Princeton, NJ: Princeton University Press, 1982), 133–137.
4 Schiffrin, *Revolutionary,* 69.
5 The main text for this and the next three paragraphs is Marius Jansen, *The Japanese and Sun Yat-sen* (Cambridge, MA: Harvard University Press, 1954), 76–78.
6 Kang had initially thought of "Baoguohui" (Protect the Nation Society), the name of a short-lived organization that he had formed in China in 1898. "Baohuanghui" was suggested by a local leader in Victoria, B.C. Kang agreed that it would be a good strategy to link the organization to the person of the emperor. The official English name of the Baohuanghui was "Chinese Empire Reform Society." In 1907, it was succeeded by the Xianzhenghui, or Constitutional Association. See Jane Leung Larson, "An Association to Save China, the Baohuanghui: A Documentary Account," *China Heritage Quarterly*, no. 27 (Sep 2011).
7 Sun's involvement with the Philippine independence movement in this and the next three paragraphs is from Jansen, *Sun Yat-sen,* 68–74, and Schiffrin, *Origins,* 167–169.
8 Schiffrin, *Revolutionary,* 67.

9   Schiffrin, *Origins*, 170–171; Hsieh Chun-tu, "Sun Yat-sen, Yang Ch'u-yun, and the Early Revolutionary Movement in China," *Journal of Asian Studies* 19 no. 3 (May 1960), 313.
10 Gloria Davies, "Liang Qichao in Australia: A Sojourn of No Significance?" *China Heritage Quarterly* no. 27 (Sep 2011).
11 Schiffrin, *Origins*, 163–164.
12 Davies, "Liang Qichao."
13 This and the next paragraph from J.Y. Wong, "Three Visionaries in Exile: Yung Wing, Kang Yu-wei and Sun Yat-sen," *Journal of Asian History* 20 no. 1 (1966), 14–15.
14 Schiffrin, *Origins*, 218–219.

CHAPTER 4: COALITION OF THE UNWILLING

1   Weihaiwei was the base of the Beiyang Fleet until the Japanese captured it in the Sino-Japanese War in 1895.
2   Hsu, *Modern China*, 348–350.
3   Ibid., 388–390.
4   Fairbank, *Chinese Revolution*, 137.
5   J.A.G. Roberts, *A History of China* (London: Palgrave Macmillan, 2006), 198.
6   Wang Gungwu, *Chinese Reformists and Revolutionaries in the Straits Settlements: 1900–1911* (Singapore: [n.s], 1953), 60. The 24th day of the 12th moon of the 25th year of the Guangxu reign is January 24, 1900, on the Gregorian calendar.
7   Yen, *1911 Revolution*, 80n129.
8   Schiffrin, *Origins*, 180.
9   Jansen in *Sun Yat-sen*, 87, identifies the ship as *Nippon Maru*.
10 See Miyazaki, *Autobiography*, 209–211, for a more detailed account of the interrogation and arrest of Miyazaki and Kyofuji in this and the next paragraph.
11 J. Kim Munholland, "The French Connection That Failed: France and Sun Yat-sen, 1900–1908," *Journal of Asian Studies* 32, no. 1 (Nov 1972): 78.
12 This and the next paragraph from Bergere, *Sun*, 115–117, and Munholland, ibid., 79.
13 Miyazaki, *Autobiography*, 231.
14 Lim Boon Keng, "The Chinese Revolutionary Movement in Malaya," *Straits Philosophical Society* (July 12, 1913), 55. Goh Kit Moh is transliterated as Wu Chieh-wu in Yen, *1911 Revolution*, 40.
15 Lim Boon Keng, *The Chinese Crisis from Within*, Rev. ed. (Singapore: Select Publications, 2006), Introduction, i-xiv.
16 Schiffrin, *Origins*, 195.

17 In some accounts, Sun is said to have been served with a five-year banishment order as well. The orders against Miyazaki and Kiyofuji appear in the *Straits Settlement Government Gazette* of July 20, 1900. If Sun had been served with a similar order, this would have been reported in the Gazette, either in the same issue, or the issue immediately preceding or following. No such order is found in any of these issues.
18 Schiffrin, *Origins*, 196.
19 Yen, *1911 Revolution*, 40.
20 The quotations from the *Daily Mail* and the *Times* are from Lo Hui-min (ed.), *The Correspondence of G.E. Morrison*, vol. 1, 1895–1912 (Cambridge: Cambridge University Press, 1976), 139–140.
21 Cheng Huanwen and Donald G. Davis, "Loss of a Recorded Heritage: Destruction of Chinese Book in the Peking Siege of 1900," *Library Trends* 55 no. 3 (University of Illinois, Winter 2007), 431–441.
22 Hsu, *Modern China*, 398.
23 This and the next paragraph from Schiffrin, *Origins*, 219 and 223–224.
24 The main text for the Huizhou Uprising in this and the following five paragraphs is Edward J.M. Rhoads, *China's Republican Revolution: The Case of Kwangtung, 1895–1913* (Cambridge, MA: Harvard University Press, 1975), 43–46.
25 Hsu, *Modern China*, 399–401.
26 The Zongli Yamen was converted to the Waiwubu in June 1901.
27 Hsu. *Modern China*, 401–404.
28 Bergere, *Sun*, 95–96.

CHAPTER 5: THE TURNING POINT

1 Marius Jansen, *Japan and China: From War to Peace, 1894–1972* (Chicago, IL: Rand McNally, 1975), ch. 5, and Ranbir Vohra, *China's Path to Modernization: A Historical Review from 1800 to the Present* (Upper Saddle River, NJ: Prentice Hall, 1987), ch. 4, cited in David Gordon, *Sun Yatsen: Seeking a Newer China* (Upper Saddle River, NJ: Pearson Education, 2010), 37.
2 This and the next two paragraphs from Schiffrin, *Revolutionary*, 90–96.
3 The mistress was Otsuki Kaori, the daughter of a Japanese merchant with whom Sun had lodged in 1898. See Chapter 16, The Man and His Legacy.
4 Hong Kong Museum of History, *Dr Sun Yat-sen and Hong Kong* (Hong Kong: Hong Kong Museum of History, 2013), 174–175.
5 Sun's meeting with Beau in this and the next two paragraphs is from Munholland, "French Connection," 79–80.

6. Jeffrey G. Barlow, *Sun Yat-sen and the French 1900–1908* (Berkeley: University of California Press, 1979), 36.
7. HK Museum of History, *Sun Yat-sen,* 58n51. However, see Barlow, *Sun Yat-sen,* 36.
8. See Harold Z. Schiffrin, "Sun Yat-sen's Early Land Policy: The Origin and Meaning of Equalization of Land Rights," *Journal of Asian Studies,* 16, no. 4 (Aug 1957), 549–564.
9. Henry George, *Progress and Poverty,* ed. and abr. Bob Drake (New York: Robert Schalkenbach Foundation, 2006).
10. Schiffrin, *Origins,* 308–309.
11. Ibid., 333–338. Marquis de Lafayette was a French aristocrat and military officer who fought in the American War of Independence on the side of the 13 colonies against British forces.
12. Yen, *1911 Revolution,* 91.
13. Schiffrin, *Revolutionary,* 101.
14. Sun's meeting at the Quai d'Orsay in this and the next paragraph is from Bergere, *Sun,* 118, and Schiffrin, *Revolutionary,* 103.
15. Schiffrin, *Origins,* 354.
16. Schiffrin, *Revolutionary,* 104.
17. Schiffrin, *Origins,* 355, and Yen, *1911 Revolution,* 91.
18. The Chinese Exclusion Act was passed by the U.S. Congress in 1882 to prohibit Chinese immigration. Intended initially to last 10 years, it was extended in 1892 and made permanent in 1902. This act was repealed by the Magnuson Act in 1943, two years after China became an ally of the United States in World War II. The 1943 act allowed Chinese immigration for the first time since 1882, and permitted some Chinese immigrants already in the country to become naturalized citizens. The ban against Chinese ownership of property and businesses continued until 1965 when the Magnuson Act itself was fully repealed.
19. Sin Kiong Wong, "The Chinese Boycott: A Social Movement in Singapore and Malaya in the Early Twentieth Century," *Southeast Asian Studies* 36, no. 2 (Sep. 1998), 230–236, and Yen, *1911 Revolution,* 64–65.
20. Teo Eng Hock sold the villa in 1912 when his business ran into financial difficulties due to neglect. After numerous changes of hands and uses, the Singapore Chinese Chamber of Commerce (SCCC) regained ownership of the villa in 1951 and in 1964 renamed it Sun Yat-sen Villa. In 1994, the Singapore Government gazetted it as a National Monument and renamed it the Sun Yat Sen Nanyang Memorial Hall two years later.

CHAPTER 6: A MARRIAGE OF CONVENIENCE

1. This and the following two paragraphs from Bergere, *Sun,* 128–130, and Schiffrin, *Origins,* 363–365.
2. This and the next paragraph from Schiffrin, *Revolutionary,* 105–106, Schiffrin, *Origins,* 358–359, and Jansen, *Sun Yat-sen,* 117–118.
3. The Zhongguo Tongmenghui is sometimes translated as the Chinese United League (Immanuel Hsu) or the Chinese Alliance (Schiffrin). The official name in English is The Federal Association of China. See Schiffrin, *Revolutionary,* 106.
4. This and the next paragraph from Bergere, *Sun,* 155–156.
5. See Shelley Hsien Cheng, *The T'ung-meng Hui: Its Organization, Leadership, and Finances, 1906–1912* (Ph.D. diss., University of Washington, 1962) for more detailed information on the Tongmenghui.
6. The membership statistics are from Bergere, *Sun,* 135.
7. The main source for this and the following two paragraphs is ibid., 135, 143–146.
8. Schiffrin, *Revolutionary,* 109.
9. Sun's meeting with Major Boucabeille and its aftermath in this and the next two paragraphs are from Munholland, "French Connection," 83–89.
10. HK Museum of History, *Sun Yat-sen,* 176.
11. Cholon was incorporated as a city in 1879. In 1931, it was merged with neighboring Saigon to form the city of Saigon-Cholon, though this official name never entered everyday discourse. Saigon was renamed Ho Chi Minh City in 1976 to honor the Vietnamese revolutionary leader.
12. Yen, *1911 Revolution,* 303, and Barlow, *Sun Yat-sen,* 37–38.

CHAPTER 7: THE NANYANG PIVOT

1. Wang Gungwu, *The Overseas Chinese: From Earthbound China to the Quest for Autonomy* (Cambridge, MA: Harvard University Press, 2000), 1 and 19.
2. Yen, *1911 Revolution,* 2–3 and 21n15.
3. Source: HK History Museum, *Sun Yat-sen,* 58. These figures are not census-based and should be taken as crude approximations only.
4. The best known of these is the Chinese Exclusion Act of 1882.
5. Constance Mary Turnbull, *The History of Singapore* (Singapore: NUS Press, 2009), 119–120, and Yen, *1911 Revolution,* xxi–xxii.
6. Yen, *1911 Revolution,* 50–51.
7. Wang, "Reformists and Revolutionaries," 18–19.
8. Tan Chor Nam and Teo Eng Hock's backgrounds and their transformation from reformism to revolution draws on Yen, *1911 Revolution,* 51–55.

9 Since Wang Gungwu's pioneering work, "Sun Yat-sen and Singapore," it was generally accepted that Sun made eight visits to Singapore between 1900 and 1911. More recently, Toh Lam Hua, chief editor of *Lianhe Zaobao*, has uncovered evidence that suggests there was another visit and that this took place sometime in the fall or winter of 1905 on his way to Europe. See *Lianhe Zaobao*, October 6 & 10, 2011. These articles have also been published in Zhou Zhaocheng (ed.), *Bai Nian Xin Hai: Nanyang Hui Mou* (A Hundred Years After the Xinhai Revolution) (Singapore: World Scientific, 2011).

10 Most records place the founding date of Tongmenghui Singapore as at the end of 1905, which lends support to the thesis that Sun visited Singapore in the fall or winter of 1905 as proposed by Zhou Zhaocheng. Tan and Teo had different recollections of the date when Tongmenghui Singapore was established but concurred that there were only three present at the founding. Yet the membership register shows that there were 15 founding members. See Yen, *1911 Revolution*, 129n29 and 130n30. The most likely explanation is that the decision to form the Singapore branch was made in late 1905 but the formalities were not performed until April 6, 1906, the date generally accepted as the founding date of Tongmenghui Singapore.

11 HK Museum of History, *Sun Yat-sen*, 181.

12 The main reference for Sun's tour of peninsular Malaya in 1906 is Yen, *1911 Revolution*, 94–100.

13 The Federated Malay States was a political union of four protected states established in 1895 by Britain, which was responsible for the foreign affairs and defense of the federation. While these states continued to be responsible for their own domestic policies, they were bound by treaty to follow the advice of the British Resident General. The four federated states were Selangor, Perak, Pahang and Negeri Sembilan.

14 Yen, *1911 Revolution*, 111–117.

15 Ibid., 100–106.

16 Ibid., 117–122.

17 Ibid., 122–127.

18 Ibid., 302.

19 The main text for Sun and the Tongmenghui's activities in Siam is Jeffrey Sng and Pimpraphai Bisalputra, *A History of the Thai Chinese* (Singapore: Editions Didier Millet, 2016), 237, 295–96 & 299–300.

20 Wasana Wongsurawat, "Thailand and the Xinhai Revolution: Expectation, Reality and Inspiration" in Lee Lai To and Lee Hock Guan (eds), *Sun Yat-sen, Nanyang and the 1911 Revolution* (Singapore: ISEAS Publishing, 2011), 138.

21 The main texts for the case of Indonesia are Leo Suryadinata, "The 1911 Revolution and the Chinese in Java: A Preliminary Study" in Lee Lai To (ed.) *The 1911 Revolution: The Chinese in British and Dutch Southeast Asia* (Singapore: Heinemann Asia, 1987), 108–124, and Leo Suryadinata "Tongmenghui, Sun Yat-sen and the Impact on Indonesia: A Revisit" in Leo Suryadinata (ed.), *Tongmenghui, Sun Yat-sen and the Chinese in Southeast Asia* (Singapore: Chinese Heritage Centre, 2006), 171–200.

22 Yen Ching-hwang, "The Confucian Revival Movement in Singapore and Malaya, 1899–1911," *Journal of Southeast Asian Studies* 7 no. 1 (Mar 1976), 33.

23 The principal text for the extraordinary experience of the Chinese in Surabaya and their revolutionary activities is Claudine Salmon, "Confucianists and Revolutionaries in Surabaya (c1880–c1906)" in Tim Lindsey and Helen Pausacker (eds), *Chinese Indonesians: Remembering, Distorting and Forgetting* (Singapore: ISEAS Publications, 2005), 130–147.

24 Tjio Poo Tjhat was the author's grandfather.

25 Yen Ching-hwang, *1911 Revolution*, 304 and 319n9.

26 There is an interesting story of how the road acquired the peculiar name. It was supposed to be Alexander Terrace after the original owner, a Mr. Alexander. Either the sign painter or the clerk who registered the name transcribed it backwards, an understandable error since the Chinese language is traditionally written from right to left. Today, the road is a pedestrian-only street in Hong Kong's Mid-Levels. In 2004, the Hong Kong government erected a commemorative plaque at the intersection of Rednaxela Terrace and Shelley Street to honor Jose Rizal. See "Stories behind Hong Kong street names" in *South China Morning Post*, July 8, 2016.

27 The main text for the case of the Philippines is Teresita Ang See, "Tong Meng Hui, Sun Yat-sen, The Chinese in the Philippines and the Filipino Revolutionists" in Suryadinata, *Tongmenghui*, 201–220.

28 Quoted in Antonio S. Tan, *The Chinese in the Philippines, 1898–1935: A Study of their National Awakening* (Quezon City: R.P. Garcia Publishing, 1972), 120.

29 C. Martin Wilbur, *Sun Yat-sen: Frustrated Patriot* (New York: Columbia University Press, 1967), 46–47.

30 Yen, *1911 Revolution*, 265 and Wilbur, *Patriot*, 43.

31 Wilbur, *Patriot*, 43.

32 Yen, 1911 Revolution, 310.

33 The HK$200,000 is the average of two estimates, one by Chen Shuqiang of HK$224,443 and the other of S$187,637 by Yen Ching-hwang. See Guan Kin Lee, "The 1911 Revolution in the Global Context: The Significance of

NOTES

Singapore" in Suryadinata, *Tongmenghui*, 166. The percentage for the rest of Nanyang is from Yen, *1911 Revolution*, 311.
34 Yen, *1911 Revolution*, 313–317.
35 Lee, "Global Context," 150n3 and 104.

CHAPTER 8: BATTLE CRIES FOR A REPUBLIC

1 Qinzhou was for many centuries the center of Chinese overland trade with Indochina. It was transferred from Guangdong to Guangxi province in 1965.
2 This and the next paragraph from Rhoads, *Republican Revolution*, 110–111.
3 Yen, *1911 Revolution*, 63 and 68n23.
4 Ibid., 63–64, 78n119 and 310.
5 The primary source for the Huanggang Uprising is Rhoads, *Republican Revolution*, 111–113.
6 The main text on the Qinuhu Uprising is Rhoads, *Republican Revolution*, 113–114.
7 Ibid., 114.
8 Yen, *1911 Revolution*, 306.
9 Schiffrin, *Revolutionary*, 129.
10 This and the next three paragraphs from Bergere, *Sun*, 177–179.
11 The primary source for the Fangcheng Uprising is Rhoads, *Republican Revolution*, 115–116.
12 The main text for the Zhennanguan Uprising is Bergere, *Sun*, 179–181.
13 This Qinzhou-Lianzhou Uprising is from Rhoads, *Republican Revolution*, 117.
14 The narrative on the Hekou Uprising is from Bergere, *Sun*, 181–182.
15 This and the next paragraph from Yen, *1911 Revolution*, 306–308.
16 Bergere, *Sun*, 182.
17 The revolutionary attempt by Xu Xilin and Qiu Jin is from Edward J.M. Rhoads, *Manchus and Hans* (Seattle: University of Washington Press, 2000), 104–105, and Spence, *Modern China*, 241.
18 Bergere, *Sun*, 183.
19 Schiffrin, *Revolutionary*, 132–133.
20 The Tatsu Maru incident and the anti-Japanese boycott are from Schiffrin, *Revolutionary*, 133–134, and Yen, *1911 Revolution*, 139n129.
21 Schiffrin, ibid., 134.

CHAPTER 9: THE WINTER OF DISCONTENT

1 The clashes between Sun and his Tongmenghui partners are mentioned in Bergere, *Sun*, 147–148.

2. Yen, *1911 Revolution*, 214.
3. Bergere, *Sun*, 148.
4. Yen, *1911 Revolution*, 214–215.
5. Yen Ching-hwang, "Tongmenghui, Sun Yat-sen and the Chinese in Singapore and Malaya: A Revisit," in Suryadinata, *Tongmenghui*, 117.
6. Bergere, *Sun*, 148.
7. Yen, *1911 Revolution*, 166–167.
8. The feud between Sun and the Guangfuhui leaders in this and the next two paragraphs from ibid., 216–219.
9. The other three old guards were Zeng Guofan (d. 1872), Zuo Zongtang (d. 1885) and Li Hongzhang (d. 1901).
10. Wilbur, *Patriot*, 65.
11. Schiffrin, *Revolutionary*, 142.
12. Wilbur, *Patriot*, 67–68.
13. Jonathan Spence, *The Gate of Heavenly Peace* (New York, NY: Penguin, 1981), 107–108.
14. Bergere, *Sun*, 185.
15. The main source for the Guangzhou New Army Uprising is Rhoads, *Republican Revolution*, 191–194.
16. Bergere, *Sun*, 185.
17. Homer Lea's background and the account of his meeting with Sun is from Lawrence Kaplan, *Homer Lea: American Soldier of Fortune* (Lexington, KY: University Press of Kentucky, 2010), 3–4, 145–157, and Schiffrin, *Revolutionary*, 137–139.
18. Schiffrin, *Revolutionary*, 142–143 and Bergere, *Sun*, 150.
19. Yen, *1911 Revolution*, 226–228.
20. The Penang Conference is from Yen, ibid., 232–233, and Schiffrin, *Revolutionary*, 143–144.
21. Schiffrin, ibid., 145.
22. Yen, *1911 Revolution*, 234.
23. Ibid., 238.
24. I have relied on Rhoads, *Republican Revolution*, 199–203, and Bergere, *Sun*, 188–189 for the account of the Huanghuagang Uprising.
25. March 29, 1911, on the Chinese lunisolar calendar was April 27, 1911, on the Gregorian calendar.
26. Schiffrin, *Revolutionary*, 147.
27. Bergere, *Sun*, 151–152.
28. Schiffrin, *Revolutionary*, 148.

NOTES

CHAPTER 10: THE SPARK THAT STARTED THE FIRE

1. These statistics are from Spence, *Modern China*, 249–250.
2. For further reading on the railroad issue, see Wakeman, *Imperial China*, 237–239, 247–248; Spence, *Modern China*, 249–253, and Schiffrin, *Revolutionary*, 149–151.
3. Rhoads, *Republican Revolution*, 205–206.
4. Bergere, *Sun*, 203.
5. See David A. Graf, *Military History of* China (Lexington, KY: University Press of Kentucky, 2002), 163–169.
6. Elleman, *Chinese Warfare*, 142–144.
7. The primary source for the mutiny at Wuchang and the fall of Wuhan is Edward A. Dreyer, *China at War, 1901–1949* (Harlow, Essex: Longman, 1995), 34, and Elleman, *Chinese Warfare*, 142–144.
8. Bergere, *Sun*, 205–206.
9. This paragraph and the next from Spence, *Modern China*, 264–266.
10. Bergere, *Sun*, 206–207.
11. Ibid., 207
12. "Dr. Sun Yat Sen" (*Singapore Free Press*, December 16, 1911).
13. The main source for this and the next three paragraphs is Kaplan, *Homer Lea*, 170–171.
14. Yen, *1911 Revolution*, 242–243. There was no revolutionary newspaper in Singapore after *Chong Shing Yit Pao* and *Sun Pao* folded in 1910.
15. Song Ong Siang, *One Hundred Years' History of the Chinese in Singapore* (London: John Murray, 1923), 471–472, and "Rebels in Singapore" (*Straits Times*, November 7, 1911).
16. This and the next paragraph from Yen, *1911 Revolution*, 239, 258n175 and 293n23.
17. "Dr Sun Yat Sen: Revolutionary Leader in Singapore" (*Singapore Free Press*, December 18, 1911).
18. Sun's Hong Kong visit in this and the following paragraph is from Bergere, *Sun*, 210–211, and Schiffrin, *Revolutionary*, 158–159.
19. This and the next two paragraphs from Bergere, *Sun*, 211–215, and Schiffrin, *Revolutionary*, 158–159.
20. The North-South negotiations and the Qing abdication are from from Rhoads, *Manchus*, 205–230.
21. Sun Yat-sen, "My Reminiscences," *Strand Magazine* 1912a vol. 1 (Jan – Jun 1912).
22. Bergere, *Sun*, 214.

CHAPTER 11: BETRAYAL OF THE REVOLUTION

1. Bergere, *Sun*, 223.
2. Hsu, *Modern China*, 477, and Spence, *Modern China*, 279. In Bergere, ibid., 224, the Jinbudang, or Progressive Party, was stated to be the party of Liang Qichao. It was actually the name that resulted from the merger of the Republican, Democratic and Unity Parties after the election.
3. Sun's visit to Beijing and the northern provinces in this and the following two paragraphs is from Schiffrin, *Revolutionary*, 169–171, and Bergere, *Sun*, 228–229.
4. Sun's visit to Japan in this and the following two paragraphs is from Schiffrin, ibid., 171–172 and Bergere, ibid., 237.
5. Hsu, *Modern China*, 477.
6. Schiffrin, *Revolutionary*, 172–173.
7. Bergere, *Sun*, 240, but Schiffrin in *Revolutionary* at 173–174 contends that both Sun and Huang Xing preferred legal recourse and had to be persuaded into taking decisive action against Yuan.
8. Wilbur, *Patriot*, 26.
9. This and the next paragraph from Bergere, *Sun*, 243–244, and Schiffrin, *Revolutionary*, 175–176.
10. Sun's letter to Okuma is from Jansen, ibid., 188–189.
11. Sun's letter to Deitrick is from Wilbur, *Patriot*, 84–91.
12. Bergere, *Sun*, 248–249.
13. The discussion on the Zhongguo Gemingdang, its organization, its policies and its membership in this and the next four paragraphs draws on Bergere, *Sun*, 256–261.
14. The narrative on Chen Qimei and Chiang Kai-shek in this and the next paragraph is from Bergere, *Sun*, 259–260.
15. The discussion on the Twenty-One Demands in this and the next two paragraphs is from Schiffrin, *Revolutionary*, 180–182 and Bergere, *Sun*, 263–264.
16. This argument was advanced by Schiffrin in *Revolutionary*, 182.
17. An account of Sun's elopement and marriage to Qingling appears in Sterling Seagrave, *The Soong Dynasty* (New York: Harper & Row, 1985), 136–139.
18. Spence, *Modern China*, 286, and Bergere, *Sun*, 266–268.
19. This and the next two paragraph from Schiffrin, *Revolutionary*, 185–186.
20. Jerome Chen, *Yuan Shih-k'ai* (Stanford: Stanford University Press, 1972), 193.

CHAPTER 12: CHAOS UNDER HEAVEN

1. Spence, *Modern China*, 288.

NOTES

2. James E. Sheridan, *China in Disintegration: The Republican Era in Chinese History* (New York: Free Press, 1975), 58.
3. Hsu, *Modern China*, 482–483.
4. Audrey Wells, *The Political Thoughts of Sun Yat-sen* (Hampshire: Palgrave, 2001), 40–43.
5. Schiffrin, *Revolutionary*, 189.
6. Ibid., 189–190.
7. Sun Yat-sen, *The Vital Problem of China* (Taipei: China Cultural Service, 1953).
8. Wilbur, *Patriot*, 94–95.
9. Puyi remained in the Forbidden City until 1924 when he was evicted by the warlord Feng Yuxiang and forced to take refuge in the Japanese concession at Tianjin.
10. The primary text on Sun's first Guangzhou government is Bergere, *Sun*, 271–276.
11. Hsu, *Modern China*, 484.
12. Wilbur, *Patriot*, 95.
13. In the same year that Sun published *The Doctrine of Sun Wen*, Mao Zedong wrote *The Great Union of the Popular Masses* in the *Xiang River Weekly Review*, which he edited. Mao was not yet a communist but he was already searching for radical solutions to China's problems. See Jerome Chen, *Mao and the Chinese Revolution* (London: Oxford University Press, 1965), 63.
14. Sun Yat-sen, *Memoirs of a Chinese Revolutionary* (Philadelphia: David McKay Co., 1927).
15. See Wells, *Political Thought*, 49–52.
16. Sun, *Memoirs*, 5–12, and 111–112.
17. This and the next paragraph from Schiffrin, *Revolutionary*, 195–197.
18. Sun Yat-sen, *International Development of China* (Shanghai: Commercial Press, 1920), iii-iv.
19. Schiffrin, *Revolutionary*, 198.
20. A copy of Paul S. Reinsch's reply dated March 17, 1919 is reproduced in Appendix II of Sun, *International Development*.
21. This and the next three paragraphs on the Paris Peace Conference, the May Fourth and the New Culture Movements are drawn from Hsu, *Modern China*, 502–505.
22. This interview was reported in the Tokyo and Osaka editions of the *Asahi* (June 22, 1919); cited in Schiffrin, *Revolutionary*, 211.
23. Schiffrin, *Revolutionary*, 211.
24. Bergere, *Sun*, 279, and Schiffrin, *Revolutionary*, 212–213.

25 This and the next paragraph from Bergere, *Sun,* 295–6, and Schiffrin, ibid., 213–214.
26 Woodrow Wilson's "Fourteen Points" speech to the U.S. Congress on January 8, 1918.
27 This and the next paragraph from Schiffrin, *Revolutionary,* 215–217.
28 Bergere, *Sun,* 299.
29 Ibid., 302.
30 Ibid., 297–298.
31 Song Qingling gave a dramatic account of her ordeal to a Chinese newspaper. An English translation is reproduced in Seagrave, *Soong Dynasty,* 168–170.
32 Built by Mitsubishi, the *Yongfeng* was the first of four Yongfeng class coastal defense ships ordered by the Qing government in 1910 but only commissioned in 1913 after the 1911 Revolution. The *Yongfeng* was renamed *Zhongshan* on April 13, 1925, in honor of Sun Yat-sen but was sunk by Japanese bombardment in October 1938. The shipwreck was salvaged in January 1997, restored and now has its own museum in Wuhan, the Zhongshan Warship Museum.
33 Jay Taylor, *The Generalissimo: Chiang Kai-shek and the Struggle for Modern China* (Cambridge, MA: Harvard University Press, 2009), 40–41, and Bergere, *Sun,* 302–303.
34 Gordon, *Newer China,* 96, and Wilbur, *Patriot,* 33.
35 Schiffrin, *Revolutionary,* 218.

CHAPTER 13: DANCES WITH BEARS

1 This and the next paragraph, Schiffrin, *Revolutionary,* 219–220.
2 Bergere, *Sun,* 306.
3 Wilbur, *Patriot,* 117.
4 Wilbur, *Patriot,* 117–118.
5 George T. Yu, *Party Politics in Republican China: The Kuomintang, 1912–1924.* (Berkeley: University of California Press, 1966), 163; cited in Wilbur, *Patriot,* 120 and 328n18.
6 Wilbur, *Patriot,* 127.
7 USDS 893.00/4651 dispatch dated August 22, 1922, Cunningham in Shanghai to Secretary of State, cited in Wilbur, *Patriot,* 128 and 331n11.
8 Wilbur, *Patriot,* 129–130.
9 Schiffrin, *Revolutionary,* 228.
10 Ibid., 228–229.
11 Ibid., 229.
12 The Chinese Eastern Railway was built by the imperial Russian government at the end of the 19th century. The southern stretch, known in the West as the

South Manchuria Railway, was the partial *casus belli* for the Russo-Japanese War in 1905. After Russia's defeat, she controlled only the northern and central segments.

13 Schiffrin, *Revolutionary*, 230.
14 A more detailed account of these exchanges is found in Wilbur, *Patriot*, 131–132.
15 Odoric Wou, *Militarism in Modern China* (Canberra: Australian National University Press, 1978), 188.
16 Schiffrin, *Revolutionary*, 230.
17 Wilbur, *Patriot*, 135, and Schiffrin, *Revolutionary*, 233–234.
18 Bergere, *Sun*, 311.
19 Wilbur, *Patriot*, 140–141.
20 Bergere, *Sun*, 312.
21 Sun's interlude in Hong Kong is from Wilbur, *Patriot*, 142–144, and Bergere, *Sun*, 312–313.
22 Schiffrin, *Revolutionary*, 236.
23 Wilbur, *Patriot*, 146.
24 Ibid., 147.
25 Schiffrin, *Revolutionary*, 238.
26 Bergere, *Sun*, 315.
27 Ibid., 317.
28 Wilbur, *Patriot*, 175–177.
29 Bergere, *Sun*, 326.
30 Bergere, *Sun*, 318, and Schiffrin, *Revolutionary*, 247.
31 Bergere, *Sun*, 325, and Schiffrin, *Revolutionary*, 248.
32 There are a number of translations of the *Sanmin Zhuyi*. One of the most widely used is Sun Yat-sen, *San Min Chu I: Three Principles of the People*, tr. Frank W. Price (Shanghai: The Commercial Press, 1938). See Wells, *Political Thought*, 61–101, which provides lecture-by-lecture summaries with the author's comments on each principle.
33 Sun, *San Min Chu I*, 95.
34 Wilbur, *Patriot*, 205–207.
35 Maurice William, *Social Interpretation of History: A Refutation of the Marxian Economic Interpretation of History* (New York: Sotery Publishing Co., 1920).
36 Sun, *San Min Chu I*, 287–288.
37 Wilbur, *Patriot*, 254–255.

CHAPTER 14: THE FINAL JOURNEY

1 Although Shanghai was part of Jiangsu province, it was not administered by the provincial authorities but by a separate defense commissioner. This

post was created by Yuan Shikai and assigned to the Anhui clique to prevent the then military governor of Jiangsu, Feng Guozhang, from becoming too powerful.
2. The Second Zhili-Fengtian War and its aftermath are from James E. Sheridan, *Chinese Warlord: The Career of Feng Yu-hsiang*, (Stanford: Stanford University Press, 1966), 130–134.
3. This and the next paragraph from Bergere, *Sun*, 398–401.
4. The source for Sun's visit to Shanghai is Wilbur, *Patriot*, 270–271.
5. Sun's visit to Kobe is from Schiffrin, *Revolutionary*, 264–5.
6. Wilbur, *Patriot*, 274–275.
7. Sun Yat-sen, *San Min Chu I*, i.
8. Wilbur, *Patriot,* 279 and 370n36.
9. Ibid., 279.
10. *Far Eastern Review* 21, 103 (March 1925).

CHAPTER 15: THE ROAD TO PURGATORY

1. Mentioned in Schiffrin, *Revolutionary,* 246.
2. See Yueh Sheng, *Sun Yat-sen University in Moscow and the Chinese Revolution: A Personal Account* (Lawrence, KS: University Press of Kansas, 1976).
3. Delin Lai, "Searching for a Modern Chinese Monument: The Design of the Sun Yat-sen Mausoleum in Nanjing," *Journal of the Society of Architectural Historians*, Vol. 64, No. 1 (Mar 2005), 22–55. Lu Yanzhi was later selected to design the Sun Yat-sen Memorial Hall, Guangzhou. Started in 1929, it was completed in 1931.
4. Taylor, *Generalissimo,* 50.
5. Ibid., 51–53.
6. Sheridan, *Disintegration*, 160–161.
7. Elleman, *Chinese Warfare*, 165.
8. Taylor, *Generalissimo,* 72–73.
9. Sharman, *Critical Biography*, 316.
10. Ibid., 315.
11. "Teakwood Funeral Coach," *Time* magazine (Vol. 13, no. 22, June 3, 1929); Gordon, *Newer China,* 111, and Bergere, 410–411.
12. The Sun Yat-sen University was founded in 1924 by Sun as National Guangzhou University. The name was changed to its present form by decree of the Nationalist government on July 17, 1926. See HK Museum, *Sun,* 145.
13. Yang Hucheng was imprisoned for 13 years. In September 1949, shortly before the Communists took Nanjing, Chiang Kai-shek ordered the execution of Yang, his family and some of his officers. Zhang Xueliang was placed under

house arrest. In 1949 he was transferred to Taiwan, where he remained under house arrest for another 42 years until 1991. He emigrated to Hawaii in 1994 and died there in 2001 at the age of 99.
14 Wells, *Political Thought*, 126.
15 The name "Greater East Asian Co-Prosperity Sphere" was coined by Kiyoshi Miki, a philosopher who was actually opposed to militarism. As originally conceived, it was an idealistic wish to free Asia from European colonial powers. Japanese nationalists soon saw it as a way to acquire resources to maintain Japan as a modern power.
16 Sun Yat-sen, *China and Japan: Natural Friends, Unnatural Enemies: A Guide for China's Foreign Policy*, ed. T'ang Leang-Li, with a foreword by Wang Ching-wei (Shanghai: China United Press, 1941).
17 Well, *Political Thought*, 129.
18 Fu Zuoyi's decision to surrender spared Beijing the damage that might have resulted from a long siege. The 25 Nationalist divisions under his command were absorbed into the PLA. It was said that the best of these troops owed their loyalty not to the Nationalists but to General Fu, who was a warlord in Suiyuan province, now part of Inner Mongolia.
19 Mao's eight points were: to punish all war criminals; abolish the 1947 constitution; abolish the Guomindang legal system; reorganize the Nationalist armies; confiscate all bureaucratic capital; reform the land-tenure system; abolish all treasonous treaties; and convene a full Political Consultative Conference. See Spence, *Search for Modern China*, 510.
20 Diana Lary, *China's Republic* (Cambridge: Cambridge University Press, 2007), 169–175.
21 The Guomindang had adopted the Gregorian calendar for the days and months but dated years from the 1911 Revolution, e.g., 1945 was the 34th year of the Republic. The flag of the People's Republic of China consists of a five-pointed gold star with four subsidiary stars on a red background. The large star represents the CPC, and the four small stars the four classes that constituted the new regime: the national and petty bourgeoisie, the workers and the peasants. See Spence, *Modern China*, 512 and footnotes, and Bergere, *Sun*, 407.

CHAPTER 16: THE MAN AND HIS LEGACY

1 Inukai Ki, "Profile of a Cosmopolitan Man" in *Asahi Shimbun*, July 22, 1930; cited in Chang and Gordon, *All Under Heaven*, 147.
2 Chang and Gordon, *All Under Heaven*, 148.
3 These incidents are mentioned in Wells, *Political Thought*, 110–111.
4 Schiffrin, *Revolutionary*, 270.

5   Ibid., 269–270.
6   Richard Wilhelm's preface to Tai Chi-t'ao's *Die Geistigen Grundlagen des Sun Yat-senimus* (The Intellectual Foundations of Sun Yat-senism) (Berlin: Würfel Verlag, 1931), 8; cited in Wells, 103.
7   Cantlie and Jones, *Awakening*, 24–25.
8   David Strand, *An Unfinished Republic: Leading by Word and Deed in Modern China* (Berkeley, CA: University of California Press, 2011), 238.
9   Letter to C. Martin Wilbur in October 1974.
10 J. Ellis Barker, "Doctor Sun Yat-sen and the Chinese Revolution," *The Fortnightly Review* (London), vol. 96 [new series, vol. 90] (Jul–Dec 1911), 778–792; cited in Chang and Gordon, *All Under Heaven*.
11 Paul M.A. Linebarger, *The Political Doctrines of Sun Yat-sen* (Westport, CT: Greenwood Press, 1973), 15.
12 Bergere, *Sun*, 282–283.
13 Ibid., 285. The Four Modernizations sought to strengthen China's agriculture, industry, national defense, and science and technology. They were first set forth by Zhou Enlai in 1963 but enacted only in 1978 by Deng Xiaoping.
14 In 2015, Shanghai handled 646,514 metric tons, South Louisiana 235,058 and New York/New Jersey 114,933 metric tons. Source: American Association of Port Authorities World Port Rankings 2015.
15 The CIA World Factbook Country Comparisons – Railways: USA 293,584 km (2014), and China 191,270 km (2014). https://www.cia.gov/library/publications/the-world-factbook/rankorder/2121rank.html. High-speed rail network is from the Guinness World Records, 2017 Edition. http://www.guinnessworldrecords.com/world-records/largest-high-speed-rail-network
16 The CIA World Factbook Country Comparisons – Roadways. https://www.cia.gov/library/publications/the-world-factbook/rankorder/2085rank.html#ch
17 U.S. Department of the Interior, U.S. Geological Survey. *Three Gorges Dam: The world's largest hydroelectric plant.* http://water.usgs.gov/edu/hybiggest.html.
18 Nathaniel Peffer, "One of Asia's Three Great Moderns, The Enigma of Sun Yat-sen, Maker of the Chinese Republic, Without Honor Save in History," *Asia* (Aug 1924), 591–94, 657–58; cited in Wilbur, *Patriot*, 5.
19 Wilbur, *Patriot*, 38.
20 Cheng Chu-yuan (ed.), *Sun Yat-sen's Doctrine in the Modern World* (Boulder: Westview Press, 1989), 80; cited in Wells, *Political Thought*, 113–114.
21 Hsueh Chun-tu, *The Chinese Revolution of 1911: New Perspectives* (Hong Kong: Joint Publishing, 1986), 34; cited in Wells, *Political Thought*, 114.
22 Wells, *Political Thought*, 114.

NOTES

23 Wou Sao-fong, *Sun Yat-sen: Sa vie et sa doctrine* (Paris: Les presses universitaires de France, 1929), 41; cited in A. James Granger, "Confucianism and the Political Thought of Sun Yat-sen," *Philosophy East and West*, 31, no. 1 (Jan 1981), 55.

24 Sometimes translated as "Great Unity," *datong* was first mentioned in Confucius' Book of Rites. It refers to a utopia that existed in the distant past but Sun Yat-sen, as did Kang Youwei, used it to refer to a future perfect world.

25 Sharman, *Critical Biography*, 310; Donald W. Treadgold, *The West in Russia and China: Religious and Secular Thought in Modern Times*, vol. 2: China (Cambridge: Cambridge University Press), 80 and 91, and Wilbur, *Patriot*, 35.

26 Sharman, ibid., 310.

27 Wu Yuzhang, who fought in the 1911 Revolution and later became President of the China People's University, recalls how the powers used the church to legitimate their aggression in 19th-century China. Missionaries protected Christian converts, who in turn used the power of the missionaries to bully their own people. The Christian churches became more powerful than the Chinese government, and often became big landlords and moneylenders and exploited the peasants by charging "even higher rent and interest than the feudal landlords of China." See Wu Yuzhang, *Recollection of the Revolution of 1911* (Honolulu: University Press of the Pacific, 2001), 45.

28 Paul M.A. Linebarger (ed.), *The Gospel of Chung Shan According to Paul Linebarger* (Paris, 1932), 26, 50, 56; cited in Treadgold, *Russia and China*, 91–92.

29 Paschal M. D'Elia (ed.), *The Triple Demism of Sun Yat-sen*, Appendix III, 718; cited in Treadgold, *Russia and China*, 93.

30 Testimony of Professor L. Carrington Goodrich, who participated in Sun's Christian funeral service. See Wilbur, *Patriot*, 281.

31 Peter Zarrow, *China in War and Revolution: 1895–1949*. (Oxford: Routledge, 2005), 192–193.

32 Chang and Gordon, *All Under Heaven*, 152.

33 *Dr. Sun Yat-sen and His Family: A Special Exhibition* (Singapore: Sun Yat-sen Nanyang Memorial Hall, 2015), 67.

34 Li Ao, *Sun Zhongshan Yanjiu* [A Study of Sun Yat-sen] (Taipei: Li Ao Chubanshe, 1987), 293–6; cited in Gordon, *Seeking A Newer China*, 138.

35 Strand, *Unfinished Republic*, 238.

36 Martin, *Strange Vigour*, 230.

37 Bergere, *Sun*, 412.

38 Ibid., 413–414.

39 Zhou Enlai (1898–1976) was the PRC's first Premier and served in that capacity until his death. A consummate diplomat, he advocated peaceful

coexistence with the West and helped to orchestrate Richard Nixon's visit to China in 1972. Zhou escaped the purges of the Cultural Revolution and attempted to mitigate the Red Guards' excesses. His effort to protect others from their wrath made him immensely popular in the later stage of the Cultural Revolution. In the early 1970s he led an internal struggle against the Gang of Four over the leadership of China but died eight months before Mao.

40 Mao Zedong, "Jinian Sun Zhongshan Xiansheng," [Celebrating Dr. Sun Yat-sen], November 12, 1956, in *Mao Zedong Xuanji* [Collected Works of Mao Zedong] (Beijing: Renmin Chubanshe, 1977), vol. 5, 311–312; cited in Joseph W. Esherick and C.X. George Wei, *China: How the Empire Fell* (Oxford: Routledge, 2014), 7 and 15n14.
41 Ceren Ergenc, "(Grand)father of the Nation? Collective Memory of Sun Yat-sen in Contemporary China," in Lee, *British and Dutch*.
42 Ezra Vogel, *Deng Xiaoping and the Transformation of China* (Cambridge, MA: Harvard University Press, 2011).
43 Peng Zhen (1902–1997) was a leading member of the CPC. He led the party organization following the Communist victory in 1949 but was purged during the Cultural Revolution. Rehabilitated under Deng Xiaoping in 1982, he became the inaugural head of the Chairman of the Standing Committee of the National People's Congress.
44 Ergenc, "Collective Memory," 221–244.
45 Baogang Guo (ed.), *Taiwan and the Rise of China* (Lanham, MD: Lexington Books, 2012), 3.
46 Chang and Gordon, *All Under Heaven*, 161.
47 Kevin Cai (ed.), *Cross-Taiwan Straits Relations Since 1979* (Singapore: World Scientific, 2011), 7–8.
48 Kyle Churchman, "Sun Yat-sen and the Future of Taiwanese 'Independence,'" *The National Interest* (March 8, 2016).

EPILOGUE

1 Wilbur, *Patriot*, 290.
2 Sun Yat-sen University in Guangzhou, Guangdong, and National Sun Yat-sen University in Kaohsiung, Taiwan.
3 Schiffrin, *Revolutionary*, 271.
4 J.W. Garver, *The Sino-American Alliance: Nationalist China and American Cold War Strategy in Asia* (Armonk, NY: M.E. Sharpe, 1997), 28.

BIBLIOGRAPHY

BOOKS

Bergere, Marie-Claire. *Sun Yat-sen*. Translated by Jane Lloyd. Stanford, CA: Stanford University Press, 1998.

Boorman, Howard L. and Richard C. Howard (eds). *Biographical Dictionary of Republican China*, 5 vols. New York: Columbia University Press, 1967–71.

Cai, Kevin (ed.). *Cross-Taiwan Strait Relations since 1979*. Singapore: World Scientific, 2011.

Cantlie, James and Sheridan Jones. *Sun Yat-sen and the Awakening of China*, 2nd ed. New York: Fleming H. Revell Co., 1912.

Chang, Hsin-pao. *Commissioner Lin and the Opium War*. Cambridge, MA: Harvard University Press, 1964.

Chang, Sidney H. and Leonard H.D. Gordon. *All Under Heaven: Sun Yat-sen and His Revolutionary Thought*. Stanford: Stanford University Press, 1991.

Chen, Jerome. *Yuan Shih-k'ai*. Stanford: Stanford University Press, 1972.

Chen, Stephen and Robert Payne. *Sun Yat-sen: A Portrait*. New York: John Jay, 1946.

Ch'i, Hsi-sheng. *Warlord Politics in China, 1916–1928*. Stanford: Stanford University Press, 1976.

Choa, G.H. *The Life and Times of Sir Ho Kai: A Prominent Figure in Nineteenth-Century Hong Kong*. 2nd ed. Hong Kong: Chinese University Press, 2000.

Dillon, Michael. *China: A Modern History*. London: I.B. Tauris, 2010.

Dong, Stella. *The Man Who Changed China*. Hong Kong: Form Asia, 2004.

Dreyer, Edward L. *China at War: 1901–1949*. London: Longman, 1995.

Elleman, Bruce A. *Modern Chinese Warfare, 1795–1989*. London: Routledge, 2001.

Elliot, Mark C. *The Manchu Way: The Eight Banners and Ethnic Identity in Late Imperial China*. Stanford: Stanford University Press, 2001.

Esherick, Joseph W. and C.X. George Wei. *China: How the Empire Fell*. Oxford: Routledge, 2014.

Fairbank, John King. *China: A New History*. 2nd ed. Cambridge, MA: Belknap Press, 2006.

———. *China: The People's Middle Kingdom and the U.S.A*. Cambridge, MA: Harvard University Press, 1967.

———. *China Watch*. Cambridge, MA: Harvard University Press, 1987.

———. *The Great Chinese Revolution 1800–1985*. New York: Harper & Row, 1986.

Fay, Peter Ward. *The Opium War, 1940–1942.* Chapel Hill, NC: University of North Carolina Press, 1997.

Fenby, Jonathan. *Modern China: The Fall & Rise of a Great Power, 1850 to the Present.* New York: HarperCollins, 2008.

Ford, Christopher A. *The Mind of Empire: China's History and Modern Foreign Relations.* Lexington, KY: The University Press of Kentucky, 2010.

Fung, Edmund. *The Military Dimension of the Chinese Revolution: The New Army and Its Role in the Revolution of 1911.* Vancouver: University of British Columbia Press, 1980.

Gao, James Z. *Historical Dictionary of Modern China (1800–1949).* Lanham, MD: Scarecrow Press, 2009.

Garver, J.W. *The Sino-American Alliance: Nationalist China and American Cold War Strategy in Asia.* Armonk, NY: M.E. Sharpe, 1997.

George, Henry. *Progress and Poverty.* New York: Robert Schalkenbach Foundation, 2006.

Godley, Michael R. *The Mandarin-Capitalists from Nanyang: Overseas Chinese enterprise in the modernization of China, 1893–1911.* Cambridge: Cambridge University Press, 1981.

Gordon, David. *Sun Yatsen: Seeking a Newer China.* Upper Saddle River, NJ: Pearson Education, 2010.

Graf, David A. *Military History of China.* Lexington, KY: University of Kentucky Press, 2002.

Grasso, June M., Jay Corrin and Michael Kort. *Modernization and Revolution in China.* Armonk, NY: M.E. Sharpe, 1997.

Gray, Jack. *Rebellions and Revolutions: China from the 1800s to 2000.* 2nd ed. Oxford: Oxford University Press, 2002.

Grieder, Jerome B. *Intellectuals and the State in Modern China.* New York: Macmillan, 1981.

Guo, Baogang (ed.) *Taiwan and the Rise of China.* Lanham, MD: Lexington Books, 2012.

Hahn, Emily. *The Soong Sisters.* New York: An [e-reads] Book, 1977.

Hawkins, Mike. *Social Darwinism in European and American Thought, 1860–1945: Nature as Model and Nature as Threat.* Cambridge: Cambridge University Press, 1997.

Hong, Lysa and Huang Jianli. *The Scripting of A National History: Singapore and Its Pasts.* Hong Kong: Hong Kong University Press, 2008.

Hong Kong Museum of History. *Dr. Sun Yat-sen & Hong Kong.* Hong Kong: Museum of History, 2013.

Hotta, Eri. *Pan-Asianism and Japan's Wars, 1931–1945.* New York: Palgrave Macmillan, 2007.

BIBLIOGRAPHY

Hsu, Immanuel C.Y. *The Rise of Modern China*. 6th ed. New York: Oxford University Press, 2000.

Issacs, Harold R. *The Tragedy of the Chinese Revolution*. Chicago: Haymarket Books, 2010.

Jansen, Marius. *Japan and China: From War to Peace, 1894–1972*. Chicago, IL: Rand McNally, 1975.

———. *The Japanese and Sun Yat-sen*. Cambridge, MA: Harvard University Press, 1954.

Kaplan, Lawrence M. *Homer Lea: American Soldier of Fortune*. Lexington, KY: University Press of Kentucky, 2010.

Khoo, Salma Nasution. *Sun Yat-sen in Penang*. Penang: Areca Books, 2008.

Kim, Hodong. *Holy War in China: The Muslim Rebellion and State in Chinese Central Asia*. Stanford: Stanford University Press, 2004.

Kuhn, Philip A. *Rebellion and Its Enemies in Late Imperial China: Militarism and Social Structure, 1796–1864*. Cambridge, MA: Harvard University Press, 1970.

Kuhn, Robert Lawrence. *How China's Leaders Think*. Singapore: John Wiley, 2010.

Lary, Diana. *China's Republic*. Cambridge: Cambridge University Press, 2007.

Lea, Homer. *The Days of the Saxon*. New York: Harper & Brothers, 1912.

———. *The Valor of Ignorance*. New York: Harper & Brothers, 1909.

———. *The Vermillion Pencil*. New York: McClure Co., 1908.

Lee, Edwin. *Singapore: The Unexpected Nation*. Singapore: Institute of Southeast Asian Studies, 2008.

Lee, Julie Wei, Ramon H. Myers and Donald G. Gillin (eds). *Prescriptions for Saving China: Selected Writings of Sun Yat-sen*. Stanford: Hoover Institution Press, 1994.

Lee Lai To (ed.). *The 1911 Revolution: the Chinese in British and Dutch Southeast Asia* Singapore: Heinemann Asia, 1987.

Lee Lai To and Lee Hock Guan (eds). *Sun Yat-sen, Nanyang and the 1911 Revolution*. Singapore: ISEAS Publishing, 2011.

Lewis, John Fulton, *China's Great Convulsion*. Heathville, VA: Sun on Earth Books, 2005.

Li, Xiaoxiong. *Poppies and Politics in China: Sichuan Province, 1840s to 1940s*. Newark: University of Delaware Press, 2009.

Lim, Boon Keng. *The Chinese Crisis from Within*. With introduction by Lee Guan Kin. Singapore: Select Publishing, 2006.

Lindsey, Tim and Helen Pausacker (eds). *Chinese Indonesians: Remembering, Distorting, Forgetting*. Singapore: ISEAS, 2005.

Linebarger, Paul Myron Anthony. *The Political Doctrines of Sun Yat-sen*. Westport, CT: Greenwood Press, 1973.

Lo, Hui-min (ed.). *The Correspondence of G.E. Morrison,* vol. 1, 1895–1912. Cambridge: Cambridge University Press, 1976.

Lu Hanchao. *The Birth of a Republic.* Seattle: University of Washington Press, 2010.

Lum, Yansheng Ma and Raymond Mun Kong Lum. *Sun Yat-sen in Hawaii: Activities and Supporters.* Honolulu: Hawaii Chinese History Center and Dr. Sun Yat-sen Hawaii Foundation, 1999.

Malone, Caroll Brown. *History of the Peking Summer Palace under the Ch'ing Dynasty.* Urbana: University of Illinois Press, 1934.

Martin, Bernard. *Strange Vigour: A Biography of Sun Yat-sen.* London: Heinemann, 1952.

McCord, Edward A. *The Power of the Gun: The Emergence of Modern Chinese Warlordism.* Berkeley: University of California Press, 1993.

Mitter, Rana. *A Bitter Revolution: China's Struggle with the Modern World.* Oxford: Oxford University Press, 2010.

Miyazaki, Toten. *My Thirty-Three Year's Dream. The Autobiography of Miyazaki Toten.* Translated by Eto Shinkichi and Marius B. Jansen. Princeton: Princeton University Press, 1982.

Ooi, Kee Beng. *The Eurasian Core and its Edges: Dialogues with Wang Gungwu on the History of the World.* Singapore: ISEAS Publishing, 2015.

Paine, S.C.M. *The Sino-Japanese War of 1894–1895.* Cambridge: Cambridge University Press, 2003.

———. *The Wars for Asia, 1911–1949.* Cambridge: Cambridge University Press, 2012.

Pan, Lynn. *The Encyclopedia of the Chinese Overseas.* 2nd ed. Singapore: Chinese Heritage Centre and Editions Didier Millet, 2006.

Pong, David (ed.) *Encyclopedia of Modern China.* Farmington Hills, MI: Gale, 2009.

Pratt, Helen G. *In Hawaii: A Hundred Years.* New York: Charles Scribner's Sons, 1939.

Reilly, Thomas H. *The Taiping Heavenly Kingdom: Rebellion and the Blasphemy of Empire.* Seattle, WA: University of Washington Press, 2004.

Restarick, Henry B. *Sun Yat-sen, Liberator of China.* New Haven: Yale University Press, 1931.

Rhoads, Edward J.M. *China's Republican Revolution: The Case of Kwangtung, 1895–1913.* Cambridge, MA: Harvard University Press, 1975.

———. *Manchus and Hans.* Seattle: University of Washington Press, 2000.

———. *Stepping Forth into the World: The Chinese Education Mission to the United States, 1872–1881.* Hong Kong: Hong Kong University Press, 2011.

Roberts, J.A.G. *A History of China.* 2nd ed. Hampshire: Palgrave Macmillan, 2006

Saaler, Sven and J. Victor Koschmann (eds). *Pan-Asianism in Modern Japanese History: Colonialism, Regionalism and Borders.* Oxford: Routledge, 2007.

Schiffrin, Harold Z. *Sun Yat-sen and the Origins of the Chinese Revolution.* Berkeley: University of California Press, 1968.

———. *Sun Yat-sen: Reluctant Revolutionary.* Boston: Little Brown, 1980.

———. "Sun Yat-sen: His Life and Time." In Chu-Yuan Cheng (ed.), *Sun-Yat-sen's Doctrine in the Modern World.* Boulder, CO: Westview Press, 1988.

Seagrave, Sterling. *The Soong Dynasty.* New York: Harper & Row, 1985.

Shanghai Museum of Sun Yat-sen's Former Residence. *Sun Yat-sen: In Commemoration of the 130th Anniversary of Dr. Sun's birth.* Shanghai: People's Publishing House, 1996.

Sharman, Lyon. *Sun Yat-sen: A Critical Biography.* Stanford: Stanford University Press, 1868.

Sheng, Yueh. *Sun Yat-sen University in Moscow and the Chinese Revolution: A Personal Account.* Lawrence, KS: University Press of Kansas, 1976.

Sheridan, James E. *China in Disintegration: The Republican Era in Chinese History 1912–1949.* New York: Free Press, 1975.

———. *Chinese Warlord: The Career of Feng Yu-hsiang.* Stanford: Stanford University Press, 1966.

Shirk, Susan. *China: Fragile Superpower.* New York: Oxford University Press, 2007.

Sng, Jeffrey and Primpahai Bisalputra. *A History of the Thai Chinese.* Singapore: Editions Didier Millet, 2016.

Song, Ong Siang. *One Hundred Years History of the Chinese in Singapore.* London: John Murray, 1923.

Spence, Jonathan D. *God's Chinese Son: The Taiping Heavenly Kingdom of Hong Xiuquan.* London: HarperCollins, 1996.

———. *The Gate of Heavenly Peace.* New York, NY: Penguin, 1981.

———. *The Search for Modern China.* New York, NY: Norton, 1990.

Strand, David. *An Unfinished Republic: Learning by Word and Deed in Modern China.* Berkeley: University of California Press, 2011.

Sun, Yat-sen. *The Fundamentals of National Reconstruction.* Taipei: China Cultural Services, 1953.

———. *The International Development of China.* London: Hutchison, 1921.

———. *Kidnapped in London.* Bristol: J.W. Arrowsmith, 1897.

———. *Memoirs of a Revolutionary.* Philadelphia: David McKay Co., 1919.

———. *San Min Chu I: The Three Principles of the People.* Translated by Frank W. Price. Shanghai: Commercial Press, 1938.

———. *The Vital Problem of China.* Taipei: China Cultural Service, 1953.

———. *Zhongshan Xuanji* (Collected Works of Sun Yat-sen). 9 vols. Beijing: Chinese Book Press, 1968.

Suryadinata, Leo (ed.). *Tongmenghui, Sun Yat-sen and the Chinese in Southeast Asia: A Revisit*. Singapore: Chinese Heritage Centre, 2006.

Sutton, Donald. *The Role of the Chinese Military in National Policymaking*. Rev. ed. Santa Monica, CA: Rand, 1998.

Tan, Antonio S. *The Chinese in the Philippines, 1898–1935: A Study of their National Awakening*. Quezon City: R.P. Garcia Publishing, 1972.

Taylor, Jay. *The Generalissimo: Chiang Kai-shek and the Struggle for Modern China*. Cambridge, MA: Harvard University Press, 2009.

Teng, Ssu-yu and John K. Fairbank (eds). *China's Response to the West*. New York: Atheneum, 1963.

Treadgold, Donald W. *The West in Russia and China: Religious and Secular Thought in Modern Times v.2 China 1582–1949*. Cambridge: Cambridge Press, 1973.

Tubilewicz, Czeslaw (ed.). *Critical Issues in Contemporary China*. New York: Routledge, 2006.

Turnbull, C.M. *A History of Modern Singapore, 1819–2005*. Singapore: NUS Press, 2009.

Ven, Hans van de. *Breaking with the Past: The Maritime Customs Service and the Global Origins of Modernity in China*. New York: Columbia University Press, 2014.

Ven, Hans van de. *War and Nationalism in China, 1924–1949*. London: Routledge-Curzon, 2003.

Ven, Hans van de (ed.). *Warfare in Chinese History*. Leiden, Netherlands: Brill, 2000.

Vohra, Ranbir. *China's Path to Modernization: A Historical Review from 1800 to the Present*. Upper Saddle River, NJ: Prentice Hall, 1987.

Vogel, Ezra. *Deng Xiaoping and the Transformation of China*. Cambridge, MA: Harvard University Press, 2011.

Wakeman, Frederic, Jr. *The Fall of Imperial China*. New York: Free Press, 1975.

Waley-Cohen, Joanna. *The Culture of War in China: Empire and the Military under the Qing Dynasty*. New York: I.B. Tauris, 2006.

Wang, Gungwu. *Anglo-Chinese Encounters Since 1800: War, Trade, Science & Governance*. Cambridge: Cambridge University Press, 2003.

———. *China and the Chinese Overseas*. Singapore: Times Academic Press, 1992.

———. *Community and Nation: Essays on Southeast Asia and the Chinese*. Singapore: Heinemann, 1981.

———. *The Chinese Overseas: From Earthbound China to the Quest for Autonomy*. Cambridge, MA: Harvard University Press, 2000.

Wang, Gungwu (ed.). *Nation Building: Five Southeast Asian Histories*. Singapore: ISEAS, 2005.

Wang, Gungwu and John Wong (eds). *Interpreting China's Development.* Singapore: World Scientific, 2007.
Wasserstrom, Jeffrey N. *China in the 21st Century.* New York: Oxford University Press, 2013.
Wells, Audrey. *The Political Thought of Sun Yat-sen: Development and Impact.* Hampshire: Palgrave, 2001.
Westad, Odd Arne. *Restless Empire: China and the World Since 1750.* New York: Basic Books, 2012.
Weston, Timothy. *The Power of Position.* Berkeley: University of California Press, 2004.
Wichler, Gerhard. *Charles Darwin: The Founder of the Theory of Evolution and Natural Selection.* New York: Pergamon Press, 1961.
Wilbur, C. Martin. *Sun Yat-sen: Frustrated Patriot.* New York: Columbia University Press, 1967.
Wilbur, C. Martin and Julie Lien-ying How. *Missionaries of Revolution: Soviet Advisers and Nationalist China, 1920–1927.* Cambridge, MA: Harvard University Press, 1989.
William, Maurice. *The Social Interpretation of History.* Long Island City, NY: Sotery Publishing Co, 1921.
Wolff, David, et al. *The Russo-Japanese War in Global Perspective.* Leiden, Netherlands: Koninklijke Brill, 2007.
Wong, John Y. *Deadly Dreams.* Cambridge: Cambridge University Press, 1998.
Woo, X.L. *Two Republics in China: How Imperial China became the PRC.* New York: Algora Publishing, 2014.
Woodhouse, Eiko. *The Chinese Hsinhai Revolution: G.E. Morrison and Anglo-Japanese Relations, 1897–1920.* London: RoutledgeCurzon, 2004.
Wou, Odoric. *Militarism in Modern China.* Canberra: Australian National University Press, 1978.
Wright, Mary Cambaugh (ed.). *China in Revolution: The First Phase, 1900–1913.* New Haven: Yale University Press, 1968.
———. *The Last Stand of Chinese Conservatism: The T'ung-chih Restoration, 1862–1874.* Stanford: Stanford University Press, 1957.
Wu, Guo. *Zheng Guanying: Merchant Reformer of Late Qing China and his Influence on Economics, Politics, and Society.* Amherst, NY: Cambria Press, 2010.
Wu, Yuzhang. *Recollections of the Revolution of 1911.* Honolulu, Hawaii: University Press of the Pacific, 2010.
Ye, Weili. *Seeking Modernity in China: Chinese Students in the United States, 1900–1927.* Stanford: Stanford University Press, 2001.
Yen, Ching-hwang. *Community and Politics: The Chinese in Colonial Singapore and Malaya.* Singapore: Times Academic Press, 1995.

———. *The Ethnic Chinese in East and Southeast Asia.* Singapore: Times Academic Press, 2002.

———. *The Overseas Chinese and the 1911 Revolution: With Special Reference to Singapore and Malaya.* Kuala Lumpur: Oxford University Press, 1976.

———. *The Role of the Overseas Chinese in the 1911 Revolution.* Singapore: Chopmen Enterprises, 1978.

Yong, Ching Fatt. *Chinese Leadership and Power in Colonial Singapore.* Singapore: Times Academic Press, 1992.

Yong, Ching Fatt and R.B. McKenna. *The Kuomintang Movement in British Malaya, 1912–1949.* Singapore: Singapore University Press, 1990.

Yu, George T. *Party Politics in Republican China: The Kuomintang, 1912–1924.* Berkeley: University of California Press, 1966.

Zarrow, Peter. *After Empire: The Conceptual Transformation of the Chinese State, 1885–1924.* Stanford: Stanford University Press, 2012.

———. *China in War and Revolution: 1895–1949.* Oxford: Routledge, 2005.

Zhao, Suisheng. *Power by Design: Constitution-Making in Nationalist China.* Honolulu: University of Hawai'i Press, 1996.

JOURNAL ARTICLES, MONOGRAPHS, ETC.

Addison, James Thayer. "Chinese Ancestor Worship and Protestant Christianity." *The Journal of Religion* 5 no. 2 (Mar 1925), 140–149.

Altman, Albert A. and Harold Z. Schiffrin. "Sun Yat-sen and the Japanese 1914–1916." *Modern Asian Studies* 6 no. 4 (1972), 385–400.

Anonymous. "Sun Worshippers." *Economist* 421 no. 9014 (Nov 5, 2016).

Armentrout, L. Eve. "The Canton Rising of 1902–1903: Reformers, Revolutionaries, and the Second Taiping." *Modern Asian Studies* 10 no. 1 (1976), 83–105.

———. "A Chinese Association in North America: The Pao-Huang-Hui from 1899 to 1904." *Ch'ing-shih wen-t'i* 3 no. 9 (Nov 1978), 91–111.

Barlow, Jeffrey G. *Sun Yat-sen and the French, 1900–1908.* Berkeley: Institute of East Asian Studies, Center for Chinese Studies, Research Monograph 14, 1979.

Brophy, David. "Five Races, One Parliament: Minority Representation in the Early Republic." *China Heritage Quarterly* no. 27 (Sep 2011).

Burdman, Mary. "Beijing Celebrates Legacy of Sun Yat-sen." *Executive Intelligence Review* 23 no. 49 (Dec 6, 1996), 17–19.

———. "China Builds Sun Yat-sen's Great National Rail Project." *Executive Intelligence Review* 29 (Jan 2010).

BIBLIOGRAPHY

Calney, Mark. "Sun Yat-sen and the American Roots of China's Republican Movement." *New Federalist* (Jan 19 & 26, 1990).

Carroll, John M. "Colonialism, Nationalism and Bourgeois Identity in Colonial Hong Kong." *Journal of Oriental Studies* 39 no. 2 (Oct 2005), 146–164.

Chan, Chi-Chao, et al. "The First Western-Style Hospital in China." *Archives of Ophthalmology* 129 no. 6 (Jun 2011), 791–797.

Chan, Lien. "Sun Yat-sen on Land Utilization." *Agricultural History* 42 no. 4 (Oct 1968), 297–303.

Cheng, Huanwen and Donald G. Davis. "Loss of Recorded Heritage: Destruction of Chinese Books in Peking Siege of 1900." *Library Trends* 55 no. 3 (Winter 2007), 431–441.

Cheng, Shelley Hsien. "The T'ung-meng Hui: Its Organization, Leadership, and Finance: 1906–1912." Ph.D. dissertation, University of Washington, 1962.

Chiu, Ling-Yeong. "Debate on National Salvation: Ho Kai versus Tseng Chi-Tse." *Journal of the Hong Kong Branch of the Royal Asiatic Society* 11 (1971), 33–51.

Chong, Key Ray. "The Abortive American-Chinese Project for Chinese Revolution, 1908–1911." *Pacific Historical Review* 41 no. 1 (Feb 1972), 54–70.

———. "Cheng Kuan-ying (1841–1920): A Source of Sun Yat-sen's Nationalist Ideology?" *Journal of Asian Studies* 28 no. 2 (Feb 1969), 247–267.

Chow, Pauline Lo-sai. "Ho Kai and Lim Boon Keng: a comparative study of tripartite loyalty of colonial Chinese elite, 1895–1912." Unpublished MA thesis, University of Hong Kong (Dec 1987).

Churchman, Kyle. "Sun Yat-sen and the Future of Taiwanese 'Independence.'" *The National Interest* (March 8, 2016).

Comber, Leon. "Chinese Secret Societies in Malaya: An Introduction." *Journal of the Malayan Branch of the Royal Asiatic Society* 29 no.1 (May 1956), 146–162.

Committee for the Centennial Celebration of the Birth of Dr. Sun Yat-sen. "Appendix: Major Events in the Life of Dr. Sun Yat-sen." *The Pictorial Biography of Dr. Sun Yat-sen*, 122–128.

Dale, Elizabeth. "Pushing the Boundaries of the Public Sphere: The Su Bao Case and Everyday Citizenship in China, 1894–1904." (April 29, 2011). Available at SSRN: https://ssrn.com/abstract=1825954 or http://dx.doi.org/10.2139/ssrn.1825954

Damon, Allen F. "Financing Revolution: Sun Yat-sen and the Overthrow of the Ch'ing Dynasty." *The Hawaiian Journal of History* 25 (1991), 161–186.

Davies, Gloria. "Liang Qichao in Australia: A Sojourn of No Significance?" *China Heritage Quarterly* 27 (Sep 2011).

De Korne, John D. "Sun Yat-sen and the Secret Societies." *Pacific Affairs* 7 no. 4 (Dec 1934), 425–433.

Doran, Christine. "The Chinese Cultural Reform Movement in Singapore: Singaporean Chinese Identities and Reconstruction of Gender." *Sojourn: Journal of Social Issues in Southeast Asia* 12 no. 1 (April 1997), 92–107.

Edmonds, Richard Louis. "The Legacy of Sun Yat-sen's Railway Plans." *The China Quarterly* 111 (Sep 1987), 421–443.

Ee, Joyce "Chinese Migration to Singapore (1896–1941)." *Journal of Southeast Asian History* 2 no. 1 (Mar 1961), The Chinese in Malaya, 33–51.

Fahlstedt, Kim. "Marketing Rebellion: The Chinese Revolution Reconsidered." *Film History* 26 no. 1 (2014), 80–107.

Freedman, Maurice. "Immigrants and Associations: Chinese in Nineteenth Century Singapore." *Comparative Studies in Society and History* 3 no.1 (Oct 1960), 25–48.

Frost, Mark Ravinder. "Emporium in Imperio: Nanyang Networks and the Straits Chinese in Singapore 1819–1914." *Journal of Southeast Asian Studies* 36 no. 1 (Feb 2005), 29–66.

———. "Transcultural Diaspora: The Straits Chinese in Singapore, 1819–1918." *Asia Research Institute Working Papers* 10 (Aug 2003).

Fung, Edmund S.K. "The Chinese Nationalists and the Unequal Treaties 1924–1931." *Modern Asian Studies,* 21 no. 4 (1987), 793–819.

Gallagher, Mary E. "Reform and Openness: Why China's Economic Reforms Have Delayed Democracy." *World Politics* 54 no. 3 (Apr 2002), 338–372.

Gamba, Charles. "Chinese Associations in Singapore." *Journal of the Malaysian Branch of the Royal Asiatic Society* 39 no. 2 (Dec 1966), 123–168.

Georg, Stefan, et al. "Telling General Linguists About Altaic." *Journal of Linguistics* 35 no. 1 (March 1999), 65–78.

George, Brian T. "The State Department and Sun Yat-sen: American Policy and the Revolutionary Disintegration of China, 1920–1924." *Pacific Historical Review* 46 no. 3 (Aug 1977), 387–408.

Goda, Miho. "Chinese Associations and the Making of Chinese Identities in Singapore." *Philippines Journal of Third World Studies* 13 no. 3 (1998), 69–74.

Godley, Michael R. "Socialism with Chinese Characteristics: Sun Yat-sen and the International Development of China." *The Australian Journal of Chinese Affairs* no. 18 (Jul 1987), 109–125.

———. "The Late Ch'ing Courtship of the Chinese in Southeast Asia." *The Journal of Asian Studies* 34 no. 2 (Feb 1975), 361–385.

Gordon, Leonard H.D. "Sun Yat-Sen and His Legacy." *The World & I* 14, no. 9 (Sep 1999), 328–341.

Granados, Ulises. "As China Meets the Southern Sea Frontier: Ocean Identity in the Making, 1902–1937." *Pacific Affairs* 78 no. 3 (Fall 2005), 443–461.

Gregor, A. James. "Confucianism and the Political Thought of Sun Yat-sen." *Philosophy East and West* 31 no. 1 (Jan 1981), 55–70.

Gregor, A. James and Maria Hsia Chang. "Nazionalfascismo and the Revolutionary Nationalism of Sun Yat-sen." *The Journal of Asian Studies* 3 no. 1 (Nov 1979), 21–37.

———. "Wang Yang-ming and the Ideology of Sun Yat-sen." *The Review of Politics* 42 no. 3 (Jul 1980), 388–404.

High, Peter B. *Umeya Shokichi: The Revolutionist as Impresario.* Nagoya University, n.d.

Horner, Charles and Eric Brown. "A Century After the Qing: Yesterday's Empire and Today's Republic." *China Heritage Quarterly* no. 27 (Sep 2011).

Horstmann, Kurt. "The Nanyang Chinese – History and Present Position of the Chinese in SE Asia." *GeoJournal* 4 no. 1, South East Asia (1980), 64–66.

Hsueh Chun-tu. "Sun Yat-sen, Yang Ch'u-yun, and the Early Revolutionary Movement in China." *The Journal of Asian Studies* 19 no. 3 (May 1960), 307–318.

Ikei, Masaru. "Japan's Response to the Chinese Revolution of 1911." *The Journal of Asian Studies* 25 no. 2 (Feb 1966), 213–227.

Jansen, Marius B. "Opportunities in South China during the Boxer Rebellion." *Pacific Historical Review* 20 no. 3 (Aug 1951), 241–250.

Karl, Rebecca E. "Creating Asia: China in the World at the Beginning of the Twentieth Century." *The American Historical Review* 103 no. 4 (Oct 1998), 1096–1118.

Kenley, David. "Singapore's May Fourth Movement and Overseas Print Capitalism." *Asia Research Institute Working Papers* 70 (Jul 2006).

Kim, Jaeyoon. "The Heaven and Earth Society and the Red Turban Rebellion in Late Qing China." *Journal of Humanities & Social Sciences* 3 no. 1 (2009), 1–35.

Krishnan, R.R. "Early History of U.S. Imperialism in Korea." *Social Scientist* 12 no. 11 (Nov 1984), 3–18.

Kung, Edmund S.K. "The Chinese Nationalists and the Unequal Treaties 1924–1931." *Modern Asian Studies* 21 no. 4 (1987), 793–819.

Kyle, James. "The Hong Kong College of Medicine (1887–1915)." *The British Medical Journal* 1 no. 6176 (Jun 2, 1979), 1474–1476.

Lai Chee-Kien. "Reclaiming the Prodigal Sun: Reconstituting the Republican Revolution in Singapore and Malaya." *Traditional Dwelling and Settlements Review* 24 no. 1 (Fall 2012), 51–52.

Lai, Delin. "Searching for a Modern Chinese Monument: The Design of the Sun Yat-sen Mausoleum in Nanjing." *Journal of the Society of Architectural Historians* 64 no. 1 (Mar 2005).

Larsen, Jane Leung. "An Association to Save China, the Baohuang Hui: A Documentary Account." *China Heritage Quarterly* no. 27 (Sep 2011).

———. "Articulating China's First Mass Movement: Kang Youwei, Liang Qichao, the Baohuanghui, and the 1905 Anti-American Boycott." *Twentieth-Century China* 33 no. 1 (Nov 2007), 4–26.

Lees, Lynn Hollen. "Being British in Malaya (1890–1940)." *Journal of British Studies,* 48 no. 1 (Jan 2009), 76–101.

Leong, Stephen. "The Chinese in Malaya and China's Politics, 1895–1911." *Journal of the Malaysian Branch of the Royal Asiatic Society* 50 no. 2 (232), (1997), 7–24.

Lim, Boon Keng. "The Chinese Revolutionary Movement in Malaya." *Straits Philosophical Society* (July 12, 1913).

Lin Han-sheng. "The Revolutionary Army: A Chinese Nationalist Tract of 1903 by Tsou Jung." *Public Affairs* 42 no. 2 (Summer 1969), 226–227.

Marx, Karl. "Revolution in China and in Europe." *New York Daily Tribune* (June 14, 1853).

Metalio, Michael V. "American Missionaries, Sun Yat-sen and the Chinese Revolution." *Pacific Historical Review* 47 no. 2 (May 1978), 261–282.

Munholland, J. Kim. "The French Connection that Failed: France and Sun Yat-sen, 1900–1908." *Journal of Asian Studies* 32, no. 1 (Nov 1972), 177–195.

Ng, Alice Lun Ngai-ha. "The Hong Kong Origins of Dr. Sun Yat-sen's Address to Li Hung-chang." *Journal of the Hong Kong Branch of the Royal Asiatic Society* 21 (1981), 168–178.

———. "The Role of Hong Kong Educated Chinese in the Shaping of Modern China." *Modern Asian Studies* 17 no. 1 (1983), 137–163.

Ng Siew Yoong. "The Chinese Protectorate in Singapore 1877–1900." *Journal of Southeast Asian History* 2, no.1 (Mar 1961), The Chinese in Malaya, 76–99.

Pang Yong-Pil. "Peng Pai from Landlord to Revolutionary." *Modern China* 1 no. 3, The Rural Revolution. Part II (Jul 1975), 297–322.

Patrikeeff, Felix, and Gregory de Cure. "Sun Yat-sen and Greater China." (2004).

Peffer, Nathaniel. "One of Asia's Three Great Moderns, The Enigma of Sun Yat-sen, Maker of the Chinese Republic, Without Honor Save in History." *Asia* (Aug 1924).

Perry, Elizabeth J. "Tax Revolt in Late Qing China: The Small Swords of Shanghai and Liu Depei of Shandong." *Late Imperial China* 6 no. 1 (Jun 1985), 83–112.

Png Poh Seng. "The Kuomintang in Malaya, 1912–1941." *Journal of Southeast Asian History* 2 no. 1 (1960), 1–32.

———. "The Straits Chinese in Singapore: A Case of Local Identity and Socio-Cultural Accommodation." *Journal of Southeast Asian History* 10 no.1 (Mar 1969), 95–114.

BIBLIOGRAPHY

Salmon, Claudine. "The Chinese Community of Surabaya, from its Origin to the 1930s Crisis." *Chinese Southern Diaspora Studies* 3 (2009), 22–60.

Santangelo, Paolo. "Renewed Interest in Sun Yatsen: Conferences on His Role and Philosophy in the Past Twenty Years." *East and West* 41 no. 1/4 (Dec 1991), 385–386.

Scalapino, Robert A. and Harold Schiffrin. "Early Socialist Currents in the Chinese Revolutionary Movement: Sun Yat-sen versus Liang Ch'i-ch'ao." *The Journal of Asian Studies* 18 no. 3 (May 1959), 321–342.

Schiffrin, Harold Z. "Sun Yat-sen: His Life and Times." In Cheng, Cho-yuan (ed.). *Sun Yat-sen Doctrine in the Modern World*. Boulder: Westview Press, 1988, 11–51.

———. "Sun Yat-sen's Early Land Policy: The Origin and Meaning of 'Equalization of Land Rights.'" *The Journal of Asian Studies* 16 no. 4 (Aug 1957), 549–564.

Shuja, Sharif M. "Western Movement in China (1557–1949): Challenges to Chinese Sovereignty." *Pakistan Horizon* 29 no. 3 (3rd Quarter 1976), 33–47.

Thomson, John Stuart. "The Genesis of the Republican Revolution in China from a South China Standpoint." *The Journal of Race Development* 3 no. 3 (Jan 1913), 316–342.

Trescott, Paul B. "Henry George, Sun Yat-sen and China: More than Land Policy Was Involved." *The American Journal of Economics and Sociology* 53 no. 3 (Jul 1994), 363–375.

Tsui, Francis. "Hong Kong: Where a Future Revolutionary Leader was Nurtured." Honolulu: Dr. Sun Yat-sen Hawaii Foundation, n.d.

Vandenbosch, Amry. "The Chinese in Southeast Asia." *The Journal of Politics* 9 no. 1 (Feb 1947), 80–95.

Wang, Dong. "The Discourse of Unequal Treaties in Modern China." *Pacific Affairs* 76, no. 3 (Fall 2003), 399–425.

Wang, Gungwu. "Chinese Politics in Malaya." *The China Quarterly* 43 (Jul–Sep, 1970), 1–30.

———. "Chinese Reformists and Revolutionaries in the Straits Settlements, 1900–1911." Unpublished thesis, 1953.

———. "Sun Yat-sen and Singapore." *Journal of the South Sea Society* 15 no. 1 (Dec 1959), 55–68.

———. "To Reform a Revolution Under the Righteous Mandate." *Daedalus* 122 no. 2, China in Transformation (Spring 1993), 71–94.

Wesser, Robert and Mark Calney "Sun Yat-sen's Legacy and the American Revolution." *Executive Intelligence Review* (28 Oct 2011), 42–50.

Wong, J.Y. "Sun Yatsen: His Heroic Image a Century Afterwards." *Journal of Asian History* 28 no. 2 (1994), 154–176.

———. "Three Visionaries in Exile: Yung Wing, Kang Yu-wei and Sun Yat-sen." *Journal of Asian History* 20 no. 1 (1966).

Wong Sin Kiong. "The Chinese Boycott: A Social Movement in Singapore and Malaya in the Early Twentieth Century." *Southeast Asian Studies* 36 no. 2 (Sept 1998), 230–253.

Worden, Robert L. "K'ang Yu-wei, Sun Yat-sen, et al. and the Bureau of Immigration." *Ch'ing-shih wen-t'i* 2 no. 6 (Jun 1971), 1–10.

World Affairs Institute. "A Short Chronology of Events in China from 1911–1927." *Advocate of Peace through Justice* 89 no. 12 (Dec 1927), 680–693.

Yang Lijun and Lim Chee Kia. "Three Waves of Nationalism in Contemporary China: Sources, Themes, Presentations and Consequences." *International Journal of China Studies* 1 no. 2 (2010), 461–485.

Yao, Souchou. "Ethnic Boundaries and Structural Differentiations: An Anthropology Analysis of the Straits Chinese in Nineteenth Century Singapore." *Journal of Social Issues in Southeast Asia* 2 no. 2 (Aug1987), 209–230.

Yen, Ching-hwang. "Ch'ing Sale of Honours and the Chinese Leadership in Singapore and Malaya, 1877–1912." *Journal of Southeast Asian Studies* 1 no. 2 (Sep 1970), 20–32.

———. "Class Structure and Social Mobility in the Chinese Community in Singapore and Malaya 1800–1911." *Modern Asian Studies* 21, no. 3 (1987), 417–445.

———. "The Confucian Revival Movement in Singapore and Malaya, 1899–1911." *Journal of Southeast Asian Studies* 7 no. 1 (Mar 1976), 33–57.

———. "Early Chinese Clan Organizations in Singapore and Malaya, 1819–1911." *Journal of Southeast Asian Studies* 12 no. 1 (Mar 1981), 62–92.

———. "Overseas Chinese Nationalism in Singapore and Malaya 1877–1912." *Modern Asian Studies* 16 no.3 (1980), 397–425.

Yong, Ching Fatt. "A Preliminary Study of Chinese Leadership in Singapore, 1900–1941." *Journal of Southeast Asian History* 9 no. 2 (Sep 1968), 256–285.

Yu, George T. "The 1911 Revolution: Past, Present, and Future." *Asian Survey* 31 no. 10 (Oct 1991), 895–904.

Zarrow, Peter. "Rethinking the 1911 Revolution: On a Panel at the Association of Asian Studies, 1 April 2011." *China Heritage Quarterly* no. 27 (Sep 2011).

Zhang, Kaiyuan, Liu Wangling and Ernst Schwintzer. "The 1911 Revolution: The State of the Field in 1982." *Late Imperial China* 6 no. 1 (Jun 1985), 113–122.

INDEX

Agricultural Study Society 50
Aguinaldo, Emilio 74–75, 160
Allen, Walter W. 190, 194–95
Anglo-Japanese Alliance (1902) 100, 108, 118, 239
Anhui (Anfu) clique 96, 253, 271, 293
Anti-imperialism 23, 108, 280–81, 294, 334

Bangkok 154–56, 336
Baohuanghui: competition with Xingzhonghui 77–79, 85, 111, 112, 162; finances of 96, 162, 168, 190; founding of 73; and Homer Lea 193; in Philippines 160; and Qing court 144, 187; in Siam 155; and *Union Times* 153
Batavia 157, 158
Beau, Paul 105
Beijing 1–2, 11, 85–86, 94–95, 207, 224, 227–28, 231–32, 250–51, 270, 292, 293–95, 298, 305, 311–12, 320
Beiyang Army 14, 71, 211, 212, 214, 215, 245, 246, 293
Black Dragon Society (Kokuryukai) 65, 126, 166, 296, 297
Blake, Sir Henry 93–94, 95
Boji Medical School 30, 327
Boothe, Charles Beach 190, 193, 194–95, 198
Borodin, Mikhail 278–81, 279, 287, 290, 294, 298, 300, 304, 307–11
Boucabeille, Major 117, 135–36
Boxer Protocol 99, 100
Boxer Uprising 84–88, 92, 94–95, 100, 108, 147, 168, 207, 328
Britain: and Boxer Uprising 94–95, 99; in Burma 28; and China trade 4–5, 9–10; and Homer Lea 216, 219; imperial retreat from China 309; and Japan 232, 239, 240, 303; and Kang Youwei 71, 88–92; and the Opium Wars 5–7, 10–11, 26; and revolutionaries 51, 60; and Sun Yat-sen 58–61, 66, 92, 93, 218, 236, 249, 253, 270, 275–77, 281, 288, 295–97, 330, 333; support for the Qing regime 46, 60, 152; support for Wu Peifu 270, 273; support for Yuan Shikai 234, 236, 249; in World War I 248–49, 257, 265; *see also* London
British East India Company (EIC) 5
Brussels 115, 116
Burma 28, 143, 159

Cai E 242
Cai Yuanpei 224, 259, 323
Cantlie, Dr. James 32, 36, 53, 55–61, 216, 324, 333
Cao Kun 251, 290, 292, 293
Chaozhou Huanggang Uprising 164, 168, 169–70, 171, 173, *183*, 186
Chen Cuifen 200, 219, 330
Chen Duxiu 258, 259, 260, 272, 280, 303
Chen, Eugene 275, 294, 298, 300, 323
Chen Jiongming 237, 238, 252, *252*, 261–65, 270, 271, 273, 274, 276, 278–90, 307
Chen Qimei 214, 238–39, 240, 243
Chen Shaobai 33, *34*, 36, 51–54, 66, 75, 87, 97, 136, 168, 330
Chen Tianhua 125, 126, 130, 153
Chiang Kai-shek: and Chen Qimei 214, 239; as Huangpu Military academy commandant 286, 289; and Song Meiling 311; and Song Qingling 331; and Sun Yat-sen 265, 267, 272, *286*, 289, 298, 311, 312–13, 322; after Sun's death 306–21, 331, 333, 345
Chicherin, Georgi V. 269
China Daily 75, 104
Chinese Eastern Railway 272, 274
Chinese Education Mission 190, 230
Chinese Exclusion laws (U.S.) 112, 120, 144, 160, 181, 317

385

Chinese Legation, Sun's kidnapping by 56–60, 107, 323, 327, 328
Chinese Nationalist Party *see* Guomindang
Chinese Revolutionary Party *see* Gemingdang
Cholon 137, 148
Chong Shing Yit Pao 153, 159, 165, 186, 187, 188, 196
Civil service examinations 2, 13, 31, 99, 102, 103, 115, 122, 212
Cixi, Empress Dowager 73; and the Boxers 85–86, 212; death of 187, 189; and the Guangxu Emperor 19, 71, 72, 73, 78, 85, 95, 99, 102, 146; and Li Hongzhang 17, 19, 37, 86; and reforms 70–71, 102, 122, 211; rise of 11, 13; and the Self-Strengthening Movement 18; and Yuan Shikai 71, 246
Cole, George 323
College of Medicine for Chinese (Hong Kong) 31, 32, 33, 35, 91, 160, 161
Columbia University 230, 241, 259, 265, 273, 332
Comintern (Communist International) 264, 268–69, 271, 273, 287, 290, 304, 307–8, 310
Communist Party of China (CPC) 268–71, 287, 310, 314–15, 331–36, 344–45
Constitution Protection Movement 251, 252, 262

Daoguang Emperor 6, 7, 187
Darwin, Charles 35
Darwinism, Social 104, 110, 193, 216
Deitrick, James 236
Deng Xiaoping 304, 325, 334–36, 340
Deng Ziyu 145, *149*, 170, 196
Dewey, John 259, 263
Diocesan School 26
Donald, William H. 224, 232
Double Tenth, insurrection of 213
Doumer, Paul 90–91, 105, 117, 189
Duan Qirui 225, 226, 246–53, 257, 293, 295, 297
Dutch East Indies 142, 143, 156, 157–59, 164, 178, 186, 198, 269

East-West Apothecary 36, 37
Eight Banners 11, 212
Equalization of land rights 106, 127, 129, 148, 185, 287

Fangcheng Uprising 167, 169, 172–73, *183*, 191
Feng Guozhang 225, 246–47, 251, 253
Feng Yuxiang 292–94, 295, 308–9, 310, 311, 314
Feng Ziyou 43, 130, 133, 192
Fengtian clique 264, 271, 292–93, 308, 310, 311
Five-Power Constitution 115, 129, 237, 255, 261, 312, 319
Four Bandits 33, *34*, 43
Four Modernizations 326, 334, 335
France: aid for Sun 90–91, 105–6, 116–17, 136, 167, 172–75, 177–79, 189, 218; concessions and territories in China 9, 11, 27–28, 82, 109, 177; conflicts with China 10–11, 17, 18, 27–29; intelligence missions in China 177, 135–36; and Japan 116, 117; in Triple Intervention 47; in World War I 248, 257; *see also* Indochina
Fujian 12, 43, 83, 93, 95, 146, 159, 160, 163, 165, 168, 169, 188, 220, 235, 252, 262
Fundamentals of National Reconstruction 285, 299, 312
Furen Wenshe (Literary Society for the Development of Benevolence) 43–44, 49

Gelaohui 76–79, 96, 114
Gemingdang 190, 195, 237–39, 252, 255
George, Henry 107, 129, 287
Germany: and Boxer Uprising 99; occupation of Jiaozhou/Qingdao 70, 82, 84, 239, 257, 258; and Sun Yat-sen 249, 253, 265, 267–68, 275, 284, 330; in Triple Intervention 47; in World War II 239, 248–50, 253, 257, 267
Giles, Herbert A. 59
Goh Kit Moh 91
Goh Say Eng 152, 196

386

Gonghedang 231
Gongjinhui 210
Government Central School (Hong Kong) 31, 44, 230
Green Gang 238–39, 311
Guangfuhui 114, 131, 132, 159, 179, 186, 188, 239, 259
Guangxu Emperor 73; and Baohuanghui 73; betrayed by Yuan Shikai 99, 229; and Cixi 71, 73, 95, 146; death of 187, 190, 193, 227; enthronement of 19; flight to Xi'an 95, 102; and Kang Youwei 69, 70, 72, 79, 89, 158; and Longyu 224; and reforms 35, 70–71, 99, 102; under arrest 71, 72–73, 85, 88, 147, 193
Guangzhou: and Boxer Uprising 94; and Huizhou Uprising 97–98; meeting with Liu Xuexun in 86, 87; Merchants' Corps strike 288–90, 332; Nationalist government (1925) 306–8; and the Opium Wars 5, 6, 10, 21; railway 207–8, 210; Sun's lectures in 282; Sun's medical practice in 36, 50; Sun's military governments in 251–54, 261–65, 267–68, 270, 273–80, 298, 332, 333; Sun Ke mayor of 265–66, 275, 276, 332; as trading port 4, 20–21
Guangzhou Huanghuagang Uprising *183*, 198–203
Guangzhou New Army Uprising *183*, 191–92, 197
Guangzhou Uprising (1895) 45–54, 75–76, 87, 97, 171, *183*, 200, 330
Guo Renzhang 167, 169, 173, 176
Guomindang (Nationalist Party): anti-Communist faction in 279–80, 286, 297; Civil War with Communists 318–21, 334; formation of 231, 261; in Guangzhou government 276, 278–80; leadership of 231, 234, 306–7; in Nanyang 239; National Congress 280, 281, 304, 307; national government (1928) 311–12; and Northern Expedition 308–9, 312; purge of Communists from 310;

reorganization of 273, 276, 278; and Second Revolution (1913) 233–36; Sun's legacy in 299, 304–5, 312; in Taiwan 336, 337; United Fronts with Communists 271–73, 281, 287, 294, 306, 308–9, 315, 331; during warlord era 245, 252

Hager, Charles 26, 29–30
Hankou 78, 79, 85, 96, 97, 207, 213, 215, 309
Hanoi 27, 105, 116, 119, 120, 167, 169, 171–77, 180
Hanyang 207, 213, 215
Harmond, Jules 90, 91
Hawaii: annexed as U.S. territory 41, 82; Baohuanghui in 73, 78, 85, 112; commemorations of Sun in 342; overseas Chinese community in 41, 50, 78, 96, 162, 165, 327; Sun's early years in 22–24, 26, 29, 41; Sun's family in 55, 200, 332; Sun's visits to 54–55, 111–12, 151, 195; Tongmenghui in 128, 195, 203; Xingzhonghui in 51, 54, 78, 162
Hekou Uprising 177, *183*, 184
Hirayama Shu 66, 68, 75, 76, 87
Ho Kai 31–32, *32*, 38, 45–46, 75, 93, 95, 224, 275
Hong Kong: anti-French actions in 29; anti-Japanese boycotts in 181; the British in 7, 11, 60, 62, 83, 208, 263, 275, 307; and Chaozhou uprisings 169–70; and Guangzhou uprisings 49, 52–53, 192, 200–203; and Huizhou uprising 97–98; and Philippine independence movement 73–75; Sun Yat-sen in 26, 31, 33, 36, 42, 44, 46, 76, 77, 87, 91, 93, 104–5, 136, 170, 190, 221, 265, 267, 275–76, 330; Sun's admiration for 35, 44; Tongmenghui in 133, 137, 161, 182, 191, 192, 222; Xingzhonghui in 43, 44–45, 51, 75
Hong Xiuquan 8–9, 12, 22, 33
Hu Hanmin 33; anti-Communist stance of 306, 307; in Guangzhou government 262, 294, 298; in Hong Kong 191, 222; involvement in uprisings 174, 175, 202–3;

387

Hu Hanmin (cont'd): in Malaya 178; as military governor of Guangdong 214, 222, 234; and *Minbao* 130, 133, 186; in Singapore 186, 187; and Sun Yat-sen 132, 174, 222, 306; and Tongmenghui 132, 150, 186, 199
Hu Shi 259, 260
Huang Naishang 93, 168
Huang Xing *114*; and Huaxinghui 14, 131; involvement in uprisings 167, 174, 175–77, 180, 198, 200–203, 214; leader of Tokyo students 124; in republican government 215, 223, 224, 230–31; and Second Revolution 235, 236, 237; and Sun Yat-sen 125, 174, 184–85, 196, 215, 231, 237, 323, 333; and Tongmenghui 126–28, 184, 191, 199, 211
Huang Yongshang 45, 49
Huanggang *see* Chaozhou Huanggang Uprising
Huanghuagang *see* Guangzhou Huanghuagang Uprising
Huangpu Military Academy 285–86, *286*, 288, 289, 294, 311
Huaxinghui 114, 125, 129, 131
Huizhou Qinuhu Uprising 170
Huizhou Sanzhoutian Uprising 97–99
Hundred Day Reform 35, 71, 76, 78, 88, 99, 102, 104, 132, 144, 147, 158, 229

India 5, 6, 10, 219, 232, 236, 250, 277, 282, 326, 342
Indochina, French 27, 69, 91, 105, 136, 143, 164, 167–77, 179–80, 178, 184, 199
International Development of China 256, 257, 263, 265, 270, 326, 336
Inukai Ki (Tsuyoshi) 65, 66, 68, 72, 74, 235, 297, 322
Iolani School 23–24
Ipoh 150, 151–52

Japan: and Boxer Protocol 99; and Britain 100, 108, 218, 239; and Chiang Kai-shek 315, 317; Chinese reformists in 71–73, 77, 78, 104; Chinese students in 102–3, 108–9, 110, 118, 119, 125–28, 132–33, 166; and Fujian 95, 98; *huaqiao* in 46, 165; and Korea 28, 40–41, 108, 118; and Manchuria 313–14; Meiji Restoration 38, 64, 70; as model for Chinese reformists 48, 69; pan-Asianism in 61, 65–66, 68, 73–75, 118, 160, 232, 256, 296; and the Philippines 73–75, 160, 342; and Russia 99–100, 108, 111, 116–18, 122, 166; Sun Yat-sen in 53–54, 61–62, 66–68, 71, 79, 85, 95, 97, 106, 121, 124, 134, 166–67, 195, 232–33, 235, 241, 295–97, 331; Sun's affinity with 38, 68, 118, 134, 182, 240, 250, 324, 330; Sun's attacks on 260, 262; Sun's supporters in 46, 68, 79, 87, *89*, 98, 126, 133, 174, 181, 185, 221, 235, 243, 296, 313; and Taiwan 66, 83, 95, 98, 345; *Tatsu Maru* incident 180–81; and the U.S. 63–64, 189, 195, 219, 317; and Wang Jingwei 316, 331; war with China (1894–95) 39, 40–42, 44, 47–48, 64; war with China (1937–45) 315–17, 331; and warlords 249, 253, 257, 273, 293, 297, 308, 311; in World War I 239–40, 249, 257–58; in World War II 317; and Yuan Shikai 243
Jiangsu (journal) 108
Joffe, Adolph 272, 273–74

Kang Youwei 70; in America 73; and Baohuanghui 73, 78, 79, 85, 96, 190; in Dutch East Indies 156; and Homer Lea 189, 194; and the Hundred Day Reform 70–71, 158; and the Japanese 71–72, 88–90; leading reformist 35, 69, 150, 155, 158; and Li Hongzhang 87–88, 95; and Liang Qichao 69, 77; and Puyi's "restoration" 251; in Singapore 89–90, 144; and Sun Yat-sen 72, 79, 87–88, 92, 93, 95
Karakhan, Lev M. 268, 272, 274, 301
Kayano Chochi 174
Khoo Seok Wan 85, 96, 144, 146, 168
Kidnapped in London 59, 61, 66

INDEX

Kim Ok-kyun 40
Kiyofuji Koshichiro 87–89, *89*, 91–93, 119
Kobe 53, 180, 294–98, 328, 342
Kokuryukai *see* Black Dragon Society
Kong Xiangxi (H.H. Kung) 298, 301, 328
Koo, Wellington V.K. 298
Korea 28, 40–41, 47, 66, 108, 111, 118, 344, 346
Kuala Lumpur 150, 151, 152, 164
Kuala Pilah 150, 188
Kung, H.H. *see* Kong Xiangxi
Kuomintang *see* Guomindang

Lea, Homer 189, 190, 193, *193*, 216, 219, 222, 330
Lenin, Vladimir 256, 268, 278, 281, 300, 304, 333
Li Dazhao 259
Li Hongzhang 37; army of 12, 246; and Boxer Uprising 95, 99, 108; most powerful man in China 14, 18–19, 36, 37; as negotiator with foreign powers 28, 40–41, 47, 100; and Self-Strengthening Movement 17, 28, 37; and Sun Yat-sen 36, 37, 39, 86–88, 93–94
Li Liejun 234, 236–37, 238, 242, 296
Li Yuanhong *213*, 213–15, 218, 220, 223, 225, 227, 231, 247, 248–51, 266
Liang Qichao 70; and Hankou uprising 78, 85, 96; in Hawaii 78, 85, 111; and Hundred Day Reform 70–71; and Kang Youwei 69–71, 72, 77–78, 79; and Minzhudang 231; refuge in Japan 71–73; and Sun Yat-sen 72, 77–78, 104, 111, 124, 135, 327; writings and ideas of 104, 106, 111, 124, 130, 209; on Yuan Shikai 244; and Zhang Binglin 132
Liao Zhongkai 262, 274, 289, 298, 306–7
Liaodong peninsula 47, 64
Lim Boon Keng 91–92, 93, 119, 158, 168
Lim Nee Soon 119, 148, *149*, 150, 159, 171, 221
Lin Shouzhi 168, 171
Lin Zexu 6–7, 15
Lincoln, Abraham *343*

Liu Xuexun 51, 86–88
London 55–61, 106, 114, 189, 216, 218, 236, 327
London Missionary Society 32
Lu Haodong 26, 30, 33, 37, 50, 53, 185
Lu Muzhen 27, 200, 219, 241, 330, 331, 332
Lu Rongting 251, 252, 254

Ma Ying-jeou 338
Macartney, Halliday 57, 59
Macau 4, 20, 21, 36, 53, 66, 180, 193, 332, 342, 343, 346
Malaya: anti-Japanese boycott in 181; overseas Chinese in 142–43, 158, 181; refugees in 171, 178; revolutionary movement in 25, 149–54, 164–65, 187, 188, 198–200, 203, 204, 219; Sun banned from 199, 218; Zhonghetang in 146
Manchuria: and Japan 42, 111, 126, 166, 256, 296, 313, 318; Manchu homeland 1; Nationalists' defeat at 320; and Russia 94, 99, 100, 108–9, 131, 272, 273, 318; warlord clique in 264, 273, 292, 311
Manila 159
Mao Zedong 259, 314, 318, 319, 320, 331, 333, 334, 340
Maring, Hans 269–70, 271–72
Marx, Karl 13, 286, 304, 333
May Fourth Movement 258–59, 260–61
May Thirtieth Incident 303
Meiji Restoration 38, 64, 70
Memoirs of a Chinese Revolutionary 255
Merchants' Volunteer Corps 288–90, 322
Mill, John Stuart 35, 115, 129
Minakata Kumagusu 61
Minbao 130, 133, 161, 185–86, 187, 188, 238
Missionaries: anti-missionary activities 18, 84–85, 120, 207, 328; and foreign penetration 10–11, 27, 82, 84; schools 16, 23, 30, 43; and Sun Yat-sen 23, 24–25, 30, 53, 169, 329
Miyakawa Fumiko 331
Miyazaki Torazo (Toten) 65–68, 71, 79, 87–93, *89*, 108, 119, 121, 124

Mongolia 209, 232, 256, 272, 273, 274, 296
Morrison, G.E. 222, 333
Moscow Sun Yat-sen University 304
Movement for the Protection of the Country *see* National Protection Movement
Mukden (Shenyang) 313
Mulkern, Rowland J. 61, 91

Nanjing: in 1911 Revolution 215; CPC capture of 320; Nationalist government at 309–13, 315, 331; Rape of 315–16; seat of provisional government 215, 222, 224, 225–27, *230*; and Second Revolution 235; Sun Yat-sen in 223–24, 302, *305*; as Taiping capital 8, 9, 12
Nanjing, Treaty of 7, 10
Nanjing Decade 312, 313
National Protection Movement 243, 252, 274
Negeri Sembilan 150
New Army 102, 115, 167, 191–92, 198, 201–3, 210–14, 242
New Culture Movement *see* May Fourth Movement
New Policy 102, 211–12
Ni Yingdian 191, 192
Northern Expedition 260, 263–64, 269, 289–90, 293, 307, 308–13, 339

Oahu School 24–25
Obama, Barack 24, 346–47
Okuma Shigenobu 65, 71, 236
Opium Wars 7, 21, 26, 83
Otsuki Kaori 104, 331

Pan-Asianism 61, 64–65, 68, 73–75, 79, 118, 132, 160, 232, 256, 296, 316
Paris Peace Conference 257, 282
Peking University (Beida) 16, 259, 303
Penang 43, 150, 152, 196–200, 203, 219, 221, 342
Philippines 73–75, 113, 142, 143, 159–61, 253, 342, 344
Pi Yongnian 76, 78, 79

Plan for National Reconstruction 248, 254, 256
Ponce, Mario 74, 160, 342
Progress and Poverty 107, 287
Puyi (Xuantong Emperor) 85, 187, 208, 227, 251, 293, 313

Qinuhu *see* Huizhou Qinuhu Uprising
Qinzhou-Lianzhou Uprising 176, *183*
Qu Fengzhi 26, 59, 75
Question of China's Survival 249

Rapallo, Treaty of 267
Reading clubs 152–54, 157, 161, 163, 165, 188, 197
Réau, Raphael 116
Reconstruction (magazine) 254, 260
Red Dragon scheme 190, 194–96, 198
Reorganization Loan 234
Revolution of 1911 (Xinhai Revolution) 137, 165, 213, 216, *217*, 242, 255, 282, 332–33, 334
Revolutionary Alliance *see* Tongmenghui
Revolutionary Army 109, 147, 153, 161, 168
Rizal, Jose 160
Rong Lu 70–71
Russell, Bertrand 263
Russia 272, 285–86, 296–98, 304, 309, 331; Comintern and 268; occupation of Manchuria 100; Resist Russia Volunteer Corps 109, 131; Sun explores relations with 267–69, 271, 274, 277; Sun's farewell letter to 299

Saigon 27, 76, 87, 88, 90, 91, 106, 121, 135, 137, 148, 171
Salisbury, Lord 58, 60
San Francisco 55, 112, 113, 120, 144, 164, 191, 195, 200, 203
Sanmin Zhuyi see Three Principles of the People
Sanzhoutian *see* Huizhou Sanzhoutian Uprising
Scramble for Concessions 48, 64, 69, 82, 122, 206

390

INDEX

Second Revolution 235–36, 238, 241, 242, 252
Self-Strengthening Movement 13, 15–18, 28, 37, 47
Seow Hoodseng 154–56
Seremban 150, 200
Shandong 70, 82, 83, 84–85, 239, 243, 257–58, 311
Shanghai: boycott of American goods in 120; and Chen Qimei 214; and Chiang Kai-shek 239, 309–11; conference in 224–25; CPC capture of 320; and Feng Guozhang 247; foreign presence/concessions in 9, 37, 109, 238, 327; Japanese capture of 315; Li Hongzhang in 95; and Lu Haodong 26, 33; May Thirtieth Incident in 303–4; radical students in 109–11; and Second Revolution 235; in Second Zhili-Fengtian War 292; and Self-Strengthening Movement 16–17; Sun Yat-sen in 135, 222, 234, 241, 243, 248, 254, 262, 265, 269, 270, 271–73, 275, 294–95, 322, 327; and Taiping Rebellion 12–13; Tongmenghui in 204
Shaoguan 289, 290, 293
Sheng Xuanhuai 208, 210
Shi Jianru 76, 98
Shimonoseki, Treaty of 47–48, 68, 69–70, 100
Siam 142, 143, 154–56, 163, 164, 198, 199
Sichuan 207, 210, 213, 235, 251, 253, 321
Singapore: anti-American boycott in 120; Chinese consulate-general in 143–44, 148, 187; Chinese revolutionary movement in, 93, 99, 114, 118–21, 145–49, 152–53, 157, 164–65, 200, 219–20; and the Japanese 46, 87, 88–92, 181; and Kang Youwei, 85, 87, 89, 96; as refuge for exiled revolutionaries, 99, 144, 145, 170, 178; Sun Yat-sen in 76, 91–93, 119–21, 144, 148, 150, 152, 167, 178, 184–87, 196, 221; Tongmenghui in 148–50, *149*, 178, 186, 188
Sino-French War 17, 49
Sino-Japanese War (1894–95) 41, 44, 46, 47, 64, 76, 111, 122, 132, 144, 206, 211, 246, 345
Sino-Japanese War (1937–45) 315–17
Social Interpretation of History 286
Song Ailing 232, 241
Song Jiaoren 125, 128, 130, 131, *133*, 134, 204, 210, 211, 214, 215, 223, 229–31, 233–34
Song Meiling 311, 331
Song Qingling 241, 242, 243, 254, 260, 265, *286*, 294, 298–99, 301, 311, 321, 331–32
Song Ziwen (T.V. Soong) 298, 300
Soong, Charles Jones 232, 241
Soong, T.V. *see* Song Ziwen
Soviet Russia/Union *see* Russia
Stalin, Joseph 309, 310
Straits Settlements 89, 147, 154, 196, 199
Subao affair 110, 132, 147
Sun Dacheng 21–22
Sun Ke 55, *199*, 200, 219, 260, 265–66, 275, 276, 289, 298, 301, 332
Sun Mei 21, 22–25, 29, 30, 41–42, 55, 78, 111, 112, 165, 200, 327, 330, 332
Sun Wan 55, 332
Sun Yan 55, 235, 332
Sun Yat-sen: during 1911 Revolution 215–16; in Bangkok 154, 155; banished from Japan 166; baptism of 26–27; birth, background and youth 20–2; and Borodin 278–81, 287, 290, 294, 298; and the British 57–60, 92, 95, 218, 249, 265, 275–77, 288, 295, 296, 298; burial at Mausoleum 312–13; character of 322–30; and Chen Jiongming 251–52, 261–63; children of 55, 199–200, 331, 332; and Chinese students in Japan 103–5, 107–8, 124–30; conflict with other Tongmenghui leaders 184–87; Constitution Protection Movement 251–53, 262; education 21–26, 29–35, 327; in Europe 114–17, 125, 148, 189, 200, 218–19; expulsion from Guangzhou 265; as Extraordinary President (1921) 262–65, 269; founding of Tongmenghui 125–30; and the French 90–91, 105–6, 116–17, 135–36, 189, 218–19;

391

Sun Yat-sen (cont'd): and Gemingdang 237–39; as Generalissimo (1922) 276; as Grand Marshall (1917) 251–54; in Hawaii 23–25, 29, 41–42, 54–55, 111–12, 195; and Hong Kong 26–27, 29–36, 43–47, 48–50, 53, 93, 104–5, 221–22, 265, 275–76; in Japan (pre-1911) 66–68, 72, 104–5, 106, 124–28; in Japan (post-1911) 232–33, 235–36, 296–97; and Joffe 272–74; kidnapped by Chinese Legation 56–58; and land policy 106–7, 127, 129, 148, 287; last days of 298–301; legacy of 333–40, 341–46; in London 56–61, 114–15, 189, 216–18; medical practice of 35–36; names of, xvi, 106; and Northern Expedition 263–64, 289–90; and pan-Asianism 61, 73–75, 79, 118, 232, 256, 296; in Penang 195–200, 219; in peninsular Malaya 150–52, 187; personal life of 330–33; petition to Li Hongzhang 36–39; and Philippines independence movement 73–75; as provisional president 223–24; and railways 194, 231–32; resignation of presidency 227; the *Sanmin Zhuyi* lectures 281–85; and the Second Revolution 235; in Shanghai 234, 243, 248, 254, 265, 270, 271, 294–96; in Singapore 91–93, 119–20, 150, 187; Tao Chengzhang's campaign against 188; in the U.S. 55–56, 112–13, 190, 193, 215–16; wives and partners of 27, 200, 241, 330–31; and Xingzhonghui, 42, 43–47

Sun Yat-sen's ten uprisings *183*; Guangzhou (1895), 48–53; Huizhou Sanzhoutian (1900), 97–99; Chaozhou Huanggang (May 1907), 169–70; Huizhou Qinuhu (Jun 1907), 170–71; Fangcheng (Sep 1907), 172–73; Zhennanguan (Dec 1907), 174–75; Qinzhou-Lianzhou (Mar–May 1908), 176; Hekou (Apr–May 1908), 177; Guangzhou New Army (1910), 190–92; Guangzhou Huanghuagang (1911), 200–203

Sun Yat-sen's writings: *The Doctrine of Sun Wen (Memoirs of a Chinese Revolutionary)* 254–55; *First Steps in Democracy* 248; *Fundamental of National Reconstruction* 285, 299, 312; *The International Development of China* 256–57, 263, 265, 270, 326, 336; *Plan for National Reconstruction* 248, 254, 256; *The Question of China's Survival* 249; *The True Solution to the Chinese Question* 113
Sun-Joffe Joint Statement 274
Surabaya 157–59, 186
Swettenham, Sir James Alexander 89, 92

Taiping Rebellion 8–14, 20, 22, 26, 27, 33, 37, 43, 46, 57, 83
Taiwan: Cross-Strait relations 321, 335–39, 344–46; and Japan 47, 66, 83, 95, 98, 345; Koxinga regime on 142, 154; relocation of Nationalist government to 321, 333, 345; Sun Yat-sen in 95; Sun's legacy in 333, 341, 342
Tan Boo Liat 220, 221
Tan Chor Nam 119–21, 146–50, *149*, 152, 153, 168, 221
Tan Kah Kee 220
Tan Sitong 70–71, 78
Tang Caichang 78, 79, 96
Tang Jiyao 242, 251–52
Tang Shaoyi 21, 225–26, *230*, 230–31, 259, 301
Tao Chengzheng 132, 159, 185, 196, 239, 323
Tatsu Maru incident 180–81
Tee Han Kee 160–61
Teng Tse Ju 164, 199, 200, 280
Teo Eng Hock 119, 121, 146–48, *149*, 152, 153, 168, 171, 200, 221
Thien Nan Shing Pao 144, 146, 147
Thoe Lam Jit Poh 113, 118, 120, 144, 146, 147–48, 153, 159
Three Great Policies 334
Three Principles of the People (*Sanmin Zhuyi*) 35, 38, 128, 130, 133, 153, 166, 237, 261, 281–88, 299, 312, 319, 332–36, *343*

INDEX

Tianjin: anti-French riots in 18; and Boxer Uprising 85, 94–95, 99; CPC capture of 320; Liang Qichao in 71; in Second Fengtian-Zhili War 292; Sun Yat-sen in 37–39, 241, 294–95, 297; as Treaty Port 10–11
Tjio Family (of Surabaya) 159
Tonking 27, 28, 90, 105, 117, 172, 174–75, 177, 180
Tongmenghui *137–41*; in 1911 Revolution 214, 220; in Burma 159; in coalition cabinet 230; in Dutch East Indies 156–59; founding of 125–30; front organizations of 152–53, 157; funding 162–65; in Hong Kong 191, 192; in Japan 195; Nanyang Regional Headquarters 186, 188, 196; in peninsular Malaya 150–52; in the Philippines 159–61; regionalism and factionalism of 130–34; relations with Hubei revolutionaries 211; reorganization as Guomindang 231; in Shanghai 204, 210; in Siam 154–56; in Singapore 148–49, *149*; and Song Jiaoren 229, 230; and Yuan Shikai 222, 226
Tongzhi Emperor 11, 13, 19, 85
Tongzhi Restoration 13–15
Too Nam 25, 151
Toyama Mitsuru 65–66, 235, 297
Treaty ports 7, 9–11, 47, 48, 95, 116, 130, 132, 145
Triads 33, 49, 76, 78, 97–98, 111, 112, 145, 172
Trotsky, Leon 310
Trump, Donald 339, 346
True Solution to the Chinese Question 113
Tsai Ing-wen 338–39, 344
Twentieth-Century China 125, 129
Twenty-One Demands 240, 241, 249, 258

Uchida Ryohei 65–66, 87–89, *89*, 92, 126, 166–67, 181
Umeya Shokichi 46, 49, 53, 313
Union Times 153, 188
United States: aid for Nationalists 317–19; anti-American boycott 120, 123, 181; Baohuanghui in 73, 112; Chinese emigrants in 56, 112–13, 143, 188, 253; Chinese Exclusion laws 112, 113, 120, 160, 317; International Settlement in Shanghai 9; and Japan 40, 63, 118, 189, 317; "Open Door Policy" in China 83; and the Philippines 74, 160, 161; and Political Consultative Committee 318–19; and PRC 337, 339, 344–46; recognition of Sun's governments 228, 253, 262–63, 270; and Self-Strengthening Movement 16; Sun Yat-sen in 55–57, 112–13, 190, 195, 200, 333; Sun's admiration for 280, 330; Sun's attacks on 277, 280; and Taiwan 337, 339, 344–46; Tongmenghui offices in *139*, *141*; in World War I 248, 250; in World War II 317; *see also* Hawaii
USSR *see* Russia

Vital Problem of China 249
Versailles, Treaty of 257–58, 267, 298
Voitinsky, Grigori 269
Volkovsky, Felix 61

Wang Heshun 172–73, 176
Wang Jingwei *133*; attempted assassination of prince regent 192, 197, 200, 205; and Gemingdang 238; in Guangzhou government 262; as head of Japanese puppet government 316; and *Minbao* 130, 186, 187; and Sun Yat-sen 294, 298; after Sun's death 306–11; in Tongmenghui 132–33; and Yuan Shikai 225
Wang Tao 37
Wang Zhonghui 113, 224
Wanqingyuan 148, *149*, 171, 196, 200
Waseda University 133, 166
Washington Naval Conference 258, 263, 268
Wen Sheng Tsai 201
William, Maurice 286, 328
Willis, Alfred 23
Wilson, Woodrow 248, 250, 256, 258, 262, 282, 325
World War I 239, 248, 256, 257, 278, 282, 330

393

World War II 241, 317, 321, 345
Wu Peifu 264, 266, 270, 272–73, 290, 292–93, 309
Wu Tingfang 224, 225, 226
Wuchang Uprising 14, 162, 164, *183*, 207–15, 219, 225, 261
Wuhan 207–8, 210, 213, 214, 309–11, 315–16, 331

Xi Jinping 338–40, 344
Xiamen 95, 98
Xiangshan 20–21, 22, 34, 41, 45, 50, 51, 230, 301
Xie Xuantai 44, 52
Xinghanhui 76
Xingzhonghui 53, *80–81*, 126, 128, 130, 132, 135; Hawaii branch 42; Hong Kong branch 43; Johannesburg branch 77; leadership tussle 44, 51; membership and sympathizers of 45–47; sources of funds 42, 45, 162; Yokohama branch 54
Xinhai Revolution *see* Revolution of 1911
Xu Shichang 264
Xu Xueqiu (Koh Soh Chew) 168–70, 173–74, 186

Yan Fu 114
Yang Heling 33, *34*
Yang Quyun *43*, 43–44, 49–53, 75–77, 87, 99, 101, 104
Ye Ju 264, 265
Yokohama 42, 53–54, 66, 73, 77, 104, 106, 125, 133, 145, 147, 149, 195, 331
You Lie 33, *34*, 76, 114, 119–20, 145, 147, *149*, 151
Yuan Shikai 99; as Beiyang Army commander 14, 71, 211–12, 215, 225, 245, 246; and Boxer Uprising 99; death of 244, 245; as emperor 241–43; forced into retirement 189, 214, 246; legacy of 246, 247, 341; as premier 215, 224, 225; as president 218, 222–30, 22–235, 240, 244, 247; and Red Dragon scheme 194; and Second Revolution 235–36, 252; and Sun Yat-sen 222, 228, 229, 231–37, 243, 249, 327
Yuanmingyuan 11, 13
Yung Wing 16, 21, 190, 194
Yunnan 27, 90, 116, 136, 164, 167, 172, 174, 177, 179, 206, 242, 251–52, 274, 276, 279, 290
Yunnan Railway Company 174, 175, 177

Zaifeng (Prince Chun) 187, 208, 209, 224, 225
Zeng Guofan 12, 17
Zhang Binglin *109*, 109–10, 125, 130, 132, 147, 178–79, 185, 187–88, 252, 259, 323
Zhang Renjie 117, 171, 238–39
Zhang Xueliang 315
Zhang Zhidong 16, 102, 189, 208, 211, 212
Zhang Zuolin 264, 271, 272, 292–93, 295–97, 308–9, 311
Zhao Sheng 167, 169, 173, 176, 191, 198, 200, 202–3
Zheng Guanying 21, 34–35, 37–38
Zheng Shiliang 30, 33, 50, 51, 53, 54, 76, 87, 97–99, 101
Zhennanguan Uprising 174–75, 177, *183*
Zhili clique 253, 264, 266, 270–71, 273, 289–90, 292–93, 308
Zhili province 14, 17, 37, 70, 97, 230, 292
Zhili-Fengtian Wars 264, 292–93, 308
Zhonghetang 145, 151, 159
Zhou Enlai 334
Zhu Qi 52
Zhu Zhixin 133, 238, 249
Zou Rong 109–10, 147, 153, 161, 168
Zuo Zongtang 12, 17